# Madam, Where Are Your Mangoes?

# Madam, Where Are Your Mangoes?

*—An Episodic Memoir—*

DESMOND DE SILVA

*with case commentaries by*
PAUL CHESTON

QUARTET BOOKS

*I dedicate this book to my parents*

First published in 2017 by Quartet Books Limited
A member of the Namara Group
27 Goodge Street, London, W1T 2LD



A catalogue record for this book is available from the British Library.

ISBN 9780704374423

Text design and typesetting by Tetragon, London

Printed and bound by TJ International Ltd, Padstow, Cornwall

# CONTENTS


*Foreword by Julian Fellowes* vii

*Preface* xi

*Acknowledgements* xvii

Part I

1 At the Bar, 1965 3

2 Target Number One: Blood Diamonds and Warlords 35

3 Pray the Devil Back to Hell 72

4 The Devil's Last Dance 87

5 Ceylon, World War II and Family 93

6 A Legal and Not So Legal Family 108

7 Madam, Where Are Your Mangoes? 126

8 The Spy Who Missed the Opera 135

9 Ambush in the Med 142

10 A Candidate of Probity and Integrity 148

11 The Moon, the Stars and Nirvana 151

12 The Royal Wedding and Poison in the Gambia 158

13 The Corruption of the Blood 168

14 'You Will Hang in the Morning' 171

15 The Caesar Photographs 177

16 The Playboy Peer 180

17 The Poisoned Daughter 183

18 Tom Clancy 184

*Epilogue* 187

Part II


19 A Newspaperman's Introduction to Desmond 191
20 The Man Who Would Be King 216
21 The Perfect Murder 226
22 The Clock Tower Alibi 232
23 The Tea Dance Murder 236
24 Brothers in Blood 240
25 The Traitor Who Never Was 255
26 The Trusted Mole 266
27 This Sporting Life 273
28 Bojangles's Handshake 281
29 Leeds and Violence 284
30 Chelsea and Violence 292
31 Cocaine and the Captain 296
32 Jamie Osborne 298
33 The Lady Jockey 300
*Afterword* 303

*Illustration Credits* 305
*Index* 307

# FOREWORD

By the time I really got to know Desmond some three decades ago, he was already hugely sought after as a Queen's Counsel in England. We were fellow dwellers in Chelsea who would run into each other at parties and, on rare occasions when he was not engaged in some high-profile murder or fraud trial, we would lunch together. In fact, in those early days, there was even a brief moment when we contemplated working together on a television series dealing with those monarchies in exile that stood, we thought in our innocence, a chance of restoration. But this subject was not our main common interest.

Oddly perhaps, we shared a fascination with murder. Not random murder, not serial killing, but crimes committed by seemingly normal people, men and women who had reached a point where murder seemed the most logical option. Men like Roderick Newall, an Army officer, who killed his parents in Jersey and was only brought to justice through Desmond's determined efforts. This was a case that fascinated us both and after many discussions with him, and reading at least two books on the subject, I feel qualified to act as his second, were there ever to be a retrial.

What made all this more beguiling was Desmond's extraordinary good humour, his buoyant talk, his sheer enjoyment of living. Personally, I have always felt that the law was the career that eluded me. Everything about it interests me now, but in my whole life I don't believe I have ever met anyone more temperamentally suited to its practice than Desmond. We share a moderately encyclopedic knowledge of history and, to some extent, an understanding of human psychology, but to that Desmond can add an astonishing and detailed grasp of crime and law. To someone who enjoys soap opera, as I do, it is hard to imagine that anyone could be a more entertaining lunch companion, as we would sit over our wine in Brooks's, dissecting every motive and nuance of past crimes and misdemeanours.

Of course, in addition to all this, Desmond is very much a heavyweight in his field by any standards, playing a major role in some of the great trials of our times, as well as making a real difference beyond his own patch. His extraordinary achievements in Sierra Leone alone make it high time that his story was told. And there is no one so qualified to tell it as the man himself.

Known as a brilliant jury advocate and deadly cross-examiner, it came as no surprise to his friends when the *Daily Telegraph*, referring to the number of people he had saved from the noose in jurisdictions with capital punishment, endowed him with the sobriquet the Scarlet Pimpernel. Not that his efforts were always successful or, given some of the countries where he would elect to take on the local powers, free from danger. Far from it. These episodic memoirs bring to life some of the more dramatic twists and hair-raising incidents of his legal life – and sometimes near death – in his relentless pursuit of justice. Such incidents form the raw materials of what is a very fascinating account.

His determination to bring Charles Taylor, former president of Liberia, to trial is just one example of why Desmond belongs in the history books. Being then the only British QC to have been appointed by the United Nations as chief prosecutor of an international war crimes tribunal, he managed to bring about the arrest of Taylor whose conviction in 2012 for war crimes and crimes against humanity was the first of its kind since the Nuremberg trials in 1946 when Grand Admiral Dönitz, who had succeeded Hitler, was tried and convicted.

The book also contains the unique story of a colonial boyhood in Ceylon, as it was then, during World War II when that part of the Empire was the frontline of the war against Japan. Lord Louis Mountbatten set up the HQ of the South East Asia Command in Kandy, where Desmond, the grandson of a minister in the Ceylon War Council, was born and where he spent his childhood. Apparently it was not long before the four-year-old Desmond began to address the Supreme Allied Commander as 'Uncle Dickie'. I do not know what Uncle Dickie's response to this was, but I do know that many years later my wife Emma was delighted to be made a godmother to Desmond's daughter Victoria from his marriage to Katarina, who, to complete one of life's curious circles, was Mountbatten's great niece.

Not only are these memoirs a rare insight into what really occurred during some of the most talked about court cases of the past fifty years, they are also a compelling account of the end of Empire and the start of the modern era. And not least, in these pages we find a fierce argument for the enduring importance of common law in England, as laid out by one of its most brilliant standard bearers.

JULIAN FELLOWES
*Lord Fellowes of West Stafford*

# PREFACE

THIS BOOK IS INTENDED AS A RECORD OF INTERESTING TIMES THROUGH which I have lived and practised law in England and in numerous jurisdictions outside the UK. It has been a journey measured in memories, friendships, political duplicity and a wealth of varied experiences. I do not propose, as some do, to take a scalpel to myself in order to dissect why I have turned out as I have. I do, however, sometimes take such an instrument to others, but sparingly, I hope. This is meant to be a light-hearted, episodic memoir of certain events as opposed to a comprehensive autobiography.

I am told that some people have found it difficult to know what to make of me. Perhaps this memoir will help. The story is something of an odyssey; from a colonial childhood in Ceylon where the imprint of Empire was still visible, to life in post-war Britain under Attlee's Labour government. Never for a moment did it occur to me that I had any other career path than that which led to the Inns of Court in London.

It is sometimes said that a person is moulded by a particular decade. In all species individuals grow within groups and these social groupings imprint their values on their offspring. If this is true, then I was perhaps influenced most by the first ten years of my life: the 1940s. Looking back, that period was my comfort zone. However, the professional life I have led since my call to the Bar has dragged me away from this arena of comfort and placed me squarely in the modern world.

A reason for my committing these memories to paper is so that my daughter, Victoria, might have an insight into my early life, both in Ceylon as it was then, and Sri Lanka as it is now. England was, however, where I spent most of my professional life and it was from England that I sallied out to other places when the finger of fate beckoned. As I only kept a diary sporadically, the account that follows is, on the whole, a series of recollections and anecdotes; a gossipy personal memoir confined to a career in the law.

Where a country has changed its name an author must choose which name to use. I have decided to use the name that applied at the time of the events about which I am writing. I hope I will be forgiven for referring to the land of my birth as Ceylon – as it was then popularly and geographically known – when I refer to events prior to 1972, after which it became the Republic of Sri Lanka. So names such as the Ceylon National Congress, which my grandfather was president of and which played such an important part in the Ceylon independence movement, will remain; as will the Battle of Ceylon in 1942 and the Ceylon War Council, which came into existence during World War II.

In a career of over fifty years at the Criminal Bar of England and Wales, with hundreds of cases to choose from, I have drawn on very few to write about. Those I have chosen, in the main, either have a relevance to my life, or sometimes even my near death, or enjoy some rare quality that does, perhaps, give them an interest outside that of the normal diet of a criminal barrister.

The Criminal Bar and the criminal justice system have undergone huge changes in the course of my career, not all of them wholly beneficial to the Bar, the public or indeed justice.

What those who knock the Bar simply fail to understand is that, in a society where people are free and presumed to be innocent, it is usually a barrister who stands between the might of the state and that – often inadequate – individual. So daily, up and down the country, the barrister plays a vital role in protecting the constitutional rights of the citizen: the right to be free unless a competent court, acting according to law, terminates that freedom. Today, that duty also falls upon solicitors who, with the changes that have taken place within the legal profession, now enjoy a much greater role as advocates.

However, the picture received by the average member of the public, encouraged by successive governments, is that the barrister is some sort of overpaid leech whose role in society is a million miles away from that of a pillar supporting the maintenance of fundamental freedoms.

The rule of law is integral to democracy itself and it is sad to see successive governments undermining the great freedoms vouchsafed by Magna Carta. The interference with the law has taken place through a mixture of Treasury-driven parsimony, fanned by envious civil servants, and political gamesmanship.

In the interest of saving money and allegedly improving efficiency of the courts, successive governments have sought to undermine the fundamental rights enjoyed by the citizens of England, Wales and Northern Ireland, which are based in the common law. The Scottish legal system belongs to a continental civil tradition. There is no such thing as British law. That is what is so silly about some politicians and commentators who, being hostile to the jury system in England, point to Scotland as an example, where a defendant has no right to insist on a jury trial and saying, in effect, 'Scotland has a perfectly good system of justice.' There, the right is that of the prosecution! I am a great believer in the jury system. There are few things more democratic than a defendant's right to be judged by his or her peers. In which totalitarian state does a jury system flourish? As Lord Devlin put it so beautifully, it is 'the lamp that shows that freedom lives.' A jury can act as a check on prosecutors, legislators and, indeed, judges.

The attack on the lay magistracy and plans of whittling down the jury system were all part of an attempt to harmonize the English legal system with that of the civil law systems of Europe. For centuries, the administration of criminal justice by local justices of the peace, in the very localities in which crimes were committed, meant that communities maintained their links with the administration of justice. With cries of a new 'strategic approach', governments have closed hundreds of magistrates' courts since 1997 and have moved the hearing of cases to centres so distant from the area of the offence that many communities are denied the local justice that successive governments have claimed to support.

The common law of England is the greatest of its exports and, according to William Blackstone, 'the jury is the principal criteria of truth in the law of England.' The jury replaced trial by battle, trial by ordeal and compurgation as a method of proof. It remains a method of bringing in a verdict acceptable to the body politic which, if not left to those on the electoral role from which juries are drawn, will lead to constant attack by the public on decisions by a judge alone or judges sitting with assessors. What is forgotten by the critics of the jury system is that judges are protected by juries. Where the verdict of the jury may not accord with the judge's views, it is nevertheless accepted by the public because the jury represents the public. If England lost her legal identity the consequences would be more pronounced than surrendering the pound for the euro. Schemes to reduce jury trials have included the proposal that the right to jury trial should be restricted to those with no previous convictions; that would be to deny a jury trial to those who most need it. I have appeared in countless cases where a jury has acquitted a defendant where the heart of the defence was that the *only* reason for arresting and charging a defendant was his previous convictions, which, according to the prosecution, if taken together with suspicious behaviour or lies, amounted to a strong case. It has been my experience that people arrested do sometimes lie; not through guilt of involvement in crime but because telling the truth might lead them to be seen in a shameful light either by the police or indeed their families.

Magna Carta sculpted the legal landscape. The liberty that is enjoyed in Britain is the result of a long historical legal process. If we are willing to overthrow the unique achievements of England's legal heritage, which spring from an intellectual tradition grounded in the Great Charter and are sustained by the concept of fairness, it would be the beginning of England losing faith in herself.

To build the great institutions that bring liberty to many is the laborious task of centuries. To weaken these institutions with ill-thought-out legislation for the sake of appearing modern can be the foolish product of a single Act. Why spend £50 million of the taxpayers' money abolishing the House of Lords as a final Court of Appeal when all that the public get for their money is a Supreme Court with the same judges? Are their judgments going to be more profound? Are the judges going to be wiser? Of course, it does separate the Lords of Appeal in Ordinary – Law Lords – or Justices of the Supreme Court as they now are, from the legislature, but it will deny Parliament the benefit of acute contributions on matters touching upon the administration of the judicial process, with new appointees not having a seat in the House of Lords.

This is not a misreading of the legal landscape. Today, in 2017, there are forces at play that have even left members of the judiciary waiting to leave in droves. Something is terribly wrong when a barrister, in order to obtain a practising certificate, is required to make a contribution to a war chest maintained by the Bar Council to finance battles with the Lord Chancellor who, until 2012 when the rot set in seriously, was a distinguished lawyer and the trusted voice for the Bar in Cabinet.

I hope I am not being overcritical; there are areas of the law in which significant advances have taken place. Advances that have truly enhanced the operation of the rule of law in the citizen's interest. One such area is the constitutional protection afforded by judicial review, by means of which the citizen can challenge the legality of decisions of public officials, including ministers. It hits at the culture of secrecy that governments are wont to protect. By the 1980s, the habit of deference had given way to accountability and those public officials making decisions had to do so within the law and with decision-making free from being arbitrary or manifestly unreasonable. This was all to the good.

The law represents a society's strengths and weaknesses. It is the duty of this and other generations to constantly monitor the law's developments to ensure that the rule of law is not eroded.

# ACKNOWLEDGEMENTS

THERE ARE MANY WITHOUT WHOSE SUPPORT AND ENCOURAGEMENT THIS book would not have been written: Rosamund Cameron, who never hesitated to carry out research for me, often at short notice; Sharmini Thiruchelvam, who had a sharp eye for expressing things; Rosemary Thomas at the Foreign and Commonwealth Office, whose guidance I sought in relation to events in Sierra Leone at the time and whose advice I gratefully received; Laura Davies, the deputy British high commissioner in Sri Lanka who, fearing possible defamation of individuals in my narration of events, kindly introduced me to her father the distinguished author and lawyer Alan Williams who became my mentor, together with my dear friend Manoli Olympitis; Lord Richards of Herstmonceux, the former chief of the defence staff and Lt. Col. Patrick Jackson, who assisted in getting my special forces story passed for publication; Brigadier James Ellery, CBE who read some of my draft chapters and encouraged me to continue; Rachel Graham for her exceptional technical support; and members of my chambers at 2 Paper Buildings (later at Argent Chambers) who kept telling me I had to put pen to paper and record what I recalled of 'the old days in chambers'.

It would be impossible for me to omit the assistance of Tracy Pettitt, my secretary in Sierra Leone, whose patience in recording a great deal of what follows knew no bounds. If it had not been for her promise to start typing up a part of these memoirs some ten years ago, I am almost certain that my inability to use a computer would have deterred me from continuing with this account. I have to extend my fullest thanks to my daughter, Victoria, who spent time revising the text instead of enjoying herself to the full during her holidays. For supplying or taking photographs I am greatly indebted to my cousins John Nell and Jennifer Hollis. Also to my sister Helga and her husband Desmond Perera.

I wish to express my gratitude to my secretary, Delarney Uyangodage, in Sri Lanka, for being so understanding and in finding the time to help me finalize these memoirs. And I would like to thank Naim Attallah, James Pulford, Grace Pilkington and Peter Jacobs at Quartet Books for getting the book in motion at breakneck speed.

Finally, my bountiful thanks are due to Paul Cheston, the former court reporter of the *London Evening Standard* whose offer to write about the trials he covered as a newspaperman, in which I either prosecuted or defended, has been gratefully accepted by me; his great contribution to this book begins at Chapter 19.

DESMOND DE SILVA, QC

*London, March 2017*

# PART I

I

# At the Bar, 1965

'Go to Downing Street at once,' said my clerk. My mind went quite numb. Before I could display my surprise, Walter Butler continued, 'Their Lordships are waiting for you in the Privy Council, so get there straight away. It's number one Downing Street. It will all be explained to you when you get there.' He put his receiver down in chambers, leaving me clutching the telephone in my flat with a pool of water spreading at my feet (caused by my leaping out of the bath to get to the telephone).

Just three days earlier I had been made a member of the chambers of Sir Dingle Foot, QC, MP – the Solicitor General. I had done only one lowly dock brief while in pupillage. Now here I was being sent by my clerk to appear before the Law Lords, sitting as the Judicial Committee of the Privy Council, the final Court of Appeal for the Commonwealth. This was the stuff of which an inexperienced young barrister's nightmares are made.

Clutching my blue bag of barrister's robes, I hailed a cab in Pimlico, arriving at Downing Street fifteen minutes later. I went up the stairs to the first floor where a sign said Robing Room. I entered. It had a musty smell to it. As I looked round I saw lockers bearing the names of great ones at the Bar who regularly practised before the Privy Council. Dumping my bag on a table I extracted a wing collar. Just as I was getting the back stud into the neckband of my shirt, the door to the robing room opened and an usher in a morning coat entered, carrying a clipboard.

'Ah,' he said. 'It's good to see that you have arrived so quickly, sir. It's very sad about Sir Gilbert,' he added, shaking his head with some feigned concern.

'What about Sir Gilbert?' I asked in consternation.

'Oh,' he said, 'it is very sad. Very sad. Sir Gilbert stood before Their Lordships this morning and instead of addressing them as My Lords,' he paused for emphasis, 'he called them My Dears.'

Here was this man telling me that a member of my new chambers, who I had not yet met, was gaga. 'What happened?' I stammered.

'Oh well,' he said in a rather superior way, 'Their Lordships decided to adjourn the murder appeal until your clerk sent down other counsel.'

He must have seen the terror all over my face.

'Come with me,' he said soothingly. 'It will be all right.'

I was shown into the court. Sitting there were my opponents, a renowned silk and a senior junior.

'Well, you're here at last,' said one of them with some asperity.

No sooner had I sat down than the judges' door opened and five Law Lords trooped into court. We stood, bowed and sat down. Lord Reid was presiding.

'Mr de Silva,' he said, looking at me.

'Go to the podium,' hissed one of my opponents.

Rising from my seat, I made my way to a lectern in the centre of the room.

'It's so kind of you to come at such short notice,' said Lord Reid. 'I am sorry to say that Sir Gilbert was feeling rather unwell this morning and we thought it right to rise so that he could go home. I take it that you are asking for an adjournment of this application for leave to appeal.'

'Oh yes, My Lord,' I heard myself say.

'Do you have any other application to make?'

'No, My Lord,' I said.

'Well, this leave application will have to be adjourned to another day, Mr de Silva. The registrar will be in touch with your clerk. Thank you again for attending at such short notice.'

We all stood up and bowed as Their Lordships filed out.

'Damned nuisance about this,' said the renowned QC to his junior, in a voice that would have carried across the hunting field. 'A wasted day. Could have been playing golf!'

I got back to the robing room and was about to telephone my clerk when the supercilious usher came into the robing room and said to me, 'You are going to the House of Lords, aren't you, sir?'

My mind went numb for the second time that morning. To the House of Lords, the highest court in the land, from the highest court in the Commonwealth? All on the same day? Surely not. My heart missed several beats. 'What do you mean, go to the House of Lords?' I said.

Seeing a haunted look on my face the supercilious one said, 'Ah,' setting out to conquer my ignorance. 'Perhaps you don't know the form, sir. When you appear in the Privy Council, you are entitled to take lunch in the House of Lords. Sir Gilbert had booked a table and I assumed you would be taking it on?'

Let me say at once that I became a barrister by accident. It was an accident of birth. I think I was biologically programmed to enter the law. I was born into a sort of genetic prison, from which I could not escape. Looking back along the trail of my family history, I come from a line of lawyers, with one break, which stretches back to 1828. Born in the colony of Ceylon, in 1939, I knew I was headed for the Inns of Court in London and a barrister's wig and gown; the only issue being whether I was to stay and take my chances at the English Bar or return to Ceylon and benefit from being the son and grandson of two exceptional advocates.

This is the story of a boy who did not return home, not for half a century anyway, apart from the occasional holiday. In a sense, my immigrant life had begun.

No barrister ever forgets his first case, or the court in which he starts that great voyage of discovery that is a full career at the Bar. My first case came to me when I was asleep.

In those days, as now, you could not practise without a pupillage, which means you had to learn your stuff by being attached to an experienced barrister for twelve months. It then cost the pupil 100 guineas. It was quite unlike today, when pupils expect to be shielded from the cold blast of market forces, pay nothing and often hope to be underwritten by chambers with some sort of handout. It is all part of the dependency culture that has become part of modern life. Again, unlike today, you could undertake court work immediately so long as you had been called and were in pupillage.

Immersed in the common law of England that has been laboriously built up around that mythical figure – the figure of the reasonable man – and full of useless legal information (such as, an imbecile is a person who is not an idiot; and an *ambidexter*, in a legal sense, is a juror who takes bribes from both parties to an action), I looked forward to my call to the Bar and my first pupillage.

While I was awaiting my call to the Bar at the Middle Temple in the Trinity term of 1964, I received a letter from my father in Ceylon informing me that he had a Red Judge – Mr Justice Rodger Winn – staying with him and that he had spoken to him about a pupillage for me. Red Judges are so called because of the predominant colour of their robes. Upon the judge's return to England I had an invitation from Lady Winn to come to supper at their house in Belgravia. At the end of the evening, I was told to be in touch with Sir Rodger's former senior clerk whose name, alas, escapes me.

'Sir Rodger has asked me to find you a pupillage,' he said when I called, and then proceeded to give me the telephone number of another senior clerk to a set of chambers in Kings Bench Walk, with whom he had had a word.

'I have fixed you up for six months with Mr Bernard Marder,' said the clerk when I called. Bernard's clerk was Mr Berry and always referred to as such. Short and rotund, he was always in pinstripe trousers, a black jacket, and a waistcoat and never without his bowler hat outside chambers. He was the epitome of an Edwardian clerk of the old school. I gave him a cheque for 100 guineas – my pupillage fee. I was now in pupillage in the London chambers of G. G. Blackledge, QC, Recorder of Liverpool.

A pupil master was the one from whom you were meant to learn the art of advocacy. I began my pupillage, as I recall it, even before I had been formally called to the Bar. Bernard Marder, who later went on to the Circuit Bench, was the most helpful of masters. Apart from town and country planning (which interested me not in the slightest), he did divorce and matrimonial work, in which I attempted to assist. I shall never forget the advice he gave me when I was trying my hand at divorce petitions which alleged violence to the petitioner; 'Desmond,' he said, 'the words blood and bleeding always look good in a petition.'

Having completed my six months with Bernard, I had the good fortune to obtain a pupillage at 2 Dr Johnson's Buildings in the chambers of the then Senior Treasury Counsel, Edward Cussen, QC, affectionately known as 'the headmaster'. As Major Edward Cussen, he was sent by MI5 to interrogate P. G. Wodehouse after the Allies captured Paris in 1944. Edward took the view that, on the evidence then available, Wodehouse had been naïve in permitting the Nazis to use him as a broadcaster, but not guilty of treason.

The highly entertaining Felix Waley (later QC and judge), who could be a deadly prosecuting counsel, was my pupil master. One of my fellow pupils was Nick Purnell, who became one of the outstanding silks at the Criminal Bar. He represented Lord Archer at the Old Bailey, a facet of which I touch upon in Chapter 10. Nick's brother, Paul, who became another successful QC, had just been taken on as a tenant, together with Richard Hawkins, who also got silk and ended up as a judge at the Old Bailey.

Those were days when one of the great perks barristers enjoyed, upon retirement, was that they took their last year's earnings tax free. I have no reason to disbelieve a story circulating at the time that the cunning old barrister Charles Du Cann (The Duke), who was then on the verge of retirement, had done so twice before with no adverse reactions from the taxman.

I followed Felix around the criminal courts, picking up court craft and getting a feel for advocacy, and generally developing the necessary skills for a barrister. Although they were becoming increasingly rare, there were still criminal practitioners trapped in a mid-Victorian mindset who believed that crime was the product of innate wickedness and depravity rather than economic or social conditions.

Days after I undertook my pupillage, I arrived at Middlesex Quarter Sessions (now the Supreme Court), opposite the Houses of Parliament, to meet up with my pupil master, who was prosecuting a case. I vividly remember having my peaceful snooze on the rear-most bench of counsel's row interrupted by the judge. Upon awaking, I realized that my pupil master and all of the other barristers who had been in court had vanished. I was the only one there in counsel's row, wearing a wig and gown, and the judge was saying, 'Mr de Silva, your moment of glory has arrived.'

Until then I had only heard of dock briefs; suddenly it dawned on me that this was it. A prisoner who had been brought into the well of the court, handcuffed by one hand to a prison officer, was pointing at me with the other, making the rash, but only, selection open to him, of his dock brief. He had no choice and neither did I. A dock brief was a direct instruction of counsel by a prisoner, armed with £2 4s 6d, without the intervention of a solicitor; a system now made obsolete by the provision of legal aid. The practice was that a defendant in the cells who needed such a dock brief would be brought up into court during a break in an ongoing trial, in order that he could make his selection of counsel. Although it could be considered bad form, all experienced barristers engaged in the ongoing trial would usually flee from court while elderly, briefless barristers in the building would rush into court on news of a dock brief, and settle themselves down on counsel's row in the hope of being selected. This, unbeknown to me, is what had happened while I snoozed in the back row. In this instance, however, no other barristers had come into court. Sometimes, if a case was likely to be complicated, or last more than a day, the court clerk would suggest to the judge that counsel should be given a legal aid brief of £4 7s 6d to represent a prisoner without representation.

When the prisoner who had picked me was taken down to the cells, I followed him, with unquenchable excitement, in order to take his instructions. Before I left to go down to the cells, the court clerk had given me the indictment and a bundle of depositions, together with a list of the youth's previous convictions, which ran on for several pages. The indictment charged my client with the felony of burglary, contrary to the Larceny Act 1916, then carrying a maximum penalty of life imprisonment.

I went down to the detention area to encounter the youth who had picked me as his counsel. My client was about twenty-three. He looked me up and down and said, 'We've drawn a bad judge, guv.'

It was quite evident to me that the young villain had had a much greater exposure to the criminal justice system at first hand than I.

'Okay guv, I will plead guilty to burglary but you just tell that bleeding judge that I want to go into the Navy. That should do the trick.'

Because this case was not going to be contested I went upstairs and informed the clerk that the defendant would be entering a plea of guilty to all matters with which he was charged.

The case was brought on at the end of the day before the chairman of Quarter Sessions, the Hon. Ewen Montagu, QC. Counsel for the prosecution opened his case very briefly and included a reference to a confession made by my client when he was interviewed after his arrest, minutes after being caught climbing out of a window of the burgled premises.

'Yes, Mr de Silva. What have you to say on behalf of the defendant?' said Judge Montagu.

Beginning with the obligatory flattery of, 'May it please you My Lord,' I went through the routine I had seen my pupil master use, which involved drawing to the judge's attention the fact that the defendant, by the acceptance of his guilt, was showing remorse for what he had done; further, he had saved the time of the court by not seeking to run some spurious defence. The judge was nodding in agreement. Things were going ominously well. Moving seamlessly into playing what I thought was my trump card, I said, 'My Lord, I am sure Your Lordship would be pleased to hear that this young man now proposes to make something useful of his life by going into the Royal Navy where he will doubtless have the benefit of a discipline his life has hitherto lacked.'

The words were scarcely out of my mouth when the judge's face tightened and his body stiffened under his judicial robes. He reacted as if I had given him an electric shock. Looking at me with thin-lipped disapproval and eyes dark with rage, he replied, 'The Royal Navy, you say? The Royal Navy?' He intervened as if my remarks invited incredulity. 'Have you seen his list of previous convictions? Do you seriously think he will be accepted by the Senior Service and what's more, what about the traditions of the Navy?'

Little did I know at that stage that my judge had been a distinguished and well-decorated naval officer during the war. Indeed, he was at that time the judge advocate of the Fleet. What is more, he had been responsible for the brilliant scheme which was the basis of his book *The Man Who Never Was*. Brought in by the director of Naval Intelligence, Admiral Godfrey, to do highly secret work for the Admiralty, Montagu's team came up with an ingenious deception – Operation Mincemeat – which, the chief of staff was to tell Churchill, the Germans 'had swallowed whole'. Using the body of a dead staff officer carrying what looked like secret papers, which Montagu and his team floated on to the Spanish coast, they saved thousands of Allied lives by fooling the Germans into believing that Sardinia and Greece were to be the next Allied targets in the Mediterranean and *not* Sicily.

'Yes, Mr de Silva,' he snorted, 'and what about the traditions of the Navy?' He banged his right fist on the judicial desk in front of him.

Taken aback by this onslaught, and in the foolish belief that I could nimbly sidestep the judge's question, I fell into the error of making things worse. A reference to Churchill having once referred to the traditions of the Navy as being 'rum, sodomy and the lash' was met with a look of utter disbelief. It was one of those moments in life when you realize in mid-sentence that you have made a terrible mistake and that some other tack would have been infinitely more profitable.

After the withering look there was a judicial explosion. To his credit, at the end of the day Ewen Montagu lived up to his reputation which was, as I subsequently gathered, for tempering justice with mercy. I was later told that while he could be beastly to counsel, he was not overly punitive in his sentencing.

When I went down to the cells to see my client, expecting a tirade, he soon banished any sense of failure with the words, 'Thanks guv. I felt so sorry for you before that bleeder.' I shook his hand and we parted. I even forgot to collect my princely fee of £2 4s 6d.

After my pupillage I was fortunate enough to join 2 Paper Buildings, a unique chambers in many ways. The head of chambers was the Solicitor General, the Rt. Hon. Sir Dingle Foot, QC, MP, who first entered Parliament in 1931 as the Liberal member for Dundee. He was a libertarian to the marrow of his bones. At Oxford he had been president of the Liberal Club and then president of the Oxford Union. A lawyer of distinction and wit, Dingle, who went on to serve in Churchill's wartime coalition government, came from a famous political family. His father, Isaac Foot, was MP for Bodmin. Dingle was one of four brothers. At one stage there were two brothers in the House of Commons and two in the House of Lords. This has not been, and is unlikely to be, equalled in politics. This remarkable achievement may have been born out of the fact that when his father returned home at weekends, 'every parliamentary speech – by Lloyd George, Asquith or Churchill – would be fully described and every scene in the Commons would be re-enacted.' Dingle was to comment: 'We were therefore left with the impression that the House of Commons is the greatest theatre in the world and that all the principal dramas of public life are enacted on its floor.' Dingle, who had been a Liberal all his life, parted from the Liberal Party and contested Ipswich for Labour in 1964 and won.

We were, in the 1960s, a very political set of chambers. Apart from Dingle, who was a law officer, we had two Liberal parliamentary candidates: John Baker, who became chairman of the Liberal Party National Executive; and Tom Kellock, QC, who entertained unfulfilled dreams of becoming Lord Chancellor in a future Liberal government. Both John and Tom were to become circuit judges.

Dick Taverne, QC, MP, the member for Lincoln, went on to become Financial Secretary to the Treasury. Then there was the whimsical and brilliant Charles Fletcher-Cooke, QC, a Conservative MP who had been a Minister of State at the Home Office in the government of Harold Macmillan. When Clement Attlee's Foreign Secretary, Ernest Bevin, required an adviser on international legal issues, he could not instruct Charles, as the Treasury considered his fees of forty guineas a day excessive. Both Charles and I were sent out to Sierra Leone in 1968 by our clerk, Walter Butler, to defend in that country's first treason trial. I represented the former Cabinet Secretary and Charles represented a very grand lady who was the only female paramount chief. I was twenty-eight and this was my first capital case. It was also the first time I was thrown in jail. More of such experiences later.

To this political mix there was then added the new Conservative member for Harlow, the irrepressible Jerry Hayes, who went on to serve at the Northern Ireland Office and then the Department of the Environment. When he was at the Northern Ireland Office at the height of the Troubles his name was discovered on an IRA hit list. Bored of being hemmed in by Special Branch officers, when he joined me for a drink at El Vino in Fleet Street we decided to give them the slip. We did and continued our refreshments elsewhere. It caused a major scare; according to my wife Katarina, apart from constant telephone calls to find out if she had heard from me there was a police helicopter that kept hovering over my address in Chelsea. Jerry's wife, Alison, was subjected to the same treatment. It was a prank we should not have engaged in and No. 10 tore a strip off Jerry.

Sir Ivan Lawrence, QC, who stood for Peckham unsuccessfully for the Conservatives in 1966, went on to win Burton in Lancashire, which he held for twenty-three years; he became chairman of the Home Affairs Select Committee. Ivan and his wife Gloria had a daughter, Rachel, who was one of the bravest human beings I knew. Despite the terrible curse of cystic fibrosis, she battled courageously in the courts as a member of chambers.

Later still, we were joined by Ivor Richard, QC, who had been a minister for the Army and later the UK's ambassador to the UN. So chambers was a patchwork of political views and a hotbed of debate that covered the issues of the day.

Dingle ran chambers in a completely autocratic fashion. He and his wife, Dorothy, were known for their formidable hospitality. Either at their flat in Ashley Court or in chambers, there would be regular parties to which members were always invited. Outside Britain it was a time of fluid and changing politics, with the march of former colonies toward independence and statehood. A man totally free of the colour prejudice that dogged the thinking of so many at the time, Dingle anticipated the stirrings for independence in Britain's colonies and made a point of getting to know the leaders of many of the freedom movements in colonial times. This had the incidental benefit of making his chambers the favourite port of call for those with legal issues from the colonies and the Commonwealth. Indeed, I got a place in his chambers because members of chambers had represented my grandfather before the Privy Council in the late 1940s.

Because his Commonwealth practice was unequalled in its breadth, at parties given by Dingle and Dorothy one met, apart from the usual range of British politicians, rather exotic people like the elegant Princess Elizabeth of Toro, the first female East African to be admitted to the English Bar. The Queen's sister, Princess Margaret, found her looks so striking that she invited her to model in a show. Elizabeth was an immediate success and it led to her becoming a hugely successful model in the UK and the US. The very insecure Kabaka of Buganda, otherwise known in England as King Freddy, was another regular guest. Commissioned as a captain into the Grenadier Guards, he was sent into exile by Milton Obote of Uganda. Sadly, he died of alcohol poisoning in Rotherhithe.

Turning up at 2 Paper Buildings it was no great surprise to see a new face, only to be told by the clerks that Dingle had run into so and so at a party the night before and invited him to join chambers. Recruiting in those days was not done by a committee with endless interviews and a debate as to a candidate's merits.

Initially, I was placed in the chambers annexe at Lamb Building, the rooms of which were immediately below the chambers of the then Attorney General, Sir Elwyn Jones, QC. On my way to see my clerk at Paper Buildings I often used to pass that great judicial figure, the former Lord Chief Justice of England, Lord Goddard. Nicknamed 'Doggy', he used to be wheeled in his chair into the gardens of the Inner Temple for an airing in the afternoon. It is hard to imagine that this stern figure of retributive justice could have had anything in common with my liberal head of chambers.

Dingle was a kindly man who, if not in court, would take any young members in chambers at lunchtime to his club. I recall that, just before the general election of 1970, he took a young member of chambers to lunch at the Garrick. On their return, I was told that when one of the club servants came up to take the order for lunch, Dingle said, 'John, I hope you will be voting Labour this time?' to which, I was told, John blithely confided, 'Sir Dingle, I would not presume to vote the same way as the members!'

The first time I went abroad on a case as a barrister was in 1967 when Dingle took me as his junior. We went to Ghana to represent the wife of a High Court judge. She had allegedly been using the judge's residence as a sorting house for the bribes that went to the former president's ministers. It appeared that the poor old judge was in complete ignorance of his wife's entrepreneurial – and illegal – activities. While in Accra, Dingle, on a whim, said he would take me to the races. So, on a Saturday afternoon we set off for the Accra racecourse from our hotel. When we arrived, we made our way toward the grandstand and came to a barrier manned by a burly Ghanaian wearing a badge of officialdom.

'You cannot enter,' he said.

'Why?' asked my rather startled head of chambers.

'Because you are not wearing ties,' was the official's reply.

'Goodness me,' said Sir Dingle. 'When I came here for the Watson Commission in 1948 I came to this very grandstand in an open-necked shirt.'

'That was in the bad old days of colonial rule,' said the indignant official. 'You must wear a tie now.'

This case in Ghana gave me a restless appetite for travel and to savour legal practice in many jurisdictions that now form the Commonwealth.

Always inspired by a passion for liberty and justice, Dingle died in 1978 as he would have wished – appearing in a case in Hong Kong. In paying tribute to him in the Privy Council, Lord Diplock described him as 'an ambassador of the common law throughout the Commonwealth.'

When I first arrived at 2 Paper Buildings I found the legendary Sir Learie Constantine as a member of chambers. He was one of the greatest West Indian cricketers of all time, who also played for the Lancashire League club, Nelson. We had wonderful discussions about the towering figures of the game. Like many of us in chambers, he too had trays for correspondence on his desk. We all had in-trays for matters that had come in and out-trays for things going out. I noticed that on his desk he had three trays: an in-tray, an out-tray and, unusually, an LBW tray. 'What does LBW stand for?' I asked innocently, thinking it had something to do with cricket. 'LBW,' said Learie, 'means "Let the Buggers Wait."'

As in my case, Dingle took into chambers others from the former colonies. It has been my privilege to share my career working with others from Sri Lanka: Harendra de Silva, QC, and Lee Karu, QC; the outstanding Aftab Jafferjee, QC, still one of the deadliest prosecutors at the Old Bailey. He was not able to get a seat in chambers as Dingle's successor Sir Charles Fletcher-Cooke, QC took the view that there were too many of us with colonial backgrounds in chambers. Aftab did better, in my view, in a prosecution set, ending up as a noted Treasury counsel. Later, among the outstanding juniors in chambers was Paul Mylvaganam, who I was to lead in numerous murder trials and a UN sanctions-busting case to do with the Iraq war. I cannot leave out the brilliant but irredeemably idle Notu Hoon, who earned the sobriquet 'No notes Notu'. He gave me diabetes; this he achieved by placing bags of sweets in front of me in court when we were doing long trials out of London and relying on my lack of resolve to resist them.

Many years later, I, too, put temptation to effective use, when prosecuting the extradition from Gibraltar of the former British Army officer Roderick Newall, wanted for murder of his parents in Jersey. Newall's yacht, the *Austral Soma*, flying the Red Ensign, was stopped by a British frigate, HMS *Argonaut*. He was asked to row across to the frigate with his papers; once on board he was arrested for the murder of his parents. Soon after this he accused the Navy of piracy as his arrest was in international waters. Held in custody in the medieval Moorish Castle in Gibraltar, which also served as a prison, Newall went on a hunger strike. We anticipated that he wanted to be taken to a hospital on the Rock, from which he could escape to Spain. Three days into his hunger strike I had a meeting with Special Branch and Gibraltarian officers and suggested that some pistachio nuts, three Mars bars and a beaker of water be left in his cell. My idea was to make Newall thirsty so that he would go for the water. There was an immediate objection to my suggestion of pistachio nuts by Special Branch. 'But sir, he could sharpen the shells and cut his wrists,' I was told sharply. In the end, just the Mars bars and the water were introduced into his cell and he succumbed to the temptation.

As luck would have it, a decade after Dingle's death and the retirement of his successor, the mantle of head of chambers came my way. I am proud to have worn it and look back on this inheritance with a degree of thankfulness. It continued to foster my love for taking on interesting cases, sometimes in dangerous places, where I almost shared the perils of my clients who were facing capital charges, or where I faced the risk of becoming a marked man when prosecuting those who saw my presence in their country as an irritant.

The Judicial Committee of the Privy Council was, in those days, a very busy court. It was the highest Court of Appeal in the Commonwealth and our chambers were the pre-eminent set in that regard. Not only were there Privy Council briefs pouring into chambers from abroad, members of chambers were often to be found flying out to some sunny part of the Commonwealth to represent clients who sought their services. Some members found the climate in these places so appealing that they accepted judicial appointments and stayed on for years.

Some years ago when I was sent off to the Bahamas to appear in a case, I found Mr Justice Kenneth Potter sitting in the High Court in Nassau. Potter had been in our chambers but had left just before I joined. Soon after meeting him I realized I had never known anyone whose consumption of alcohol was so great. Before he came to Nassau, he had served as a judge in the Court of Appeal in Kenya. I ran into him in the Muthaiga Club in Nairobi when I was there to defend in a treason trial in 1982. Such was his legendary capacity for drink that, upon his departure from that posting, I understand, they named a bar after him: Potter's Bar. He was a brilliant and erudite lawyer who suggested to me that we should write a book about our chambers called *Liber Amicorum* – a book of friends. I readily understand why he suggested that title, for when I joined chambers, over fifty years ago, it was essentially a group of friends.

In the mid-1960s, life at the Criminal Bar was very different from life at the Bar now. Anyone who has practised at the Bar in England for over half a century, certainly since the early 1960s, has lived through huge legal and social changes that have impacted today's practising barristers, judges and those arrested on suspicion of crime. Previously, it was a much smaller pool of barristers – about a quarter of the number at the present day. Many young barristers supplemented their meagre incomes by lecturing or libel reading for newspapers. I would not wish it to be thought that I am praising the Bar of old and decrying the profession of the moment. The changes made in the past half-century have ushered in a more equitable, democratic and less elitist way of legal life, but some great values have been sacrificed in the process. In recent times, certainly in the twenty-plus years I was head of chambers, the constant talk has been that we have to run as if we were a business. The values of the Bar worth upholding are not contiguous with those of business. If I wanted to do business I would not have come to the Bar.

It was in 'the Mags' that fledgling criminal barristers first cut their teeth. They soon realized that stipendiary magistrates (known as the Stipe or the Beak) came in two sorts: the charming and able, or the simply dreadful. One for the former category was David Hopkin, who was a senior magistrate at Bow Street. Prior to taking to the stipendiary bench, David had spent years in the office of the Director of Public Prosecutions. In my first months at the Bar my uncle, Dr Michael Hollis, who was at Cambridge with David, rang him to see if a place could be found for me in the director's office.

'David is very clever,' said my uncle. 'He learned Japanese in three months and was able to interrogate Japanese prisoners of war.' I am glad I did not depart from private practice as, looking back, I have had all the fun, excitement and thrills of both prosecuting and defending nationally and internationally without having been a civil servant to whom, on the whole, such excitements were denied. However, we now have a Crown Prosecution Service composed of civil servants who only prosecute and a Public Defender Service, again, composed of civil servants, who defend.

In the simply dreadful judicial category there featured a number of London magistrates. One of them had a glass eye so perfectly made that it was impossible to tell it from the real one. The story goes that a young barrister sitting beside a more senior one in counsel's row whispered to his senior, 'Tell me, which one is the glass one?' The emphatic reply was, 'It's the one with the little bit of humanity in it, dear boy.'

The magistrates' courts were always a wonderful source of amusing stories which young members of the Bar regaled each other with on their return to chambers at the end of their legal forays. Mr Justice Sweeney tells the story of appearing for a motorist in the magistrates' court in his early days at the Bar. When the case was called on there seemed to be no prosecutor. The chairman of the bench looked around the court and said, 'Who is making the allegation?' There was no answer. On the third occasion these words were uttered a large officer in jack boots stepped into the well of the court and when asked by the chairman, 'Are you making the allegation?' replied, 'Yes, your worship, I am the alligator.' Needless to say Sweeney won his case.

A stipendiary magistrate known for getting through his list of cases expeditiously was once confronted by a police officer seeking an adjournment of a case so that the substance found in the possession of a defendant he had arrested the night before could be analysed. 'I know all about drugs,' said the Stipe, 'let me see what you found.'

The officer opened a sealed exhibit bag and handed over a small package.

Tearing it open the magistrate removed the contents and put a piece on his tongue. 'This is cannabis resin,' he said smugly, 'and where was it found?'

'In the defendant's anus,' was the embarrassed constable's reply.

Mike McElligott, who was a stipendiary at Old Street Magistrates' Court in the late 1960s, was never one to waste time. A busy prosecutor before he went on the bench, he was once prosecuting a fraud case in which the defendant, who had numerous convictions for dishonesty, had given evidence over two days trying to explain away a web of manifestly false transactions. In cross-examination McElligott asked but one question. 'When you die Mr Whelan, who will be the biggest liar in the county of Essex?' A rightful conviction of a guilty man was secured by a question that would today get counsel hauled up before the Bar Council.

Some judges were always a good source of hilarious pronouncements in court. However – and thankfully – many judicial remarks from yesteryear would no longer be tolerated today. The 1970s saw the high watermark of untoward judicial observations that would today invite ridicule or worse. I was a witness to some of them.

The awful Judge Gwyn Morris, QC, who sat at the Old Bailey, publicly stated in 1975 that he would like to put football louts 'in the stocks'. This was a punishment abolished in 1872. I was once defending a pharmacist in a fraud trial that had begun with four defendants, three of whom pleaded guilty before the jury was sworn to try my client. When the prosecution case against my client concluded, Gwyn Morris said to prosecuting counsel, 'It is only right that the jury should know that the three defendants who have pleaded guilty are of the Jewish faith.' Observations on immigration and race often found a place in his sentencing remarks; despite his ferocious prejudices he soldiered on undaunted.

The power of the Lord Chancellor to remove a judge had been used so sparingly for centuries that that it had almost fallen into disuse. In 1993, Judge Bruce Campbell's private yacht, *Papyrus*, was detained by Ramsgate customs with some 10,000 cigarettes and 125 litres of whisky. Campbell's companion, on what was manifestly a smuggling trip from Guernsey, was a second-hand car dealer. I received a telephone call from John Blackburn Gittings, then the senior partner of one of London's busiest firms of solicitors, informing me that he was with Judge Bruce Campbell, who had just been charged with attempting to evade customs duty. Because the press were camped outside he asked me if I could do a consultation at the Carlton Club, of which I was a member. I declined to hold a meeting at my club but agreed to speak to him. The rules of confidentiality prevent me from revealing the advice I gave; what I can say is that Bruce Campbell had distinguished himself in World War II and I came to the conclusion that, like many who had seen wartime action, he must have found life on the bench rather pallid. In due course, represented by Sir David Napley, he pleaded guilty, was fined and then removed as a judge by the Lord Chancellor, Lord Hailsham. It was the first time such a punishment had been meted out in recent times.

In another case, when an eminent counsel was mitigating on behalf of his company director client, who had committed an act of bestiality, defence counsel ended his plea to Judge John Maude with these words: 'Your Lordship has seen the medical reports. Alas, as Your Lordship will observe, my client has a split personality. My Lord, he is a Jekyll and Hyde; he is in fact two people.'

'In that case,' said Maude, 'they will both go to prison!'

In being merciful to an Irish labourer with pages of previous convictions for offences often associated with drink, he was to say, 'Promise me that you will not take another drink, even the smallest sherry before lunch.' The defendant nodded vigorously from the dock, seeing where his best interests lay.

Whether these utterances did in fact fall from the lips of Judge Maude, I do not know, but having appeared before him in the very first case I prosecuted at the Old Bailey, fifty years ago, I can well believe them. In this case the defendant, who had the unfortunate name of Sexious, was represented by my dear friend Nigel Murray, later a High Court master, whose first appearance at the Old Bailey this was. Nigel had an uphill task trying to persuade the jury that his client had not caused grievous bodily harm to a police constable by seriously damaging his testicles. In fact, the alibi in defence was essentially that at the time the constable suffered his testicular damage Sexious was in bed with a certain lady.

The alibi witness having given her evidence for the defence, it fell to me to cross-examine her. I put it to her that she was lying to assist the defendant. Standing in the witness box she threw her arms up in supplication to the heavens and declared loudly, 'God strike me dead if I tell a lie.' To this, the reply from John Maude was, 'Madam, compose yourself, He never interferes in my court.' I refrain from reporting the method used by Sexious to accomplish this injury to the officer, but suffice it to say that the defendant was convicted and the judge, having sentenced him to a term of imprisonment, invited both Nigel and me for a sherry. When the court clerk ushered us into the judge's room, we were met with the greeting, 'Children, I understand that this is your first case at the Bailey.'

A story I heard about Maude from more than one source had to do with when he was at the Bar and appearing for a defendant in a case with a number of other counsel. It was normal, in those days, for the High Sheriff of the county to be present on the first day of the assize sitting. On this particular day the scheduled trial in which Maude was appearing could not take place. All counsel involved in the non-effective trial were invited to lunch at the High Sheriff's manor house. Everyone was assembled in the High Sheriff's library at noon when, standing with his back to a roaring log fire, the incumbent of this ancient office began addressing the assembled company about his colonial experiences in Matabeleland. After half an hour Maude could take it no more. 'High Sheriff,' he said, 'do you speak any Matabele?'

'Yes, a little bit,' was the reply.

'Oh good,' said Maude, 'I would love to hear you say something in Matabele.'

'What would you like me to say?' said the puzzled High Sheriff.

To which Maude said, 'High Sheriff, what I would love to hear you say in Matabele is, "would you like a whisky and soda?"'

Judge Michael Argyle, QC, another Old Bailey judge, was also given to unconventional judicial utterances. Addressing a female police constable in the witness box in the middle of her testimony, he said, 'You are much too attractive to be a police woman – you should be a film star.'

I was once representing the manager of a major bank in a fraud trial who, depending on one's view of the evidence, was either duped by his criminal co-defendants or wholly central to the perpetration of the fraud. Returning from lunch in the Bar mess I was handed a message by the court usher. It was from Judge Argyle. The note said, 'If your client pleads guilty I will not send him to prison.' I was duty bound as counsel to alert my lay client to this communication and the judge's assurance of a non-custodial sentence. The bank manager leapt for joy and immediately agreed to plead guilty. All other defendants, when convicted by the jury, were sentenced to long terms of imprisonment. On this occasion my client had benefitted from rather erratic and errant judicial behaviour which was adversely commented on by the Court of Appeal when the others, who were sent to prison, sought to have their sentences reduced on appeal.

My heart always sank if I was informed that in a trial at the Old Bailey my judge was going to be Judge Edward Clarke, QC. The grandson of Sir Edward Clarke, QC, who was the counsel for Oscar Wilde at the Old Bailey in 1895, he was quite preposterous on the bench, but charming otherwise. When acting as defence counsel before him you felt he was incapable of being fair. One always had to prepare for a rough ride. He had a strong theatrical streak which he unfailingly put to use in court. When addressing a jury in a final speech I noticed some of them were distracted by something outside my line of vision. They were looking toward the judge. I, too, turned toward Judge Clarke momentarily and caught him pulling faces at the jury. Knowing his reputation for conduct of this kind I stopped addressing the jury and asked if he was feeling unwell. There was the inevitable judicial uproar, titters from the jury and an undeserved acquittal of the accused at the end. The average London jury takes against what it perceives to be unfairness on the bench. Edward Clarke's son, my very good friend Peter Clarke, QC, is now an excellent circuit judge who proves that sons are not necessarily destined to inherit their fathers' shortcomings.

Judge Murray Buttrose, who used to sit at the Old Bailey, had at one time been Solicitor General of Singapore before becoming a High Court judge there. It was said that he was once accused of sentencing eighty-six people to death before lunch during the Malayan Emergency. He robustly rounded on his accuser, saying, 'That is a gross exaggeration, it was only eighty-three.' Like it or not, many of these judges provide a vivid flavour of the times in which those at the Criminal Bar then functioned.

However, there were also some excellent Old Baily judges. Judge Christmas Humphreys, QC, was known as the Gentle Judge. Having been influenced by the writings of a Sri Lankan philosopher in his teens, he became drawn to Buddhism and was the author of many fine works on the faith. He had been the prosecuting counsel in a number of *causes célèbres* that saw the defendants go to the gallows. Some of them subsequently received posthumous pardons and those cases played a significant role in the abolition of capital punishment in the UK.

When I started at the Bar, the chairman of the Inner London Quarter Sessions was the unsmiling Reggie Seaton, QC, before whom I often appeared. The story is told that an old lag came up for sentence before him armed with a very favourable probation report recommending a non-custodial disposal of his case. In addition, the defendant had the good fortune to have a lady who ran a hostel who told the judge that, as the defendant was now a reformed character, she had no hesitation in offering him employment if given the chance to do so. In sentencing the defendant, the judge began by saying how greatly impressed he was by the kindly lady with the hostel. The old lag promptly perked up at this and smiled. 'Well,' continued the judge, 'she seems ever such a nice lady that I am sure she will not mind waiting for four years before employing you.'

With the possible exception in 2003 of an Old Bailey judge who adjourned his court so that he could go to Royal Ascot to watch his horse Counsel's Opinion in the 2.55 p.m. race, things have changed. The days when an Old Bailey judge intrigued juries by taking snuff in court instead of a note, or dashed off the bench to watch the 2.30 p.m. at Sandwich on the television in his room – returning either smiling or scowling depending upon the outcome of the race – are all gone. Gone too are the days when a judge would say at 3 p.m., 'Members of the jury, evening is drawing nigh. I think this is a convenient moment to adjourn.'

The days are also past when a senior judge at the Old Bailey who had been a fellow officer with my brother-in-law in the Coldstream Guards, seeing a defendant in the dock wearing a Household Brigade tie, decided that that alone was sufficient for the man's 'character to go in'. In those days, evidence as to the previous convictions of the defendant was not admissible in judicial proceedings, on the grounds that a defendant should be shielded from undue prejudice in the eyes of the jury. One circumstance in which it would be admissible is when a judge took the view that a defendant had put himself forward as a man of good character. Mervyn Griffiths Jones, the Common Sergeant of London, took the view that the tie the defendant was wearing was sufficient to throw away his shield.

All of us barristers were, when starting, very dependent on the clerks in chambers. The senior clerk ruled the roost and wielded great power. They could make or break a young barrister. Solicitors had to be carefully nurtured by our chambers clerks. We were not allowed to have business cards setting out our profession of Barrister-at-Law, as that would amount to advertising. Apart from Walter Butler (of whom more is to follow), I cannot leave out the names of Gordon Breadmore and Robin Driscoll, who succeeded Walter in turn and to whom I also owe a very great debt of gratitude for any success that has come my way as a barrister.

The principal concern of solicitors, then and now, was the late return of a brief that counsel had found himself unable to do. A barrister often finds himself in an impossible position through no fault of his own. A trial may overrun its estimate and he or she may be prevented from appearing in some new matter that clashes with the current commitment. Sometimes solicitors became so enraged that, despite all efforts by the clerks, they have been known never to instruct chambers again and, indeed, remove all their existing work from a set of chambers. It was all left to the clerks to smooth things over.

Those were the days when the power of a chambers' senior clerk was immense. He (there were no female clerks that I was aware of in the early 1960s, although some very able ones were around ten years later) could make or break a young entrant to the Bar. At the Criminal Bar the first thing a senior clerk would do, if he could, would be to get his 'guvnor' on to the Yard List, the 'Yard' being Scotland Yard and the 'List' being a list of counsel who were authorized to take on a 'Yard brief'. I was extremely lucky to be put on the Yard List within a few days of joining 2 Paper Buildings. One could start making a living as, if the Yard liked you, you could receive four or five briefs a day at 'the Mags'.

However, the power of an ordinary senior clerk was nothing to the power of a senior clerk in the chambers of one of the law offices of the government. In the chambers of the Solicitor General, which I had joined, the great Walter Butler was my senior clerk, and was one of the Temple's most remarkable and best loved figures. He was world renowned, to an extent that could never have been achieved by any other barrister's clerk. Starting as a junior clerk in chambers in 1923, Butler became senior clerk in 1937. With the development of air travel English counsel were increasingly flown all over the Commonwealth to defend or prosecute in important cases. Because chambers had a monopoly on work before the Privy Council, which was the highest Court of Appeal for the Commonwealth, it often happened that chambers would take in pupils from the Commonwealth, who would then go on to hold high office in their own countries. They always maintained their links with chambers. Walter was the centre of this international legal community.

According to Dingle, Walter's finest moment was in 1955 when a telegram arrived from northern Nigeria. It was addressed simply to 'Butler London'. There were several well-known bearers of the Butler name. No fewer than thirty-one were then listed in *Who's Who*. One of them was the Chancellor of the Exchequer, R. A. Butler. Nevertheless, the telegram was delivered to Walter at 2 Paper Buildings. His greatest friend was the other legendary senior clerk, Stanley Hopkins of 5 Kings Bench Walk, who had at one time been the junior clerk in the chambers of the great Norman Birkett, QC, and the legendary Sir Edward Marshall Hall at 3 Temple Gardens.

In 1992, one of Stanley's 'guvnors' was appointed Solicitor General by Prime Minister John Major. Sir Derek Spencer, QC, MP, had won his first seat by only seven votes. When Derek came into chambers one day, Stanley had just finished reading the names of MPs who had voted in favour of capital punishment. That list included Derek. The story was told at El Vino that Stanley said to him, 'Sir, with a majority of seven I would be trying to keep them alive!'

Walter, together with Eric, the Attorney General's clerk, controlled a vast array of 'nominations'. These were usually high-profile and well-paid prosecution briefs that lay in the gift of the law officers which, in reality, meant in the gift of their clerks. I remember Walter and Eric debating as to who would get the leading and junior briefs for the prosecution in the case of the Moors Murderers, Ian Brady and Myra Hindley.

One evening Walter and I were sitting at El Vino in Fleet Street, at a table which was reserved for our chambers, when a bottle of champagne arrived with a waitress who proceeded to whisper in Walter's ear. It was obvious she was telling him it came with someone's compliments. Walter and I looked round to see who our benefactor was, only to observe an eminent silk at another table raising his glass to Walter. Sitting next to him was Barry Hudson, QC, squinting at us through the smoke curling up from the cigarette pendant between his lips.

'I've got a good nomination for you, sir,' said Walter, thanking the QC for the champagne.

No doubt Walter kept his word. Our benefactor later went on to become the Attorney General and, after that, Lord High Chancellor of Great Britain. That night he was after a brief!

Apart from persuading solicitors who are in the habit of instructing chambers to try a new barrister, the clerk could give a young barrister a junior brief to sit behind leading counsel, usually a silk. This was known as 'being led'. The very first time I was led was by Dick Taverne, QC, MP. To this day I can recall a few aspects of that case as it if were yesterday, although the case itself took place in the first months of my tenancy at 2 Paper Buildings, over fifty years ago.

'I have got you a case with a decent fee,' Walter said to me one morning. His motto was no case is too small and no fee is too high.

I was delighted.

'What sort of case is it?' I asked.

'It's a charter-party case,' he said.

'But I know nothing about shipping law,' I pleaded.

'Don't worry,' said Walter. 'Just sit behind Mr Taverne and keep a good note.'

Clutching some papers, I arrived in the Admiralty Division of the High Court in the Strand with Dick. We'd had a working breakfast in a cafe in Fleet Street, where, not to Dick's discredit, the efforts he made to explain the intricacies of this case were lost on me. Rather like the former Conservative cabinet minister Ken Clarke, QC, Dick loved wearing Hush Puppies. In those days, the dress code for barristers was rigidly enforced and some traditionalist judges took great exception to counsel wearing what was considered unusual attire.

Of course, it was just my luck that in the first moments in court things started to go wrong. Somehow the judge, who wore a monocle, spotted that Dick was not wearing black leather shoes. When my leader got up to address

His Lordship he was met with a frosty stare. No sooner had Dick spoken the traditional opening line of counsel, 'May it please you My Lord,' than the judge intervened with the remark, 'I cannot hear you, Mr Taverne.'

'I am sorry My Lord,' said Dick, 'I shall speak up.'

'I still cannot hear you,' said the scowling figure on the bench.

'I shall speak louder still,' shouted Dick.

'No, Mr Taverne,' said the judge. 'I cannot hear you until you are properly shod.'

For a moment I was gripped with a terrible panic. I thought Dick was going to turn round and say to me, 'Take over while I go and get a pair of shoes.' I was getting ready to feign a sudden attack of something when I heard the usher's voice in the distance saying, 'All rise.' My spirits rose too. All was well. The judge rose to give Dick a chance to go to Ede & Ravenscroft in Chancery Lane to get a pair of black shoes.

'Silly bugger,' said Dick, when the monocled figure was out of earshot. 'Hang on in court for twenty minutes while I get myself a pair of shoes.'

The case lasted some four days and was so complex that it remains, to this day, totally incomprehensible to me. Apart from some divorce work and a foray into libel, when I was led by David Hirst, QC, who became a Lord Justice, I told Walter Butler that I proposed to stick to crime, both national and international.

In the mid-1960s there were just four courts at the Old Bailey. The stalwarts of the Bailey Bar mess were Jeremy Hutchinson (now Lord Hutchinson), Victor Durand, Dick du Cann, Robin Simpson, Michael Corkery, Brian Leary, Bill Howard, Sir Harold Cassel, James Crespi, John Marriage, Barry Hudson, John Matthew and Edward Cussen. They were some of the more colourful characters on the commanding heights of the Criminal Bar. Half of those named were regulars at El Vino and most were yet to take silk. It was a delight to be in a trial with any of these advocates – all remarkable, charismatic and quite distinctive in their styles. George Carman and Gilbert Gray, both outstanding northern practitioners, had yet to make their mark in London. George did it with his successful defence in 1979 of the Liberal leader Jeremy Thorpe, which was a prelude to his phenomenal success in the decades to follow. Apart from Cussen, who was on the bench, it has been my privilege to have shared the illustrious company, in and out of court, of all of these outstanding advocates.

I recall Dick du Cann telling me of a murder in which he had been junior counsel, where the lay client had been sentenced to death. In conversations with his leader he learned how agonizing some decisions could be. There was an arguable appeal, but the danger lurked in the fact that the hearing would inevitably come before the Lord Chief Justice Goddard. If the Appeal Court rejected the appeal and Goddard chose, as he often did, to make some trenchant remarks about the appellant, there was no chance of a successful appeal for clemency to the Home Secretary. Was it wiser to avoid the Court of Appeal altogether and place the fate of the doomed man in the hands of the Home Secretary? The agony, of course, lay in having to advise one's client and deal with the inevitable question, 'what do you think will happen?'

In 2001, long after capital punishment had been abolished in the UK, I was instructed to appear in Botswana, where the first white woman to be convicted of murder had been sentenced to hang. I will never forget Mariette Bosch putting her rather frail hand into mine when I went to visit her in the death cells and her saying to me, 'If my appeal fails, will you promise to be near me when I stand on the threshold of eternity?'

In those days El Vino did not admit unaccompanied ladies. It was not just a watering hole for the Bar and Fleet Street journalists, but also acted as a bank where, in those pre-ATM days, we cashed our cheques.

Barry Hudson – who in his later years would send juniors scurrying back to the Temple to look for the false teeth he had left in chambers before going to the Bailey – together with James Crespi, dominated a table at El Vino. Barry, who prosecuted in my very first jury trial at Middlesex Quarter Sessions and who did a great deal of prosecuting for the Yard at that time, was once driving back home after a late session at El Vino when he found himself being followed by a police car. Try as he might, he could not shake off the tailing vehicle. He eventually took a turn which lead into a cul-de-sac. Fearing arrest and disqualification for driving while unfit, he jumped out of his vehicle and did a runner. Despite the fact that in his youth he had been a long distance runner of note, gaining a blue at Cambridge for athletics, two panting policemen finally caught up with him. One of them placed a hand on his shoulder and saved Barry the ignominy of arrest by saying, 'Mr Hudson, sir, let us drive you home.' Barry had the unusual distinction of having a very successful career at the Bar without passing his Bar finals. His plan to sit for his finals in 1939 was interrupted by the outbreak of war; he was mobilized as a subaltern in the Royal Artillery. Understanding examiners gave him a dispensation from further exams.

The unstoppably indiscreet James Caesar Crespi was a brilliant lawyer, a great wit and perhaps the last of the great eccentrics at the Bar. We took silk together in 1984. He weighed over twenty-seven stone; when the IRA detonated a bomb outside the Bailey in 1972, he was caught in the blast and survived because of his bulk. When Lord Hailsham visited him in hospital, Crespi said proudly, 'Lord Chancellor, I put myself between the bomb and the Bailey.' Rather like being decorated for gallantry in battle he was appointed a Recorder on the spot.

James, who had a photographic memory, slept little and frequented the dubious Eve's Club off Regent Street, where he met a girl whom he married. The marriage sadly only lasted some weeks. In later years, when James wanted to be a permanent judge at the Old Bailey, his short marriage to the club hostess at Eve's proved an insuperable barrier. When a deputation of his friends sought to persuade the Lord Chancellor about a permanent judicial appointment, they were met with the objection, 'but she has form for tomming [prostitution] and what's more, he is still married to her.'

Our chambers had its own table at El Vino and any new member was taken there to get to know other members over drinks. The round tables were seen as circles of fellowship. Our senior clerk always repaired to 'EV's' at 5 p.m. and juniors in chambers were bidden to attend. On joining chambers I was taken up to EV's, where Walter informed me my annual rent in chambers would be £150, but my EV's expenses would be about £500. A heavy evening at El Vino was often followed by a dinner at Rules or at one's club. Then back home to prepare for court the following day unless Tom Kellock persuaded you he had a feeling that we would be lucky at Crockfords or the White Elephant on the River.

Another jovial eccentric at the Bar who frequented El Vino was the baronet Sir Lionel Thompson, who was arrested for drunk driving and taken to Cannon Row Police Station where, putting his experience as an Oxford boxing blue to good effect, he laid out the desk sergeant and two other police officers. My recollection is that he was tried for assault occasioning actual bodily harm and was triumphantly acquitted by a jury at the Inner London Quarter Sessions.

There was a brief period when Lionel started coming to El Vino with a Gladstone bag which contained a python. It turned out he had formed a relationship with a Spanish girl who had a cabaret act in which this reptile played an important part. Leaving for Spain for a week, she entrusted the creature to Lionel. Unfamiliar with how to deal with it, he used to come to the bar at El Vino, reach into the bag, squeeze the base of the reptile's head and pour a double gin down its throat. The romance with the Spanish girl had an unhappy ending. On the day she returned from Spain, her prop breathed its last and died of alcohol poisoning.

Michael Worsley, QC, who had been an outstanding senior Treasury counsel was, when he retired, the Old Bailey's most experienced prosecutor. Scrupulously fair and with a phenomenal legal brain, he kept a copy of *Archbold Criminal Pleading, Evidence and Practice* in his lavatory. In an appeal before the House of Lords, Michael's submissions were interrupted by Lord Diplock who said to him, 'Mr Worsley, this is nonsense, the case of Brown is against you.'

Michael replied, 'Has Your Lordship read the case?'

'Yes,' said Diplock tersely.

'Recently?' inquired Michael.

He was another of the Old Bailey stalwarts with whom I took silk in 1984.

Some of the great advocates I had the privilege of co-defending alongside included the legendary George Carman, QC, and those two celebrated raconteurs and wits Gilbert Gray, QC, and Rodney Klevan, QC. Rodney went on to the High Court bench shortly after he had successfully defended the Liverpool goalkeeper Bruce Grobbelaar, and I had defended Hans Segers, the Wimbledon goalkeeper. That was Britain's first football match-fixing trial, which came to be called football's trial of the century. Rodney and I had the pleasure of having Jerome Lynch and Trevor Burke, both yet to take silk, defending with us. Prosecuting for the Crown in this case was David Calvert-Smith, later to become the Director of Public Prosecutions and a High Court judge.

~

For some five centuries the Old Bailey has been one of the world's most famous criminal courts. Renamed the Central Criminal Court in 1834, it is still more popularly known as the Old Bailey. The present building dates from 1907 and, despite it no longer being the hub of the most celebrated trials taking place in London, judges and lawyers from abroad are still some of its most appreciative visitors. The training school for many eminent advocates and judges, the Bailey, to me, was the place to be. The methods of advocacy at the Old Bailey, which had been held up to ridicule by certain supercilious civil practitioners and writers of fiction, have now given way to advocacy that is neither too oratorical nor theatrical. However, there is a connection between the Bar and the stage. Many members of the Bar are members of the Garrick Club, situated in the heart of Theatreland and named after the great eighteenth-century actor. Some barristers even became accomplished dramatists themselves, the most famous of whom in recent times was Sir John Mortimer, QC. Lord Havers, the former Lord Chancellor, co-wrote *The Royal Baccarat Scandal*, the first night of which I attended at the Haymarket Theatre.

A military coup in Ghana in 1966 resulted in the fall of its elected leader, Kwame Nkrumah. This event led to my first junior brief in the House of Lords and my first junior brief at the Old Bailey. Our lay client, Kwesi Armah, having given up his diplomatic post in London, had gone back to Ghana to become minister of trade. He took refuge in England after the coup and the new government in Accra sought his extradition from England.

It was a case that took me to the House of Lords and twice to the Divisional Court in my first year in proper practice at the Bar. I was led by Tom Kellock, QC, in our chambers. On both occasions we succeeded in preventing our client from being extradited and sent back to Ghana. When we had our first victory before the House of Lords, Their Lordships ordered Armah's immediate release from custody. Our solicitors took me and Tom to El Vino for an alcoholic celebration and then on to Crockfords for dinner and a bit of gambling; Tom lost his entire brief fee playing roulette that night. Then, at about 11 p.m., a message came through that Armah had been arrested again. Fuelled by a great deal of champagne, we rushed back to chambers to make a midnight bail application.

During the vacation, when no judge is sitting in court, a bail application may be made to a judge anywhere he can be found. Fortunately, a number of High Court judges resided on the upper floors of our buildings. The only problem was that Tom and I had drunk so much we could not make it up the stairs to the upper floors. Walter Butler managed to track down Louis Blom-Cooper, QC in our chambers to make a sober application, as Tom and I settled ourselves at the bottom of the steps leading to the judge's flat. Having made the bail application to a judge who was in his pyjamas, Louis came down with a handwritten order, directed to the governor of Brixton Prison, authorizing bail. Tom, myself and the solicitors continued with our revels that night.

The second extradition request by the authorities in Ghana ended up in the Divisional Court which refused leave to appeal to the House of Lords. Once again, I was fortunate enough to be junior counsel to Tom. The government in Accra was so incensed when Home Secretary Roy Jenkins refused in January 1967 to return this former minister, on the grounds that the second request for extradition was politically motivated, that suggestions started being made in Accra that Ghana, the first of Britain's African colonies to receive independence, should leave the Commonwealth. A decision was made in London to pacify Accra by the prosecution of Armah at the Old Bailey for theft. After a conference in chambers, my instructing solicitors decided we needed to have the leading criminal silk of the day for the jury trial at the Old Bailey.

Jeremy Hutchinson, QC was the greatest criminal barrister in the country, whose impact as an advocate, in a variety of cases, was to change social perceptions. While Jeremy led me for the defence of Armah, the Crown was represented by my head of chambers, Sir Dingle Foot, QC, who led John Matthew, then senior Treasury counsel.

I could not have had a finer leader than the donnish Hutchinson, with his immense charm and razor-sharp mind. Watching him perform in court was like being at a command performance. With a lifetime's interest in the arts, he was married to a famous actress. The trial went well for our client and Armah, the former Ghanaian minister and high commissioner to the Court of St James's from 1961 to 1965, was triumphantly acquitted.

Many, particularly American lawyers, find it hard to understand how two people in the same chambers can be on opposite sides without there being some conflict of interest. They would find it inexplicable that I could be defending a client with my head of chambers acting for the prosecution. It is testimony to the strength of the English judicial system that such appearances by counsel, in my experience, have never impinged upon their duty to their respective clients; nor has justice been seen to fail in such circumstances.

There seemed to be a *joie de vivre* around in those days that is much less noticeable now. I recall the most spectacular ball in 1965 to commemorate Wellington's victory over the French 150 years before. The Waterloo Ball took over the entire Gothic-style Royal Courts of Justice in the Strand. There were two bands, one at each end of the Great Hall, and there was even a casino set up in the Lord Chief Justice's Court. Lord Parker and his American wife presided over this extravaganza. The dress code for men was meant to be period costume which, with a little licence, turned out to be that of the Regency period. My outfit had been made for Albert Finney, which he wore in the film *Tom Jones*. With a few tailoring adjustments, it fitted me perfectly. Rosamund Cameron, with whom I went, wore a dress made for Jane Asher for a period film, together with a wimple. The billionaire Paul Getty was there dressed as a Regency buck with Robina Lund; the striking magnate Nubar Gulbenkian, and a host of guests who made London hum in the sixties, gathered to celebrate the outcome of the battle that saved Europe from Napoleon's domination. Michael Corkery, who became a good friend and senior Treasury counsel in later years, was there too, with some of the other great figures from the Bar who I had not yet met.

In the 1960s and 1970s there was a deal of corruption in the Metropolitan Police. Suspects used to be verballed, which meant confessions were ascribed to them while in police custody and without a solicitor present. This often proved fatal to a defence raised in court. It took skilled advocacy to penetrate to the truth. Happily, early and prompt access to free legal advice by a suspect, which is central to a fair trial, was introduced in 1984. The days of sudden confessions to a police officer came to an end.

For the rest of the twentieth century we saw the criminal justice system operating at its best. The citizen accused of crime, whose liberty or reputation was at stake, had access to the finest and most talented barristers through legal aid. It was then the best legal system in the world, envied across the globe. In a modern, civilized society, a healthy justice system stands side by side with good medical care available for all. The twenty-first century has seen an unhappy reversal of all that was good about the criminal justice system. With modern Lord Chancellors knowing nothing about the practice of law and seeing in the administration of justice a method to advance their own political careers, the downward spiral in the criminal justice system continues.

Legal aid has been slashed. Salaried civil servants from the Public Defender System now oppose other civil servants of the Crown Prosecution Service. With civil servants to prosecute and civil servants to defend, true independence in legal practice has been eroded. The truly independent advocate is being squeezed out of the system, leading to far fewer competent criminal barristers representing those whose lives and reputations may be destroyed. Elite chambers have emerged, but not for those of modest means. Be it an Army officer wrongly accused of betraying his country's secrets or a public figure accused of shoplifting, the consequences of being arrested and charged can be ruinous. Where reputation was at stake there was in place a system of independent representation that protected citizens to the utmost. That has been eroded. In my view, that which increases the chances of miscarriages of justice strikes at the rule of law itself.

The role of independent barrister lies at the heart of justice. If prosecuting, he was totally in charge of the case he was presenting. In the event that he formed the view, having heard a cross-examination of his principal witness by the defence, that he could not properly ask the jury to convict, he would inform the judge that he would not be seeking a conviction and offer no further evidence. The jury would then be directed by the judge to bring in a verdict of not guilty. This was independence and integrity combined.

Today, prosecuting counsel would be wondering if the Crown Prosecution Service would brief them again if they were seen to throw in the towel. As for a Crown Prosecution Service civil servant prosecutor, would the lure of promotion impede bold independence?

Looking back to my call to the Bar in 1964, with over half a century of practice thereafter, I am more than ever convinced the law has been one of England's greatest exports to the world. The rule of law, habeas corpus and the concept of due process of law are inseparable from human freedom. Today these principles are on the lips of every lawyer professing an interest in the liberty of the subject worldwide. They have their origins in England, and Magna Carta is the single most important document produced in England. For centuries it has been seen as the guiding star by which freedom has been guaranteed in the English-speaking world. Nowhere are the basic concepts of the rule of law and due process more clearly stated than in Magna Carta. Chapter 29 of the Great Charter of 1215 is the most powerful of statements, which has guided my footsteps as a barrister.

> No freeman is to be taken or imprisoned, or be disseised of his freehold, or of his liberties, or free customs, or be outlawed, or exiled, or any other wise ruined, nor will we go against such a man, nor condemn him save by lawful judgment of his peers by the law of the land. We will sell to no man, we will not deny or defer to any man either justice or right.

The Charter, signed by King John at Runnymede, was the precursor to many of the civil and political rights to be found in the European Convention on Human Rights and Fundamental Freedoms, signed in 1950 by the member states of the Council of Europe.

While the rule of law is integral to democracy itself, it has been a sad experience for me to sometimes witness at close quarters its perversion in the hands of those whose systems maintain all the trappings of the law but nevertheless ensure that the practice of it serves sinister and political ends. In succeeding chapters I deal with my experience of being jailed more than once, and being the victim of more than one attempted assassination, in certain jurisdictions where those in authority saw the administration of justice as a method of ensuring the destruction of political opposition.

~

Five decades after my first unnerving experience in the Privy Council and after countless murder trials, some capital murder cases in the Commonwealth, football celebrity trials, endless fraud cases, treason trials, drugs cases and a spy trial or two, I found myself, in 2012, sitting in a courtroom in the International Criminal Court (ICC) in The Hague, which had been allocated to the Special Court for Sierra Leone.

All eyes were on a door through which a man awaiting judgment was about to enter from the detention in which he was being held. He was someone against whom I had signed an eleven-count indictment and whose arrest I had brought about after the Secretary-General of the United Nations had appointed me the chief prosecutor of the Special Court of Sierra Leone, which was required to try those who bore the greatest responsibility for war crimes arising from a decade-long, savage civil war. They were hideous crimes and their methods of commission so evil that their investigation and prosecution took us to the very heart of darkness. The immaculately attired defendant entered the court and sat in the dock. All eyes now turned to the entrance through which the judges were about to enter.

The night before this judgment, David Crane, the founding chief prosecutor of the Special Court of Sierra Leone, hosted a splendid dinner in The Hague. I succeeded David, who had signed the first seventeen-count indictment against this defendant. In turn, I was succeeded by Stephen Rapp, who went on to become President Obama's ambassador for war crimes issues in 2009. Also present at the dinner was Brenda Hollis who had succeeded Stephen and to a large extent carried the heat and burden of the trial. It was an anxious time for all those who had laboured for many years to bring a brutal head of state and war criminal to justice.

We all stood as the judges entered and took their places on the bench. Mr Justice Lussick delivered the judgment of the court. The man in the dock was ex-president Charles Taylor of Liberia, whom I had once described as Africa's Hitler. Was history going to be made on this day in 2012? The last head of state to have been convicted by an International Criminal Tribunal was Grand Admiral Dönitz, who had succeeded Hitler as Führer, and faced the judgment of the International Military Tribunal in Nuremburg in 1946.

## 2

# Target Number One: Blood Diamonds and Warlords

LITTLE DID I REALIZE IN 2002 WHAT CHANGES THAT YEAR WOULD bring to my career. But then life, as I have learned, has its own agenda. It was the start of a process that would eventually throw me into the heart of darkness and unimagined adventures in the international legal and political firmament.

In the 1990s, the United Nations set up two ad hoc international criminal courts; one to deal with the crimes committed during the conflict in what had formerly been Yugoslavia (ICTY) and the other to deal with the genocide in Rwanda (ICTR). These were the first attempts by the international community to bring to justice those responsible for war crimes and crimes against humanity since the Nuremberg and Tokyo tribunals that followed World War II.

In 2002, the international community created the Special Court for Sierra Leone. This court had been structured differently by the international community in order to eradicate some of the failings that appeared inherent in the setting up of the other two international courts. I was invited to become the deputy prosecutor at the level of an Assistant Secretary-General (ASG) of the UN. Given my interest in world affairs I accepted it as an irresistible posting.

In answering the call of international justice I was exchanging the richer prospects of the Bar for the considerably leaner rewards of the salary at a level of an ASG – with no pension entitlement. There had to be cutbacks in England. Luxuries such as the racehorse had to go. My trainer, Jamie Osborne, had informed me that the name I had originally chosen for the Irish colt, Reasonable Doubt, was not an option, as a horse with a similar name had raced before. So, Trusted Mole became the registered name of the horse. As moles are not very fast, the reason for the selection of this unusual name came at the insistence of my former client, Major Milos Stankovic, MBE, of the Parachute Regiment, who had been wrongly accused of breaches of the Official Secrets Act. He was then just about to publish his military memoirs that dealt with his experiences during the Bosnian war. Its title was *Trusted Mole.* With the concurrence of my instructing solicitor, Steven Barker, the colt was registered as Trusted Mole.

The delightful Sharon Baxter from my chambers agreed to come out to Sierra Leone as part of my team. She had the advantage of knowing Africa well. Alas, her valuable contribution had to be foreshortened when, in 2003, it looked as if her husband, Brigadier James Baxter, might have to deploy to Iraq in what became Operation Iraqi Freedom; she wanted to return to England to be with him before his possible deployment. As a legal secretary, I had the good fortune to have the very experienced and engaging Tracy Pettitt, who was to meet her future husband, Lt. Colonel Duncan Bruce, in Freetown. He later went on to command his regiment in England. The rest of my core team in Freetown consisted of two highly experienced British close protection officers: Malcolm Hutchinson from the Royal Ulster Constabulary in Northern Ireland and Robbie Franks who was in the Royal Marines.

Friends who read the diaries I kept while I was deputy prosecutor have suggested that any memoirs I write should incorporate my notes from the time for two reasons. First, they give a feel for the moment and, secondly, they provide a sharp insight into the sort of work done and the decisions that have to be made by those who represent the Office of the Prosecutor and the tensions that were ever-present in the new model of court. From my own point of view, the keeping of a diary enables me to reflect on past mistakes in the hope that they will not be repeated.

The Office of the Prosecutor is the engine that drives the train of justice. It is the prosecutor and the deputy prosecutor who decide if war crimes and the like have been committed and, if so, by whom; they also decide what charges should follow and what evidence needs to be called upon to prove a case. It comes after a process known as conflict mapping.

What follows is a narrative, interspersed with my diary entries as deputy prosecutor. I hope the latter will give the reader a flavour of my life on this mission, with some of the problems, and something of the mirth, that attended our lives at the time. Of course, I was answerable at all times to my

American boss, David Crane, who was the chief prosecutor of the Special Court.

I should point out that war crimes courts are institutions designed to be a part of an accountability process based on the concept that justice is the cornerstone of peace and reconciliation. Nowhere was this truer than in Sierra Leone where, on my arrival, I found 17,000 UN troops keeping the peace. In addition, there was the British-led International Military Advisory and Training Team, then commanded by Brigadier Patrick Davidson-Houston.

David Crane and his senior staff took up residence at Seaview House, which had been the HQ from which Operation Barras (also known as Operation Certain Death) was planned. It was a brilliantly successful SAS jungle raid in September 2000 to free British forces held captive by the drug-crazed and unpredictable militia known as the West Side Boys. Their cry was, 'What makes the grass grow? Blood, Blood, Blood.' The SAS was assisted by elements of the 1st Battalion Parachute Regiment, together with other specialist units. Huge credit for the planning of this successful operation must go to Brigadier David Richards (now General Lord Richards) and Brigadier John Holmes (now Major General Holmes).

After a very short stay elsewhere, my team and I were moved to Union House, overlooking Freetown. It had been the home of Brigadier Patrick Davidson-Houston which, thanks to both him and the Ministry of Defence in the UK, was made available to me. There was a high perimeter wall, an underground escape tunnel beneath the swimming pool and a six-inch-thick steel door in the corridor leading to my bedroom. Today, law and lawyers have become an essential part of any peacekeeping operation.

When I arrived in Freetown in early 2002, two of the people we were looking at as possible indictees outside Sierra Leone were Muammar Gaddafi, the ruler of Libya, and Charles Taylor, the president of Liberia. Taylor was a former student at Gaddafi's university of terrorism in Tripoli and someone who had spent a decade at the epicentre of destabilizing West Africa. He was responsible for the deaths of tens of thousands. Gaddafi and Taylor both had hit squads and the former also had an effective intelligence system, against which we had to guard.

Protecting ourselves involved creating a windowless sterile room at Seaview which we called the Bubble, within which no interception from outside was possible any more than any contact from within could be communicated to the outside. Once inside the Bubble its entry point was sealed electronically and remained sealed until a predetermined time we had set. There was one moment of crisis when, through an electricity failure, the electronic door failed to open and for some reason the generator failed to kick in. Al White, our chief of investigations, formerly of the FBI; Gilbert Morissette, formerly of the RCMP; two others and I began to try to work out how much air we had left, with suggestions being made that we should lie down on the floor to use less oxygen. Luckily for us, someone did eventually get the generator working for some different purpose and this led to us freeing ourselves, but not before we had spent an unnerving time contemplating an unpleasant fate.

Diamonds have been used in a strategic and systematic way by rebel groups to fund some of the most savage wars in Africa; al-Qaeda cells began a massive diamond-buying operation in Sierra Leone and Liberia following the crack-down on al-Qaeda finances after the US Embassy bombings in East Africa in 1998. Diamonds have proved to be the easiest way for al-Qaeda to convert their cash into an easily transferrable commodity, which can be hidden from those looking for a financial trail. In Sierra Leone a number of Lebanese diamond dealers are Shi'ites from Tyre and south Lebanon. Many Lebanese who control the diamond business in Sierra Leone are sympathetic to the aims of al-Qaeda and Hezbollah. For al-Qaeda and, no doubt, Hezbollah, trading in underpriced, looted Sierra Leone diamonds and fencing them in Europe has been a source of considerable revenue. A number of known al-Qaeda operatives – some indicted by the FBI for the bombing of the US Embassy in Nairobi, yet still on the loose – did, until 2001, turn up in Sierra Leone on a regular basis, in pursuit of funding via the diamond business.

Shortly after I arrived in Sierra Leone in 2002 I began to ask myself what on earth I was doing there. The last time I had been in Freetown I was jailed and shot at. That was thirty-four years earlier when I was twenty-eight; a different part of my life. Now I had to travel between Freetown, London, New York and Washington to do the work the international community, and David Crane, required.

18 SEPTEMBER 2002
*Mammy Yoko Hotel, Freetown*

'Your boss is target number one,' said Colonel David Blizzard to my PA, Tracy Pettitt, the day she arrived from London.

'Why is he target number one?' she asked.

'Because he is well known in Freetown, easily identifiable, someone who knows a great deal about the background to the civil war,' was the grizzled colonel's reply.

16 NOVEMBER 2002
*Freetown, Sierra Leone*

'Good evening sir,' said Terry Spearman, from the Office of the Prosecutor (OTP). Terry, formerly US special forces, is now on the Security Committee of the OTP. 'A matter of operational security. Can you come to the OTP immediately?'

David Crane, my American boss, is abroad and I am in charge.

On my arrival at the OTP in Seaview House I chair a meeting of the Security Committee, at which I am informed that US intelligence sources have passed information on to us that a female close to President Charles Taylor of Liberia has, in the past twenty-four hours, shepherded a quantity of rocket-propelled grenades and their launchers into Freetown. I am further informed that the original source is credible. I have had to alert Robin Vincent, the superb and unflappable registrar of the Special Court. His is a position of vital importance and I am so glad someone of his calibre has come to us from the Lord Chancellor's Department.

Is this delivery to be used to attack us at Seaview? Or the Registry at King Tom? Is it to be used on the occasion of the swearing-in ceremony of the judges of the new international war crimes tribunal? A few well-placed RPGs and the Special Court for Sierra Leone would be stalled in its tracks. In UN terms this is a hazard posting and there would be little enthusiasm for the international staff here to return after an emergency evacuation.

Keith Biddle, the British Inspector General of Police, is on his way back to Freetown from the provinces. I decide to await his arrival at the OTP.

19 NOVEMBER 2002
*Seaview House, Freetown*

In 2000, when Tony Blair ordered that British troops being held hostage by the murderous West Side Boys had to be freed, in what turned out to be one of the most daring SAS/Para missions ever, it was at Seaview House, a former British military HQ, that a great deal of the planning for Operation Barras took place.

The Office of the Prosecutor is now situated here.

I am at my desk at the OTP. On my left, on the wall, is a detailed map of Sierra Leone. To my right and behind me is a large window of bulletproof glass with a one-way view. The window overlooks a colonnaded colonial-type terrace. The large trees in the garden below have been cut down to give us a line of sight to the British high commission. The dining table in the far corner of the terrace has been screened off with bamboo matting to make it more difficult for a sniper to take someone out while we have lunch. In front of me is Security Council Resolution 1315, under the authority of which I am here. Immediately behind me stands a bookcase with files containing the details of some of the most savage and abominable war crimes and crimes against humanity that have devastated this diamond-rich former British colony over the past ten years, and that have made Sierra Leone synonymous with vile brutality.

Security Council Resolution 1315 of August 2000 states that the situation in Sierra Leone continues to constitute a threat to international peace and security in the region and calls upon the UN Secretary-General to set about negotiating the creation of an independent international special court to exercise jurisdiction over crimes against humanity, war crimes and other serious violations of international humanitarian laws.

The prosecutions are be carried out 'in theatre' in the middle of the killing fields where thousands of ex-combatants and their victims live side by side in explosive proximity. Some of the warlords, too, are still about. As my American boss once put it, 'Desmond, we are surrounded by the bad guys. We might have to lean forward in the saddle to get out of dodge fast!'

20 NOVEMBER 2002
*Seaview House, Freetown*

As I walk back to my desk from the terrace I spot a local newspaper lying on a table in the OTP. 'THE AGE OF IMPUNITY IS NOW OVER – JUSTICE ROBERTSON' screeched the headline. 'There should be no hiding place for those who commit crimes against humanity.' The paper goes on to attribute the published phrase to Geoffrey Robertson, QC, a fellow British silk and the new president of the Special Court for Sierra Leone.

To help bring an end to the cycle of impunity? Is this what has brought me here? Or is it that after fifteen years of being head of chambers in London I need a break? Is it that I was once the pupil master to the Cardiff University graduate and Lincoln's Inn-educated barrister, President Kabbah, the democratically elected leader of Sierra Leone, who is desperately trying to lead his people out of an incessant cycle of military rule? Or perhaps it was that five-year-old amputee girl whose arms were hacked off by rebels, saying to her mother, in Krio, 'Mummy, when will my arms grow again?'

Am I a part of a team that may yet play a role in the successful transition of Sierra Leone from brutal violence to democratic peace? Are we about to meet the expectations of those who say there is no peace without justice? I think that the rule of law demands that a man responsible for killing tens of thousands does not escape justice, particularly when someone who steals a loaf of bread is hauled before the courts. The most culpable of these monsters, at the moment, are free to walk the same streets as their victims' families.

I am constantly reminded that this is the first time since World War II that a court has been set up to try war criminals 'in theatre'; this is yet another attempt by the international community to break the cycle of impunity that has enabled despots and warlords to escape the consequences of their crimes against international law for decades; it is all part of the movement away from appeasement, an attempt to bring grave violators of crimes against humanity to book.

The Sierra Leone war crimes tribunal represents the next step in the evolution of the international response to criminality with impunity.

The ability of the warlords of Sierra Leone to purchase weapons depended, to a large extent, on their control of Sierra Leone's diamond-producing areas.

Before I left London for Freetown I was made aware of a shadowy diamond route to al-Qaeda, whose involvement in these tragic events in Sierra Leone forms part of our investigations. In September 1998, Abdullah Ahmed Abdullah, a senior al-Qaeda operative and one of the FBI's twenty-five most wanted men, came to Liberia and met with President Charles Taylor and senior Revolutionary United Front (RUF) representatives. The object of the meeting was for al-Qaeda to buy large quantities of Sierra Leone diamonds from the RUF in return for weapons.

Over the past two years the official value of diamond exports from Sierra Leone has halved. In the same period diamond exports by Liberia – a country with few diamonds – has risen dramatically, indicating the flow of conflict diamonds to Taylor's Liberia.

The Liberian president, Charles Taylor, is a Boston-educated warlord and a descendant of the freed American slaves who founded Liberia. He won elections in his country in 1997 after a devastating seven-year civil war. My brief is to investigate him for his part in the bloody conflict in Sierra Leone. A predatory actor in the West Africa region, he has been described by the US State Department as being at 'the epicentre of a system of conflict'. In his civil war, Taylor was supported and backed by the president of Libya, Muammar Gaddafi. Taylor has become Gaddafi's protégé; and without doubt, Taylor launched West Africa's cycle of bloodshed in 1989 when he began his civil war.

Twenty years ago, Charles Taylor was a government procurement officer in Liberia. His sticky fingers earned him the nickname Super Glue. Accused of embezzling $1 million in 1983, he fled to the US. Arrested in Massachusetts in 1984, he escaped from jail the following year, surfacing in Liberia four years later.

All our information indicates that Gaddafi himself was involved in promoting the fighting and thus the chaos in Sierra Leone. He set up training camps for the RUF (one of the principal rebel groups in Sierra Leone) in Benghazi in the late 1980s and early 1990s. Gaddafi is setting his sights south of the Sahara and, as the Arab world has begun to ignore him, he has decided to flex his muscles in Africa.

He is yet another head of state whose activities in Sierra Leone we are investigating. Article 6(2) of the Statute of the Special Court reads:

> The official position of any accused persons, whether as head of state or government... shall not relieve such person of criminal responsibility nor mitigate punishment.

We know that the intelligence services of both dictators have mounted a form of surveillance on what we are doing at Seaview House.

In March 2001, the UN imposed an arms ban on Liberia on account of the Taylor government's backing of the RUF (members of which entered Sierra Leone from Liberia in 1991) in its involvement in the illegal arms for diamonds trade.

The RUF, and another group, the AFRC, committed crimes of unbelievable horror. Psychological abuse and teasing were utilized so as to maximize terror. Victims were sometimes given the choice as to how they wished to be killed, or were forced to listen to rebels arguing as to what atrocity was to be committed against them. Pregnant women had their stomachs cut open as rebels placed bets on the sex of the unborn children. Boy soldiers were forced to shoot their parents dead to be initiated into the RUF. All this in addition to mass execution, sexual slavery, the amputation of the limbs of children, and compelling other children to take mind-altering drugs and forcing them to fight and commit atrocities alongside adult insurgents.

For the past two months David Crane and I have been in regular contact with Brigadier James Ellery, chief of staff (force) United Nations Mission in Sierra Leone (UNAMSIL) and Brigadier Patrick Davidson-Houston, commander of British Forces in Sierra Leone, about military measures to protect the personnel of the Special Court and to ensure their safety when we decide to move in on those presently at large and carry out their arrests. Some of the Sierra Leonean targets are still in positions of considerable authority. They command large numbers of armed men who could, on instructions, launch an attack on us or take us hostage. Fortunately, apart from the British contingent in the International Military Advisory and Training Team there are some 17,000 troops in blue berets – the largest UN military mission in the world – an indication of the international community's recognition of the explosive environment we are working in.

Brigadier Ellery, who expresses himself in forthright terms and who is wholly devoid of political correctness, has become a regular dining companion at the Lagoonda, which overlooks Man of War Bay.

A Royal Naval frigate, HMS *Westminster*, has made a stopover in Freetown. This is all part of the signal that Britain intends to communicate to those who may wish to disrupt the efforts of the Special Court.

5 DECEMBER 2002
*Seaview House, Freetown*

It is 6 p.m. I have just walked on to the terrace of Seaview House and I can hear the bugler playing the Last Post at the British high commission. Time to go home. Home is now Union House, until recently the residence of Brigadier Patrick Davidson-Houston. When I first visited the house in October, Patrick was sharing it with Lt. Col. Jeremy Stadward and Patrick's orderly, Cpl. Riddler, who has an almost shaven head and a large silver nipple ring which I noticed as he made his way to the swimming pool when we were all having a drink on the terrace. The house overlooks Freetown, Lumley Beach and the Atlantic beyond. The security people say the house is as safe as one can get in Freetown. There is a five-inch-thick steel door in the corridor leading to my bedroom that would take a very high explosive to penetrate and there is another steel door in the garden wall, through which a path leads downhill to Cockerill Barracks and possible safety, unless the occupants of those barracks have turned to the rebels and are heading up the hill.

18 DECEMBER 2002
*Seaview House, Freetown*

We are getting ready to leave Seaview House for Christmas. Our most sensitive material is being moved into the Bubble. Quite a lot has been shredded. We cannot risk any unauthorized access into the OTP over the Christmas holidays.

We were informed today that one of our targets has a cache of arms coming in on a freighter. We are further informed that this weaponry is to be used to disrupt the work of the Special Court. Hopefully this cache can be intercepted.

13 JANUARY 2003
*Seaview House, Freetown*

There has been a raid on the military depot at Wellington, which is in the east of Freetown. Is this the beginning of a full blown *coup d'état*?

11 FEBRUARY 2003
*Seaview House, Freetown*

I received a rare treat from the UNAMSIL chief of staff, Brigadier Ellery: a parcel containing a copy of yesterday's *Times* and a packet of Turkish cigarettes made from the finest blend of Izmir and Samsun tobaccos.

On his arrival in Freetown he began an address to his officers in which he referred to his last posting by saying, 'Gentlemen, the day I arrived in the Congo, they ate the zoo!' The package also contains a part of James's wittily written journal, which relates to the events of the recent attack on Wellington Barracks:

> Keith Biddle, the avuncular Mancunian Inspector General of Police, called me one evening to say that 'something was going on'. And while this was unsupported by intelligence, he stated robustly that 'he had never been wrong'. And he wasn't. At 2230 hours on a Sunday he warned of an imminent attack involving a Republic of Sierra Leone Armed forces (RSLAF) barracks and the Pademba Road Prison, where Foday Sankoh and 600 RUF, AFRC, West Side Boys and others reside. The plan failed – but only just. At 0100 hours a gang of twenty or so attempted to seize the weapons held at the RSLAF Engineer Regiment's Wellington Barracks in Freetown. Had they succeeded – and they nearly did as the barracks guard had no ammunition (!) – their intention was probably to alert the Pademba Road prisoners by mobile telephone (they have them) to riot and kill their unarmed guards. And with several hundred prisoners on the loose in Freetown, armed with weapons stolen from the barracks, who knows what they might have achieved in a city which feeds on rumour? Most of these prisoners face the death penalty when convicted – they will not be tried until the Special Court decides which they intend to indict – so they really have nothing to lose.

At the last breakout (in 1998) the prisoners killed every one of their warders, the prison gates having been blown open by the firing of an RPG-7 at point-blank range. We are confident that our Nigerian Guard Force would significantly reduce the number of escapees in a repeat operation. But prisons the world over are notoriously porous if a high proportion of inmates are minded to leave simultaneously.

16 FEBRUARY 2003
*Seaview House, Freetown*

'MORE BRITISH TROOPS ARRIVE' screams a headline in a local newspaper.

A deployment of British troops is proof of the fantastic training opportunities offered by Sierra Leone! Of course, all this is designed to protect us when we move against our targets.

Brigadier James Ellery came to lunch at the OTP, bringing with him the latest part of his journal. It is relevant to what we are doing.

8 MARCH 2003
*Seaview House, Freetown*

I arrived at the OTP at 8.15 a.m. David called me aside looking very excited.

'All the indictments have been confirmed in London and the arrest warrants have been issued – including one against President Charles Taylor!' Drifting melodramatically into American hunter speech, he says to me, 'We have to be loaded for bear!'

I expect he is referring to Taylor's hit squads. The president of Liberia knows we are on his trail. It does not help that US Senator Russ Feingold has made a speech in Wisconsin saying, 'I think the current president of Liberia is a war criminal and I hope to see him held accountable for his actions in a court of law.'

We have set up a sting operation to cause him to come to Burkina Faso. I have drafted a secret treaty with the government of Burkina Faso, which has been concluded by the registrar, that may lead him to being handed over to us if he crosses the border.

10 MARCH 2003
*Seaview House, Freetown*

Operation Justice is to be launched today. We hope to accomplish the arrest of our targets before the day is out. The Hon. Sam Hinga Norman, Minister of the Interior, is one of them and the one for whom the armed guards at my gate work!

The names and number of the people we are about to arrest today have been kept a very close secret. Keith Biddle, the British Inspector General of Police, and three British brigadiers, Bill Moore, Adrian Freer and James Ellery, are in the know. The last named, who is the UNAMSIL chief of staff (force), has taken steps to keep the arrest date even from Ambassador Adeniji, a Nigerian national and Special Representative of the UN Secretary-General (SRSG). Two of our targets have to be arrested before they leave Freetown. We are aware that they were due to go to the bank today to draw out a substantial sum of money, no doubt to finance their flight from the country. Even the president of Sierra Leone has been kept in the dark as to what we are doing today.

Thank goodness for Alan Jones, the British high commissioner, who has been marvellously supportive. He is also a bon viveur. He recently discovered that I had taken Ian Gleeson at the Africa Desk of the FCO to dinner at Brooks's and then on to Annabel's until 3 a.m. Tongue in cheek, he accused me of corrupting young FCO officials. Alan has developed a reputation for informality and sometimes goes to Paddy's Bar, which is much frequented by women who by midnight all start looking like Naomi Campbell! They are also known as 'night-fighters'. Paddy, who has been here forever, received an MBE last year for playing his part in keeping the British troops happy.

HMS *Iron Duke* is at anchor off Lumley Beach. Her 4.5 inch guns, with a range of twenty-two kilometres, are trained on Freetown. Her missiles can strike targets up to 130 kilometres away.

'C' Company of the Royal Ghurkhas is conducting a setpiece firepower demonstration at Hastings. They will use Milan antitank guided missiles and medium range mortars.

The projection of power is good and a signal is being sent out that any attempt to interfere with the arrests to be carried out, or any attempt to come to the aid of the indicted war criminals, will be met with force.

11 MARCH 2003
*Seaview House, Freetown*

The arrests have been carried out seamlessly without loss of life. The Minister of the Interior, Chief Sam Hinga Norman, was arrested at his desk in his ministry. We have five indicted war criminals in the bag. We are missing Sam 'Mosquito' Bockarie, who presently commands a large mercenary force fighting for President Charles Taylor in the Côte d'Ivoire where Taylor plans to overthrow the existing regime and replace it with one of his nominees. One of those whom we have arrested is called Gullit, so called for his propensity for slitting throats!

We have not revealed to the public our sealed indictment against President Taylor in the hope that he will step outside Liberia and we may be able to collar him!

12.30 P.M., 18 MARCH 2003
*Brooks's Club, London*

The House of Commons is to debate Iraq this afternoon. A war with Iraq is inevitable. Three hours ago I arrived at the House of Commons to give oral evidence on the Special Court for Sierra Leone before the Select Committee for International Development. The Special Court was created by the United Nations and the government of Sierra Leone, with Britain as a significant financial contributor to the court.

I was seated at the end of a large horseshoe table around which sat several MPs who fired questions at me.

In his concluding remarks, after my evidence, the former Foreign Office minister, Tony Baldry, MP, the present chairman of the Committee, said, 'There were reports of pregnant women being bayoneted and the soldiers taking bets as to whether the child was going to be male or female. Horrific stuff. There are various messages that come before this committee. First, we all recognize that you are undertaking this task at not a little personal danger to yourself and we would all wish you well in that. Obviously it is some consolation to know that UK forces are around…'

17 APRIL 2003
*Seaview House, Freetown*

I am looking forward to going to Marlands for Easter. My joy is somewhat reduced by a communication from Katarina yesterday that many old trees in the wood there are afflicted by honey fungus and, what's more, deer are eating seventy-five saplings that my gardener, Allen, planted in January. As regards the second problem, I suggested that she goes to the zoo or Longleat and collect some lion dung. Carefully placed, that should see the deer off – they must have some primeval instinct for survival that the lion dung is bound to provoke. As regards the first problem, I have not the slightest idea what honey fungus is and I must get Tracy to download information about it from the Internet.

21 APRIL 2003
*Marlands House, Horsham*

Had Stephen Lamport, Prince Charles's former private secretary, to luncheon together with Brian and Susan Jubb. The roast lamb was divine and Katarina's *îles flottantes* were magnificent.

Had a call from Anthony Cavendish* as to whether I had seen the latest *Private Eye* and its reference to Le Cercle, of which we are both members.

22 APRIL 2003
*Brooks's Club, London*

Saw Norman Ramsbottom in his surgery at noon. His doctors have banned him from coming to lunch with me. When I was over in March and took him to lunch at Mark's Club in Mayfair he had a partial stroke and started listing heavily to his left. A world-famous heart surgeon sitting at the next table did nothing to help!

* Former MI6 officer and author of *Inside Intelligence*

I make this diary entry waiting for Brigadier James Ellery and my nephew, Detmar Blow, to arrive for supper. I hope Detmar keeps off his impending divorce to Issie, who I adore. Issie, who discovered Alexander McQueen and Philip Treacy, is never seen in public without some traffic-stopping hat. Indeed, she wears a hat indoors at most times.

23 APRIL 2003
*Carlton Club, London*

After a very good supper at Brooks's last night we went on to White's. I had much too much Armagnac. Detmar was very good and kept off his divorce. James was in marvellous form.

Back to Freetown at the crack of dawn tomorrow!!!

7 MAY 2003
*Seaview House, Freetown*

Meeting chaired by David. Others present are myself, Robin Vincent, Alan White, Bruce Mackay, Lt. Col. Bob Parnell and James Ellery.

Our discussions revolve around the news received yesterday that General Sam Bockarie, aka Mosquito – who was indicted by us on 10 March 2003 and who was a senior commander in the RUF – has been killed or executed in Liberia. His unequalled ability to induce deep trauma and fear into the civilian population made him one of West Africa's most feared warlords. His body is allegedly in Monrovia. We have asked for the body to be turned over to us for tests and identification; two years ago he spread a rumour he was dead only to surface again. Our other indictee still on the run is Johnny Paul Koroma (JPK). Although President Taylor of Liberia denies it, we know him to be (according to US intelligence sources) in Liberia, in a place called Foya where, with Taylor's approval, he is at the head of some 3,000 troops. We discuss whether this is going to be just one prong of an incursion into Sierra Leone to destabilize the Special Court. Alan Jones, the British high commissioner, called David and I to the residence three days ago to inform us there was good intelligence that an anti-aircraft gun stolen by rebels from UNAMSIL is to be brought into Freetown to be used against the Special Court. James Ellery believes if this is mounted on the back of a flatbed truck it could be used to devastating effect at ground level.

'Of course it will be a suicide mission,' he says, 'because we will get them.'

Given the fact that some of the barbarities during the civil war were committed by combatants who believed they were invincible and untouchable if they took a particular potion handed out by a juju man, it is not necessarily comforting to know that using an anti-aircraft gun against the Special Court should impinge upon their minds as suicidal.

The village sorcerers still have the capacity to persuade believers that, with the proper juju, a bullet directed at them will stop in mid-air and fall harmlessly to the ground.

Yesterday I was told of a rebel battlefield commander who informed his troops that he was now impervious to bullets as he had taken a potion given to him by the juju man. So convinced was he of the efficacy of the magic potion and the occult powers of the juju man that he handed his revolver to his best friend saying, 'Now shoot me.' Confident that his commander was not flirting with death, his best friend pulled the trigger. As his fighters gathered around his corpse, the next in command said, 'Let's go and kill the juju man; he must be a crook.' Off they all went to the juju man's hut and as they levelled an AK-47 at his head, the quick-thinking rogue said, 'You're making a terrible mistake. What happened?'

When the story of their commander's death was recounted to the now condemned man, the rascal rounded on his assembled assassins, saying, 'Don't you see how foolish you all are? My potion was to protect him from the bullets of his enemies and not those fired by his own revolver!' Bowled over by the force of this logic a hush fell upon his would-be executioners and they left the juju man, apologizing for having caused him so much distress.

Taylor of Liberia has declared that if he is indicted (which of course he has been by way of a sealed indictment) he will cross the border to Sierra Leone with 10,000 troops. Ellery says he cannot wait and relishes the prospect of taking them on.

10 MAY 2003
*Union House, Freetown*

David Crane is away in the States until the end of the month. I am in charge again and something was bound to happen.

I have seen pictures in local newspapers of a body on a mortuary slab in Monrovia. It is said to be that of the barbaric General Sam Bockarie. As he has resurrected himself before to cause untold evil, the public will not be satisfied unless we see the body and perhaps do a DNA profile.

I spoke with Robin Vincent, the registrar, who is trying to get the Liberian authorities to release the body – we will make the flight arrangements. As the Special Representative of the Secretary-General of the United Nations (Ambassador Adeniji) is being so unhelpful in every way, Brigadier Ellery suggests that I write to him immediately so that the mortuary facilities under UNAMSIL control in Freetown can be used by us to house the body.

I discussed with Alan White, our chief of investigations, whether we could get some DNA from Bockarie's mother, wife and children.

Alan Doss, who is the DSRSG, and his wife Soher (he is Welsh, she Egyptian) gave a delightful party to say farewell to the British high commissioner, Alan Jones, who is about to leave us.

James Ellery told us an amusing story of when, at the end of a dinner in London given by General Sir Charles Guthrie, the US ambassador lit up a Cuban cigar. The urbane Foreign Secretary, Malcolm Rifkind, asked quizzically, 'Smoking a Cuban cigar, ambassador?'

'Yes, I am helping to burn the enemy's crops!' said the diplomat winsomely.

13 MAY 2003
*Seaview House, Freetown*

The Liberians are playing silly buggers over Bockarie's body. Alan White informs me this morning that we have intelligence that Bockarie was executed on President Taylor's orders. Apparently, General Benjamin Yeaten, the head of Taylor's security services, telephoned Bockarie and asked him to come to a meeting with the president. It was then that he was executed, at the Executive Mansion (Taylor's residence) in Monrovia.

Is this why the Liberians are chary about letting us have the body for forensic examination? Because we may be able to detect that this is not a body that was hit in a shoot-out, as has been the official Liberian line?

14 MAY 2003
*Union House, Freetown*

Gave a dinner party last night at Union House for the retiring British high commissioner, Alan Jones. Ellery was on terrific form and came out with a gem in relation to the deadly SARS virus that is sweeping China and Canada. 'I believe,' he said, 'that there should be an illness called TSARS, for the grander people!' Apparently life at UNAMSIL has been enhanced by the arrival of two chimps, Maurice and Molly, who hurl mangoes at passers-by.

Robin Vincent, Tracy and I drank brandy until 3 a.m.

15 MAY 2003
*Seaview House, Freetown*

Informed this morning by Alan White that General Bockarie's family, who had left Ghana and settled in Liberia, are being hunted down and killed by President Taylor's security people. If true, is this to stop any DNA profiling if ever they gave us the body? Al White maintains that JPK is still in Liberia.

18 MAY 2003
*Union House, Freetown*

We have just come back from Hamilton Beach where I heard that JPK is not, as the Americans tell me, in Liberia. In fact, I am informed that JPK was having medical treatment in Freetown after 7 May. My informant and I both agree that had the warlord Bockarie fallen into our hands he could have revealed too much of Taylor's involvement in Sierra Leone's bloody war, and I am totally satisfied that Monrovia was a transit point for the blood diamond trade between the RUF and Taylor's people on the one hand and the Taliban / al-Qaeda on the other. It must be the case that Taylor knows that if there is firm evidence of Monrovia's involvement with al-Qaeda's business network prior to 9/11 then the full wrath of the US will be turned on him. This is why, I believe, the likelihood is that the body in Monrovia *is* that of the brutal Bockarie.

22 MAY 2003
*Seaview House, Freetown*

I have just met with the investigators who are back from the provinces. Evidence has been gathered that Kondewa, the high priest of the CDF*, not only ran initiation ceremonies with human sacrifices and enforced cannibalism, but also burned people alive so that their ashes could be used to make those marked with such ashes invulnerable to bullets. This monster Kondewa preferred the ashes of women in the later stages of pregnancy.

Amidst all this grim stuff there are a few rays of humour. One of them is the name of the French Consul – Rene Revoltier! He called me up to find out the names of the nine we had indicted. I told him, on the prompting of my PA, to look up our website.

23 MAY 2003
*Union House, Freetown*

Gave a very successful farewell dinner party for Keith and Sue Biddle last night. We will miss him sorely as Inspector General. Usually, at the onset of the rainy season, we bring the dining tables from the terrace indoors. However, on this occasion it was not because of the rain but because of the arrival of all manner of unwelcome winged creatures of various sizes and shapes that were

* Civilian Defence Force under the control of Chief Sam Hinga Norman.

attracted to the lights and candles. This will probably be the last terrace dinner party until the rainy season is over. Brigadier Freer joined us, arriving with the bubbly Captain Pippa Davis and Lt. Col. Dick Austin, who was in Freetown for a week and was looking none too well at dinner. He confined himself to a carrot and a sip of water.

24 MAY 2003
*Seaview House, Freetown*

9 a.m. meeting at the OTP. Intelligence reports just came in of a possible *coup d'état* tomorrow. Tomorrow is the anniversary of an earlier coup and I am made to understand that the plotters intend to break into Pademba Road Prison to release some of the people presently on trial for treason. JPK is behind this, but where is he?

His wife gave birth to their fifth child two weeks ago in Freetown. I am told that JPK and his wife are very close, so I have agreed with Alan White that he should pay her a visit and inform her that her husband's best chance of survival is to surrender himself to us and face a trial that will not involve the death penalty. We believe that this is bound to spawn a contact between her and him, which may enable us to get a fix on where he is.

Yesterday the British high commissioner called as he wanted to see me, together with the US ambassador, at the residence at 12.15 today.

28 MAY 2003
*Union House, Freetown*

Had a call from Peter Chaveas, the US ambassador, yesterday. I had previously informed him that I was likely to be seeking the arrest of three people, one of them the high priest, Kondewa. I told him that I was going to endeavour to have the arrests carried out today. Two of the suspects are in the provinces and Peter was concerned that there were some Americans in the Bo and Kenema areas who might be caught up in any backlash against the arrests. Yesterday afternoon the US Embassy, following our conversation, sent out a signal through their wardens and their 'phone tree' warning all Americans to exercise watchfulness and caution.

Had dinner last night at the residence of the US ambassador. Robin Vincent, the registrar, filled me in on his trip to New York and informed me that he wanted my second close protection officer, Robbie Franks, to work for him. Keith Biddle made a very good farewell speech.

29 MAY 2003
*Union House, Freetown*

Rather delightfully, the retiring British Inspector General of Police, Keith Biddle, has been crowned paramount chief of the Jawei Chiefdom, in a traditional ceremony that attracted hundreds of onlookers.

30 MAY 2003
*Union House, Freetown*

Arrived at the OTP this morning in driving rain where we held our Friday 'all hands', an amusing meeting on the terrace. I had to do it today as David was away. On my desk I find a note from Bruce Mackay. It reads, 'The rains will have spawned swarms of hungry mosquitos. We may have an obligation to feed our staff but we have no obligations to offer up our staff as food for others!'

We had a very successful operation and have three more defendants in detention – including the CDF high priest, Kondewa and their former director of war, together with the self-styled Brigadier Brima Kamara, a former member of the AFRC junta that overthrew the legitimate government of Tejan Kabbah in 1997. Kondewa, as part of his initiation ceremonies, compelled Kamajor fighters to eat human brains and intestines. I am not at all sure that we will be able to cater for his dietary needs in the detention centre on Bonthe Island!

31 MAY 2003
*Seaview House, Freetown*

The Liberian government has finally decided to turn the body of General Sam 'Mosquito' Bockarie over to us. It is coming in tomorrow. We have arranged for an autopsy at Connaught Hospital and the taking of DNA samples at 10 a.m. on Monday 2 June.

1 JUNE 2003
*Union House, Freetown*

Today, Sunday, Tracy and I were guests at the spectacularly beautiful Buretown Beach. It was a farewell to the British high commissioner at his favourite weekend retreat. Among those present were the affable Egyptian ambassador, the US ambassador and his wife, Lucile, and the Lebanese ambassador, all old friends of Alan Jones. The suckling pig and the steaks were delicious.

2 JUNE 2003
*Seaview House, Freetown*

David has just returned from Washington where he had talks with the State Department. During our discussions this morning Walter Kansteiner, the Assistant Secretary of State for African Affairs in the State Department, called. The position is that President Charles Taylor, who has $4.5 billion in Switzerland, is willing to step down in Liberia if we do a deal with him and do not indict him. France has indicated that it is willing to give him asylum. The United States has expressed the view that a NATO force under European command could be put into Liberia until the elections in October in the event of Taylor leaving the stage. Taylor will be in Ghana tomorrow for peace talks. We have two main options.

The first: 'unseal'* the indictment against him when he is in Ghana. But

* The process of making public that which has hitherto been hidden.

will the Ghanaian government do anything about arresting him? Will the unsealing imperil the peace talks? It is clear that the State Department and the FCO do not want us to rock the boat. Yet I take the view that those who participate in the peace talks are dealing with an indicted war criminal. Could the unsealing of the indictment lead to a palace coup in Monrovia while Taylor is in Ghana?

The second: do nothing and let him go back to Liberia and await military developments in his country, where the Liberians United for Reconciliation and Democracy, and Movement for Democracy in Liberia rebels seem to be gaining the ascendancy. If he flees to Burkina Faso I have in place a secret treaty with that government under which he can be handed over.

3 JUNE 2003
*Seaview House, Freetown*

We have reports that President Taylor has left Liberia for Ghana. We have other reports that he may go via Burkina Faso. Will the president of Burkina Faso, as Crane puts it, 'have the testicles to detain a fellow head of state and hand him to us?' No incumbent head of state has ever been arrested before in a third country. If Taylor falls into our hands we would like to test the principle of head of state immunity before the Special Court. If we succeed, it will have a significant bearing on the development of law – bringing tyrant heads of state within the grasp of international criminal law.

I have just finished a letter to our Foreign Secretary, Jack Straw, indicating what we propose to do in relation to Taylor. Spoke this afternoon with Frank Marshall, the deputy high commissioner, and informed him that Tracy would be coming to see him tomorrow carrying the letter I have drafted, to be sent by the secure line to Straw.

At a late-afternoon meeting we consider the possibility that Taylor has sleeper cells in Freetown. Will he activate them in revenge if we unseal the indictment against him?

4 JUNE 2003
*Seaview House, Freetown*

At 8 a.m. Robin Vincent served an international arrest warrant for President Taylor at the Ghana high commission in Freetown. At the same time my letter to Jack Straw was taken round to the British high commission where Frank Marshall was in charge pending the arrival of a new high commissioner. I spoke with Frank and Harriet Mathews at the FCO. Both expressed grave concerns at the decision we had taken to go public on the indictment of Charles Taylor when he is in Ghana. Both Britain and the US have helped broker the peace talks in Ghana, where Taylor is now. There is a fear that our unsealing of the indictment may be seen by some as an Anglo-American plot to get Taylor out of his country in order to have him arrested in Accra. I relayed these concerns to David Crane and he agreed to brief the press at 11 a.m. that it was he alone that made the decision as an independent international prosecutor, without consultation with any government.

The 11 a.m. press briefing at UNAMSIL HQ goes well when David calls upon the international community to help in bringing Charles Taylor to justice.

At our late afternoon meeting Al White informs us that one of our assets in Monrovia, codenamed Jungle, was executed on Monday 2 June on the instructions of Taylor.

5 JUNE 2003
*Seaview House, Freetown*

Great disappointment: the government of Ghana has given President Charles Taylor safe passage back to Liberia. We do not feel that Taylor can last long anyway. David's view is that 'he will come out of Monrovia in a box or in chains!'

I am not too sure. We have intelligence reports that France or Nigeria may give Taylor asylum. Perhaps even South Africa, where we know he has a girlfriend and property. It would be appalling if, in this day and age, governments give indicted war criminals refuge. It is precisely this kind of conduct that has made tyrants feel they are immune to the reach of international criminal justice.

7 JUNE 2003
*Union House, Freetown*

The rebels are pushing on to Monrovia and Taylor is increasingly penned in. There are reports of his ministers and their families leaving the country. Yesterday, military helicopters began evacuating French and US nationals from Liberia's besieged capital to a waiting French warship.

9 JUNE 2003
*Union House, Freetown*

At 10.30 a.m. I flew with General Syed Athar and Brigadier Ellery to near the Liberian border where a firepower display has been organized. Helicopter gunships are the most feared weapon in Africa and four Mi-24s, firing cannons, rockets and guided missiles were used on static targets. We hope that anyone on the other side of the border considering crossing into Sierra Leone will have second thoughts.

Went aboard an Mi-26, out of the vast belly of which two large Russian trucks rolled down. The trucks acted as an observation platform for us to watch this impressive display put on by UNAMSIL.

Returned to the OTP covered in dust and mud.

At an evening meeting, Alan White informed us that information had started to come through that the Liberian president has now executed the former Sandhurst-trained major, Johnny Paul Koroma, another one of our indictees. If this is true then this is another incident which demonstrates how desperate Taylor is that certain people do not fall into our hands.

The Liberians United for Reconciliation and Democracy (LURD) has issued an ultimatum giving Taylor until midnight on 11 June to vacate power or face further onslaughts. Liberia itself is at risk of complete disintegration and in Monrovia there is heavy artillery fire across the city.

12 JUNE 2003
*Seaview House, Freetown*

Taylor is still holding out in Monrovia and I am leaving for London this afternoon for consultations with the FCO tomorrow, and then, on Monday, I go on to the swearing-in of the new prosecutor for the ICC in The Hague. I wonder if Taylor will still be in power when I return to Freetown in a week's time?

As the UK led in Sierra Leone and the French in the Ivory Coast, the Americans must give a lead in pushing Taylor out of power and help establish a post-Taylor government in Liberia.

An Agence France report has just been shown to me in which Taylor calls for the withdrawal of the indictment we have brought against him as a precondition to peace talks and accusing us of being politically motivated.

13 JUNE 2003
*London*

An exhausting overnight flight from Freetown. Arrived in England to read that Blair has abolished the Keeper of the Queen's Conscience, aka the Lord Chancellor, and intends to replace him with a Secretary of State for Constitutional Affairs! Could hardly keep my eyes open at the FCO meeting.

15 JUNE 2003
*Marlands House, Horsham*

The rhododendrons are looking lovely. We have, however, got hornets and moths.

Anthony and Elspeth Cavendish came to lunch. He, in particular, wanted to consult me on behalf of Lady Falkender and the book *Glimmers of Twilight: Harold Wilson in Decline* by Joe Haines, in which she is disparagingly referred to throughout. I gave him an informal opinion. He told me that he had just received an inscribed watch from President Putin.

16 JUNE 2003
*The Hague*

Attended the swearing-in of the new prosecutor for the ICC at the Palais de la Paix. I sat immediately behind the very attractive Princess Máxima of the Netherlands, whose ADC was sitting next to me and whom I asked to nudge me if I dropped off to sleep. One of the seventeen judges – who were all sitting at a raised table – started to vomit violently when the new prosecutor began to make his speech. After the ceremony I had the opportunity to have a chat with my old friend Sir Adrian Fulford, QC, Britain's judicial appointee to the ICC.

Heard from a senior prosecutor at The Hague Tribunal that some Belgrade lawyers who represent Serb clients before the ICTY split their fees with the defendants. One defendant and his counsel are apparently now joint owners of a bar in The Hague! To a Balkan lawyer the daily rates of pay at The Hague would seem huge – hence these deals with the defendants.

23 JUNE 2003
*Seaview House, Freetown*

With the assistance of the government of Switzerland we have frozen the Swiss bank accounts of President Charles Taylor and his relatives. We have yet to learn from the Swiss the extent of his wealth, which is estimated in billions of dollars. This must send a cold shiver down the spines of other tyrants who loot the wealth of their countries and are indifferent to the sufferings of their people.

25 JUNE 2003
*Union House, Freetown*

Very good dinner at Brigadier Freer's, at Kaladan House, Leicester Square. Our SIS station chief was there and assures me that the American information about JPK having been executed is wrong and that this is just being put about by JPK's friends so that we will give up the hunt for him. It looks as if Charles Taylor will be toppled as fighting intensifies in Monrovia. A few days ago some US

Navy SEALS passed through Lungi heading up toward the Liberian boarder. Is it to save Americans in Monrovia? Help overthrow Taylor? Or get him out alive?

5.50 p.m.: A report has just come through that tens of thousands of refugees have been let into the US Embassy compound and that mortar shells are now beginning to fall on these terrified people. All UN personnel are also in the US compound.

4 JULY 2003
*New England, Freetown*

Yesterday we moved from Seaview to our new offices in New England. I have been put in a prefabricated building – OTP1. It is surrounded by high walls with razor wire and I begin to get the feeling of what it must be like in a prisoner of war camp.

Today we had a visit from the Security Council Mission to West Africa, headed by Sir Jeremy Greenstock, our urbane Head of Mission in New York, who is shortly to head the British administration in Iraq. Included in the group were ambassadors Richard Williamson of the US, Alexander Konuzin of Russia and Stefan Tafrov of Bulgaria.

National Day celebrations at the US Embassy.

5 JULY 2003
*New England, Freetown*

Had lunch with Ray England, who is on the SAS Council. Discussed my Gambian chapter with him. Ray wants a draft of it for SAS approval.

20 JULY 2003
*Union House, Freetown*

Had a very successful dinner party at Union House last night to say farewell to James Ellery, who is leaving us tomorrow. Brigadier Freer and the acting British high commissioner, Frank Marshall, regaled us with tales of how they were caned at school and the ploys of the masters to make the punishments more painful. Tracy looked on askance while the lovely Captain Sally Glazebrook, who was just about to run across Morocco for charity together with a friend, watched with faint amusement.

26 JULY 2003
*New England, Freetown*

Readying ourselves for any sudden developments in Liberia. Will Taylor be taken by the LURD, flee to another country or be killed?

An Amphibious Readiness Group centred on the USS *Iwo Jima* with the US Marine Corps' Marine Expeditionary Unit has been diverted from the Mediterranean and could be off Liberia within three days.

11 AUGUST 2003
*Marlands House, Horsham*

President Charles Taylor has gone into exile in Nigeria, apparently to a colonial mansion in Calabar. It seems to me that if the international community wants to stop rogue tyrants from unleashing savage wars it must find ways of preventing these people from looting their own country's resources. It is by seizing the nation's cash box that Taylor found the money to buy the weapons and the support that has led to the deaths of hundreds of thousands in the region. We are picking up the pieces in Sierra Leone.

13 AUGUST 2003
*Marlands House, Horsham*

Had lunch at the Cavalry & Guards Club with Brigadier Ellery. Other guests were the American broadcaster Jennifer Glasse, Colonel Hamon Massey and Lt. Col. Robin Vickers. Hammond tells us that George Bush is due to make an official visit to London in October and US Secret Service people are objecting to the president riding in a state coach on the grounds that it is not bulletproof. It has been pointed out to them that in fifty years the Queen has not lost a single one of her guests.

14 AUGUST 2003
*Marlands House, Horsham*

Gave James Ellery lunch at Mark's Club and we discussed Liberia. Benazir Bhutto gave an excellent dinner party at Alexandra Court. I was delighted to see Norman Lamont, Bitu Bhalla and the striking and accomplished Clio Rochas. Norman was fiercely defensive of Margaret Thatcher, who has recently been the subject of a cruel comment alleging she was going gaga and had only received three cards on her birthday. Bitu told us a lovely story: when the conman Robert Maxwell was awaiting the outcome of a judgment in a legal action he had brought in the High Court, his solicitor sent him a fax saying, 'Justice has been done.' To this the crooked owner of the Mirror Newspaper Group replied immediately – 'APPEAL!'

31 AUGUST 2003
*Marlands House, Horsham*

I am returning to Freetown tomorrow and have failed to keep a diary for the past two weeks – largely through social exhaustion. Some highlights: had a very good and informative dinner at the In and Out with Harriet Mathews, Rosemary Thomas, Caron Röhsler and Gavin Hood of the FCO. Gavin is working on a court for Iraq.

A very entertaining dinner with Norman Lamont at Mark's led him to invite me to address Le Cercle in Washington in December. I agreed.

11 SEPTEMBER 2003
*OTP, New England, Freetown*

I have just had a report about a mass grave at Tombudu in Kono District. The report is from the UNAMSIL Human Rights Section, which is reporting on the skulls and bones in a house where over 100 people were burned alive by a rebel named Colonel Savage. The town chief is anxious that the bones be collected and removed, as the locals believe that if any of the bones should prick their feet, the wounds will never heal; the chief himself believes that until the bones are buried, the yield from farm produce and diamonds will be affected.

26 SEPTEMBER 2003
*OTP, New England, Freetown*

David Crane has just returned from Washington where, among other things, he met General Jacques Klein, the Secretary-General's new representative to Liberia. Klein, according to David, said, 'Taylor was a vampire and the indictment was the stake that would be driven through his heart.'

Christopher Staker, a delightful and brilliant Australian lawyer, is staying with me at Union House and being a tower of strength to us in the OTP.

29 SEPTEMBER 2003
*OTP, New England, Freetown*

Watched General Obasanjo, the president of Nigeria, on CNN News at 8 a.m. It does look as if he may be willing in due course to surrender Taylor to us. He made references to the possibility of Taylor being brought to book.

Had lunch with Brigadier Freer at Hamilton Beach who told me an amusing story arising from the organization of the hugely successful party he had given up at Leicester Square (the International Military Assistance Training Team HQ in Freetown) two nights ago. A newly arrived officer had been put in charge of the guest list and he, unsurprisingly, had been in touch with the British high commission for a selection of suitable British and Sierra Leonean guests. On the eve of the invitations being sent out the brigadier was studying the list and to his horror discovered that one of his proposed guests was none other than the indicted war criminal Chief Samuel Hinga Norman, who for the past six months we have had under lock and key in a securely guarded detention centre. The high commission still had him down as the Minister for the Interior.

7 OCTOBER 2003
*Union House, Freetown*

I am utterly exhausted. For the past two weeks we have been either preparing for or taking part in the critical preliminary hearings before the Appeals Chamber. On 31 October the members of the chamber, presided over by Geoffrey Robertson, QC, took their seats on the bench in a temporary courthouse to a fanfare of trumpets contributed by UNAMSIL. The first motion before the court was one by the absent ex-president Charles Taylor claiming head of state immunity for his acts and seeking to strike down our indictment, which had been approved when he was still Liberia's head of state. His counsel, Terrence Terry, made a spirited attack on what he claimed was our non-observance of international law. For the prosecution I did Taylor's motion, together with the other major attack on our jurisdiction, which sprang from the purported amnesty given to the defendants by the Lomé Peace Accord, to which Britain was a moral guardian.

For the best part of two weeks I have not left the OTP before 8 p.m. In this heat, it has become a crippling working day.

8 OCTOBER 2003
*Union House, Freetown*

I met my first witch doctor, a transvestite. He was beside a motorcycle which was laden with bags containing small packets of his potions. Standing by his machine on a dirt track road, dressed in a frock in the middle of a rainforest, he was a most unusual and riveting spectacle. On the back of the motorbike was his advertising – Dr Nico, it said on a board. My close protection officer promptly bought some of Dr Nico's powder – his equivalent of Viagra, which he called, 'manpower powder for mummy-daddy business.' Paul shared the powder with Osman, my driver. Another potion was bought by Lt. Col. Graham McKinley, a former British defence attaché.

We went on to Tokeh – a heavenly beach.

11 OCTOBER 2003
*Union House, Freetown*

Woke up this morning with a dreadful hangover. We had Robin Vincent and Wendy Hart to supper last night and Adama's excellent meal was washed down with too much wine and brandy.

The 11 a.m. appointment I had with the assistant chief of the general staff – Major General David Richards – was cancelled as his flight was delayed at Gatwick. I was looking forward to him coming to the OTP for a briefing, as the last time I saw him was ten years ago in 1993 when I was a guest at a regimental ball in Colchester and he was commanding his regiment.

Tracy and I attended a reception at Kaladan House where I had my first long chat with the new British high commissioner, John Mitchiner. He is a Sanskrit scholar and an authority on llamas. My knowledge of these creatures was greatly enhanced when he told me that llamas are very good at protecting sheep. 'You see, they adopt the sheep as their own and if any fox attempts to interfere the llamas will chase it away. If the fox does not beat a hasty retreat the llama can kill it with a single kick!' I thought to myself that this alternative to keeping foxes down or at bay was bad news for the pro-hunting lobby.

14 OCTOBER 2003
*Union House, Freetown*

David and I are luncheon guests at Runnymede – the residence of the British high commissioner. The HC John Mitchiner and Derek Smith of the FCO make up the four for lunch. They want to know what our plans are for Charles Taylor. Derek feels that the Nigerians will toss him to us for trial. We discuss local security issues. Excellent lunch.

20 DECEMBER 2003
*Marlands House, Horsham*

An eventful week. Saddam Hussein was found in his burrow on my birthday. Following this I was interviewed by Sky about what sort of court would be needed to try him. It was strange watching a replay later when I saw myself on one half of the split screen talking about bringing Saddam to trial while on the other side of the screen Saddam's mouth gaped open as a US medic extracted DNA.

The Foreign Secretary's reception on 17 December in the Locarno room of the FCO was a terrible crush. Ran into Elizabeth Butler-Sloss, who told me that she was off to Nepal for Christmas.

Yesterday, the PM announced that Colonel Gaddafi had agreed to destroy his WMDs. It appears that many months of negotiations lay behind this important Libyan concession. No wonder there was great concern shown last year when the FCO learned that Gaddafi might end up as one of our indicted war criminals. It now appears that in August 2002 the FCO minister, Mike O'Brien, raised the WMD issue with Gaddafi in a Bedouin tent during the very first visit by a British minister to Gaddafi. I still feel that there is something in what was said by a former president of the Sudan, who described Gaddafi as being 'a man with a split personality – both evil.'

26 DECEMBER 2003
*Marlands House, Horsham*

Received a report that fifteen of our protectors, UNAMSIL troops, were killed on Christmas Day. Apparently their West Coast plane on its way to Dubai plunged into the sea, having clipped the control tower in Benin. The plane was overloaded, largely with Lebanese. A plastic bag containing $6 million was found floating on the surface of the water. I expect the diamonds that were being illegally removed from Sierra Leone sank to the bottom.

8 JANUARY 2004
*OTP, Freetown*

Received a communication from John Evans, legal adviser to Sir Jeremy Greenstock, inviting me to suggest what role I could envisage for myself in the Iraqi war crimes tribunal. Having consulted the Statute of the Iraqi Special Tribunal I have responded. The temporal jurisdiction of the court is to run from 17 July 1968 to 1 May 2003. My own view is that this court is flawed in that it will be seen as an American court. It should have been created by an international treaty between the Arab League or, at the very least, by a treaty between Iraq, Kuwait and Iran.

4 FEBRUARY 2004
*Union House, Freetown*

Good dinner party by Brigadier Simon Porter at Kaladan House. I met the new defence adviser, Lt. Col. Desmond Bergin. He and his wife are mad-keen golfers. I explained to them that the sixteenth hole at the Freetown Golf Club is known as 'alligator hole' as there is a mangrove swamp ten yards away. He trumped this by saying that a golf course in Zimbabwe had a crocodile-infested rivulet running through it and many of the caddies had lost arms or more while unwisely trying to retrieve balls! The high commissioner quizzed me about delays to which the trial process was being subjected. I told him, quite truthfully, that in my view the delays were being caused by some of the judges, who were spinning the proceedings out by delaying the delivery of rulings and judgments.

10 FEBRUARY 2004
*Union House, Freetown*

Today we had the ceremonial opening of the Special Court building in which the monsters we have in detention will be tried.

Late last night I was roused from my bed by the arrival of Solicitor General Harriet Harman, the legal editor of the *Times* Frances Gibb and veteran *Times* photographer Chris Harris. They were all here for the court opening. Upon their departure after many glasses of wine, Tony Baldry, who was staying with me, suggested that we should have a midnight feast of pâté de foie gras with truffles, which he had kindly brought me from Fortnum's. After this feast and considerably more wine I retired to wake up feeling marvellous this morning.

Following a speech by the Secretary-General of the UN we were treated to the most moving singing by the Milton Margai Blind School. I had to choke back tears as I listened to the joyous voices of the children; they had not been born blind, rather they were deliberately and wickedly blinded during the terrible civil war.

# 3

# Pray the Devil Back to Hell

THE TAIL END OF THE TWENTIETH CENTURY SAW THE BEGINNING OF TWO savage and brutal civil wars in which the people of Liberia and Sierra Leone endured more than their fair share of suffering. The title for this chapter is drawn from the prayer of Liberian women who came together in their thousands to call for the end of the agony to which the people of Liberia were then subject. It is also the name of the award-winning documentary by Gini Reticker released in 2008. The war in Sierra Leone was one in which monstrous signature crimes were committed against the civilian population, threatening the security and stability of West Africa. Both wars were driven by a lust for power and an unquenchable thirst for diamonds by bloodthirsty warlords, the most evil of whom was Charles Taylor, the man behind the misfortunes that befell the Liberian people.

With no method of death considered out of bounds you enter a world of deeds so dark that one is ashamed to be a member of the human race; for instance, the intestines of the disembowelled were stretched across the road to act as a signal to stop and, elsewhere, pregnant women were cut open to settle wagers made as to the sex of the unborn child.

In 1991, an attack was launched on Sierra Leone from neighbouring Liberia. It was a conflict directed toward terrorizing an entire population and looting the diamond wealth of the country by means of slave labour. It was a war that lasted a decade, with crimes that shocked the conscience of the world.

In 2012, in a courtroom in The Hague, the first completed trial against a former head of state since the conviction of Grand Admiral Karl Dönitz by the International Military Tribunal at Nuremburg in 1946 took place. The trial of Charles Taylor had been transferred to The Hague from Freetown for security reasons in 2006.

Power comes in many forms. The chief prosecutor of an international criminal tribunal is mandated with the jurisdiction to indict and issue warrants of arrest for heads of state, heads of government and, of course, others falling within the jurisdiction of the tribunal. With such power it is possible for a chief prosecutor to bring about regime change. As the chief prosecutor of an international criminal tribunal investigating and prosecuting war crimes and crimes against humanity, you are pitched into the front line of international justice, where success or failure can have profound political implications. You are an amalgam of Attorney General, ambassador, strategist and CEO all rolled into one.

In addition, you sometimes need to seek the help of national intelligence services. When Carla Del Ponte was appointed chief prosecutor of the International Criminal Tribunal for the Former Yugoslavia, one of the first things she did was go to the CIA HQ at Langley, Virginia, to speak to George Tenet, the then director of the CIA, to seek his help in capturing General Ratko Mladić and Radovan Karadžić, who were then indicted war criminals on the run. I am sure she would have approached the Russian FSB if the Russians had not been so hostile to The Hague court. In the event, she got very little help from the CIA and it took another eight years to get Karadžić and eleven to get Mladić.

The chief prosecutor is required at all times to act independently and not seek or receive instructions from any government or from any other source. This is not to say that the holder of that office cannot seek the assistance of the UN, foreign governments or their agencies, or indeed anyone who may be able to assist the accomplishment of the objectives of the Office of the Prosecutor.

Above all, a chief prosecutor has to have a high tolerance to criticism. Sometimes it is plain ignorance and at others it can be a carefully orchestrated political campaign directed at rendering ineffective the discharge by the prosecutor of his or her mandate. In particular, such obstruction is used to protect powerful figures, both political and military, or the interests of a great power.

Save for the Criminal Bar giving me an intimate familiarity with human nature, nothing at the English Bar can really prepare you for the role of chief prosecutor of an international criminal court. Quite apart from being the face of the court to the international community, which looks to the prosecutor to bring to justice the perpetrators of atrocities, the prosecutor is also expected to be a diplomat, who has to deal regularly with the United Nations and the foreign ministries of a host of interested countries. In our case we had to organize safe houses in Europe for witnesses and their families to avoid them being murdered. I was personally responsible for obtaining passports in fake names from certain European missions so as to protect the identities of threatened individuals as they took up residence in safe countries.

With the explosion in the number of NGOs and issue-driven members of civil society that now have such a significant impact on domestic and international affairs, a prosecutor's responsibility includes dealing with civil society organizations that are often pressurizing the prosecutor for information. Outreach programmes were started by us in Sierra Leone, where the prosecutor is often confronted by great assemblies of people who rightly feel that they have a stake in the ongoing process and need to hear from the prosecutor himself. This is an important political role for the prosecutor, who needs to carry the people with him on the legal journey. As a court of this kind is often seen as the cornerstone of peace building, there is a vital need for the prosecutor to keep in close contact with the UN military presence. Above all, your 'clients' are the hundreds and thousands of victims of war crimes and crimes against humanity, whose cruelly ended lives cry out for accountability.

Initially, as a deputy prosecutor, I had been fortunate enough to do an apprenticeship under David Crane, who was the founding prosecutor of the Special Court for Sierra Leone. (This was the third international court to be set up by the international community after the Tribunal for the former Yugoslavia (ICTY) and the Tribunal for Rwanda (ICTR); the first following the horrors of the Balkan war, and the second after the genocide in Rwanda.)

The horrors of the decade-long war we had to investigate and prosecute were rendered even more sinister by the quirky *noms de guerre* that leapt from the pages of evidence to do with Sierra Leone and Liberia. Commander Bomb Blast, Captain Blood, Captain Eagle, Superman and Rambo were all monsters who featured in the gory saga we had to examine in detail. As for the Liberian Commander General Butt Naked, he got his name from going into battle without a stitch of clothing, with a view to terrifying the enemy. However, he had an epiphany moment when Christ spoke to him and asked him to repent. Since then he has, I am told, become a clergyman, lovingly caring for his flock.

In bringing the Special Court for Sierra Leone into existence the international community, for the very first time, decided to hold trials 'in theatre'. Holding the trials in Sierra Leone meant that for all of us that came in from outside, and, indeed, for those Sierra Leoneans who worked for us, there were lurking dangers. There were many who faced possible indictment and long terms of imprisonment who clearly would not want us there. In short, there were those who wanted us out of Sierra Leone. Whether you are a peacekeeper or a prosecutor, when you are operating in potentially hazardous regions secret intelligence takes on an added importance which calls for special skills in intelligence gathering. The UN, being a highly transparent organization, had banned the word 'intelligence' from its lexicon because the word connotes undercover operations.

The Peacekeeper's Handbook (1984) goes so far as to state:

> A new form of covert intelligence is likely to create prejudice and suspicion. The UN has resolutely refused to countenance intelligence systems as part of its peacekeeping operations; intelligence having covert connections is a dirty word.

Tragically, this approach to proper covert intelligence has resulted in many failures in UN field operations that could have been avoided if these operations had a stronger mandate and better information-gathering systems. In 1994, in the Rwandan genocide that claimed millions of lives, Major General Roméo Dallaire, the Canadian Force commander of that ill-fated mission, complained of being 'deaf and blind' without an adequate intelligence capability. It was part of the UN policy not to carry out undercover activities. Hundreds of thousands died as a result.

In 1992, Major General Lewis MacKenzie, Sector Commander in Sarajevo, said,

> I was also upset that I had to get my intelligence from the BBC. The UN was still following its outdated rules. Here we were, almost 300 kilometres from the nearest semi-secure border and we scarcely had the foggiest notion what was going on around us.

To a large extent, controlled as we were by a management committee based in the United Nations in New York, our procedures were meant to mirror UN practices. However, David Crane decided that we would not be handicapped by an absence of proper procedures. With his intelligence background he organized our affairs to make up for UN deficiencies.

So we decided that only proper undercover operations could protect our court and its personnel. We could not be blind to plots to disrupt the work of the OTP, nor fail to preserve the lives of potential insider witnesses, without tipping off the perpetrators. Insider witnesses and spies enabled the OTP to penetrate the political circles among West African leaders. As David was to say in an interview, 'We developed probably the finest information assets system – far better than MI6 and the CIA.' This may have been an overstatement, but it is true to say that there were times when both MI6 and the CIA came to us for help.

As the UN had not adequately prepared itself to deal with secret intelligence in a systematic fashion, we did in fact receive a certain degree of intelligence material from the services of friendly governments. At its most active our intelligence operation encompassed a number of well-placed assets throughout West Africa. Our list of assets even included the brother-in-law of the president of Liberia – our principal target.

Having escaped from a maximum security American prison with, as he was to claim, the assistance of the CIA, Charles Taylor slipped out of the US, winding up at Gaddafi's school in Libya nicknamed the Harvard and Yale of terrorism. Apart from the Sandinistas of Nicaragua, the other alumni included a who's who of budding African tyrants: Foday Sankoh of Sierra Leone; Blaise Compaoré, who seized power in Burkina Faso; Idriss Déby, strongman of the Chad; and my old quarry Kukoi Samba Sanyang, the Marxist revolutionary who escaped from the Gambia in 1981 following an abortive coup, after which I had been sent out from London to prosecute the plotters for treason. Taylor then progressed to become a ruthless West African warlord and gangster, amassing power and wealth and using terror to become the president of Liberia. With his followers chanting, 'He killed my Ma, he killed my Pa, but I am going to vote for him anyway,' Taylor was elected on a wave of fear that worse might follow if he was not elected. He supported rebel forces in Sierra Leone and in return for diamonds looted from that country he gave them weapons. It was a conflict characterized by a systematic and random mutilation and murder of civilians.

The case the prosecution team had assembled against Charles Taylor showed that he was the main individual beneficiary of blood diamonds, often brought to him in mayonnaise jars by child soldiers. We felt we had a cast-iron case against Taylor's instigation of attacks on the diamond areas of Kono, as well as aiding and abetting the chillingly named Operation No Living Thing and Operation Spare No Soul. These involved the massacring of citizens of Freetown and other settlements in an orgy of terror, the use of child soldiers, forcing children to execute their parents, sexual slavery, cannibalism and forced labour.

The urgency for the court to take Taylor into custody, to face justice and to thereby bring peace to the region, had never been greater; the catalogue of atrocities committed by the rebels, aided by Taylor, could not have been graver.

On 3 March 2003, in the OTP, David signed the first seventeen-count indictment against Charles Taylor alleging war crimes, sexual slavery, the recruitment of child soldiers and crimes against humanity. But the indictment was kept under seal. On 4 June 2003, the OTP in Freetown unsealed the indictment as Taylor left Liberia for Ghana. This was his first visit abroad since he was indicted. The hope in the OTP was that, as he was now an indicted war criminal, any state which he visited would surrender him to our court. Because of the unsealing of the indictment, Taylor fled Ghana and returned to the safety of Liberia.

However, in Liberia things were not that safe for Taylor either. There was a civil war taking place and with a rebel force trying to topple him in his own country, President George Bush called upon Taylor to step down from the presidency to assist in a peace process.

On 4 August 2003, under intense pressure from rebels closing in on Monrovia, the embattled Taylor went into exile and was offered asylum in Nigeria by President Obasanjo. Taylor was escorted out of Monrovia by no fewer than four African presidents; of Nigeria, of Ghana, of South Africa and of Mozambique. I have no doubt that the unsealing of the indictment against Taylor played a strong part in destabilizing him and his regime and bringing about his departure from Monrovia.

We in the OTP in Freetown were distraught. The most wanted war criminal in the world appeared to be slipping through our fingers. On his arrival in exile Taylor took up residence in a villa on the Calabar coast of Nigeria. The position adopted by the president of Nigeria regarding the handing over of this indicted fugitive war criminal to the international court in Freetown was expressed by him in these words: 'I will only hand him over if the government of Liberia asks me and then only to the government of Liberia.'

With the president of Nigeria showing no willingness to surrender this fugitive and the new government in Liberia not prepared to help, David and I had a crisis meeting. Despite the fact that we had indicted and arrested a number of other war criminals in Sierra Leone, Africa's most wanted war criminal seemed to be enjoying impunity through powerful political friends and a section in the US State Department, the latter presumably due to a prior relationship between Taylor and one of the US intelligence agencies.

With the departure of Taylor from Monrovia, David decided to exploit his absence by sending our chief of investigations, Alan White, to Monrovia to uncover the extent of Taylor's assistance to Osama Bin Laden's al-Qaeda. David took the view that perhaps the discovery of such evidence might swing the White House more decisively in our favour.

Alan White returned from Monrovia with stunning information. What he had uncovered seemed to suggest that, following the al-Qaeda bombings of the US embassies in Nairobi and Dar es Salaam on 7 August 1998, two of Bin Laden's al-Qaeda operatives wanted by the US for being involved in the attacks – Ahmed Khalfan Ghailani and Fazul Abdullah Mohammed – had arrived in Liberia in March 1999 to coordinate al-Qaeda's diamond-purchasing operations, with the blessing of Charles Taylor. In the meantime, Taylor had settled down to exile in great luxury, with an estimated $4 billion accumulated by looting Liberia.

It did not surprise us at the OTP that Taylor was becoming increasingly confident of the protection of the Nigerian president, who remained deaf to powerful international calls for him to surrender the fugitive. Taylor now spent most weekends at the Nigerian president's farm. At dinner parties each would sit at the end of the table addressing each other as Mr President and regaling the assembled diners with their anecdotes.

In order to rid himself of the dangers to his freedom we presented, Taylor decided on a pre-emptive legal strike. A motion was filed before the Special Court seeking to set aside the indictment against him on the basis that as he was indicted while being a sitting head of state. As such, it was argued, he enjoyed absolute immunity from criminal prosecution. The doctrine of sovereign immunity which was being invoked had been developed at the time when the head of state was a sovereign and any distinction that existed between the state and the head of state was an extremely fine one. However, the absolute nature of sovereign immunity had been eroded by the explosion of the birth of republics around the world, which drew a sharper distinction between the state and the head of state.

To me, at any rate, it was an exquisitely fraught legal issue. The importance of the judicial decision in this case led to the motion being fast-tracked to the Appeals Chamber to save time. The court had appointed as amici curiae two world-famous legal professors – Philippe Sands, QC, a member of Matrix Chambers and University College London and Diane Orentlicher, from Washington University.

Feeling quite dwarfed by the towering reputations of Philippe and Diane, I was tasked with the job of defeating this Taylor motion, which was presented in court by Taylor's attorney, Terrence Terry. I did my humble best to repel the argument based on sovereign immunity.

In putting the case for the prosecution I made the obvious point that Taylor could not simultaneously seek to evade the processes of the court by refusing to appear before it and at the same time seek to use the processes of the court to file a motion to strike down the indictment. In any event, it was our case that there was a distinction between national and international courts, and as the Special Court was an international criminal court Taylor could not claim immunity from its jurisdiction any more than Grand Admiral Dönitz, who succeeded Hitler as Führer, was able to successfully claim so at Nuremberg. Indeed, the statute setting up the Special Court expressly provided that the official position of head of state or government would not relieve such a person of individual criminal responsibility.

It was music to my ears when I listened to both Philippe and Diane addressing the court on a basis that broadly supported the arguments I had placed before the Appeals Chamber. The judgment of the Appeals Chamber was that, 'The principle seems now established that the sovereign equality of states does not prevent the head of state from being prosecuted before an international tribunal or court.' This put an end to Taylor's legal attempt to rely on sovereign immunity to escape the consequences of the massacres, mutilations and terror he visited upon the people of Sierra Leone in his personal quest for power and blood diamonds. Although we won this round, Charles Taylor was still physically beyond our grasp and justice.

On 24 February 2005, the European Parliament unanimously passed a resolution calling on Nigeria to transfer Charles Taylor to the Special Court for Sierra Leone (SCSL). It had no effect. On 4 May 2005, the US House of Representatives passed a resolution, 421-1, that called upon Nigeria to transfer

Charles Taylor to the court in Freetown. It, too, had no effect. This was also the case when, on 11 May 2005, the US Senate passed a unanimous resolution that Nigeria transfer Charles Taylor to the court in Freetown.

On 24 May 2005, the United Nations Security Council added its voice to the cause. That had no effect either. Even a bounty of $2 million posted by the US Congress for the surrender of this fugitive to justice did not produce results.

There was a growing realization in the OTP that Taylor might get away with his crimes because the international funding for the court was likely to finish at the end of 2005 and there was no chance of transferring the case to the newly-formed International Criminal Court in The Hague, as its jurisdiction was limited to crimes committed after July 2002.

After hundreds of millions of dollars had been spent by the international community on setting up the SCSL, it seemed as if Taylor himself was never going to face justice. With international funding for the court running out, it now became a race against time. To Taylor it must have seemed that he could outrun justice.

With the retirement of David in June 2005, Kofi Annan, the Secretary-General of the UN, appointed me as the new chief prosecutor of the SCSL. On my appointment I made a pledge to the people of Sierra Leone that, 'I will exert every nerve and sinew to bring about the arrest and trial of Charles Taylor.'

I called a meeting of my senior staff, which included the outstanding Australian lawyer Christopher Staker, the deputy prosecutor, the ever loyal Jim Johnson, the very experienced Luc Coté and other senior figures involved in investigations and intelligence. I informed them that as all political persuasion directed at Nigeria had failed, the OTP now had to change its strategy and rely on an intelligence-driven plan exploiting any opportunity that presented itself if we were to bring this war criminal to book.

On 7 June 2005, I went to the United Nations in New York to persuade donor states not to give up on funding the court. John Bolton, the no-nonsense US ambassador to the UN, said to me, 'Mr Prosecutor, your heartburn is at an end, we will back you.' I then went to the State Department in Washington to spell out my new strategy and to coordinate US support for securing the arrest of Charles Taylor. Unlike my visit the day before, I found the State Department officials wreathed in smiles that morning.

'Why are you in such good humour?' I asked, teasingly.

'We got al-Zarqawi,' they said, referring to the al-Qaeda leader in Iraq responsible for suicide bombings and, also, for personally beheading Nicholas Berg, an American businessman.

I explained to George Taft and John Bellinger, the latter being legal adviser to the State Department and the National Security Council, the strength of the case the prosecution had assembled against Taylor and the links uncovered between Taylor and al-Qaeda operatives in Liberia and Sierra Leone. One of the more uncomfortable moments I had in the State Department was when I called on Cindy Courville, then special assistant to President George Bush and previously a senior intelligence officer in the Defence Intelligence Agency (DIA). She was a formidable woman who told my assistant Pin Athwal and me, 'The day you get Taylor you had both better get out of Freetown.'

After that outburst I began to wonder if Taylor had in fact been run by the DIA. Is that why she appeared anxious to deter us from getting him?

Unlike ICTY and ICTR, which received their funding from the UN, the Special Court was set up differently and had to rely on national contributions from donor states whose ambassadors formed a management committee at the UN to oversee our spending requirements. Of course, our budgetary requirements depended on what we were going to do and how we were going to do it. As chief prosecutor, in order to get further funding, I had to satisfy them and their foreign ministries as to the reasonableness of our plans, projected timelines and our financial requirements. Naturally, the strength of a case against an indictee was, in broad terms, something they all wanted to know. After all, they had to explain to their finance ministers that they were satisfied their national exchequers should underwrite our required budget. The problem I faced was that different countries do their budgets at different times and thus I was, as David before me, constantly faced with having to come up with figures to fit the timings of national budgets.

In seeking to lay hands on the war criminal Taylor, good fortune came my way when, in January 2006, Ellen Johnson Sirleaf took office as president of Liberia, the first female president in Africa. She had once been imprisoned by Taylor. A golden opportunity had arrived and the moment had to be seized.

I paid a secret visit to Liberia where, with the help of Alan Doss, the Special Representative of the Secretary-General, I met with President Johnson Sirleaf in

Alan's apartment in Monrovia. When I requested her to ask President Obasanjo to surrender Taylor for trial, the poor woman looked utterly terrified. Taylor, she told me, still had a power base in Liberia and any return of Taylor to Liberia or indeed neighbouring Sierra Leone, had the possibility of destabilizing the region. I gave her the undertaking that if she was willing to call for the return of Charles Taylor, I would ensure that Taylor would not be tried in neighbouring Sierra Leone, but in The Hague.

On the basis of this assurance, President Johnson Sirleaf called upon President Obasanjo to surrender Taylor, but not before I had been to London and Washington to ensure that if any trial of Taylor were to take place, the US and the UK would support, in the Security Council, such a trial taking place outside of Freetown. Both capitals agreed.

Coincidentally, at the same time as Johnson Sirleaf summoned up the courage to call on Nigeria for the surrender of Taylor, the US announced a $30 million economic package for Liberia. (Some years later when I was having dinner with Donald Duke, the former governor of Cross River State in Nigeria where Taylor had been in exile, he was to tell me he had received a telephone call at 3 a.m. from Charles Taylor demanding an immediate meeting with him. Taylor arrived shortly afterward, immaculately dressed, and said to the governor, 'It is Judas Iscariot all over again. The only difference is that thirty pieces of silver have now become $30 million. This is inflation for you!')

At the OTP we received information that President Obasanjo was planning a state visit to Washington in the third week of March 2006. One of the principal purposes of this visit was to enhance President Obasanjo's prestige by seeking American support for Nigeria to be made a permanent member of the Security Council, based on the fact that Nigeria was Africa's most populous country and that, of all African countries, Nigeria had made the biggest contribution by way of troops for peacekeeping operations.

I came to the view that it would benefit us to create a delicate political situation, a situation in which Obasanjo had to wrestle with the conflict between the pain of betraying a friend and the enhancement of his own legacy.

Together with my senior associates in the OTP we decided this was the moment to spring into action. I informed President Obasanjo through Nigeria's high commission in Freetown that I was going to object to Nigeria being considered for permanent membership of the Security Council, on the basis that

Nigeria had failed to surrender a wanted war criminal. The diplomatic trap was now set.

My precedent for such a course was the chief prosecutor of the ICTY, Carla Del Ponte, who had objected to Serbia being considered for membership of the European Union on the basis that it had failed to surrender the war criminals Mladić and Karadžić. In my view this was both legally and politically a parallel case.

Two days later the OTP received some vital intelligence. While there were normally sixty to a hundred personnel around the Taylor villa in Calabar, we were now told his protection had evaporated and there was just a single sentry on duty.

Interpreting this information in the OTP, we came to the obvious conclusion that the path was being made easy for Taylor to escape. President Obasanjo could then visit Washington and seek to excuse himself from having to surrender Taylor on the basis that the latter had, alas, absconded. In order to prevent President Obasanjo advancing this excuse, I transmitted to the Nigerian president the message that he must take all necessary steps to ensure Taylor did not escape and called upon the Nigerian authorities to take Taylor into custody by executing the arrest warrant that the OTP had sent them.

I issued a press statement on Sunday 26 March 2006 saying the world was watching to see if Taylor was going to succeed in using his wealth and associates to give justice the slip, and I personally called on President Obasanjo 'to take all necessary steps to ensure Charles Taylor is unable to abscond.'

On Monday 27 March, information began emerging from Nigeria that Taylor had disappeared. On Tuesday 28 March, when President Obasanjo arrived in Washington, he was informed that the meeting at the White House was in jeopardy and may not happen. He was further informed that President Bush was not going to meet him until Taylor was arrested and handed over. At that moment we had an overwhelming advantage. The White House was fully onside. In a manner of speaking we had the Nigerian leader in a headlock.

Wednesday 29 March was the day set for the meeting of the two presidents at the Oval Office. President Obasanjo was now trapped: should he arrest and surrender Taylor and incur the wrath of African leaders who were disapproving of international courts and had little wish to see the chill wind of international justice blowing through the corridors of their own fiefdoms? Or should he refuse to surrender Taylor and incur the anger of President Bush, on whom he relied for getting Nigeria considered for a permanent seat on the Security Council? Could he face the snub if President Bush did not see him?

We had made human nature our weapon of choice. A good grasp of human nature in all its manifestations is, fortunately, something that a member of the Criminal Bar in England acquires in the course of a knockabout criminal practice.

On that day, unsurprisingly, I received information that Taylor had been arrested on the Cameroon border by Nigerian officials, and that the arrest had been carried out on the orders of President Obasanjo. Taylor was to be flown immediately to Liberia.

All preliminary difficulties having now been ironed out and the obstacle to their meeting having been removed, President Bush welcomed President Obasanjo to the Oval Office, with the usual press briefing that followed. The US president congratulated Obasanjo on having secured the arrest of Charles Taylor and the president of Nigeria thanked President Bush for his warm welcome and went on to emphasize that any suggestion that Nigeria had been negligent over the issue of Taylor was wrong and that Taylor would, in fact, be arriving in Liberia shortly.

The trap was now shut.

Taylor's arrival in Freetown was a galloping news story. It was quite amazing to me how quickly the world's press arrived on the scene, even though there was little or no evidence twenty-four hours previously that Taylor would be flown into Sierra Leone.

I was aware that the initial touchdown by the aircraft carrying Taylor would be in Liberia and I was determined that, once it landed there, Taylor was handed over immediately to Special Court personnel. These included my personal close protection officer Robbie Franks (a former Royal Marine), with instructions to get Taylor to us in Freetown as soon as possible.

Normally, in dealing with Liberia, I would be in touch with Alan Doss, the personal representative of Kofi Annan, the then Secretary-General of the UN. Alas, Alan was out of station and his deputy informed me it was UN procedure that in these circumstances the rules required Taylor to have a medical before he was handed over. I was even more disturbed to learn that this medical clearance involved an electrocardiogram (ECG). Now every minute began to matter as the weather started to close in and there were restrictions on UN flights at night. President Johnson Sirleaf of Liberia wanted Taylor off Liberian soil as soon as possible and I was anxious to get Taylor into our detention centre in Freetown before UN flights were shut down for the night. Knowing there was an ECG machine in the US Embassy in Freetown, I called the ambassador and begged him to lend it to us, which he agreed to do. I then managed to persuade the deputy SRSG in Monrovia that an ECG would be carried out upon Taylor's landing in Freetown. The deputy gave in.

An hour or so later, I walked on to our newly-constructed helicopter pad next door to the detention centre in Freetown and looked up at the sky. I saw two dots in the distance. Helicopters. Word had spread through Freetown like wildfire that we were bringing Taylor in to face justice; there was scarcely a rooftop to be seen as people clambered up to the highest points to witness for themselves the arrival at our detention facility of the man they all regarded as the Devil.

The dots in the sky got bigger and bigger and finally I watched as a dishevelled and handcuffed Charles Taylor was escorted off a UN helicopter, while a helicopter gunship circled overhead. He emerged with my close protection officer, Robbie Franks, beside him.

That day, by pure chance, I had in my office in Freetown a number of people who over the years had helped me in various ways to get to this point. There was Stadler Trengove from the UN, James Roscoe from the British high commission, Rob Luke, head of the war crimes section of the FCO, and a multitude of others.

Once Taylor was admitted to his cell there were significant celebrations in my office at the OTP. Champagne corks popped and glasses were raised and drained many times. It was an historic moment; it had taken us three years to finally get this war criminal to face justice.

However, there was to be a further delay. On this occasion I was the culprit. My obligation as the prosecutor was to get Taylor before the Special Court as soon as possible, for certain formalities to be completed. These included the not unimportant duty of the court to seek the accused's answer to the counts on the indictment. This was to occur at the initial appearance. However, I received a plaintive message from Taylor in the cells as to whether I would use my discretion to delay proceedings for his appearance before the court, in order for him to receive clothes from London and Rome. I knew that when he stepped into the dock at this initial appearance his picture and any utterance by him would be relayed worldwide. Going against the rules, I agreed to indulge him. So it came to be that on 3 April, when Charles Taylor made his initial appearance before the Special Court, he was immaculately attired and every inch the dandy he aspired to be.

The day Charles Taylor appeared at his initial hearing and pleaded not guilty to all charges was at a point when the trials of the other defendants indicted by us were finished or in their concluding stages. Taylor would have to be tried on his own and, because of the fears entertained by President Johnson Sirleaf of Liberia and, indeed, the Security Council, he was going to have to be tried by the Special Court sitting in The Hague.

The symbolic impact of having a former African head of state in custody for war crimes and crimes against humanity sent shockwaves through the continent.

I thought everything was now accomplished and we could proceed to his trial, but I was wrong. The government of the Netherlands, one of the greatest supporters of our court, threw a small spanner into the works. They were unwilling for Taylor to be tried in The Hague unless they could get a guarantee of another state being willing to imprison him in the event of his conviction. The sort of crimes Taylor was charged with would carry enormously long sentences on conviction. It is thus a very expensive process and a huge burden on the taxpayers of the country where the prisoner is housed. It may well be that the Netherlands, the home of international criminal justice, felt that it had done enough in this regard.

Try as I might, I simply could not get any country on the continent of Europe to accept him. Africa, I was told, was out of the question, given Taylor's skills at escaping. It took a great deal of persuasion to finally get the UK to agree to take him as a prisoner. Only when this assurance was given did the Netherlands make it possible for the trial of Taylor to go ahead in The Hague.

On 18 June 2007, the UK passed the International Tribunals (Sierra Leone) Act, under the provisions of which Taylor, if convicted, could serve his imprisonment in England.

# 4

# The Devil's Last Dance

No stranger to celebrating birthdays in style on the French Riviera, in May 2010 the supermodel Naomi Campbell once again lived up to her reputation as a party girl. She was celebrating her fortieth birthday with the most lavish of all her parties in the iconic Hotel du Cap Eden Roc. The star-studded celebrations then moved to the sixty-five-metre-long *Silver Angel,* a yacht belonging to her billionaire Russian boyfriend, Vladislav Doronin. The guest list included Eva Herzigova, Jennifer Lopez, Sarah, Duchess of York and her daughter Princess Beatrice. The following night the party moved on to the Billionaire Club in Sardinia where Campbell's guests included the English billionaire Sir Philip Green, top fashion model Elisabetta Gregoraci and Leonardo DiCaprio, the star, among others, of the film *Blood Diamond*. Significant absentees were her old friends Mia Farrow and Carole White, Campbell's agent for nearly two decades. She was someone Campbell once referred to as her 'surrogate mum'.

Despite her outward gaiety in all these celebrations, Campbell was haunted by an inner fear. It was a fear that first raised its head when Brenda Hollis, the then chief prosecutor of the Special Court for Sierra Leone, wished her to give evidence in relation to having received rough diamonds at the home of Nelson Mandela in South Africa. Campbell's fear was not of the court, or of being imprisoned for contempt if she defied a court order to testify; her fear was born out of the brutality of the defendant and his long and unforgiving reach were she to testify.

A desperate Campbell told millions of viewers on the Oprah Winfrey show, 'I don't want to be involved in this man's case – he has done some terrible things and I do not want to put my family in danger.' The man she was expressing her terror of was none other than Charles Taylor, the brutal Liberian warlord we had put in the dock who was now standing trial in The Hague.

The trial had begun in June 2007. The indictment now contained eleven counts, or charges, as I had reduced the number from seventeen in March 2006, and the Special Court had approved the amendment on 16 March 2006. Taylor pleaded not guilty to all eleven counts.

On 4 June 2007, Stephen Rapp, who had succeeded me as chief prosecutor, made the opening statement in Trial Chamber II of The Hague, setting out the prosecution case on five counts of war crimes, five counts of crimes against humanity and one count of other serious violations of international humanitarian law, which included the recruitment and use of child soldiers. Taylor caused a drama by sacking his legal team, which led to an adjournment so that he could find new representation.

Stephen was not able to see the trial through to an end as the prosecutor; when Barack Obama became the 44th president of the United States in January 2009, Stephen returned to Washington to become the ambassador for war crimes, and his place as chief prosecutor was taken by my old friend Brenda Hollis. A more thorough and no-nonsense prosecutor would be hard to find. Brenda, who was leading Kathryn Howarth, Nicholas Koumjian and Sigall Horovitz, had an encyclopedic knowledge of the case.

As for Taylor, he selected the highly successful Courtenay Griffiths, QC, from England, who had for two decades been one of the leading advocates in some of the highest-profile cases. Griffiths was heading a defence team that included Terry Munyard and Morris Anyah.

In the trial of Taylor the prosecution called some ninety-one witnesses to the crimes committed, with a good sprinkling of insider witnesses and some experts. These witnesses testified to horrendous crimes that Taylor was party to in Sierra Leone.

Taylor himself gave evidence on his own behalf and was cross-examined by Brenda Hollis. Throughout his evidence Taylor totally refuted suggestions he had supported rebel groups in Sierra Leone in return for diamonds. Indeed, he testified that he had never possessed rough diamonds and denied any suggestion that he had given diamonds to Naomi Campbell. Thus, the issue of whether rough diamonds were ever in the possession of Charles Taylor became a crucial one in this war crimes trial. Indeed, in view of his persistent denials, it went to the heart of Taylor's credibility as a witness.

In light of Charles Taylor's evidence, the prosecution applied to call three witnesses in rebuttal of Taylor's testimony. They were: Naomi Campbell, Mia Farrow and Carole White, Campbell's agent. The defence were aware that Carole White was on record as saying she had overheard Charles Taylor promise Naomi Campbell diamonds over dinner and that they were rough diamonds.

Still trying to prevent some terrible retribution from Taylor and doing her best to avoid being called as a witness, Campbell was to say, 'I did not receive a diamond and I'm not going to speak about that,' before storming out of an interview with ABC News when the subject was touched on. An observation, perhaps unsurprisingly made, to protect herself.

The court granted the prosecution a subpoena. For Campbell to refuse to obey a writ of the court to attend and testify would have amounted to her facing punishment which could have included imprisonment.

In the same way as Campbell had good reason to be fearful of Taylor, who had murdered anyone who stood in his way or might do him harm, Taylor too had good reason to fear Campbell. He knew that she could give deadly evidence against him: evidence that could ensure he would never again see the light of day as a free man. Before I gave up being the chief prosecutor, we had already assembled a mass of evidence on those Taylor had assassinated or executed, fearing if they came into our hands their information might be harmful to him. However, we were then unaware of the dinner party at Mandela's residence attended by Taylor.

When Taylor became president of Liberia in 1997, the war he had unleashed against Sierra Leone, to obtain its diamonds in return for weapons, was at its height. In September of that year Nelson Mandela held a house party at his residence in South Africa. Among the guests staying were the great cricketer Imran Khan, with his wife Jemima. So too were Naomi Campbell, Carole White and Mia Farrow. Campbell, at the time, was an ambassador for the Nelson Mandela Children's Fund, and the dinner was held in connection with Mandela's charity. The hostess was Graça Machel, the wife of the deceased president of Mozambique, whom Mandela was later to marry.

An unexpected guest arrived. The suddenness of his arrival is underlined by the fact that all guests were seated and the dinner had already begun. It was Charles Taylor, who had taken office as president of Liberia the previous month. Mandela, as president of South Africa, was obliged to extend the hospitality of his house to a fellow president. Yet, Graça Machel, Mandela's future wife, was to whisper to Mia Farrow, 'The Liberian president is not welcome,' adding, 'you don't want to be photographed or be around this man.' What happened during and after dinner that night became a vital component in the prosecution's case against Taylor.

Taylor's legal team fought valiantly to prevent the evidence of the supermodel from being placed before the court. But they failed. On 29 July 2010 the court ruled that the fresh evidence the prosecution proposed to call was highly probative and gave the prosecution permission to call the three additional witnesses to ensure a fair trial. Naomi Campbell was to be the first of those witnesses and the day fixed for her evidence was 5 August 2010.

Anxious to protect herself from harm, Campbell filed a request in court that she should be the beneficiary of such protective measures as the court could grant. Lord Macdonald, QC, of the English Bar, whom she had retained to represent her on this application, managed to secure for her the protection that no person could photograph or video Campbell entering or exiting the court building. This was probably the only time that a court order has come into existence stopping the photography of the most photographed supermodel in the world.

Brenda Hollis had been kind enough to invite me to join her on counsel's row in the court on 5 August. Sitting there I watched this tall, world-famous, but sometimes controversial beauty, make her way across the court and into the witness box. Wonderfully composed, she raised the Bible and, having repeated the oath after the usher, sat down.

'Good morning,' said Brenda Hollis for the prosecution; thereafter, Campbell's version of the story of the Mandela dinner and the rough diamonds began to emerge. It was a curious tale, to say the least; unless, of course, one factored in the dread she must have felt as the man in the dock, on whose orders so many had been killed, made notes as she spoke.

She testified that she did not want to be in court and that she feared for her life because she had discovered through the Internet that Taylor had killed thousands and she did not want to put her family in harm's way. However, that did not help prove the case against Taylor. She was being called specifically to assist the court on the issue of rough diamonds.

Asserting that she had never met Taylor before in her life, she told the court that once she had retired after the Mandela dinner, she went to her room and fell asleep. There was then, according to her, a midnight knock on her bedroom door. On opening the door she was presented with what turned out to be 'a pouch of dirty stones' by a man. She placed it beside her bed and went to sleep again. There was no explanation and no note, just the remark, 'It is a present.'

'I am used to seeing diamonds shiny and in a box,' said Campbell, to drive home the point that she did not know what the contents of the pouch were.

In total contradiction of Campbell's testimony, Mia Farrow gave evidence of an 'excited' Campbell arriving at breakfast the following morning and telling her, even before she sat down, that Taylor had sent her diamonds during the night. In addition, Carole White told the court that she had heard Taylor tell Campbell during dinner that he would send her some diamonds, adding that she was also present when the diamonds were brought in by two men and that, while waiting for them to arrive, 'Naomi was very excited' and was in touch with someone on her telephone as she awaited their arrival.

The reason why this present of diamonds to Campbell by Taylor in September went to the heart of the case against Taylor was he was alleged to have been carrying a cache of rough diamonds while on an arms-buying trip that took him from South Africa to Libya, from where arms were bought and shipped, via Burkina Faso, to the RUF rebels. The shipment landed at Sierra Leone's Magburaka airfield in October 1997. It is believed that the value of diamonds looted from Sierra Leone and traded for weapons through Taylor could have been as high as £950 million.

In delivering the judgment of the court, the presiding judge described Campbell as, 'A reluctant witness who openly expressed fear of testifying against the accused', and went on to say, 'The Trial Chamber is of the view that Ms Campbell deliberately omitted certain details out of fear of the accused. The evidence establishes beyond reasonable doubt that two men sent by the accused delivered uncut diamonds to Naomi Campbell… following a dinner they both attended on 26 September 1997 at the Presidential House of Nelson Mandela in Pretoria.'

Taylor was convicted. In sentencing Taylor to fifty years' imprisonment, the presiding judge said, 'The accused has been found responsible for some of the most heinous and brutal crimes recorded in human history.'

Charles Ghankay Taylor, the 22nd president of Liberia, became, in 2012, the first head of state to be convicted of war crimes since 1946. Taylor's appeal against his conviction for war crimes and other grave offences was rejected in September 2013 by the Appeals Chamber of the Special Court for Sierra Leone, sitting in The Hague.

In case, dear reader, you are wondering what happened to the pouch of diamonds, I am able to satisfy your curiosity. They were given by Naomi Campbell to the chief of Mandela's Children's Fund.

# 5

# Ceylon, World War II and Family

My grandfather, George, was born in Ceylon (now Sri Lanka) in 1879. He was a remarkable man. He was self-made, handsome and a dandy; a true Singhalese patriot who not only fought for independence but did so with a fervent desire to benefit all people. He challenged injustice wherever he encountered it and, in the political language of the time, was classed as a Fabian socialist. Against revolution, but in favour of gradual reform, he became a figure loved by many and reviled by few. A statue to him in his beloved Kandy, erected using contributions from the public, is testimony to the affection in which he was held. Courage, strength and vitality flowed out of his mere appearance. Some say that his fight for the rights of the less fortunate makes him one of the most significant figures the Kandyan provinces had seen in the first half of the twentieth century. He also wooed most women in sight, regardless of their marital status and had a tendency to crush them to his body when dancing. In matters of the heart he committed himself with characteristic energy.

Life to him had to be lived passionately and his conversation, mostly a monologue, was used to dominate the dining table. Some found him too controversial, others insufferable. He was given to spending money rashly and did, as a consequence, have to pay regular calls to colourfully dressed men who lent money at usurious rates of interest. They disappeared when Ceylon got independence.

My grandmother Agnes Nell was a strong-willed woman and an early motor enthusiast. The first car was imported into Ceylon in May 1905 by Edward, the playboy son of the philanthropist Sir Charles de Soysa. When driven from the docks, thousands lined the streets to view the marvel of the automobile. By 1906 Agnes was driving a Belgian five-horsepower chain-driven Belgian Minervette that made a terrible puffing sound that attracted the unwelcome attention of local dogs who clearly mistook the vehicle for some form of mechanical beast. Rumour has it that these motoring pioneers discharged pistols to scare off canine interest.

When my grandfather George began to court my grandmother Agnes, he did so in the teeth of opposition from those of pure Dutch decent who, as Burghers – as they were called in Ceylon – occupied some of the highest positions in the judiciary and elsewhere under the British colonial administration. As Jane Russell says in her biography of my grandfather, *Our George*:

> They considered the upstart George had no business seeking the hand of the beautiful bearer of a distinguished name in the Burgher community. Agnes's grandfather, Louis Nell, had been deputy Queen's advocate, a post later converted to Solicitor General. Apart from his legal prowess he was known as an erudite scholar and one of the earliest followers of Darwin… Charles Ambrose Lorenz, the Supreme Court judge, H. L. Wendt and Sir Richard Morgan who became Attorney General were among her uncles.

A former Attorney General of Ceylon, Sir Samuel Grenier, and his brother Joseph Grenier, KC, were her in-laws. They saw my Fabian-socialist grandfather as someone who imperilled their secure colonial world. After their marriage in 1908, my grandmother became one of her husband's most ardent supporters and remained at his side in all his political battles.

After their marriage, George and Agnes lived in the house they had designed and built on one of the serrated hills that ring the town of Kandy. This is where my father, Frederick, was born. The eminence of the hill had been flattened to build a rambling house with cool verandas. To reach the house involved a perilous journey by car up a steep and winding road.

Houses often acquire an aura. This is sometimes attributable to the personality of the man who chooses the spot and creates a house that reflects his needs and attitudes. My grandfather, who always saw himself as coming from a rather heroic mould, called the house St George's. It certainly had an aura.

My father wanted me to be a barrister. My mother wanted me to take to the church. I am very glad that I did not become responsible for the souls of others entrusted to my care. Looking back, it was difficult enough dealing with rogues and rapists, muggers and murderers, traitors and terrorists, treachery and treason, sanctions busting and espionage – with the odd footballer and war criminal thrown in for variety. The responsibilities of priesthood were quite beyond my limited capabilities.

Born into a legal family, it was inevitable I would follow my father and my grandfather into the law. And there was not the slightest doubt that it would be the Criminal Bar that would attract me in the end. This was probably fashioned in my mind while watching my father's impassioned jury addresses in court, snatches of which were often tediously practised on my mother, my sister and myself at breakfast.

I do recall at the age of about seven taking down from the shelf in my father's legal library, Sidney Smith's *Forensic Medicine*. Within those pages I had my first encounter with intimate pictures of the female body and the still unknown mysteries of a woman's anatomy. I seemed to have taken a healthy interest in their bodies, after which I developed a terrible crush on a girl called Flavia with slightly protruding teeth. So taken with her was I that I spent a great deal of time forcing my tongue against my own front teeth so that we might have protruding teeth in common. Unfortunately, I succeeded only too well, and my teeth had to be put into braces by a German dentist who had been interned in Ceylon during World War II. Not only did I set about disfiguring myself, I also began to steal my mother's jewellery, with which I made presentations to Flavia from time to time. Unfortunately, her mother discovered this hoard of love tokens and she was grilled by her parents. Broken by this parental interrogation, she made a confession as to where the jewellery had come from. All items were returned to my mother. Two of our servants, who had been sacked as thieves, were promptly sent for and re-employed with suitable apologies. I was severely beaten by my father, who felt that a series of blows might quell my rather precocious ardour for the opposite sex.

Kandy, in the central highlands of Sri Lanka where I was born, has been described as one of the most entrancing cities of east Asia. It is also the crossroads of many faiths: the meeting place of those who worship Buddha, Vishnu, Mohammed and Christ. The Temple of the Tooth still houses the eyetooth of the Buddha, the most sacred of Buddhist relics. A drumming, which can still be heard today, wafted up from the temple, across the Kandy lake and up the hillside to my parents' home. In my early years at the Bar in London, I was instructed to defend at the Old Bailey the son of the former keeper of Buddha's tooth, who faced charges of living off immoral earnings in Mayfair; the story ended happily with his triumphant acquittal at the hands of a London jury.

St Paul's, the Victorian Gothic Anglican church in which my grandfather married Agnes Nell, is not a hundred yards from the Temple of the Tooth. In this church, where I was confirmed by my godfather, the bishop, are burnished brass memorials to the Ceylon Planters Rifle Corps that go back to the Boer War and the more recent, pre-World War II commemoration of the Ceylon Mounted Rifles.

After their arrival in Ceylon in 1796, it took the British nineteen more years and many military reverses to finally capture Kandy, the last royal capital of Ceylon, in 1815. The King, who was taken prisoner, was sent into exile in India. So ended the oldest monarchy in the world. The country now became a fully-fledged British colony.

With the old royal capital as his base, Grandfather George began to build his political career, which never wavered from his commitment to improve the lot of the people he served. To them he was affectionately referred to as Our George.

In 1931, he contested and won a seat for the Central Province in the State Council. He remained at the heart of national politics for the rest of his life, playing the most significant part in persuading the colonial office in London that Ceylon should be given universal adult franchise ahead of any other non-white colony.

Visitors to St George's included the former British prime minister, David Lloyd George, the poet Rabindranath Tagore, the former Indian prime minister Jawaharlal Nehru with his wife and daughter, and future Indian prime minister Indira Gandhi, who had just finished schooling in Switzerland. Ramsay MacDonald, who was to become the first Labour prime minister of Britain, was another visitor. Indeed, between the wars, anyone in mainstream British politics who visited Ceylon, or those national leaders in India who looked to the day they could lead their own people, beat a path to my grandfather's home.

In 1927, when Mahatma Gandhi arrived in Kandy with his wife, Kasturba, he was already a highly controversial figure. A wholehearted pacifist whose sincerity was never in doubt, he was held by many in Britain to be the victim of naïve delusions. Indians saw him to be a patriot and a great teacher who had a message for the world. His wife Kasturba was, according to my aunt Minnette, someone who was rarely noticed or considered while accompanying her husband. My grandmother Agnes took her out for a drive to watch elephants bathing and Kasturba Gandhi began to cry like a child. Worried that something awful had happened, my grandmother's enquiries into this tearfulness elicited the explanation that she was overcome with emotion. Astonishingly, she explained to my grandmother that no one had ever been so considerate as to take her out for a drive before. Perhaps it was a case of a husband so high-minded that he neglected to understand the simple needs of his own wife.

The following year, George left for England in pursuit of his aim to make Ceylon the first non-white British colony to win adult universal franchise from Britain. It is in large measure due to his indefatigable efforts that Ceylon succeeded in achieving this objective.

Arriving in England with their daughters – my aunts Marcia and Minnette – my grandparents felt that Marcia, being of the right age, should be launched into London society as a debutant. In due course she was presented at court, as was the custom at the time. She later went into the film world and worked at Pinewood Studios cutting and scripting for Alexander Korda. From Pinewood, Marcia went into journalism and had her own byline in the *Daily Express*. A vivacious beauty, she was often likened to the actress Merle Oberon, a great star in the 1930s and 1940s who married Alexander Korda. In 1937, Marcia returned to Ceylon, having married Lieutenant Commander Robert Nicholl-Cadell, RN. Minnette, meanwhile, was sent to boarding school at St Mary's Hall, Kempton, which was one of the first public schools for girls. Her going to St Mary's was at the insistence of her step-grandmother, Mrs Louis Nell, who was then aged ninety-nine and had been a pupil there in 1832. Minnette became a brilliant and talented architect and worked with Le Corbusier. She made close friendships with other architects, artists and actors who included Jane Drew, Denys Lasdun, Henri Cartier-Bresson, Laurence Olivier, Picasso and Feliks Topolski. According to an obituary in the *Independent*, in her architecture Minnette made it her 'mission to preserve local (Sri Lankan) traditions and to join their craft base to modern Western technology.'

Both my aunts were possessed of bohemian attitudes and feisty intelligence. Genuinely interested in all things artistic and the avant-garde, with little time for those they regarded as philistines, they were the dominant females on my father's side of the family.

In 1928, the British Labour Party elected my grandfather to represent the colonies at the International Socialist conference in Brussels. At the conference my grandfather disagreed with the more flagrantly anti-imperialist speeches made by some of the delegates. However, with his natural affability he was able to cement his friendship with George Lansbury, who was to become a cabinet minister in Ramsay MacDonald's government of 1929, alongside Arthur Henderson who became Foreign Secretary. Herbert Morrison was another who became a lifelong friend, together with Lord Pethick-Lawrence, an old Etonian and Fabian socialist who became Secretary of State for India and Burma during Clement Attlee's Labour government, after the war.

While in Belgium, my grandfather met the King and went on to Holland to see the 1928 Olympics in Amsterdam. On his return to Ceylon, he set about preparing seriously for a parliamentary career. To quote Jane Russell,

> There are several reasons why George decided to make politics his profession. Vanity certainly played a part. George was never a man to assume a false modesty about either his achievements or his capabilities. But there was no trace of superciliousness in his self-esteem. It was like the conceit of a clever, attractive and precocious child, entirely without affectation. More important, though, was the urge to serve. George's *amour propre* was merely a thin top-soil to a deep and solid character founded in a bedrock of idealism. His need to bring about a social regeneration and to improve the living conditions of the poor, the old, the sick, the illiterate and the unemployed was a much more powerful impetus.

Finally, in 1931, largely through his efforts, the people of Ceylon were granted adult universal franchise; no mean achievement, considering that in Britain it wasn't until 1928 that all women over twenty-one received the right to vote.

In February 1934, the British government received a resolution proposed by my grandfather – and passed by the State Council – that the crown and the throne of the Kandyan Kings be returned to Ceylon from Windsor Castle where they had been stored for over 100 years. King George V expressed his desire that these ancient symbols of sovereignty be restored and they were brought to Ceylon by his son, the Duke of Gloucester. In a ceremony of unusual interest held in the Audience Hall of the future Kandyan Kings, the governor, Sir

Reginald Stubbs, took possession of these national heirlooms on behalf of the people of Ceylon.

They came to be exhibited at the Colombo Museum, established in 1877. Alas, unforeseen trouble lay ahead. In the 1960s, the Kings' golden crown was transferred to the Kandy Museum where, it was thought, it properly belonged. On the morning of 19 September 1961, the assistant curator opened the doors of the museum and was shocked to discover that the Kings' crown was missing; the intruder had entered through the roof and removed the crown by forcing open the glass showcase within which it was displayed.

Acting on a tip-off, the police apprehended the culprits but sadly, in an act of vandalism by the thieves, the jewels had been removed from the crown and the crown itself had been cut up into 300 pieces of gold and smelted down. So ends the story of the centuries-old crown of the Kings of Kandy, which my grandfather had succeeded in getting back to its home.

George loved declaiming. When I used to stay with my grandparents at St George's, I used to visit my grandfather's room at 6 a.m. every day, just before he would go for a walk in the garden opposite his wing of the house. I would accompany him on his perambulations to inspect the plants and the glorious variety of flowers that had burst into bloom with the first rays of the sun. He would pause and look across the valley to the wooded hills beyond, to Hantana Peak and to land covered by the immaculate green mantle of tea bushes. Sometimes he would hum. Sometimes he would sing rousing Sinhalese songs, such as 'Danno Budunge', and sometimes he would practise a political speech. The garden was lovingly tended by Archie, the female gardener. When Archie died, my grandmother insisted she was buried beside the roses she had so lovingly cared for in life.

From the lawn opposite his wing we would go to the garden at the entrance to St George's. Here, the hill had been cut to make a triangular lawn, while the hillside that had not been cut rose as a sheer bank and towered over the lawn. It was very dramatic and spectacular. Whether disturbed by my grandfather's singing or not it was impossible to determine, but often a flash of electric blue would leave a neat hole in this bank and take to the air; the kingfisher was off. Grandfather George would walk purposefully toward his beloved orchids. Some grew at eye level from baskets suspended from the branches of trees. Others sprang from the earth. He examined the scorpion orchids with care. Not a day went by when he did not have his lapel adorned with a scorpion orchid. The one for that day would be plucked with care and then a servant would be sent for to take charge of this sinister but exotic flower, to be kept fresh for his next change of attire. The gardens of St George's, laid out by my grandmother, were deeply influenced by the terraced wilderness of the gardens created by Count de Mauny on Taprobane Island, which I came to inherit in 1993. Those gardens were themselves inspired by Axel Munthe's San Michele.

Granny Agnes was the sweetest of women and adored her husband. Over the years she put up with all of my grandfather's infidelities by turning a blind eye. When he died, she was the kindest person to all manner of women who turned up from time to time with children allegedly fathered by my grandfather. Her generosity of spirit was undoubtedly inherited from her father, Paul Nell, who once, when out riding near Dambulla in the 1880s, found a child still trying to feed at the breast of his dead Tamil mother. This was probably an example of a woman having walked from the north of Ceylon in search of work as a tea-plucker on an up-country tea estate. My great-grandfather, Paul, picked up the child, took it home and for some eccentric reason christened him with the name of Denmark, and brought him up in his household.

Marion Hill, Tipperary, Deanstone and Kobonella were the names of my grandfather's tea and rubber estates, on which I grew up. The distinctive and unforgettable smell of the sheets of crepe rubber coming off the press at Marion Hill, the large rocks on Tipperary to the top of which I used to climb, the gin-clear streams at Deanstone, the rock pools and waterfalls of Kobonella, together with the rich aroma of the tea factory produced by the rolling and curing of tea leaves are the haunting memories of my boyhood. It was a secure and protected world. After my grandfather's death the estates were divided between his three sons. One of the greatest gifts that life can endow is to give one a chance to turn back the clock. To return temporarily to a childhood paradise full of the memories of youth is to achieve just that. Alas, as a result of nationalization by ultra-nationalistic and short-sighted governments in the 1970s, all these dream places of my early youth now lie in neglect, disrepair or ruin.

My father had two brothers: the feckless George (Sunny), a truly happy person, and Percy, the youngest, who also went into the law. Due to Percy's fondness for drink, when he died his many grieving friends diverted his funeral cortège, removed his coffin and took it to the Ceylon Rugby and Football Club where it was placed on the bar; Uncle Percy had got drunk there for the better part of his life. He was a brilliant parliamentary draftsman with an acute legal mind. I am told he never had less than thirteen pink gins before he settled down to drafting some complex piece of legislation.

George (Sunny) became a tea planter and ran the family tea estates. Another relation by marriage, Dickie Hurst, ran the rubber plantations. I loved going to stay with Uncle Sunny on the estate, as he was always full of fun, very indulgent and never took life too seriously.

I was born in Kandy in 1939, two and a half months after Britain and the Empire went to war with Hitler. Things remained quite tranquil in Ceylon until after the Japanese attack on Pearl Harbor in December 1941.

In a political speech to the Ceylon National Congress, in 1941, my grandfather voiced his sentiments in the following terms:

> We must place our whole-hearted support on the side of England and other democratic countries, so that their grim fight against the aggressor countries of the world will end in triumph for world freedom. We are entirely with them in the noble war in which they are engaged at the present time. We have provided all we can to expedite the defeat of Germany and Japan, so that small nations like our own can live their own lives.

After the Japanese entry into the war, Ceylon became a frontline base. Pro-Marxist politicians in the country, who opposed the war and agitated against Britain, were interned.

At the beginning of 1942 things were looking grim for the Allies. In January, Erwin Rommel (popularly known as the Desert Fox), the German commander in North Africa, was advancing in Egypt. In February, Singapore fell to the Japanese. An entire convoy making for Malta was sunk and in the Java Sea the British Far East striking force had been completely destroyed. In March, the Japanese took Rangoon. By April 1942, the Japanese were in the Bay of Bengal and all the major rubber-producing countries in the East had now fallen to the Imperial Japanese Army.

With the fall of Singapore in February 1942, the anticipation was that Ceylon would be the next target for the Japanese. Given this looming danger from Japan, Churchill sent Vice Admiral Sir Geoffrey Layton to Ceylon, with dictatorial powers. All fighting services were united under Layton's command and he took charge of the War Council, on which my grandfather served as the minister of health.

The formal meetings of the War Council took place at Queen's House, the official residence in Colombo of the then governor, Sir Andrew Caldecott. This rambling but dignified house was the most attractive building in Colombo. Originally built by the Dutch in the mid-eighteenth century, it had been extended by successive British governors, ending up with a kindly facade, irregular roof levels and gardens which faced the sea.

Sir Geoffrey, the new commander-in-chief of Ceylon, and his service chiefs, loved to escape the sweltering heat of Colombo and take refuge in the cool of the Kandyan hills. As my grandfather was the only member of the War Council living in Kandy, St George's became home to endless unofficial meetings of the War Council. Here my sweet-natured grandmother's exquisite hospitality never flagged. The kitchens were constantly on the go as servants brought food to those who came by day and night.

Such were the troubled expectations of an imminent Japanese attack that a large sea turtle coming ashore one night was reported as a Japanese amphibious vehicle. These expectations were, however, soon realized when, at the end of March 1942, intelligence was received of the expected Japanese attack. On 4 April a Catalina flying boat on patrol reported a large enemy naval force on its way. Vice Admiral Chuichi Nagumo, whose First Air Fleet had attacked the Americans at Pearl Harbor, was approaching with orders to seek and destroy the British Eastern Fleet, which he hoped to find at anchor at Colombo or Trincomalee. A huge air armada of fighters and bombers took off from Nagumo's aircraft carriers to attack Colombo on Easter Sunday 1942. So began the Battle of Ceylon.

One man understood the significance of these events: Churchill. At the end of a dinner in the British Embassy in Washington in 1946, he was to say,

> The most dangerous moment of the war, and one which caused me the greatest alarm, was when the Japanese Fleet was heading for Ceylon and the naval base

> there. The capture of Ceylon, the consequent control of the Indian Ocean, and the possibility at the same time of a German conquest of Egypt would have closed the ring and the future would have been black.

As with Pearl Harbor, the Japanese selected a Sunday for the attack. Once again it was Commander Mitsuo Fuchida who commanded the Japanese aircraft. But the War Council had moved very fast. The racecourse at Colombo had been turned into an airfield and the Chief Justice's residence had been demolished to extend the runway. Every elephant available was pressed into war service. When on 5 April the Japanese attacked Colombo, Emperor Hirohito's pilots got the shock of their lives when two squadrons of Hurricanes came up to greet them from this unexpected landing ground. The ack-ack guns too subjected the Japanese to a withering fire.

Although a number of ships were sunk in Colombo harbour, the Japanese attack was beaten off. Of the attacking Japanese aircraft, twenty-five had been shot out of the sky and another twenty-five had been damaged. This was the first real reverse they had suffered in the Far East and the first major setback to their all-conquering progress. Naturally, in the Ceylon War Council there was a certain amount of self-congratulation. There was, however, one minister who did not want to join in the congratulations – my grandfather. 'Your grandfather took it very badly and flew into a towering rage,' Sir Geoffrey Layton said to me many years later.

According to Layton, before the Japanese attack on Ceylon, my grandfather had, as minister for health, issued instructions that all hospital roofs were to have the symbol of the Red Cross painted on them, so that they might be spared from aerial bombardment. His orders were meticulously carried out, except in the case of the principal mental asylum in Colombo, which was somehow forgotten in the rush to prepare for the impending attack. The Japanese mistook it for a power station and it received a number of direct hits. According to the commander-in-chief, the only thing that quelled my grandfather's anger over the incompetence of certain officials was the report he received from the chief medical officer of health stating that the Japanese bombing of the asylum had achieved some unexpected medical results. A number of patients, previously thought incurable, seemed to have had the balance of their minds restored by the primitive shock treatment occasioned by the Japanese explosives.

On 8 April 1942, a radio message was received from another Catalina flying boat that a large Japanese force had been sighted heading at full speed toward Trincomalee. Admiral Sir James Somerville, commander-in-chief of the Eastern Fleet and another member of the War Council, was under strict instructions from the Admiralty to keep the Eastern Fleet 'in being' and not to risk fighting a fleet action with superior Japanese forces. He spent a lot of his time manoeuvring the fleet so as to keep clear of the enemy's probable search area by day. There were, however, some ships at anchor in Trincomalee. Orders were given for the harbour to be cleared of all shipping. The Japanese attacked on the morning of 9 April. Heavy bombing of Trincomalee, its docks and airfields began. Once again, every available aircraft was airborne, engaging the enemy.

That day Admiral Nagumo missed his real prize: the Eastern Fleet. However, many ships that sailed out of Trincomalee harbour on the night of 8 April were spotted by Japanese reconnaissance aircraft the following day and eventually sunk. These included the aircraft carrier *Hermes*, which was attacked by waves of Japanese bombers. In the final result Admiral Somerville did succeed in preserving the bulk of the Eastern Fleet, which had received orders to scatter and then rendezvous at the secret British naval base at Addu Atoll in the Maldives.

I have often wondered why Churchill regarded the Battle of Ceylon to be the most dangerous moment of the war. There were, I believe, two reasons other than those he stated. One was to do with oil and the other to do with rubber. If Ceylon fell to the Japanese, the Strait of Hormuz would have been within their grasp, together with oilfields in Bahrain, Kuwait, Basra, Qatar and Saudi Arabia. This would have left the Allies badly short of oil.

As regards rubber, with their Army moving remorselessly westward, every major rubber-producing country in South East Asia had fallen to the forces of Imperial Japan by April 1942. If Ceylon fell, where were the Allies to get the rubber from to roll the troops across Europe after D-Day? Mechanized warfare needs rubber for tyres, tanks, hoses and a hundred other needs. Japanese military success led the United States into a hurried programme to produce synthetic rubber, with President Roosevelt appointing a committee in August 1942 to make recommendations on how to enable its production. If Ceylon fell, the Allied invasion of Europe in the summer of 1944 may have been significantly delayed through lack of this strategic commodity. The fact is that a delayed Operation Overlord, which in fact took place in June 1944, may have exposed the Allies to all the wonder weapons the Nazis were furiously working on, including atomic weapons. Evidence used at the Nuremberg trial suggests that among the weapons the Germans were developing were five-kilogram tactical nuclear weapons on their V-2 rockets, which were the world's first long-range guided ballistic missiles.

I now realize it was my grandfather who has been the biggest influence in my life. He had an unshakeable self-belief. His dynamism and enthusiasm instilled in me a passion to live life to the full. I am told, alas, that the only thing I seem to have actually inherited directly from him is his extravagance. It may be that, as the first grandchild, I was particularly spoiled by him. He denied me nothing that I wanted. I loved travelling with him in his black Ford Sedan, with a flag fluttering from a pole attached to the left mudguard. During the war I have vivid recollections of going with him toward the red facade of the Galle Face Hotel, with the sky above the esplanade in front of the neo-Palladian State Council thick with barrage balloons as a part of the air defences. Right through the war my grandfather maintained a suite at the Galle Face Hotel due to its proximity to the State Council. And I now realize that these war years were perhaps the busiest of his life. As Jane Russell, his biographer, was to say:

> His reorganization of the health services was appreciated by the military authorities as well as the help which he rendered to the armed forces in establishing the enormous camps in and around Kandy town. He was able to render great assistance liaising between the civil and military population, reducing the possibilities of tension as the huge influx of allied personnel poured into the hill country. St George's became open house to the officers of the Asia Command based in Kandy, with a procession of jeeps continually climbing the steep hill… Apart from the army personnel milling in and out of the house… there was a stream of callers, constituents and others… Always an early riser, he began his work in the ministry at 6.30 a.m., even before the caretaker arrived.

Admiral of the Fleet Lord Louis Mountbatten, as he was known when he arrived in Ceylon in 1944, was the great-grandson of Queen Victoria. He set up the

HQ of South East Asia Command (SEAC) in the beautiful botanical gardens at Peradeniya, just outside Kandy. He was another regular visitor to St George's, my grandparents' home. So frequently did he come that I began to call him Uncle Dickie. I must have been the only child with a khaki battle dress. I even had a helmet he had specially made for me as a present. In 1977, when we were both attending a dinner in London and our conversation turned to the war and Kandy, Mountbatten told me that there was considerable opposition to his choice of Kandy for the HQ of SEAC, but that he was totally satisfied that he had been vindicated in moving it from Delhi.

I never cease to be amazed by the degree to which our lives are shaped by coincidence. Years later I married his great-niece, Katarina, who was the last member of his family to plant a tree at Broadlands, Earl Mountbatten's home in Hampshire, before his assassination by the IRA. She told me that at the end of a family dinner party at Broadlands, Mountbatten took her into the grounds in driving rain to plant the tree. A story that emerged from that same evening highlighted an incredible vanity my grandfather and others had observed about him. The Earl of Harewood had arrived for dinner with a present for his host. It was a board game which had the logo 'MB' on the box. 'Look,' said Mountbatten, as the wrapping paper was removed from the gift and his eyes fell upon the logo, 'they have named this game after me – Mountbatten of Burma.' There was a guffaw and an immediate intervention by the Duke of Kent. 'Don't be a fool, Dickie. It stands for Milton Bradley!' Mountbatten, who had clearly never heard of the famous games manufacturer, was rather miffed by the remark.

With the surrender of Germany in May 1945, my grandfather began to address the issue of the political independence of Ceylon. On 15 August 1945, he wrote to the new British prime minister, Clement Attlee, with the following plea:

> Ceylon has now reached a stage in its political development where it demands freedom as a right. We have begun to create a welfare state, and the plans for industrialization will radically alter the nature of our society. Politically and socially the whole country has come alive. Yet still the masses are poor. Landlessness is the cause of poverty and poverty the cause of disease. Freedom alone will give us the power to change the economic structure, which forces large

> sections of the population to live in misery even though the country is endowed by nature with all that man needs. I feel this is an appropriate time for me to appeal to the British people, after the victory of the Labour Party at the recent elections. I recall with pride that when I attended the Labour Party conference in 1928, the party decided that Ceylon was entitled to self-government. On behalf of the people of Ceylon, I appeal through you to the people of England to concede us the right to be free.

My grandfather had been president of the Ceylon National Congress, which paved the way for the formation of the United National Party, the winner of the first parliamentary general election in 1947. Independence followed in 1948.

## 6

# A Legal and Not So Legal Family

I ENTIRELY AGREE WITH THE MAN WHO SAID EVERY FAMILY TREE PRODUCES some lemons, some nuts and a few bad apples. In my case, the really bad apple in my family was someone who faced penal servitude for life, for the felony of forgery. And he was a priest in Holy Orders to boot.

Many have a hunger to know who they are and where they come from. That knowledge may enrich us or, occasionally, depress us. It always educates, as a man is the sum total of his ancestors.

After the revocation of the Edict of Nantes in 1685, a branch of the French Protestant Noell family settled in Holland. In due course, they changed their name to Nell. From Holland they went on to settle in the Cape of Good Hope with other Huguenot families. My paternal grandmother, Agnes Nell, was an outstanding beauty. Her ancestor, Frederick August Nell, fled South Africa in the 1790s, having fought a duel and killed his opponent when duelling had just been made illegal. To escape prosecution he teamed up with a famous Swiss mercenary, Count de Meuron, who had been awarded a contract with the Dutch East India Company to raise his own regiment. The regiment came to Ceylon to fight for the Dutch, whose colony Ceylon then was, as the Dutch were getting rather rattled by the British, who were planning to take over Dutch possessions in the region. Count de Meuron, his regiment and my ancestor Frederick August Nell, switched sides and ended up fighting for the British. In addition to winding up on the winning side, Nell married a Portuguese heiress, Catharina Petronella de Fonseca, in the Dutch Reformed Church, Colombo on 8 December 1793 and lived in great splendour in a mansion near Galle on Ceylon's south coast. They had a son, George, born in 1797. He was my great-great-great-grandfather.

It is with George Nell's sons that my legal heritage begins. Two of his sons became barristers. George Frederick, who was born in 1828, was called to the Bar at Lincoln's Inn and became deputy Queen's advocate, an office that was later converted to Solicitor General. His brother Louis, from whom I descend, was born in 1830 and was also called to the Bar of England. He too went on to become a deputy Queen's advocate. There have been something like five generations of lawyers since 1828, with one break: three generations of de Silvas and two prior generations of Nells. This I think is relatively rare. I am the fifth, and my nephew, Detmar Blow, represented the sixth when he was called to the Bar at the Inner Temple.

While I – like my own father, and his father, George, before him – chose the Criminal Bar, the earlier generations of Nells preferred to make their mark in the civil courts. Not only did the Nells produce a number of lawyers of distinction, the Nell girls married some of the most distinguished legal figures in Ceylon at the end of the nineteenth century and beginning of the twentieth century. I went into law simply because I was going into the family business. I had been greatly influenced by the biographies of Sir Edward Marshall Hall, KC, and of Sir Patrick Hastings, KC, which I read at the age of ten. They were all part of a fine library of legal biographies my father kept in his study together with a series of volumes called *Famous British Trials*.

At the outbreak of World War I, my great-uncle, Paul Nell, left Ceylon aged seventeen for England in order to sign up to fight. He joined the Royal Flying Corps, the predecessor of the RAF, and served in France where he was tragically killed in April 1917. He is buried in the Commonwealth Cemetery at Longuenesse (St Omer). Fifty years later when my father was presenting his credentials as ambassador to France at the Élysée Palace, General de Gaulle, the then president, who had been briefed as to Nell's sacrifice, embraced my father, saying, 'Monsieur l'ambassadeur, votre oncle a donné sa vie pour la France.'

Toward the end of her life, my grandmother Agnes used to lie in bed propped up by large pillows, with a bowl of grapes in front of her, surrounded by stacks of detective novels which she devoured as eagerly as the grapes. Her ambition was to see me become a famous amateur detective. Not only did she introduce me to the works of Sir Arthur Conan Doyle, she introduced me to his son Adrian, who was once staying at St George's. He spoke at length about big-game fishing and continuing the exploits of the eccentric detective Sherlock Holmes with his deerstalker, fiddle and tobacco in his slipper. To my grandmother Agnes, a real detective was a combination of Dorothy L. Sayers's

Lord Peter Wimsey, Sapper's Bulldog Drummond, Agatha Christie's Hercule Poirot and, of course, Sherlock Holmes.

When I was about thirteen years old I recall her saying to the then prime minister of Sri Lanka, who had come to St George's for tea, 'Now Dudley, I want Desmond sent to Scotland Yard for proper training in due course.' To this, the rather startled prime minister said, 'Of course, Mrs George, of course.' They always called her Mrs George, never Mrs de Silva. The only reason I can think of is that my grandfather George was such a dominant political figure in his day that, while he was popularly known throughout the country as Our George, she became Mrs George. She was a very kindly, loving, broad-minded and generous-spirited woman.

By contrast, Grandfather George had a ferocious temper. When I was eight, my parents took my sister Helga and myself on holiday to the seaside resort of Weligama on the south coast of Sri Lanka. My mother's sister, Lorna, came with us, together with the brilliant and amusing leader of the Communist Party, Peter Kueneman. He had been president of the Cambridge Union in 1939 and was described in a well-known American magazine as one of the most dangerous men in the world; this was at a time when the US was paranoid about communism. He was quite keen on Aunt Lorna and they used to perch on the rocks, smoking cigarettes and generally behaving in a smoochy manner. I was very fond of Peter; we would sit on the beach and he would tell me racy and captivating stories about pirates and smugglers.

When my grandfather discovered that my father had taken a leader of the Communist Party on a family holiday his anger was too awful to behold. Yet during World War II when a number of prominent Marxist politicians were interned in the main prison in Kandy, he had ordered that food should be sent to them daily from the kitchens of St George's, much to the annoyance of some of his ministerial colleagues.

My grandfather took infinite pains with his dress and I remember him wearing spats in the late 1940s, long after they had been abandoned in England. When he died in 1950, my grandmother gave me his silk topper and a collapsible opera hat, together with his evening dress, so that when I came to England I would be properly attired. Granny had not been to England since the early 1930s and failed to realize that by the time I came to school, what with the war and the Labour government of 1945 – and the awful austerity that came in its wake – the world of opera hats had disappeared. It all goes to underline the fact that some of those who lived in the colonies tended to hang on to traditions and customs long abandoned by the colonial power that once ruled over them.

In 1950, the world-famous French photographer, Henri Cartier-Bresson, came to Kandy. His photographic journey through the East had been marked by momentous events. He was there taking photographs when Mao took over in China, and he was there in time to photograph Gandhi an hour before his assassination. In March 1950, he asked my grandfather to pose for him. A few days later, my grandfather was dead.

Nowhere in the world are astrologers taken more seriously than in Ceylon. From the humblest to the highest, palms are read and stars consulted. Our senior houseboy, Elias, once told me a story that illustrates the grip astrologers have over their clients. Another servant working for friends of my parents had consulted an astrologer and had been told that his expectation of life was limited, as the 'lifeline' on his left palm was very short. Tormented by the thought of an early demise, he decided to alter his fate. Taking a nail he began to scratch a furrow in the palm of his hand to extend his lifeline. Within the week he developed blood poisoning and died.

Knowing of my grandfather's date and time of birth, an astrologer sent him an astrological chart. He was informed that death would come to him over the Ides of March. That same year my grandfather had decided to have a crack at the Kandy Golf Championship and had spent a number of hours practising on the lovely course at Peradeniya. On 12 March he went out for an early round in the morning with an English planter. They completed a four-hour session and were just coming to the clubhouse when my grandfather felt a crushing pain in his chest. A waiter brought him a double brandy. His car was called for and he was driven home. As he swept up the drive he suffered another massive heart attack and lay slumped in the back seat. To quote Jane Russell:

> As his sons came out to help him he asked 'What day is it?' 'The $12^{th}$' was the reply. 'The Ides tomorrow then, I'm done for.' Characteristically, George had mixed up the date. The Ides of March is not until the $15^{th}$ but, believing the $13^{th}$ to be the traditional day of doom in the calendar served only to confirm to him that his end had come. However, despite the appalling pain from these

two massive heart attacks, George insisted on having a bath while his doctor was called for.

It was apparent to everyone that he was dying. When his personal physician arrived, my grandfather was lying in bed fighting for breath and he began to develop a bluish pallor. Still conscious when the physician arrived, my grandfather gasped out words so characteristic of him: 'Dammit Wilfred, can't you save my life?' Jane Russell described it as 'the despairing plea of a man reluctant to relinquish his hold on life. A few minutes later he was dead.'

He was the first person I saw die. I was at his bedside. From all his other difficulties, financial and political, he always arose with an iron-winged determination. I am still enormously proud to be the grandson of a man who championed his causes with such vigour, had a passion for liberty and brought an indefatigable enthusiasm to everything he did in life. He saw it as a moral duty to dedicate his life to the welfare of people. In 1980, a postage stamp was issued in Sri Lanka to commemorate his remarkable life.

Until my grandfather died, my father had dedicated his life to helping his father pursue his political aims. This death marked a watershed in the fortunes and times of our entire family; my parents decided to spend an extended period in England, taking my sister, Helga, and me with them.

My mother had trained at the Slade School of Art in London during the great days of Sir Henry Tonks. She did most of her finest portraits in charcoal and two of her best were of Lord Sankey, the Lord Chancellor; and Aldo Castellani, the Italian bacteriologist, whose daughter, Jacqueline, Lady Killearn, kept a copy in her bedroom until her death at the age of 105.

My mother's interest expanded to sculpture and wood carving, which she pursued at a school in Thurloe Place, South Kensington, which was under the chairmanship of Sir Edwin Lutyens. Her brother, my uncle Ray, went on to become a brilliant architect who worked around the world, from Libya to the Bahamas.

There came a point when my mother fell under the spell of the famous German World War I artist Arnold Busch who invited her to work in his studio in Germany. With the rise of the Nazis in the 1930s, my apolitical mother did a number of portraits in charcoal of young German officers. She also painted many landscapes in oils. It was at the insistence of her father that she was dragged away from Germany where she had been so intensely happy. Perhaps her father had an inkling of the horrors that were to come and was alert to the fact that his daughter had a trace of Rothschild-Worms blood.

The names of the Worms brothers who settled in Ceylon from Frankfurt will forever be associated with the story of Ceylon tea. In September 1841, Maurice Worms brought seedlings from China to Ceylon and formed a nursery of them on his Rothschild estate – named after his mother's family, which was by then perhaps the greatest banking dynasty the world had ever known. Maurice and his brother, Gabriel, pioneered the production of manufactured tea and family legend has it that in those early days it cost £5 to produce one pound of tea. The immense value of tea at the time explains why Victorian tea caddies had padlocks.

Like their cousins, the Rothschilds, they came to be ennobled with a Hapsburg title. The Emperor Francis Joseph conferred the title Baron of the Austrian Empire on the eldest of the brothers by Imperial Letters Patent in Vienna on 23 April 1871 and, as they had become naturalized British subjects in 1874, Queen Victoria, by Royal Licence, granted him and his descendants permission to use the title of baron in Britain and the Empire, owing to the contribution made by the family 'to the development of the colony of Ceylon.'

In 1895, Baron Henry de Worms (the family had by then adopted the particle) went into politics after a brief stint at the Bar. He succeeded Gladstone as the member for Greenwich and later became Secretary of State for the Colonies. Eventually he was raised to the peerage as Lord Pirbright. Henry was a good speaker, an accomplished boxer, a fine shot and showed an interest in an improbable variety of subjects; yet he is also recalled as an immense bore. His published works were said to be so learned that they were generally incomprehensible and he himself was said to be so boring he was nicknamed Baron de Book-Worm.

Late in the 1970s, my only remaining de Worms kinsman, Baron Charles de Worms, invited Rosamund Cameron and me to his home in Woking. A renowned lepidopterist, he had been given the right to set up a mercury-vapour light trap in the gardens of Buckingham Palace. Upon my expressing an interest in collecting butterflies, we were treated, over lunch, to a learned discourse on them, from the rare Camberwell Beauty to the Painted Lady. He then turned to moths, saying, 'If you want to take this up, cyanide is the best for killing!'

Between large helpings of lamb he went on to tell me that all I needed was a good killing jar with a wide mouth and a cork bung. 'The best method of killing butterflies is potassium of cyanide buried in plaster of Paris,' he added firmly. Fearing some tragedy were I to take his advice, I inquired after some less dangerous method of collecting specimens. 'Yes,' he said, 'You could use ammonia, but this would only take the colour out of some butterflies.'

Then, changing the subject, he returned to the gardens of Buckingham Palace and the moths to be found there. 'Do you know?' he said, 'there have been forty moths seen in the grounds of the palace which are not to be found anywhere else in London?'

'Really?' I exclaimed, with genuine interest.

'Yes, and there are several newcomers in the palace gardens.'

'Such as?' said I.

'The Common Footman, the Scarce Footman and the Marbled Coronet,' he replied, rattling the names off as if they were members of the palace household staff.

After lunch we went to his study, where he kept a vast selection of Lepidoptera in a magnificent collector's cabinet made of polished satin walnut. 'Now, let me show you two: the Red Carpet and the Shoulder-striped Wainscot,' said he, pulling out a specimen drawer. He then pointed to two of twenty moths lying beneath the glass and added: 'They are also palace moths. Sometimes,' he said, 'the mercury-vapour light trap in the palace grounds catches specimens wholly foreign to the British Isles.'

'But how do they get there?' I asked.

'Ah,' he said with a glint in his eyes, 'I once caught a moth only to be found in East Africa. I wracked my brains as to how it could have made its way into the palace grounds, until I discovered that President Kenyatta of Kenya had visited the Queen two days before. I assume it travelled in his clothes or in his beard.'

After more talk about the Cloaked Minor, the Common Carpet and the Minor Shoulder-knot, I returned to London. This was the last time I was to see the great naturalist alive. He was due to dine with me in London a week later. On that day, I had a call from his niece, Rosamund Williams, who gave me the sad news, 'Uncle Charlie has just passed away.'

Sometime before, he and I had gone to stay with my sister, Helga, and brother-in-law, Jonathan Blow, at Hilles House near Stroud. The last thing he had to say to me before we left Woking was, 'Remember, I would love to set up my light traps on Painswick Beacon', which was on the Hilles estate. With his death, the Painswick moths were to elude the baron's traps and not form part of his vast collection of Lepidoptera, which he bequeathed to the Royal Scottish Museum in Edinburgh.

Hilles House, built of lovely Cotswold stone by the architect Detmar Blow, nestles high on an escarpment, with its shoulder to the hillside, and has the most magnificent views down into the Severn Valley and beyond. On a bright day, seven counties can be seen from the terrace.

My sister had met her husband-to-be at a fashion show at Berkeley Castle when she was modelling for the House of Worth. Berkeley Castle is the oldest inhabited castle in England and the scene of the murder of King Edward II. After a courtship in which Jonathan followed Helga across Europe, they married in 1962. Alas, Jonathan committed suicide in the 1970s, tormented by the thought that his inheritance of the Hilles estate had enforced upon him obligations that destroyed his desire to exploit his talent as a writer. I have two nephews, Detmar and Amaury, from that marriage, together with the talented fashion designer Selina as a niece.

Hilles House is also the place where I nearly met an untimely end when attending birthday celebrations for Selina. Shortly after my marriage to Katarina, we were spending the weekend there. Katarina and I had retired one evening as the rest of the house party and guests continued their riotous enjoyment downstairs. Suddenly we were both awakened by the sound of our bedroom door being flung open. Standing in the light of the hall outside was Daniel Chadwick, with a sword in his extended hand, coming toward the four-poster bed. Katarina, taken aback by these sudden developments, disappeared under the blankets.

'Where is she?' said Daniel, advancing upon me menacingly with wild staring eyes. 'I know she's in bed with you.' This was, of course, not an unsurprising venue for such an accusation, but the need for a speedy denial became pressing. Such denials, however, only enraged him further. He was on the point of running me through when Katarina flung aside the bedclothes to show the intoxicated Daniel that his girlfriend was not in bed with me. Numerous drunken apologies followed Katarina coming to my rescue. In the morning, it turned out that my nephew, Amaury, had secured the attentions of Daniel's girlfriend that night and the pair had sloped off to some quiet and convenient place, unwittingly leaving me to run the risk of assassination at the hands of an intoxicated and inflamed Chadwick.

~

At the age of six I was sent to boarding school, St Thomas's, a prep school in the hill country of Ceylon. It was an isolated but beautiful place, with rolling green hills and gin-clear streams. It rained a lot and could get very misty. In many respects it resembled parts of the Scottish highlands.

I think I must have been unhappy at St Thomas's, as I do not recall having made a single friend. When I was about eight, I was brought back to Kandy and I boarded at Trinity College, although it was only a twenty-minute drive away from our home, which was then called Rhynern, after a small village in Germany where my mother had lived when she was studying painting.

I do not think that I was a very conscientious schoolboy. All I was interested in was cricket, rugby, tennis and going to the estate over the holidays, where I could indulge my interest in shooting and naturalism. While my father clearly wanted me to come to the Bar and take to politics, he was beside himself with anger at my lack of interest in study and obsession with wildlife.

My love of nature, I believe, came partly from my Worms heritage and partly through my Cleland ancestors. As everyone knows, there are no snakes in Ireland. The experiments of my ancestor, James Rose-Cleland with snakes, in order to test the theory that the soil and climate of Ireland were fatal to the serpent tribe, ended up causing feelings of bitter indignation in County Down in the late-eighteenth century. Of course, as legend has it, St Patrick had banished the reptiles from Ireland's shores by chasing them into the sea. Driven by a spirit of inquiry, my ancestor, during a holiday in London, purchased six harmless English snakes in Covent Garden and on his return to Ireland he released them in the grounds of his estate at Rathgael – and awaited the results.

Three weeks later one of the snakes was killed some three miles away from the point at which it was released by a person who believed it must have been a curious kind of eel. Taking the creature to the celebrated naturalist, Dr J. L. Drummond, he discovered to his horror that the good doctor pronounced the creature to be a reptile and not a fish.

When news spread that a real serpent had been killed within a short distance of St Patrick's burial place, consternation reigned among the country folk, many of whom were too afraid to venture from their homes after dark. One local clergyman preached a sermon in which he referred to the presence of the snake as heralding the beginning of the end.

Sums of money were offered for the discovery and destruction of any other snakes that might be found in the county. Excited seekers after the rewards formed themselves into hunting parties and spent weeks searching the fields and woods of County Down. The remaining five snakes were found and disposed of. But the searches continued with undiminished enthusiasm, until my ancestor had it put about that a prankster had introduced six snakes. I do not believe that he let it become known that he was the culprit.

When, in 1951, my parents brought me to England, we sailed from Colombo on the SS *Himalaya* and everybody, as they did in those days, came on board to see us off; the servants appeared to be sobbing at the imminent departure of my sister and myself. Friends and well-wishers came aboard in large numbers to say goodbye. It was all very touching. There were trunkloads of packets of tea from our estate, which my parents felt would make welcome presents in post-war Europe.

After Colombo the next stop made by the P&O liner, which had started off in Australia, was Bombay. When the *Himalaya* docked there we were met by a Parsee couple who were great friends of my parents. For dinner they took us to a restaurant on Malabar Hill which overlooked the city. Looking around from the terrace of the restaurant I saw a circular enclosure with walls some twenty-five to thirty-feet high. Perched on top of these walls were a large number of vultures. Asking about the structure I learned that this was the Tower of Silence, where the Parsees left their naked dead to be picked clean by the birds. I promptly expressed a desire to be shown round the place, but was met with stony looks and an immediate rebuke from my parents who informed our hosts, unfairly I thought, that I was 'a thoroughly morbid child.' At this, our Parsee hosts began to look at me with very disapproving eyes. Matters were made worse when out of the night sky there dropped something that looked remarkably like a human finger, which was quickly gathered up in a napkin by a member of staff.

Now eleven, I began to have the first real stirrings of sexuality during this three-week voyage to Southampton. On board was an Australian girl of thirteen, travelling with her aunt and an Indian girl of eleven, who had boarded with her parents in Bombay. Alas, the latter's father got pneumonia and died during the voyage. While her mother lay sedated in her cabin, the girl clung to me, burying her face in my shirt and sobbing uncontrollably as we looked at the bundle of her father's body draped in a Union Jack. After prayers, which were conducted by the ship's chaplain, the ship was stopped out of respect, and the body was tipped into the sea.

In England I was sent to Dulwich College Prep School as a boarder. The school, founded in 1855, was a solidly middle-class institution. Unsurprisingly, it even had a boy named Bourgeois in my time. The headmaster was John 'hold your ankles whilst I beat you' Leakey. When I started school in England it was during the period of the post-war Labour government and we were all subject to strict rationing: one egg a week and a coupon so one could buy a packet of Polo mints in Dulwich Village. It was austerity Britain. However, London cheered up with the Festival of Britain in 1951 which, I was to learn, was the first real manifestation of joy after VE Day.

At Brightlands, the house in which I boarded, we took a keen interest in the activities of our sports master, Captain Fraser, because of his obvious and constant advances on a rather pretty young school matron. He used to come along to supervise our evening prep and would then linger well beyond any honourable time for departure. We also watched, in youthful fascination, as a tender relationship grew between the housemaster and a spectacularly good-looking young boy who was showered with presents and always driven by the housemaster in his car if ever we had to go anywhere. The rest of us had to travel less comfortably.

During my school holiday my father took my sister and me to Holland. My mother, meanwhile, was determined to look up the friends she had made in Germany before the war. We crossed the Channel on a ferry, taking the new car my father had just bought in London. Its boot was stuffed with one-pound packets of loose tea from our estate; the teabag had not yet been invented. Broken Orange Pekoe was a rarity in post-war Germany and there was no gift that was more welcome to our German hosts. Almost everywhere we parked the car, the Germans would gather round to take a look at this latest British model.

It was just six years after the war and Germany still looked ravaged by the bombing to which it had been subjected. I remember seeing bombed-out buildings in which large clocks still hung at drunken angles, their unmoving hands showing the time the bombs came down.

Looking back, I discovered that my family abounds in adventurers. Besides Frederick August Nell, who came to Ceylon to avoid being tried for duelling, an English ancestor also set out for the East in 1765. Richard Rose left Abingdon, then in Berkshire, to seek his fortune in the East as an officer in the regiment of the East India Company. In June 1766, he married Agnes Cleland at Fort St David, Cuddalore, on the Coromandel Coast of India, having survived no fewer than three shipwrecks and being seriously wounded in the head by a musket ball when attempting to storm the fort at Colocunda.

The following year he commanded a storming party at another fort, when he was shot through the left wrist. This kept him out of further action for six months. In June 1768, he died at Trichinopoly of wounds received at the siege of Attoor and his body lies buried in a cemetery in Madras. His son, my great-great-great-grandfather James Dowsett Rose, was born at Fort St David, Cuddalore on 24 March 1767 and brought back to England at the age of four by his mother, Agnes. James eventually succeeded to his uncle's estates in Berkshire and County Down. As a result of a name-and-arms clause in the will of his uncle (Agnes's brother), James was required to add his mother's surname of Cleland to that of Rose and assume the Arms of Cleland. Rathgael House in Bangor, County Down became his seat. There my ancestor lived as a devout Protestant landowner. Indeed, Rathgael House was where the first Sunday school was held in Ireland – in 1788.

The name Rathgael is derived from two words, 'rath' (fort) and 'gael' (stranger) – The Fort of the Stranger. The house itself was built on the remains of an old fort and was typical of those spacious Irish mansions built of stone. It was encircled by woods and overlooked a beautiful panorama of country and sea. Cleland's Lake was used as a skating rink during a particularly hard winter.

Another branch of the same Cleland family lived in the Victorian Gothic Stormont Castle. When, in 1979, my old friend, Sir Maurice Oldfield, who had been head of MI6, was sent by Prime Minister Thatcher to Northern Ireland as Security Coordinator, he went to stay at Stormont, which had passed out of the Cleland family in 1922.

On 11 July 1798, my ancestor, James Rose-Cleland, received a letter from Viscount Castlereagh, who had been entrusted with the duties of the Chief Secretary (in the absence of the Earl of Chichester), indicating that the lord lieutenant, Lord Camden, had been pleased to approve of him raising a regiment of infantry. The regiment came to be called the Rathgael Yeoman Infantry and my ancestor maintained it at his own expense in the service of his sovereign. The uniform was dark blue with gold facings, the rosette, which fastened the gorget, was a maroon red as was the knitted silk sword scarf. Sadly, all that remains of the regiment, apart from the written records, is a dark blue and gold regimental drum in Bangor Abbey, County Down.

In 1805, as High Sheriff for County Down, my ancestor presided at the contested election for that county between Viscount Castlereagh and Colonel John Meade, which lasted twenty-one days. In due course, as Foreign Secretary under Lord Liverpool, Castlereagh reached the zenith of his greatness when he became the very soul of the coalition against Napoleon. From Rathgael, the seven Rose-Cleland sisters ran the successful Rathgael Hunt.

James's grandson, the Reverend John William Gregg MacGregor, whose mother was a Rose-Cleland, was my great-grandfather. Having had a brilliant academic career at Trinity College Dublin, where he read not only theology but also law, he was ordained as a clergyman into the Church of England. Sometime later, when he had the souls of many in his care, the Reverend J. W. Gregg MacGregor embarked on conduct that, until 1831, could have sent him to the gallows. Not satisfied that the parish registers of St Helens, Abingdon, were sufficiently detailed about our Rose ancestors, who had lived in that parish for 300 years, my great-grandfather inserted additional details about baptisms and marriages of our family in the records of the church.

The clergyman's 'felony' was detected by the noted local researcher and historian, Meineke Cox, with whom I once studied these ancient parish records.

It is clear from his letters that have survived, that it was my great-grandfather who tampered with these inviolable records and put himself within the reach of the criminal law.

Through the marriage of Agnes Gregg of Parkmount to William Cairns of Magheraconluce in the eighteenth century, my great-grandfather was a cousin to Earl Cairns, twice Lord Chancellor. Perhaps the Reverend John felt protected by his family connections? In the West and in the East the advance of the family in legal achievements continued. While Cairns was a Victorian Lord Chancellor in Britain, in Ceylon my great-grandfather, Louis Nell, was appointed by the governor, Sir Hercules Robinson, as Solicitor General, a position then known as the deputy Queen's advocate.

If indicted, did my clergyman ancestor have a defence to a charge of forgery? I believe he did. The offence under the English Forgery Act of 1861, of altering parish registers, could only be committed if the entry was false. None of them were. Where he believed the parish records were deficient in detail he had merely added such descriptions as had socially significant connotations in those earlier days. Although vanity may be classified as one of the seven deadly sins, it has, as yet, not been made unlawful.

~

My cousin, the late Walker Macran, whom I did not really get to know until my father became Ceylon's ambassador to France in 1966, had left England in the late 1940s and settled in France. Douglas, who was one of the founders of the English School of Paris, then lived in the chateau Monte Cristo, built by Alexandre Dumas. Douglas maintained the chateau and lived very well on the considerable earnings of Cleopatra, his basset hound; she was enormously photogenic and was the symbol of Hush Puppies. A chauffeur-driven limousine with a nurse would arrive at Monte Cristo and Cleopatra would be whisked away to one of her photo shoots like a superstar! Her fame spread so widely that in due course a newspaper based in San Tropez started a Cleopatra gossip column, concentrating on what Cleopatra would have seen from being under the table.

My father gave up the Bar temporarily to become Ceylon's ambassador to France. I remember flying to Paris in 1968, to spend a few days at the residence in Neuilly. On my arrival, I found my father in the walled garden engaged in pistol practice. My father felt he needed to become more skilled in these deadly arts in the event that the atmosphere of revolution in Paris that year took a more threatening form.

It was during that stay in Paris that my father took me to the Élysée Palace to meet President de Gaulle. De Gaulle could scarcely believe that someone of twenty-seven wanted to talk to him, when others of my age were responsible for barricades and the burning of his effigy in the streets of Paris. With de Gaulle was the prime minister, Pompidou, and the elegant foreign minister, Couve de Murville. When I complimented the latter on his wonderful command of English, de Murville informed me that he had been a male au pair in England. 'At Sissinghurst Castle, with the Nicolsons,' was his reply when I asked where.

It was during my stay in Paris that my mother invited to luncheon the young Aga Khan, who had recently succeeded his grandfather. Unlike his grandfather, Karim Khan neither drank nor smoked and held up the American astronauts as supreme examples of healthy manhood. During lunch he expressed his desire to sell the stables he had inherited from his grandfather. I think this must have been my earliest contribution to the turf when I said to him over lunch, 'It is unthinkable that you should sell the greatest racing stables in the world.' I am sure that others must have expressed similar sentiments to him, for he never sold the stable and eventually became one of the most enthusiastic and successful racehorse owners in the world.

When my sister Helga's eldest son, Detmar Blow, emerged from schooling, my father began looking to the next generation of the family to come to the Bar. He put Detmar under great pressure. Although I did not think that Detmar's interest lay at the Criminal Bar, he joined the Inner Temple when he finished at the London School of Economics. After his call to the Bar, my father was very anxious that I should take him into our chambers and we subsequently spent a great deal of time in various hostelries and nightclubs debating whether he was cut out for life at the Criminal Bar.

Late one night at Annabel's when we were discussing the merits of him joining a matrimonial set instead, we spotted Alexander of Yugoslavia with his wife, Katherine, dining with the flamboyant Baron Enrico 'Ricky' di Portanova and his wife. Going over to greet my in-laws and their guests, the Portanovas, and taking my unsteady nephew with me, was a terrible mistake. Detmar dropped a cigarette lighter, which fell from his hand and vanished down into the depths of the ample cleavage of the seated Baroness Portanova. Without a moment's hesitation, my nephew thrust his right hand straight down in pursuit of the vanished lighter which, after some fumbling, he retrieved with an air of triumph. The startled baron looked on horrified. Just days before when he was shooting in Scotland, I had been told, a strong gust of wind had carried his toupee high into the sky, where it was riddled with holes by someone who thought it a rare pheasant. An ugly scene was avoided by my profuse apologies for a tipsy nephew.

Not long after passing his Bar exams he met and married Isabella, the daughter of the baronet Evelyn Delves Broughton. Issie's grandfather, Sir Jock Delves Broughton, one of the most prominent members of the decadent Happy Valley set in Kenya during the war, had been charged in 1941 with the notorious murder of the 22nd Earl of Erroll, who had been his wife Diana's lover. A conviction for murder would certainly have resulted in him being hanged. The killing became the subject of the film *White Mischief.* In the film, Greta Scacchi, playing Diana, and Charles Dance, playing Erroll, vividly portrayed the sexual hedonism that prevailed among the rich British ex-pats who were sheltered from the dangers and the shortages of the war in Europe. When Sir Jock was triumphantly acquitted of the murder, a racing friend of his at White's sent him a telegram that read, 'Won by a neck!'

At our home in Chelsea, Katarina and I once gave a dinner party bringing together Merlin, the present Lord Erroll and grandson of the murdered peer, and my niece Issie, the granddaughter of the baronet charged with the murder. They got on famously.

Issie Blow was a fashion icon for many years before she committed suicide by drinking the same weed killer that my nephew's father had drunk to do away with himself. She understood both the key to being a muse and the value of being immediately recognizable by an item of fashion, rather like Jackie Kennedy and her dark glasses. The late Princess Margaret used to call Issie The Hat, on account of her sometimes stunning – and often startling – choice of headgear.

As history has shown, Detmar was not cut out to be the next generation of the family to earn his living sporting a barrister's wig. He gave it all up in favour of owning a contemporary art gallery in Hoxton.

When I was called to the Bar at the Middle Temple in 1964, little did I think that in the years that lay ahead the range of those I would represent, or advise, would span the realms of royalty, spies, heads of state, governments, jockeys and stars from the worlds of entertainment and football; and the second man on the moon. For years I lived on the basic and staple diet of criminal barristers: murder, rape, drugs and fraud, before I developed my passion for international law.

I was into my eleventh year of practice when, rather to my surprise, I received a communication that I was to be appointed a deputy circuit judge, meaning I had to sit as a non-permanent judge in the Crown Court for a certain period. In the early days of my sitting as a judge, my mother used to come to the Knightsbridge Crown Court to see how I was doing. In my judge's room, before the hearing began, I introduced her to the clerk and ushers, who would find her a good seat. During the course of a contested trial I caught sight of my mother passing a note to the usher, then whispering something to him. To my horror, everything seemed to stop while counsel and the jury watched the usher approach me on the bench carrying the note. It is as well they could not hear what the usher said to me. 'Your Honour, your mother would like you to read this note urgently,' he whispered. I unfolded the note and it read, 'Darling, I do not believe a word this witness is saying. I hope you don't either!'

If this early judicial appointment was an indication that the powers that be had singled me out for what is now called fast-tracking, I failed to live up to their expectations. I believe I failed in two ways. Among the things the decision makers look to determine is if you are towing the line in respect of sentences one imposes on convicted persons. I am totally satisfied in my own mind that doing justice sometimes does mean going against the trend of the tariff penalty by imposing a sentence which does meet the justice of the case, even though it may be thought to be too lenient by others. It is the initial clanging of the prison doors behind a convicted person that has the most impact on a criminal. However, as time passes, they settle down to a prison routine that blunts the memory of that clanging door. I know that by going against the tariff I did sometimes incur the disapproval of civil servants in the Lord Chancellor's Department. In addition, I did not temper my lifestyle to fit in with the dull sobriety that is looked for in those who are being tested on the lower rungs of the judicial ladder.

After I had been sitting for a number of years, mainly at the Knightsbridge Crown Court, I was called into the Lord Chancellor's Department where, referring to my perceived lifestyle, the Permanent Secretary observed rather sardonically, 'De Silva, you are not an average cocoa-drinking member of the British public are you?' I agreed and did not seek to repel the attack. As it was, I had no great passion to go on the bench and be a sort of umpire between the prosecution and defence, before delivering homilies to those I was about to sentence. It was much more exciting to be a gladiator in the ring with an encircling net and short sword.

# 7

# Madam, Where Are Your Mangoes?

EVENTS IN SIERRA LEONE IN 1967 WERE TO LEAD TO ME BEING INSTRUCTED to defend in that country's first treason trial in 1969; my first capital case. The only penalty for treason was death. I had been in active practice for just four years. Such is the wheel of fate that another 'first' came, some thirty years later, when it fell to me to prosecute for war crimes someone whose life I had helped to save in Sierra Leone during this very trial.

In March 1969, four members of chambers were instructed to appear before the Supreme Court in Freetown, where sixteen men and one very grand female paramount chief were on trial for treason. She was represented by Charles Fletcher-Cooke, QC, with Tom Kellock, QC representing the former Attorney General. It fell to Nigel Murray to lead for the defence of the former Army commander, while I had the former Cabinet Secretary as my client.

Some at the Bar in England may well have raised their eyebrows at two very junior juniors doing a capital case. In fact, this very subject had received an airing in the Hanratty case not long before. In 1962, James Hanratty was convicted of murder at the Bedford assizes and sentenced to death. The murderer, alleged to be Hanratty, had discovered two lovers in a lay-by near Bedford. He shot Michael Gregsten and then raped and shot his girlfriend, Valerie Storie. She survived to give evidence from a wheelchair. Hanratty denied he was the killer. It was a trial that gripped the nation and the brilliant Michael Sherrard (later QC) who was undertaking his first murder case, fell to be criticized by some who felt that a capital case warranted more than a member of the junior Bar as defence counsel. In my case I had no choice. My client, George Panda, the former Cabinet Secretary in Sierra Leone, was a civil servant of limited means, as was Nigel Murray's client, Brigadier David Lansana. We were all they could afford from Britain.

The allegation against all these defendants was that in March of 1967 they had attempted to prevent Siaka Stevens, the former leader of the opposition, from forming a government, after an election which he narrowly won. All those in the dock were people to whom Britain had handed over power when Sierra Leone received its independence in 1961. They constituted the political and military elite of the country. One man who was absent from the dock was Sir Albert Margai, the former prime minister, who had lost the election to Stevens. Margai was in London.

It was a case that took us all on a voyage through the English Treason Acts of 1351, 1553 and 1695. My learning curve was steep and this early, rather esoteric knowledge stood me in very good stead when I was later sent off to Kenya, the Gambia and Tanzania for capital cases where the allegation of treason lay at the heart of the indictment.

On the first day of the treason trial the acting Chief Justice took his seat in court number one of the Supreme Court in Freetown. He looked around at counsel, the all-male jury and then at the defendants in the dock, and finally the packed public gallery behind the dock. On the wall behind and above him were the Royal Arms, as always present in Her Majesty's courts. The Queen was still head of state. Sierra Leone was yet to become a republic.

Fixing his eyes on counsel's row, the acting Chief Justice addressed the barristers. 'Good morning, gentlemen,' he said, giving us all a beaming smile. Then, looking beyond the defendants at the public gallery, he began to scowl as he noticed a number of ladies who he felt were inappropriately attired. 'Will the ladies who are not wearing hats please leave the public gallery?' was the judicial order.

He waited. No one moved. Adopting a sterner tone Chief Justice Cole spat out the words, 'Very well. Will the women who are not wearing hats leave immediately?'

No one in the gallery stirred.

'Tipstaff,' he said, 'remove the women from the public gallery who are not wearing hats.' He rose and went to his room while his sartorial orders were put into effect.

All the ceremony and some of the trappings of a long-forgotten age of English trials were in place. But as we were all to discover during this travesty of a trial, fairness and justice found little place.

'Behave yourself, Mr de Silva. Show more respect to the witness you are cross-examining.' This outburst, directed at me by the acting Chief Justice, came just a month into the trial.

There are moments when, as cross-examining counsel, you realize that not only have you got a lying witness in the witness box, but that appropriate questioning can demonstrate to the court the perjury the witness is committing. This was one of those moments. Unfortunately for me the witness was the foreign minister in Siaka Stevens's government, who was falsely testifying about overhearing an alleged conspiratorial conversation between some of the defendants in a place called Moyamba. The art of destroying a lying witness, I had learned, was to take him along the path of his evidence, getting him to confirm its salient points, and then close the gate behind him so that there is no escape from his perjury.

The judge could see where I was going and that I could establish that the witness was 200 miles away from Moyamba at a public meeting at the time. I treated the witness as I would any other perjurer. Sheer panic prompted the judge's reaction in calling me to order. This was, after all, a political trial in which he had to get a result for the government and here was a cabinet minister about to be unmasked as a liar in an open and packed courtroom.

The notes made by some counsel record my reply to the judge as, 'My Lord, the witness should command respect and not demand it through Your Lordship.'

Three days later, shortly after court adjourned for the day, I was arrested on a trumped-up charge in the bar of the Paramount Hotel. It is something I had been warned of by opposition supporters; fortunately I had a good friend in the form of the local Governor-General, the late Sir Banja Tejan-Sie, who himself had to go into exile in England a few years later when he fell out with Prime Minister Stevens. He would send me messages to keep me abreast of what he had picked up at State House.

My arrest and prosecution, largely at the insistence of the prime minister, Siaka Stevens, and Cyril Rogers-Wright, the prosecutor, was the first time I experienced how getting at the truth, the fight for justice and the rule of law can carry some perils in certain jurisdictions. This experience, while in my twenties, was to occur again and again.

Even the manner of my arrest was reminiscent of a bygone age. I was sitting at the bar of the Paramount Hotel having a much-needed drink with

Nigel Murray at the end of a day in court, when the local commissioner of police, Malcolm Parker, accompanied by two policemen carrying Lee-Enfield 303 rifles, came up to where I was sitting. Having saluted smartly, he said, 'Mr de Silva, sir, I have a warrant for your arrest.'

'Commissioner,' said Nigel Murray, 'do join us for a drink.'

'No thank you, sir,' said the commissioner, 'I will wait until you finish.'

Once I finished my drink I was arrested and taken to a police station where my braces and shoelaces were removed. I was charged with the criminal offence of smuggling a small amount of cognac into the prison when I went to see my client for a conference on 26 April 1969.

Fortunately, after being held in custody for a couple of days, my application for bail was granted by a magistrate. When I was given bail I was invited by the British high commissioner to lunch at his residence – Runnymede. After lunch, Sir Stanley Fingland said to me, 'Desmond, of course I understand your difficulties but this is a friendly Commonwealth country and there is little that the Foreign Secretary can do to help.'

Despite the inability of the Foreign Office to assist, the US State Department now took a hand. Within twenty-four hours of my luncheon with the British high commissioner, I had a message from Bob Minor, the US ambassador, who invited me to the embassy for dinner. What a different attitude. He informed me that if I felt I was in any real difficulty or danger I could take refuge in the US Embassy. With that reassurance, I continued defending in the treason trial.

My own case came up and I was tried by a magistrate who dismissed the case against me. Some days later I was re-arrested in relation to the same matter. Once again, despite protestations about double jeopardy, I had to go through another trial and I soon realized that the whole object of the exercise was to harass me to the point I would give up defending my client and return to England. Of course, the government realized they could not just throw me out of the country; that would leave my client unrepresented, with the very good argument in an appeal before the Judicial Committee of the Privy Council that he had been denied natural justice.

When I was tried and discharged by the second magistrate, the anger of the government took the form of an appeal against my acquittal and on 15 July 1969, I found myself in the dock in the Supreme Court before a High Court judge who, saying that the magistrate was wrong to discharge me and without hearing any evidence, declared that this was, in his opinion, a matter 'that required an exemplary sentence'. However, I neither paid my fine nor served my sentence of three months in lieu, as he suspended my sentence pending my appeal.

By the time I appeared before the Court of Appeal I was shaking with the return of malaria, which I had first contracted when incarcerated in a cell nine feet long and five feet wide, with a stone floor, not a stick of furniture and a tiny aperture high up in the cell wall through which mosquitoes came in by the cloud. When I appeared before the court I had only one ground of appeal which was that, although I had been sentenced, no one had ever convicted me of anything. The Court of Appeal was the West African Court of Appeal, presided over by the English Chief Justice of the Gambia – Sir Phillip Bridges.

'My Lords,' I said, 'I hope Your Lordships will find that a powerful argument.'

They did and my sentence was quashed.

All defence counsel in the treason trial that began on 4 March 1969 and ended on 14 April 1970 knew that the verdict was likely to be rigged. Our suspicion that evidence was being manufactured by the prosecution was underlined by the court's finding that it was deplorable of prosecuting counsel to interview, in his chambers over a weekend, a prosecution witness who was then undergoing cross-examination by the defence. When, during the trial, it was discovered the leading counsel for the prosecution had done this, Nigel Murray obtained a subpoena to force the prosecutor, Cyril Rogers-Wright, into the witness box to explain this monstrous behaviour. Of course, the inevitable happened. The Supreme Court ducked the issue and set aside the subpoena, 'on the ground that there were errors in the Royal Style and Title appearing on the face of the subpoena.' Prosecuting counsel was let off the hook on the most technical basis imaginable.

The trappings of wigs and gowns, the traditions encrusted with rituals and old-time courtesies, were just window dressing for political executions and the destruction of the opposition. All the defendants were convicted by the jury and sentenced by the acting Chief Justice to suffer the supreme penalty.

An indication that the verdicts were fixed before the trial even began was to be found in the foreman of the jury receiving, on the recommendation of the then President Siaka Stevens, the Order of the British Empire in the next lot of the Queen's honours and the acting Chief Justice being made permanent.

After those death sentences were imposed, of course, the question of appeals arose, and in the following year I went out with Noel Gratiaen, QC to appeal for Brigadier David Lansana, who was the first appellant. Indeed the arguments we proposed to deploy, if accepted by this court, would have led to the quashing of all the convictions.

Gratiaen and I had travelled from Lungi airport by cab and ferry. Having crossed the sea estuary we set off on the dusty journey to Freetown. When our taxi got us to the Cotton Tree in Freetown it turned left and went uphill, past the colonial Supreme Court building and up to the Paramount Hotel. At the reception we were told that they had no reservations for us and that the hotel was full. Was the government trying to make our lives difficult? The prime minister, Siaka Stevens, was desperate to have the convictions confirmed, to ensure the execution of his political opponents and pave the way for him to set up a republic and a one-party state.

Unable to get rooms at the Paramount Hotel, we spent a considerable time at the bar drinking brandy, while I ran through my experience of the year before with my leader, Noel. Following this we caught a taxi outside.

'Take us to another hotel,' Noel said to the driver. The driver acknowledged this instruction with a nod and off we went. In a few minutes we pulled up at a rather low-built building. Little did I realize, but this establishment was a haunt of ladies of the night. It was now about 9 p.m. in a hot and steamy Freetown.

'Yes, we have two rooms,' said the receptionist. 'They are across the compound. I will have your luggage taken there.'

'Where is the bar?' enquired Noel.

'It's just round to the left,' said the receptionist.

'Come on Desmond,' said Noel. 'Let's have a nightcap.'

Noel Gratiaen was a great trencherman and bon viveur. He believed life was best approached with a stiff drink at the ready. If not in court, El Vino in Fleet Street was his principal watering hole until it closed or until he reached a state of fuddled bonhomie. His other great love was food. Sitting in El Vino, between great gulps of claret, he would wax eloquent about a curried partridge with saffron rice followed by a dark chocolate soufflé that he treated himself to the night before. His vast girth was testimony to his passion for food and drink. In the bar of our new quarters we had several drinks, with Noel being a rumbustious, if slightly inebriated, raconteur. A covey of gaudy and revealingly dressed bar girls sat around the room chattering between themselves, occasionally shooting glances at a few men perched on bar stools. They were girls who knew how to connect with their eyes.

'The bill,' said Noel to the barman.

As we were making ready to leave, rather unsteadily, a few girls got up, straightened their tightly fitting skirts, and left the bar area.

To get to our beds we had to cross a tree-fringed compound, beyond which lay our rooms. As we crossed the compound toward our quarters, I noticed a number of ladies standing beneath the trees. One of them, wearing a very tight-fitting top that could barely contain her cleavage, stepped out into the light percolating through the windows of the reception area. Sidling up to the very rotund QC, and with a surprisingly delicate choice of phrase not usually associated with her profession, she posed a question I shall recall to the end of my days, 'Excuse me, sir, would you like some mangoes tonight?'

In the armoury of possible lines of approach, the girl could not have made a better choice so far as this QC was concerned.

'Yes. Yes,' said Noel. 'Just the thing. Bring them to my room at once.'

We walked on. He is eager for passion tonight, I thought to myself.

'I wonder if they are Alphonsos,' he said to me in raptures. 'They are aromatic and wonderfully delicious. Some say that before they are eaten they should be massaged like a woman's breasts to make them more succulent,' he observed, with his gift for conveying the sensuous pleasures of the edible. Supposing to myself that this must be some subliminal association between food and sex, we continued our journey across the compound.

Entering our living quarters we passed through a door which led to a corridor, off which were our rooms. I bid him goodnight and entered my room. No sooner had I unpacked my bag when I heard loud and angry voices in the corridor outside. Perplexed by this din I opened the door, looked down the corridor and was met with a wonderfully theatrical moment.

Standing in the open doorway of Noel's room was the visual delight who had spoken to us ten minutes before and whose figure would not have disgraced the chorus line at the Crazy Horse in Paris. I was seized with a fit of uncontrollable laughter as Noel, with his true passion now torn to tatters, towered over this nubile beauty, who was naked to the waist, while he wailed gloomily, 'But madam, where are your mangoes?'

She did not earn a living that evening, but I got the title for this book.

The appeal hearings of the treason cases began in April 1971. Seventeen people were in the dock, sentenced to death. To determine their fate was the West African Court of Appeal, consisting of Sir Phillip Bridges, the English Chief Justice of the Gambia; Justice of Appeal Tambiah (seconded) from Ceylon; and Justice Beccles-Davies from Sierra Leone. During the course of preliminary argument we contended that our grounds of appeal went to the root of the case and that they should be heard first, as they would be decisive of all convictions. If we were correct, not just Brigadier Lansana, who we were representing, but all accused, would walk away from execution. For the respondents, Mervyn Heald, QC agreed.

In our view their fate turned on the principles spelt out by Mr Justice Avory in the case of Rex v Molloy at the Court of Appeal in London in 1921, which had to do with a broken grate. Together with the principles to be found in Rex v Disney, where the defendant's conviction for an offence contrary to the Night Poaching Act 1828 was quashed by the Court of Appeal and, also, a case that had to do with 'destroying game or rabbits', I realized that it is among broken grates and dead rabbits that some of the fundamental principles of English law are to be found.

Having heard our submissions and those of Mervyn Heald, QC for the respondent, the West African Court of Appeal quashed all the convictions. Sixteen men and one woman stepped out of the shadow of the gallows that day.

David Lansana was a true gentleman, a devoted friend to Britain and one of the first West Africans to get into the Royal Military Academy Sandhurst. Immediately after the judgment of the court had been delivered, I went down to the death cell from which the elated Lansana had not yet been released. He said to me, 'When you return to England, if you happen to see Lord Mountbatten, please do give him my regards and tell him I hope to see him in England soon.'

The story does not end happily, however. All others who had been cleared by the Court of Appeal were released, but not David Lansana. In 1971, the country was declared a republic and in November 1974 the BBC World Service announced that Lansana had been sentenced to death again, allegedly for treason.

I wrote to Mountbatten on 29 November and acquainted him with the fate that was now facing Lansana. Little did I know at the time that Mountbatten had got to know him well when he was chief of the defence staff. On 3 December I was engaged in a trial at the Old Bailey when a special messenger arrived in court, bearing a letter addressed to me with a great wax seal on the envelope. In the letter Mountbatten said he considered David Lansana to be, 'one of the most exceptional, if not the most exceptional soldier West Africa had produced.' Mountbatten and I wrote letters to President Siaka Stevens of Sierra Leone pleading for clemency, which were sent by the head of the FCO Sir Thomas Brimelow 'by bag' to Ian Watt, the British high commissioner in Freetown, and delivered to the president by hand.

Richard Hough, in a biography titled *Mountbatten: Hero of Our Time*, wrote, 'When they hanged the brigadier, and publicly exposed his body, Mountbatten was heartbroken.'

But then the practice of hanging individuals and displaying their bodies outside the gates of Pademba Road Prison became a Siaka Stevens speciality.

# 8

# The Spy Who Missed the Opera

THE HALLOWED PHRASE 'BEYOND REASONABLE DOUBT' REPRESENTS THE standard of proof that the prosecution's evidence must reach before a jury is entitled to convict in a criminal case in England. This leaves a defence barrister free to deal with legitimate doubts that arise about the evidence or proper inferences that can be drawn from evidence before the jury.

Thus, a criminal trial may sometimes never uncover the truth. When, as a defending barrister, your lay client receives a not guilty verdict at the hands of a jury, you are satisfied, as you have upheld his or her constitutional right to be free from punishment unless his guilt has been proved to the required standard. However, as an advocate you do sometimes hanker after the truth about some aspect of the case that features prominently in a trial and is not satisfactorily answered by convincing evidence during the trial.

One such trial took place at the Knightsbridge Crown Court. The client was charged with obtaining money by deception. The prosecution was conducted by Treasury counsel, David Tudor Price.

Alan and I happened to be defending someone who turned out to be a master fraudsman, convicted in this case of cruelly deceiving a grieving widow – Ewa Shadrin. It was no ordinary case of fraud because it brought into sharp focus the bizarre twists in the espionage battles of the Cold War. Then, as now, the collection of information and the spreading of disinformation played a key role in conflicts. Ewa was the widow of a spy who was a double agent working for the CIA during the Cold War.

The story began in Gdynia, a port city on the Baltic coast of Poland and an important Polish naval base. In Soviet times, it formed part of the Warsaw Pact. It was here, in Gdynia, that the pretty, dark-haired Polish dental student, Ewa, met and fell in love with a thirty-one-year-old charismatic Russian naval officer. By the age of twenty-seven, Nikolai Fedorovich Artamonov had become the youngest destroyer captain in the Soviet fleet. With advanced training in nuclear missiles he was tipped by many to become the youngest vice admiral in the Soviet Navy. In 1959, he was to be the most senior Russian naval officer to defect to the West.

In 1981, Henry Hurt published a detailed account of Artamonov's life in *Shadrin: The Spy Who Never Came Back* but did not come to any conclusive view as to what actually happened to the defector spy.

The case that unfolded in a courtroom in London in 1979 was that Artamonov was a Soviet naval officer who had fallen in love with Ewa when he was on a training exercise in Gdynia. Pretending to be going on a fishing trip, they took a naval launch, crossed the Baltic, avoided Soviet patrols and finally ended up in Sweden. No sooner had they got to Sweden and disclosed their arrival than the CIA made arrangements for the couple to be flown to Frankfurt where they were lodged in a safe house for some weeks.

Artamonov and Ewa were flown secretly to Andrews Air Force Base where they were met by Walter Onoshko, a CIA officer whose codename was Benson. Artamonov presented this officer with a bottle of vodka that had a plant floating in it. This small gift was to assume a great significance in the trial.

In the US they were married and he changed his name to Nicholas Shadrin. Ewa became a dentist with a successful practice. With the support of Admiral Rufus Taylor, later director of the CIA, Shadrin came to be employed by the US Defense Intelligence Agency (DIA) where he made a huge contribution to matters such as Soviet naval intelligence and anti-submarine warfare. In the community in which they lived they were a popular and gregarious couple. However, trouble lay ahead.

In the summer of 1966, Igor, a Russian diplomat and a KGB officer, approached Shadrin in a supermarket and suggested he should work for the Soviets. Shadrin promptly reported this contact to the FBI. The CIA, too, then entered the picture and decided that he should continue contact with Igor and become a double agent. In this new role, Shadrin, who was now codenamed LARK, passed to the KGB material that was sanctioned by the CIA. All meetings he had with KGB agents, either in the United States or such cities as Montreal, were observed by CIA surveillance teams at all times. There came a time when the KGB required Shadrin to visit Vienna.

On 18 December 1975, Shadrin and Ewa went to Vienna where they booked into room 341 of the Bristol Hotel. Ewa, in giving evidence in court in London, confirmed that Shadrin told her he had a meeting at 5 p.m. on the steps of the neo-Gothic Votivkirche in Rooseveltplatz, quite close to the US Embassy in Vienna. Her husband, having met with two KGB agents, returned to the hotel where he joined his wife and his CIA case officer, Cynthia Haussman, operating under the name Ann Martin, who debriefed him. One of the KGB agents had told Shadrin that he had been promoted to the rank of colonel in the KGB. This was a piece of information that he shared with Ewa, but was unknown to the defence at the time of the trial. Looking back, this was quite clearly a KGB ploy to allay any of Shadrin's concerns as to the motives of the KGB.

Ewa was to say in evidence that two days later, on 20 December, Shadrin told her he had another meeting at the Votivkirche that evening, after which he would meet her at the Opera House to watch a performance. He left the hotel at 6.30 p.m. to meet two KGB agents, Kuryshev and Kozlov. Shadrin never joined his wife at the Opera House that evening and she was never to see him again. A tearful Ewa was to say in the witness box that things were made worse when her frantic efforts to get hold of her husband's CIA case officer, Ann Martin, proved impossible that evening. Her husband having seemingly vanished, a very depressed Ewa Shadrin left Vienna for Washington on Christmas Eve.

On her arrival in Washington, she set about the difficult task of trying to uncover the truth about her husband and endeavoured to galvanize the US government to support the search for his whereabouts. This even involved taking the matter up with the White House. On 5 November 1976, she met with President Ford. Following that meeting the jury at Middlesex Crown Court were fascinated to hear the contents of a letter written by President Ford to Soviet leader Leonid Brezhnev. Unsurprisingly, Brezhnev's reply, according to the given evidence, was that Shadrin had never turned up at the meeting.

Something that struck me then and concerns me still, is this: how could Brezhnev have been so positive about Shadrin not keeping the meeting? After all, Shadrin may have been under CIA surveillance. And if he was not, why not? All the other evidence was that whenever Shadrin had meetings with KGB agents they were always subject to CIA surveillance. Why was this different? Ann Martin, Shadrin's CIA handler, was not called by the prosecution but an FBI agent called Ralston, who could not deal with this aspect of the matter, was.

My client Joseph Flynn eventually ended up in the dock of the Middlesex Crown Court against the background of this complex Cold War spy drama as a result of publicity attached to the fact that Ewa Shadrin had employed the tenacious Washington lawyer Richard Copaken. Copaken was skilled at using the press in his campaigning work and Mrs Shadrin's case was to be no different.

Copaken told the jury that on the morning of 5 August 1977, some three weeks after the Shadrin story broke in the newspapers, his telephone rang at the Washington office of the law firm Covington & Burling. The caller used the name Benson and told Copaken that he was in a position to trace Shadrin through a man called Agnew, who had suppled Shadrin with false travel documents before he disappeared in Vienna. Benson made clear to Copaken that, for money, Agnew might lead Mrs Shadrin to her husband. Agnew, Benson said, could be contacted by a coded message, which he dictated and was to be placed in the *International Herald Tribune.*

According to Copaken's evidence, the printed message was to be, 'Harry wants bank notes of 17$^{th}$ century origin.' This message was to be accompanied by an unlisted number connecting to Copaken's office. He was told that when Agnew called, Copaken should tell him that, 'the man who gave me your name is the same man who he once gave a bottle of vodka to with a plant in it, some years ago.'

Copaken was sufficiently alert to the fact that this had all the hallmarks of a confidence trick. The court was told by Mrs Shadrin and her lawyer Copaken that when this information was conveyed to the CIA, it appeared there were aspects of that conversation known only to the CIA and Ewa Shadrin.

First, the name Benson was the code name of the Russian-speaking CIA officer who had welcomed Shadrin at 2 a.m. at Andrews Air Force Base on his arrival in the US. Second, Shadrin had indeed given that officer a present of a bottle of vodka with a plant in it. The possibility of anyone having guessed or having invented these two facts was regarded as well-nigh impossible; the conclusion was that the caller simply had to have possessed inside knowledge.

The court heard that Mrs Shadrin and Copaken placed the advertisement as Benson had suggested. The response to it was a call from Saint-Jean-Cap-Ferrat in the south of France. The caller, who purported to be Agnew, informed Copaken that he had supplied Shadrin with travel documents and that Shadrin was well and living in a Western country. In another call a few days later from

Beaulieu-sur-Mer, Agnew informed Copaken that Shadrin wanted to return to his wife, but he feared unspecified reprisals from the CIA. Agnew asked for the sum of $3,000 to be transferred to the account of W. Flynn in the National Bank of Paris in Monaco to cover expenses. The money was sent immediately and withdrawn in Monaco by a man who produced a passport in the name of William Joseph Flynn. That passport, on subsequent inquiry, turned out to be forged.

Following the payment, Ewa Shadrin and Copaken waited for news. There was none. Suspecting they were the victims of a scam, Copaken and his client set off for the south of France where, with the assistance of the French police, they managed to track Flynn down to a yacht called *Rodi's Island*. Adding another bizarre twist to the saga, they found him with a woman called Karen Steadman, whose brother had been recently convicted of selling RAF secrets to the Soviets.

After insisting he had told the truth about the existence of Agnew, Flynn agreed to come to London and take a polygraph test. He failed the test. This may have been the first instance that such a machine had been used in the UK.

Flynn left for Vienna and later called Copaken to meet him there, saying it would be to the advantage of his client, Mrs Shadrin. In December 1977, FBI special agent Leonard Ralston, who gave evidence in the trial, arrived in Vienna. Unknown to us at the time of the trial, Ralston met up with Gustav Hohenbichler, an Austrian policeman who was working for the KGB under the codename ZAC. Ralston met up with Flynn and managed to get him to fly to London, where Flynn was arrested by the British police and charged with obtaining money by deception. Having been convicted by the jury, Flynn was sentenced by Judge Phelan to eighteen months imprisonment, with the words, 'You have preyed most callously on the desolation of that desperate woman.'

My purpose in recounting this case is not to deal with Flynn's criminal behaviour but to invite the reader to consider the circumstances of the disappearance of Shadrin, on 20 December 1975, when he failed to turn up at the Opera House in Vienna to join his wife.

In 1985, Oleg Gordievsky, a colonel in the KGB and a long-time asset of MI6, was smuggled out of Russia by MI6 when the Soviet net was closing in on him. He has resided in England ever since. Some years after he arrived in England I made an enquiry of him as to Shadrin's disappearance. He wrote to me in February 2000 to say there is little doubt that Shadrin was kidnapped by the KGB when he kept the meeting at the Votivkirche and that he had been killed after being over sedated in an effort to get him across the Austrian-Czech border. Another KGB colonel, Vitaly Yurchenko, who defected to the West in 1985, told of hearing about the abduction of Shadrin, and that his accidental death was the result of the administration of too much chloroform.

In the 1990s, after the fall of communism in Russia, Oleg Kalugin, a former major general in the KGB, went into exile in the US and became a US citizen. In Moscow he had been head of K Branch of the First Chief Directorate of the KGB, responsible for foreign operations.

In 1992, Kalugin admitted to Ewa Shadrin that he had been part of the operation in connection with her husband and that he was dead. Indeed, Kalugin was in fact in charge of the plan to abduct Shadrin and was later to admit that at the meeting with KGB agents on 20 December, Shadrin had been abducted, drugged and bundled into the boot of a car that was to take him over the Czech border where Kalugin himself was waiting to receive Shadrin. The plan was to get Shadrin back to Moscow, where he would face a firing squad unless he collaborated with the Soviets by attending a press conference, at which he would admit being a loyal KGB mole within the CIA, thereby winning a propaganda victory for the KGB. Unfortunately the sedative was too much and Shadrin died at Kalugin's feet on the Austrian-Czech border. If true, this is the only eyewitness account of Shadrin's death.

The problem I have with all these accounts is that they rely on the abduction of Shadrin by KGB agents. As I have said before, why was there no surveillance on Shadrin by the CIA that evening? Further, all these accounts are totally inconsistent with the position of Leonid Brezhnev, that Shadrin never showed up for the meeting. For Brezhnev to have been certain that Shadrin never showed up would mean he knew there was no CIA surveillance on Shadrin that evening. Is this something he would only have known with certainty if the CIA and the KGB collaborated in the Shadrin disappearance? The Votivkirche is in an unobstructed line of sight from the US consulate, yet we're led to believe there was no surveillance.

I can understand why the KGB would want Shadrin back in Moscow. After his defection he had been sentenced to death *in absentia*. My research, since Flynn's trial, indicates that the CIA may have been brilliantly hoodwinked by a KGB ruse to lay their hands on Shadrin and take him back to Moscow.

It emerged during the trial in London that in June 1966, Richard Helms, the director of the CIA, took an urgent telephone call from a man who identified himself as Igor Kochnov, requesting a meeting with him. Kochnov was a known KGB operative working in the Soviet Embassy. In the meetings with the CIA that subsequently took place, Kochnov came up with a deal that involved him working for the CIA. Emphasizing that he had a bright future within the KGB, and the CIA being alert to the fact that in Kochnov they had no lesser a person than the grandson of Yuri Andropov – who was soon to become head of the KGB – the CIA could not have had a better placed mole in the KGB. The carrot he dangled before them was irresistible. Kochnov was given the codename Kittyhawk.

Kochnov then informed them he was interested in Shadrin. If he could be seen as having turned Shadrin to supply intelligence through him to the KGB, his standing in the KGB would be enhanced, enabling him to climb the KGB ladder to better serve the interests of the CIA. The CIA agreed.

When Shadrin reported to the FBI that he had been approached by a KGB agent named Igor to assist the Soviets, little did he know that it was by someone who was being then jointly run by the FBI and the CIA. Despite his reservations, the CIA encouraged Shadrin, now codenamed LARK, to become a double agent, supplying doctored material to Moscow. Shadrin was now on the KGB hook.

Not long afterward, Kittyhawk returned to Moscow, leaving Shadrin to deal with other KGB controllers. All that remained was for the KGB to reel him in. It does not seem to have struck the CIA that there was absolutely no tradition in the KGB of forgiving a defecting senior officer, particularly one, as in this case, who had been sentenced to death.

Gradually the KGB required Shadrin to make visits outside the US to meet with his KGB controllers: Montreal in 1971, Vienna in 1972 and then, finally, Vienna again in 1975, from which he never returned. In going along with Kochnov's request to get Shadrin working for the KGB, did the CIA walk into a trap which led to the death of Shadrin, whose loyalty to his adopted country never wavered?

It might interest the reader to know that Major General Oleg Kalugin, who was waiting for Shadrin to be delivered on the Austrian-Czech border, was decorated with the highly coveted Order of the Red Banner.

# 9

# Ambush in the Med

IN 2010, I WAS UNEXPECTEDLY THROWN INTO THE CENTRE OF THE SNAKE pit that is Middle Eastern politics. For the first time in my life I came face-to-face with certain ambassadors who made direct and improper attempts to influence my thinking, away from the independent report I was appointed to produce for the UN, and in favour of agendas being promoted by their own national interests.

The great Dr Samuel Johnson was to say in 1758, 'When war is declared truth is the first casualty. Among the calamities of war may be jointly numbered the diminution of the love of truth, by the falsehoods which interest dictates and credulity encourages.' What was said in 1758 sums up perfectly the strains to which those on missions of this kind can be subjected.

One need look no further than the case of Richard Goldstone, a distinguished international jurist and the former first chief prosecutor of the International Criminal Tribunal for the former Yugoslavia and Rwanda, who was appointed in 2009 to head a UNHRC fact-finding mission investigating allegations that Israel had violated human rights in Gaza during Operation Cast Lead. There was outrage in Israel when the mission concluded that Hamas and Israel had both potentially committed war crimes and crimes against humanity. He was subjected to intense personal attacks made more virulent by him being a Jew by birth.

The story ended with Goldstone revising his findings in light of evidence subsequently brought to his attention by Israel. I make no comment on the correctness or otherwise of Goldstone's change of heart, save to say that this is one of the problems a UN fact-finding mission is confronted by when a country initially refuses to cooperate, waits for the report to emerge and then pounces on what it claims to be incorrect conclusions.

There is a finely honed technique in certain parts of the world that starts with personal attacks on individuals who are appointed to determine the

*Top left*: My paternal grandfather George E. de Silva, 1935

*Top right*: My maternal grandfather Arthur Holman Nathanielsz, 1934

*Below*: My paternal grandmother Agnes Nell at the wheel of her Belgian Minerva, 1906

*Top*: My great-great-great-great-grandparents: James Dowset Rose-Cleland and Sarah Eaton Andrews. Painted by William Grimaldi, 1790

*Middle*: Seven of the eight Rose-Cleland sisters with their pack of harriers at the Rathgael Hunt, 1890s

*Bottom left*: My maternal grandmother Elaine Gregg MacGregor, at 17

*Bottom right*: My parents, my sister and me, 1947

*Top left*: The Waterloo Ball at the Royal Courts of Justice, 1965

*Top right*: A Buckingham Palace garden party, 1975

*Bottom left*: With my clerks at the House of Lords taking silk, 1984

*Bottom right*: At the Royal Palace in Belgrade, 2016

*Top*: My wedding to Princess Katarina of Yugoslavia, 1987 (see p. 305 for full caption)

*Bottom*: Introducing Katarina to Prime Minister Margaret Thatcher at 10 Downing Street, 1987

*Top left*: With Kofi Annan, then UN Secretary-General, New York, 2006

*Top right*: Pinning medals on UN peacekeeping troops, Sierra Leone, 2006

*Left*: Charles Taylor – African warlord and former president of Liberia

*Bottom*: Dr Nico, a transvestite witch doctor, Sierra Leone, 2003

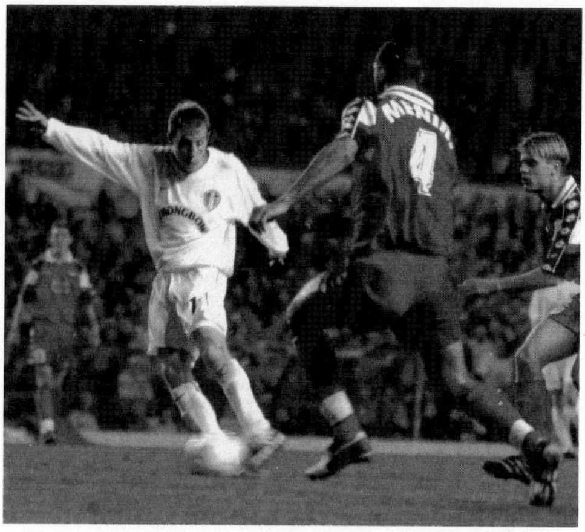

*Top left*: Leaving Middlesex Crown Court with John Terry after his acquittal, 2002

*Top right*: Lee Bowyer scoring a goal during a game that took place at the time of his trial, 2001

*Bottom*: Jockey Jamie Osborne with John Major and Charlie Brooks.
He was cleared of race-fixing in 1998

TIMES 2

**books**
The war between science and religion will never cease
Pages 8 – 15

**lifestyle**
Why bother reading a woman's mind?
Pages 4 & 5

**property**
A farmhouse or a flat in W11: what you get for £385,000
Pages 24 – 27

**plus Crème**
16 pages of office life and top jobs every Wednesday

**A very colonial murder**
The woman who will hang for Botswana's White Mischief
pages 2 & 3

*Top left*: Front cover of *Times 2* reporting the case of Marietta Bosch in Botswana, 31 January 2001

*Top right*: Roderick Newell in custody at the Moorish Castle, Gibraltar

*Bottom left*: Professor Hugh Hambleton, the KGB spy in NATO

*Bottom right*: Nicholas Shadrin, the Russian double agent

*Top right*: With my daughter Victoria at a Buckingham Palace garden party, 2015

*Right*: Taprobane Island, Sri Lanka

*Bottom left*: With Victoria on Taprobane Island, 2017

*Bottom right*: With Her Majesty the Queen, 2003

factual truth by those in whose interest it lies to cloak it. Sometimes the cover of parliamentary privilege is used, as it was against me in Sri Lanka, so as to avoid an action in defamation with consequent damages against my detractor.

The achievement of peace is a process: a process with a goal. The path to that goal must involve all parties recognizing the wrongs they themselves have perpetrated. Sometimes this forms part of the work of an independent fact-finding mission; at other times in post-conflict situations, we turn to a truth and reconciliation commission, as South Africa did in coming to terms with the aftermath of Apartheid.

On 1 June 2010 there was an emergency session of the Security Council called in New York. The meeting was occasioned by a perceived threat to peace and security triggered by an Israeli Defence Forces (IDF) attack on a group of six civilian ships calling themselves the Gaza Freedom Flotilla. The ships were carrying humanitarian aid and construction materials to Gaza, which was subject to an Israeli blockade. It was the clear intention of the organizers of the flotilla to attempt to break the Israeli blockade on the Gaza strip and draw attention to the plight of the citizens of Gaza. Unquestionably it was a political move intended to hit the headlines of the world's media.

The humanitarian situation in Gaza, resulting from the imposition of the Israeli blockade, had become a matter of growing concern to the international community and the Security Council stressed the need for a sustained and regular flow of goods, as well as unimpeded distribution of humanitarian assistance.

The military interception of the flotilla by Israeli forces took place in international waters, leaving nine civilians dead (another was to die later) with some fifty others wounded. The lead ship of the flotilla was the *Mavi Marmara*, a cruise ship like the other five vessels in the convoy. There were NGOs of some thirty-seven nationalities, with a very large number of press and film crews, aboard these ships.

At about 10.30 p.m. on 30 May, the Israeli Navy got in radio contact with each of the ships in the convoy and they were warned that they were approaching an area of hostilities under naval blockade. The captains of the various vessels stated that their destination was Gaza and that the blockade of Gaza being referred to by the Israeli Navy was illegal.

One of the questions that fell to us to answer was whether the Gaza blockade was in fact illegal in international law and, for reasons that will emerge below, whether the IDF used excessive or disproportionate force.

This unarmed motley flotilla was confronted by an Israeli interception force which included a number of corvettes and missile boats, helicopters, zodiacs, surveillance aircraft and two submarines. Israeli special forces took part in this attack, which was code-named Operation Sea Breeze, or Operation Sky Winds.

Israeli forces made an unsuccessful attempt to board the *Mavi Marmara* by attaching ladders to the ship's hull. The efforts of their special forces to get aboard by climbing the ladders were repelled by the passengers, who used the ship's water hoses on them. Other attempts by the special forces to climb aboard were defeated by passengers, who dropped dining plates on their heads.

Completely foxed by this unusual form of response, Israeli helicopters then hovered over the *Mavi Marmara* and used smoke and stun grenades to clear the top deck so that the soldiers could abseil down. But when the first rope was lowered for the soldiers to make their descent, some passengers got hold of the end of the rope and tied it to a part of the top deck, effectively making abseiling impossible.

From the helicopter, Israeli commandos now started firing live ammunition on to the top deck. This certainly had the desired effect. Soldiers were then landed from three helicopters. There followed a struggle with passengers who were resisting capture. One of the passengers killed by Israeli soldiers was a photographer recording the scene. Our forensic analysts demonstrated that two of the passengers killed were shot at close range while lying on the ground.

With most of the dead being Turkish citizens, the Turkish foreign minister Ahmet Davutoglu claimed, 'this is tantamount to banditry and piracy. It is murder conducted by a state.' Israel's deputy ambassador, Daniel Carmon, by contrast, told the Security Council that the flotilla was anything but a humanitarian mission and that its organizers 'cynically used the guise of humanitarian aid to send a message of hate and to implement violence.' So the battle lines were drawn. Turkey and Israel were poles apart.

The Security Council, which for these purposes had the agreement of Britain, France, Russia and China, called for a 'prompt, impartial, credible and transparent investigation conforming to international standards.' The following day, the United Nations Human Rights Council (UNHRC) in Geneva decided to 'despatch an independent international fact-finding mission to investigate alleged violations of international law, international humanitarian law and human rights law' resulting from the ambush of these six ships making their way through the Mediterranean.

I recall that on my collecting my mobile telephone from the prison officer, to whom it had been entrusted on a visit to a client in a detention facility, I noticed a missed call from abroad. On my calling the number I was put through to the personal assistant to the president of the United Nations Human Rights Council who informed me that, if I agreed, I was to be appointed as one of a three-person team to participate in a fact-finding mission for the UN.

So in August 2010 I found myself in Geneva, with Karl Hudson-Phillips, a former judge of the International Criminal Court (ICC), and Shanthi Dairiam, who had a formidable record of fighting for women's rights worldwide.

The day I was appointed, I was personally criticized by an Israeli newspaper and the entire mission was attacked as being biased. Israel did have one legitimate grievance, in that the language of the resolution passed in Geneva did presuppose that Israel was at fault. Of course, as lawyers we rephrased the resolution to be neutral, so that when we started our fact-finding we did so with a clean slate and no preconceived views.

However, what I had not expected were visits by ambassadors and other representatives, who shamelessly asked me to take other considerations into account in approaching my task. One ambassador said to me, 'there are talks going on in Washington at this very moment between Israel and the Palestinians and don't you realize that at this point a report such as yours might interfere with the delicate balance of the negotiations? Can I appeal to you to try and delay the final conclusions of this report?' Trying to make me feel as if we would be standing in the path of an impending peace agreement was, of course, an absurd attempt. Whether the other two members of the mission were similarly targeted, I never discovered.

In order to create confusion, another ploy was brought into being. Somehow, the Secretary-General of the UN, Ban Ki-moon, had been persuaded to appoint another panel of his own, in the same month as our appointment. This was to be under Sir Geoffrey Palmer, a former prime minister of New Zealand.

I was quite incensed that the Secretary-General had appointed a Secretary-General's panel as I could, with a cynical eye, see that someone's game plan may have been to have a bundle of conflicting conclusions from which cherry picking could take place to further a national point of view. My two colleagues, however, were not willing to take this matter up in New York.

In case two missions appointed under UN auspices covering the same factual matrix were not going to cause sufficient confusion, Israel decided to set up its own commission under an Israeli judge, Jacob Turkel. To this commission were added others, who included Lord Trimble, the former chief minister of Northern Ireland. I saw nothing wrong in this commission, as Israel was perfectly entitled to examine the conduct of its own armed forces.

So as not to feel left out of this international legal jamboree, Turkey set up its own commission. Once again, as they were mainly Turkish citizens who were shot it was perfectly sensible that there was a legitimate Turkish interest in a national commission.

To get to the truth of what happened on 31 May 2010, Karl, Dairiam and I had a secretariat of outstanding specialist UN employees, who had been drafted in from all over the world to help us uncover the facts and circumstances of the flotilla incident, and to view our factual findings in the light of the applicable international law, international humanitarian law and international human rights law. In addition we had external specialists in forensic pathology, military issues, the law of the sea and the laws of armed conflict.

We conducted interviews with over 100 witnesses in London, Geneva, Istanbul and Amman. These were people who could give us first-hand accounts of the events before, during and after the Israeli intervention when, apart from those killed, the 700-odd passengers were taken captive, a number in handcuffs, and taken to the Israeli port of Ashdod. There were complaints that they were denied access to lawyers or consular officials.

All of the photographic and video images covering the interception of the flotilla, and the conduct of the Israeli soldiers, by journalists and others, were confiscated and never returned. As our report says, we were satisfied that this was a deliberate attempt by the Israeli authorities to suppress or destroy evidence that challenged their version of events.

We sought the right to visit Gaza. This was refused by the government of Israel. In view of the permanent representative for Israel informing us that the position of his government was one of non-recognition of and non-cooperation with our mission, we had to look for our evidence elsewhere.

We were satisfied that the blockade of Gaza was unlawful, making the interception of the *Mavi Marmara* and other vessels in international waters unlawful. Further, that the actions of Israeli forces were 'disproportionate' and 'betrayed an unacceptable level of brutality', with clear evidence of execution-type killings.

As for the Palmer Report, commissioned by the Secretary-General, even that found that the degree of Israeli force used against the *Mavi Marmara* was 'excessive and unreasonable' and that the way Israel treated detained crew members violated international human rights law. That said, Palmer held that the blockade of Gaza was legal. The Turkel Report, set up by the Israeli cabinet, 'cleared the government and the military of wrong doing' and held that the 'passengers were liable for the violence'.

A lot of time, energy and money has been expended in an attempt to come to grips with the truth. In 2013, Prime Minister Netanyahu of Israel spoke to President Erdogan of Turkey and a statement from the prime minister's office said that, 'the tragic results regarding the *Mavi Marmara* were unintentional and that Israel expresses regret over the injuries and loss of life.' In addition, 'in light of the Israeli investigation into the incident, which pointed out several operational errors, Prime Minister Netanyahu apologized to the Turkish people for errors that could have led to loss of life and agreed to complete the agreement on compensation.'

In June 2016, Turkey and Israel decided to normalize relations, with Israel paying $20 million to the families of those killed on the *Mavi Marmara*. Is it cynicism on my part to believe that apologies are now no more than a tactic employed by political leaders to put the past to bed; that leaders weigh up the costs of not apologizing against the cost of doing so and only do so if there is a political cost benefit? Are most political apologies of this kind motivated by personal or national self-interest? Sadly, yes.

## 10

# A Candidate of Probity and Integrity

AT THE BAR ONE GETS USED TO A CURIOUS SHORTHAND SLANG THAT sometimes baffles outsiders. I shall never forget the look of bewilderment on the face of a fellow guest at a party who asked me what I was doing the following day. I lapsed into barrister speak and replied, 'doing a murder.'

On 28 June 2001, I was 'doing a murder' at the Old Bailey and the jury had been out for three days considering their verdict. I had just emerged from court number nine on the third floor when a shrill voice came over the tannoy: 'All parties in Archer and Francis to court eight, please.' A door to a conference room opened and Lord Archer came out with his solicitor. When he caught sight of me he gave me a weak smile and walked purposefully to the lift to get down to the first floor, where he was on trial for attempting to pervert the course of public justice.

A week earlier I had found myself alone in the same lift. The doors had just started to close and my finger was on the down button as Archer pushed his way in through the closing gap.

'Going down, Jeffrey?' I said, unthinkingly.

A wry smile came to the lips of the peer who was, not long afterward, convicted and sent down for four years.

There is no doubt that the scandals attaching to Jeffrey Archer were part of the sleaze factor that so damaged the Conservatives, both in office and in opposition. Despite this, he was described by William Hague, the Conservative Party leader, as 'a candidate of probity and integrity' when Hague endorsed Archer's candidature for the mayoralty of London in October 1999.

Lord Archer's road to a dock at the Old Bailey, and subsequent prison sentence, sprang from his ambition to be the Mayor of London and the resolve of his former friend, Ted Francis, to stop him in his tracks. In Francis's view,

Archer's character rendered him unsuitable for high office in public life. It is an intriguing premise that Ted Francis may not have told his story, and there may have been no conviction and consequently no imprisonment, if I had played the part that at one stage appeared to have been mapped out for me.

In the summer of 1998 a former Conservative MP, Sir Timothy Kitson, suggested that the Ethics Committee to be established by the Conservative Party should be used to investigate Lord Archer's colourful past, particularly in light of the excoriating biography just written by Michael Crick, which threw a deep shadow over the peer's probity. Short of a senior figure, such as former Prime Minister John Major, persuading Archer not to run, it was thought by some that an unfavourable finding by the Ethics Committee might be the only way of dissuading him from standing. It was also a method by which the party could use an adverse finding against the peer as a basis for not backing him as the Conservative candidate.

Soon after Conor Burns put my name forward for the new Ethics Committee, I received a call from Cecil Parkinson. After some initial pleasantries he asked me if I was interested in helping the party by going on to the committee. I told him I would think about it.

'Are you coming to the Blue Ball on 9 July?' he asked.

Once I told him that I was, he said, 'Good, we will talk more about it at the Hilton.'

That day I called a number of friends in the party, at least one of whom informed me that I should have no hesitation in joining the Ethics Committee, if only to stop Lord Archer from standing for the mayoralty of London in the Conservative interest. Thereafter I called two former Conservative ministers, who also suggested that I should join the committee.

Despite having reservations about the whole notion of such a committee – it could leave itself exposed to legal proceedings should it reject someone who considered it a smear on his or her character – I made up my mind to join and subject the novelist to a grilling about the allegations contained in Crick's book.

The Blue Ball on 9 July 1998 was attended by all the usual Conservative grandees, MPs and would-be MPs and hangers-on. Cecil Parkinson, the former chairman of the party, was the president of the ball and the programme recited that our 'host for the evening is Lord Archer of Weston-super-Mare.' At the end of the dinner and before dancing began, Conor Burns left my table and made his way over to Parkinson's, in order to get him over for a chat. Conor was one of those who felt the party could be hurt by an unsuitable candidate.

'I hope you will consent to joining the Ethics Committee,' Parkinson said.

Once I had agreed, Cecil looked over to where Jeffrey Archer was at a microphone, just about to begin another successful money-raising auction for the Tories. Then, nodding in Archer's direction, he said to me, 'Desmond, he will be your first customer.'

Cecil then listened without a flicker of a muscle when I told him I thought Archer utterly unsuitable and that, so far as I could see, Michael Crick's allegations were unanswerable. I added that I would do everything in my power when on the Ethics Committee to block Archer, as I took the view that he was unfit to be the Conservative candidate for the mayoralty of London. On that note we parted, with Parkinson saying he would be in touch soon. I had no further communication from Parkinson, or indeed anyone else from the Conservative Party about the Ethics Committee.

In retrospect I now realize that I was probably expected to whitewash Archer, and that the sentiments I expressed were not to the taste of the party hierarchy. In the event, the Ethics Committee, set up under the chairmanship of another person, let Archer go forward. I am unaware of how thorough the investigation of the millionaire author was by the committee or how plausible he may have been, if questioned.

If it was in fact the intention of the party bigwigs to sanitize Archer, then the views I had expressed to Lord Parkinson had clearly put me out of the running. This must be so, as at the Conservative Party conference William Hague endorsed the former Tory deputy chairman as 'a candidate of probity and integrity'.

Just weeks later came the revelation in the newspapers about the peer's lies on oath during the High Court battle with Express Newspapers. The efforts made by some within the Conservative Party to stop Archer had failed.

The decision to let Archer run as the Conservative candidate came to be bitterly regretted later by William Hague, who subsequently confessed he wished he had stopped Lord Archer of Weston-super-Mare before he brought the party into disrepute.

## 11

# The Moon, the Stars and Nirvana

IN 1954, THE FRENCH JOURNALIST VERONIQUE PASSANI, A FRIEND OF my aunt Minnette's, came to Ceylon in search of woven fabrics. She was also in search of a husband in the form of Gregory Peck, the Hollywood idol and future Oscar winner, whom she subsequently did marry. I met them both at St George's where my aunt lived after Granny's death. Peck was there to make his second British film, *The Purple Plain*, a wartime story with the script written by Eric Ambler, based on a book by H. E. Bates. It was a story of a Canadian squadron leader whose nerves were shot to pieces in the Burma campaign during World War II, but who recovered during an epic journey of escape. When, later, Peck came to my parents' home, it turned out that the film he had made immediately before this one, *The Million Pound Note*, was being shown at the Regal Cinema in Kandy. In that light-hearted comedy Peck played the male lead.

'I never saw the completed film,' he said. 'I only saw the rushes.'

The suggestion that we should go and see it locally was met with enthusiasm. A week later Peck, Maurice Denham (who was also in *The Million Pound Note* and was to appear in *The Purple Plain*) and I went off to see this film, in which Peck reveals unsuspected comic genius. He was a great Hollywood heart-throb at the time and when he was spotted going into the cinema with us he was mobbed by his admirers and importunate autograph hunters who, on our way out, proffered handkerchiefs for his signature.

Anna, the female lead in *The Purple Plain*, was played by that ethereal Burmese beauty Win Min Than. She was staying with us, together with her short, rich and burly Burmese husband, who was thirty years her senior and insanely jealous. He insisted on going on to the set every day. I gathered subsequently that there was much hilarity on the set one morning during a scene involving a passionate kiss between Peck and Win. No sooner had she melted into Peck's arms than the irate husband, shouting loudly in Burmese, rushed on to the set, waving his arms, and pushed them apart. Nothing would induce him to permit the kissing scene to take place. I believe in the end the scene had to be shot from such an angle that, while giving the impression of a kiss, the husband's jealousy was assuaged by their lips never touching; a sort of romantic fade-out.

*Cape Fear*, a film made by Universal that Peck appeared in, together with Robert Mitchum, Polly Bergen and Telly Savalas, played a significant part in a murder case which I was subsequently to be involved in. In August 1992, the former British Army officer Roderick Newall took a Brazilian beauty, Helena Pedo, to Miami, where they watched *Cape Fear*. It was after seeing that film that he confessed to her his guilt in murdering his parents in Jersey five years earlier. This confession proved vital in proving the case against this former public school and Sandhurst-educated double murderer.

Among Aunt Minnette's many friends in the theatre and film world was Vivien Leigh. She came to Ceylon to make *Elephant Walk*, during the filming of which she visited our home many times with Peter Finch. At that stage I did not know that she was having an intense and passionate affair with Finch. I do recall Laurence Olivier, her husband, at St George's with Vivien, before he took her away for psychiatric treatment abroad. Vivien was replaced by the young Elizabeth Taylor. *Elephant Walk* was the first film I saw being made.

Many years later I dined with Laurence Olivier's son Tarquin, by his marriage to Jill Esmond; Tarquin had decided to make a film on Kemal Atatürk and was looking for film finance, which he hoped I may have been able to facilitate through connections in the City. In the course of this dinner Tarquin told me an amusing story that touched upon his father and Noel Coward, his godfather.

The story was that at a dinner party attended by Coward, Olivier, Larry Adler and James Robertson Justice, the conversation got round to discussing their homosexual experiences at school. Upon James Robertson Justice saying he had been buggered twice during his first term at boarding school, Coward, in his inimitably clipped way, said, 'I hope your friends gathered round to see Justice being done!'

The brilliant director, David Lean, came out to Ceylon to make the Oscar winner *The Bridge on the River Kwai*, his first international film. On a visit to the set of *Kwai* I was fortunate to meet some of my favourite actors: William Holden, Jack Hawkins and Alec Guinness, whose masterly portrayal of Colonel Nicholson depicted a man with a high sense of duty that collided with the outlook of the POW camp commander, Saito. In this classic tale of the use of forced labour to build a bridge across the River Kwai, Nicholson shows a willingness to make the men under his command collaborate with the enemy, in order to keep them sane during their brutal incarceration.

Through being in school in England, I missed out on Carol Reed's *Outcasts of the Islands*, which was also shot in Ceylon, with other legendary actors such as Ralph Richardson, Trevor Howard and Robert Morley.

It was my aunt Minnette who introduced me to the zany world of the Marx Brothers. A cousin and I were so captivated by the lunatic antics of this brilliant trio that not only did we see every film they made but while he used to dress up as Harpo, I, using my late grandfather's morning coat, used to imitate Groucho.

When I was an elected councilman for the City of London in the early 1980s, I had a call from Mel Frank, the veteran American writer, producer and director who won Academy Award nominations for *Road to Utopia* and *The Road to Hong Kong* with Bob Hope and Bing Crosby. He scripted, directed and produced the Danny Kaye films, *Knock on Wood* and *The Court Jester*. Known as the director who brought class to comedy, he will, perhaps, best be remembered for his British-made *A Touch of Class* with George Segal and Glenda Jackson. I had been introduced to him by the beautiful and brilliant Sharmini Thiruchelvam. He was over in England to make *Not a Penny More, Not a Penny Less* based on Jeffrey Archer's bestselling novel of that title.

'Can you do dinner tomorrow at Grosvenor House?' he asked.

I accepted.

Dinner with Mel involved trying to solve a pressing financial problem that had beset the production. 'One of our principal backers has died,' he said. 'Can you use any contacts you have in the City to try and find someone who will step in to back this production?' Although I was not able to find the required backing for the film, Mel and I became friends. It turned out we knew a number of poker players in common. He used to play with my chambers colleague Raymond Lewis, the banker Manoli Olympitis and the bestselling author Larry Collins. One night during dinner at the Ritz he asked me if I could help him with a matter of the heart. It turned out he had fallen madly in love with the Filipino housekeeper at Grosvenor House. Alas, her permission to remain in

England was about to expire and he was desperate to ensure she did not have to leave the country. Fortunately, in this area I was able to help via a ministerial friend at the Home Office, through whose intervention Juliette obtained an extension of stay. After many months together in London the happy lovers left for Hollywood.

Thirty-five years ago he was one of the most famous men in the world. His photograph was in every newspaper; President Nixon described his achievement as the greatest thing since Creation. The first thing I noticed about Colonel Edwin 'Buzz' Aldrin was his West Point bearing and huge, saucer-like hands. Lady Michèle Renouf had invited me to dinner at the Dorchester, where Buzz and his wife Lois were among the guests.

On 20 July 1969, in what was probably the most significant moment in television history, 600 million viewers watched as Buzz followed Neil Armstrong down the ladder on to the moon. Buzz was the second man to walk on the moon and, as is sometimes forgotten, the very first words spoken from the lunar surface were those of this sprightly astronaut. He also held the first communion on the moon, having taken a wafer, some white wine and a small silver goblet.

We soon picked up on the fact that he was a great friend of Arthur C. Clarke, who I had recently taken Katarina to meet when we were in Colombo, where he lived with a unique tax-free status granted him by the government. Waving his huge right hand, on which he wore a signet ring depicting the moon and a star, Buzz told us that when they took off there was no great certainty that they would return and that his greatest moment of loneliness was when they were passing round the dark side of the moon and they lost all contact with the Earth.

Buzz, who never touched a drink during the evening, is now a reformed alcoholic. It appears that after the lunar journey of half a million miles, Neil Armstrong took to God and Buzz to drink. Whether this was due to the number of near-death experiences they survived on that epic journey, it is difficult to tell. With the assistance of Alcoholics Anonymous, he recovered from his alcoholism and was then planning space tourism for the masses.

After dinner Lois said to me, 'I understand from Michelle that you are an attorney.' I was asked, 'Can Buzz consult you in relation to a problem that has arisen?' Buzz, Lois and I retired to a quiet corner of the suite. As he fell into the category of an overseas client, I did not need the intervening presence of a solicitor. The problem he related to me was that a certain watch manufacturer had been studying the pictures taken inside the Apollo 11 capsule and had noticed that Neil Armstrong was not wearing a watch. A further study of the pictures revealed to the manufacturers that Buzz Aldrin was wearing one of their watches and, therefore, it was the first watch on the moon. They began an advertising campaign with photographs of the inside of the capsule with Aldrin wearing their watch, and others of him landing on the moon. I was told that this advertising campaign was being conducted without any reference to Buzz.

'Is there any action I can take against them in law?' I was asked. 'I was told in the States that I had no cause of action,' he said. Initially, I was concerned as to whom these images from the moon actually belonged. However, I decided that the best advice I could give him was that he should sue for libel; anyone seeing such advertising could conclude this scientist and brave astronaut had surrendered himself to base commercial instincts. I am happy to say that the watch manufacturers, having received warning of impending litigation, desisted from further advertising and paid Buzz a substantial sum of money.

~

Long before the arrival of the institution of same-sex marriage, Robin Maugham introduced me to a very manly English tea planter with the words, 'Meet my wife.' I might have been startled at such an introduction to a man, had I not read Robin's revealing autobiography, *Escape from the Shadows*. The shadows that blighted his life were his uncle, Somerset, with whose works his writings were constantly compared; his father, the daunting Lord Chancellor, who pushed him into the law for which he had neither the aptitude nor love; and, finally, the homosexuality which had caused him so much angst as a young man.

Some two hours before, as a result of an early finish at the Old Bailey, I had returned to chambers to be informed by my clerk, Gordon Breadmore, that Viscount Maugham had telephoned and wished me to be in touch as soon as possible. When I called the number that Robin had left, he was most insistent I should join him for lunch at the Ritz at 1.30. It was when I arrived that he introduced me to his wife, Christopher.

It turned out that the whole purpose of my being invited to lunch by the prolific author, who set his literary plots in exotic places, was so that he might rent Taprobane, my island house. He told me he wished to write a second volume of autobiography called *The Search for Nirvana*. 'I saw it some years ago and fell in love with it,' he exclaimed, 'and you simply must let me have it.'

Taprobane is a tiny, magical island off the south coast of Sri Lanka on which the Frenchman, Count Maurice de Mauny, built his dream house, surrounded by 'towering palms and tropical foliage of every kind.'* From the southern terraces there is no land between Taprobane and the South Pole. I am told it is the greatest expanse of water in the world with no land in between.

Having married Lady Mary Byng, the daughter of the $4^{th}$ Earl of Strafford, on 24 June 1898, the couple left for the eighteenth-century Palladian house, Wrotham Park in Barnet, which had been built by Lady Mary's ancestor, Admiral Byng. My life has been full of coincidences and some of them spring from this wedding. Lady Mary was maid of honour to Queen Victoria, who is my daughter Victoria's great-great-great-great-grandmother. One of my dearest friends, the brilliant and hugely witty Julian Fellowes, won an Oscar for the best original screenplay for the film *Gosford Park*, which was shot entirely at Wrotham Park. Above all, Lady Mary's husband Maurice de Mauny created the paradise home that I inherited – Taprobane.

Eventually the de Maunys left for France and took up residence at the chateau of Azay-le-Rideau, near Tours. There, however, things started to go wrong. Gossip began as to the goings-on at the chateau. In 1900, Viscount Esher's son, Oliver, went to stay in order to learn French. 'It was not a success,' wrote Lees-Milne in *The Enigmatic Edwardian*, 'the count made advances to Oliver, who vigorously repelled them.'

Returning from France in 1900, de Mauny suffered a number of financial crises and had, possibly by 1912, made his first visit to Ceylon where, eventually, he came to live as a 'remittance man', building the house and creating the gardens on Taprobane Island. In 1973, when I was lunching with Maugham, Taprobane belonged to my father, from whom I held a long lease. 'You see,' said Maugham, 'Taprobane is my nirvana.'

* *Count de Mauny: Friend of Royalty* by S. Chomet.

Of course, I knew that, due to the then political situation in Sri Lanka and the constant threat of nationalization by a socialist government, the house built by de Mauny had been allowed to deteriorate and was now in an appalling state. 'If we maintain the Taprobane property,' said my father, 'it will only get taken over as an island retreat to which ministers will take their girlfriends.'

Maugham was not put off by my warnings and so insistent was he on getting Taprobane that we drew up an agreement on the back of a Ritz menu. As it happened, when he eventually went to Sri Lanka he didn't settle on the island as a result of a bad heart attack. However, such was his love for it that when in 1975 *Search for Nirvana* was published, Taprobane appeared on its cover.

When my father died in 1993 and the island became mine it appeared that the threat of nationalization had receded so I decided to restore the octagonal house on the island's peak, with its unrivalled views and romantic gardens. I am extremely proud of the fact that the island of dreams created by the count has been rescued from oblivion and that my friend, Geoffrey Dobbs, the present incumbent, has taken on the mantle of maintaining this rare jewel.

Alas, the hawksbill turtles that swam around the island's rocks have disappeared. So, too, happily in this case, have the large bats that occasionally flew straight into the house, across the domed Hall of the Lotus and out again. Such was the fear that these creatures instilled in some of those who stayed in the house that Arthur C. Clarke, in his book *The Reefs of Taprobane*, called it Castle Dracula.

# 12

# The Royal Wedding and Poison in the Gambia

29 July 1981 was a red-letter day for many. In London, Lady Diana Spencer was getting ready to set off from Clarence House in the ceremonial glass coach to her wedding at St Paul's Cathedral. Katarina, my wife to be, was preparing to attend the marriage of her cousin, the Prince of Wales, to Diana. For my old friend Colonel Sir Ronald Gardner-Thorpe, the 653rd holder of the ancient office of Lord Mayor of London, it was probably the high-water mark of his mayoralty. Christopher Wren's great cathedral lies at the heart of the City of London and it fell to him, watched by millions around the globe, not only to pass the Pearl Sword to his sovereign at Temple Bar but also to receive, on the steps of St Paul's, royalty, heads of state, prime ministers and the highest dignitaries from all over the world who were attending Britain's most spectacular wedding of the second half of the twentieth century.

At the same time, 3,000 miles away in the small former British colony of the Gambia, Marxist rebels under the leadership of the Kukoi Samba Sanyang were getting ready to overthrow the pro-Western government of Sir Dawda Jawara who, as president of the Gambia, was at St Paul's, together with most other Commonwealth leaders.

As the main route of the wedding procession to St Paul's cathedral lay at the heart of the ancient ward of Farringdon Without, an area for which I was the elected member, I too was getting into a morning coat to watch the wedding from a favoured position reserved for councilmen of the City of London.

As I watched the British and foreign royals arrive, together with world statesmen, little did I realize that in a matter of months I would be appointed the chief special prosecutor for the Gambia and be sitting in State House in Banjul, discussing with the re-installed Sir Dawda the events that had occurred in his country while he was in Britain for the royal wedding.

After the wedding, a high-commission vehicle drove Sir Dawda from the steps of St Paul's to Haywards Heath, where this devotee of golf was to spend the weekend. But there was bad news from back home. In the early hours of the morning of 30 July, rebels, with the support of some of the Gambia's paramilitary Field Force, seized the principal defence establishment at Bakau and then took over and closed Yundum airport. The rebels stormed the central prison and released the inmates. The Marxist coup had begun. Checkpoints were set up and Denton Bridge, the only way of entering or leaving Banjul by road, was secured by the rebels. After a fire fight, State House was taken and the new Revolutionary Council announced over Radio Gambia that they had established a dictatorship of the proletariat and that the country was now under Marxist rule. Parliament was dissolved, the constitution suspended and banks and courts were closed. All tourists were ordered to remain in their hotels.

By midday on 30 July blood donors were being urged to come forward by Radio Gambia, in view of the large number of casualties. On the morning of 31 July, Sir Dawda, accompanied by a number of journalists, arrived in Dakar, Senegal from Britain. In a speech to the people of the Gambia he made clear that those guilty of treason would have to face the consequences.

This is how I came to find myself in the Gambia as the chief special prosecutor in a Special Court set up for dealing with the aftermath of the coup.

As I was to discover when I arrived in Banjul, a degree of panic had set in at the British high commission. Sir Phillip Bridges, the English Chief Justice of the Gambia, had been admitted into the mission but the gates remained firmly closed to some British tourists caught up in the events who had sought sanctuary in the compound.

The Marxist rebels, calling themselves the Gambia Revolutionary Socialist Party, issued an invitation to the Russians to come in. This, of course, was at the height of the Cold War when one of the dominant political themes of the time was that the Soviets must not be allowed to establish any further footholds in West Africa. All students of history know that for 250 years it was Russian foreign policy to seek what was called 'a warm water port'. The consequences of this coup were many. A 200-mile-long river on the west coast of Africa, which might have served as a Soviet naval base on the Atlantic, sent shivers down the spines of those in Washington and Whitehall.

But the rebels had made the mistake of failing to render Yundum airport unusable. As a result of a call for assistance to the Senegalese government by Sir Dawda, it was not long before hordes of Senegalese paratroopers arrived with a view to securing the airport for future troop-carrying flights.

In addition to this, Margaret Thatcher had authorized the use of the SAS, whose special skills in hostage situations had been so brilliantly demonstrated during the Iranian Embassy siege in London the year before. In Banjul, another hostage situation was developing. The president's wife, Lady (Chilel) Jawara, and her four children had been taken by the rebels and were held prisoner in the Bakau police depot.

With the failure of attempts by Colonel Gaddafi, the plotters' mentor, to persuade the Senegalese not to intervene, and with the arrival of more Senegalese troops and Mirage jets screaming across the skies of Banjul pouring fire into rebel positions, the coup was on the verge of being crushed, with some 2,000 civilians killed. The rebels had only one card left to play – the hostage card. Lady Jawara and the president's children were hostages. But of them, more later.

First, after the ill-fated coup was initially put down, and large numbers of rebels had been rounded up, Sir Dawda was re-installed at State House. It was then decided to create a Special Court to try those who had planned and effected the short-lived coup.

The coup leader, Kukoi Samba Sanyang, who had been trained by the Soviets and was supported by Gaddafi, fled to Guinea-Bissau on 2 August and then, later on, to Castro's Cuba. I was appointed chief special prosecutor and I arrived in the Gambia from London, to find 500 people in custody without a single file on any detainee. Once again, I was confronted with a situation in a former British colony where the English Treason Act of 1351 and other medieval legislation was the primary applicable law. The only penalty for high treason was death.

When I flew into Banjul I went straight to see the newly re-installed president at State House. In the course of our discussions, when I informed him of the inevitable sentence on conviction for high treason, he seemed rather taken aback.

'But Mr de Silva,' he said, 'we have not executed anyone for eighteen years – in fact, since independence.' Then, for good measure he added, 'What's more, the hangman is dead.'

I went on to inform Sir Dawda that in the event of a conviction he could always exercise the prerogative of mercy and avoid an execution. He went very quiet and said nothing further on the subject.

I was unwilling to undertake the appointment of special prosecutor unless I had guarantees that the presiding judges in the treason trials that were to take place were from other Commonwealth countries and not from the Gambia. As a small country where most families had been touched by the events of the coup, it seemed vital that if justice was to be seen to be done, the judges and prosecutors must come from outside the country. Thankfully these conditions were agreed to and, with the help of others, I set about putting together a team of prosecutors and investigators. Gradually, too, we built up files on all those in detention. We also sought to track down those who had participated in the coup who had undergone training in Libya and Moscow.

Sometime after I arrived in the Gambia I sent for the outstanding John Causer, then in my chambers, to come out and join me. Rarely have I been blessed with such an excellent companion. Industrious and disciplined but with a connoisseur's appetite for the absurd, John also had certain skills that I thought might come in handy – he was an expert pistol shot, having represented England as an under-sixteen. On one occasion John got quite carried away with the authority he enjoyed, which included the power to have anyone arrested. Irritated by slothful officials when we were trying to collect some cash from a bank, I heard him shout, 'Eddie, arrest that man!' The manager, who was the object of John's wrath, had just stepped out of his office on his way to the lavatory. He was spotted by John, who lost no time in calling upon Inspector Eddie Gomez to effect an arrest. Gomez, who had been called to the Bar in England before joining the police, promptly galvanized lethargic officials into rapid action. Yes, somehow they found that elusive hard currency that John and I so badly needed.

During our tour in the Gambia, John and I got to know a delightful Lebanese man called Joe Abraham, who had for ten years received a substantial grant from the University of Leiden so that he could try to grow those tiny red-hot birds-eye chillies to the size of chilli peppers. 'How is it going?' I once asked him. 'Oh,' said Joe, 'I have been growing them for years but don't tell Leiden – they won't pay me any more.'

On another occasion, at a barbecue held by a local judge, John and I were surprised to find that his hospitality extended to a lady of the night for each male guest. We made our excuses. 'Sorry, judge, but we cannot pass 10 per cent of this on to our clerk.'*

Now, for some answers to tantalizing questions. Why had the plotters chosen 30 July 1981 as the day on which to launch their coup? Was it because the president would be out of the country? In fact, there was considerable dispute among the conspirators as to when the coup should be launched. As the result of the interrogation it became apparent that the plotters had decided to consult a marabout (Muslim holy man) for the most auspicious moment to bring about a successful power grab. They told him their plans and he came up with the date. On the face of things the marabout, by playing his mystical part in this treasonable conspiracy, had certainly brought himself within the shadow of the gallows. On any basis he was guilty of treason.

John and I had the marabout traced and interviewed. He immediately confessed to the fact he had been approached by the plotters. When the interrogating police officer pointed out to the worried marabout that his advice about the date had not proved too good – because the rebellion was crushed and the coup had failed – the marabout, with self-deprecating charm, replied by saying, 'Yes, I must be forgiven because I am only a trainee marabout!'

Both John and I decided to take pity on the man and spare his life. He was never charged.

In the aftermath of the short-lived coup, and during the trials for treason of the confederates before the Special Court, a state of emergency existed in the Gambia. Because I was made a 'competent authority', if during the interrogation of a person in custody he implicated another not in custody, all I had to do was write the name of that other on a form and he or she would be promptly arrested. Indeed, I was even invested with the power to commandeer property. The exercise of this authority, however, did lead to a problem – namely, my own arrest.

While enjoying supper one evening at the Atlantic Hotel I was joined at my table by the detestable minister of justice, Lamin Saho. I used to avoid him

* Clerks were then entitled to 10 per cent of what a barrister received.

like the plague, for whenever we met he used to badger me with requests, such as, 'Can you get me another lot of kippers from England?' On this occasion, however, he had a much taller order.

Having called for a bottle of brandy and brandy balloons, he turned to me, glass in hand. 'Now, Mr de Silva,' he said, raising his glass in salutation, 'I need you to do me a favour.'

'Not more kippers?' I said.

'No, this is serious,' he replied. 'In Banjul there are several hundred citizens from Guinea-Bissau.' He paused and studied me closely. Then, continuing, he said, 'If you were to order their arrest we could hold them and demand the return of Kukoi Samba Sanyang, whom the Guineans will not otherwise return.'

When I told him that the request he had made of me was downright criminal and that he should be ashamed of even contemplating anything so vile as taking hostages, all he did was laugh and say, 'I am serious in my request, Mr de Silva.'

'In that case, Minister,' I said, 'you have my immediate resignation.'

Sitting at a nearby table was the captain of a British Caledonian flight that was taking off in a couple of hours. As I had met him on a number of previous occasions I called out to ask if his flight was full. When he informed me it was not, I turned to my orderly, Corporal Cassa. Cassa was a handsome man reputed to have a wife in every town in the Gambia. However, his greatest love was the Kalashnikov rifle, which he certainly shared his bed with. He had once been a sergeant, but that was before he was sent by the police to the All Gambia Freestyle Wrestling Competition. Finding the declared victor to be inadequate, Cassa propped the Kalashnikov against the corner post and stripped himself down to his underpants, issuing the challenge, 'Now wrestle with me!' Ten minutes later, Sergeant Cassa became the All Gambia Freestyle Wrestling Champion and the next day, for some unfathomable reason, he was reduced to the rank of corporal. The loser clearly had friends in high places.

I ordered Cassa to go to my suite, pack my things and bring them down to the lobby. The minister watched me making these arrangements without saying a word. When my orderly returned and told me all my bags were in the lobby, I informed the minister that on my return to England not only would I inform the Foreign Office of his outrageous plan, but that I would be writing to the president explaining why I had left.

Luckily, all I had to do was sign my hotel bill and leave. Unluckily, I had told my driver to take my official car home so I found myself standing on the outside steps of the Atlantic Hotel with my bags and my orderly. Seeing a government Mercedes parked by the hotel I told my orderly to put my bags in its boot. I got in and told the driver to take me to Yundum airport. At the check-in I produced an open ticket to Gatwick and got myself and my bags checked in. Ten minutes before boarding I was still in the departure lounge when two police officers walked up to me and said, 'You are under arrest, sir.'

'What for?' I asked, struggling to keep my temper.

'We had a report that you have stolen the minister of justice's car and we are required to take you back to Banjul,' was the policeman's reply.

Much to the irritation of other passengers the flight was delayed while my bags were found and unloaded from the aircraft. I was then driven back to Banjul in a police vehicle, but not to a police station. Instead, I was taken back to the Atlantic Hotel and to the table I had left an hour earlier. Still sitting there was the minister. 'Sit down, Mr de Silva,' he said, pouring me a large brandy. 'Please forget everything I said about having the Guineans arrested. I must also apologize for having had you arrested.' It was now almost midnight and I was too tired to engage this man in conversation. I left him and went back to my suite, taking the glass of brandy with me.

Not long afterward the minister of justice lost not only his ministerial job, but his leg. He came to England, where he perpetrated some fraud, was arrested and detained on remand at Brixton Prison. While in custody he developed an infection that resulted in his leg having to be removed. Poetic justice?

Four months prior to the minister of justice's wicked suggestion that innocent hostages should be taken, I was told about a real hostage situation. This one was defused by a brilliant ruse, conceived by a specialist British Army unit, in which the president's wife, Lady Jawara, who had been threatened with death, played a significant part. While being held in captivity by the increasingly jittery rebels, a message was somehow smuggled to Lady Jawara that she was to demand her captors permit her to take her four children to a particular doctor, as she suspected they were becoming seriously ill. Alongside the smuggled letter was a laxative to be given to the children to simulate the symptoms of a serious gastro-intestinal ailment. Once the children played their unwitting part in this necessary charade, the rebel guards were sent for and the president's wife begged that she be allowed to take them to see their usual doctor. After a great deal of discussion the rebels realized that if the children died they would lose some of their hostages; they agreed to Lady Jawara's request. So, under the armed escort of three rebel guards, they set off to see the physician who had already been secretly alerted to the scheme by members of the specialist unit.

After an examination of the children at the surgery in the presence of their captors, having given them some innocuous substance, the doctor informed Lady Jawara and impressed upon her guards that it was imperative the children were brought back the following day at a given time, as their condition was serious. When Lady Jawara arrived with her children the following day she was carrying the youngest in her arms. Inside the surgery members of the specialist unit were concealed and in wait. As three guards with their rifles stood vigil over their hostages, Lady Jawara attracted the attention of one of them by tossing the child she was carrying toward the guard, who instinctively dropped his rifle and caught it. At this moment of distraction a number of shots rang out. All three guards were killed outright and the president's youngest child was caught for the second time, before it fell to the ground.

Lady Jawara and her children were first taken to the British high commission before being reunited with the president. Once again, members of this famous unit could congratulate themselves on another superbly executed operation.

The first trial for treason that I prosecuted began on Monday 30 November 1981. There were seven plotters in the dock. I had spent much of the first day opening the case for the prosecution, which included informing the court that treason was an offence against allegiance and that, prior to the Gambia becoming a republic, this allegiance was owed to Her Majesty the Queen, but that it was now owed to the president of the republic.

As the second day of the trial dawned – and before I got out of bed – I heard the front door to my suite open. A few moments later my bedroom door opened and in walked a woman who looked as though she was one of the staff. I switched on the light beside my bed and it took me a moment to get her face into focus. I noted that the features of this woman were vaguely familiar to me, but I could not tell how or why.

Later that day in court I happened to turn around and look at the defendants in the dock. Suddenly, I was jolted into the realization that the seventh accused, though male, had the features of the girl who had entered my room that morning. I was staggered by the likeness. The surname of the seventh accused was Corr. At the end of the day's hearing, I called Commander Riley of Special Branch and asked him to get me the names of all female staff at the Atlantic Hotel. By the time I returned to my suite, Riley was waiting for me with the list. Sure enough, there was a floor maid with the name Annie Corr. It turned out that she was the twin sister of the seventh accused who, if convicted, was facing a death sentence. Denis Monk, the English manager of the Atlantic, and Commander Riley, both took the view that given the possible security implications Annie Corr should be dismissed by the hotel. I interceded on her behalf, saying that she may be the only member of her family in employment, and that I would be content if she was moved to a different floor. She was. At the end of their trial the defendants were found guilty of treason and the trial judge, having sent for and placed the black cap over his wig, sentenced her twin brother and the six other defendants to death, and called upon God to have mercy upon their souls.

Some months later, while in the middle of another batch of prosecutions, I returned to the Atlantic at about 8 p.m. On this occasion I had asked John Causer to come back with me so that we could have a chat about an aspect of the case. It had become my practice, when returning to my suite in the evening, to pick up a bottle of brandy and a brandy balloon and go straight to my balcony that overlooked the Atlantic Ocean, where I would unwind with my drink. On this occasion, however, having a guest with me, I turned on the lights to find another brandy balloon for him. But no sooner had I poured his drink and given him the glass than I noticed a slight discolouration of the brandy. Telling him not to touch it, I called Commander Riley to come to my suite. On his arrival I gave him John's glass and the bottle from which I too had been about to pour myself a drink. I informed the commander that I wanted a government analyst's report on the contents as soon as possible. When it came through the following day it made unpleasant reading. The brandy had been poisoned. Not only were the contents of the bottle highly toxic, but death as a result of consuming it would have been slow and painful, with no antidote.

Was it Annie, whose job in the hotel I had saved? Or was it someone else? It was something we never discovered. What we did discover pretty rapidly, however, was how hard it was to live when we could never drink anything except from bottles taken at random that we opened ourselves. Was it going to be the food next? John and I decided to get out of the Gambia as fast as we could. We both agreed with that old maxim: better to be a coward for a moment than dead for the rest of your life.

## 13

# The Corruption of the Blood

I WAS HAVING SUPPER IN THE MUTHAIGA CLUB IN NAIROBI WITH THE late Kenneth Potter, then a Justice of Appeal in Kenya and a former member of our chambers in London. He was one of many barristers who, in those days, had left England to serve the cause of law in the Commonwealth. We had just finished our first course when the judge's attention was drawn to someone who had entered the dining room. 'That's Nicholas Harwood, your prosecutor,' said Potter, sending one of the club servants to bring Harwood over. Moments later he arrived and Kenneth insisted he join us for supper.

After we had been introduced, Nicholas asked me, 'Are you ready to start the trial on 7 March?'

'Not the trial proper,' I said, 'because I have a legal submission to make that goes to jurisdiction upon which I will require a judgment.'

'You're a bit too late for that,' said Harwood. 'The prosecution is entitled to fourteen days' written notice of any point of law you intend to argue!'

Neither my instructing solicitor nor my junior from the Kenyan Bar had alerted me to this requirement. Indeed, I could not possibly have complied with it, as I had only been instructed the week before and this supper at the Muthaiga Club was taking place on Friday 4 March.

'Look here, Nicholas,' said Potter. 'This is a capital case and as you have heard, Desmond has only just been instructed. I think it is your duty to go to court and seek an adjournment so that the defence can serve you with their written legal arguments. Anyway, you must help because he is a member of my old chambers in London!'

The judge's entering the lists on my behalf succeeded and, on 7 March 1983, Nicholas Harwood told the morning session of the High Court in Nairobi, 'Some matters relating to the case have come up,' and asked for an adjournment of four weeks. As happens when respected counsel make an application of this kind, judges tend not to question their judgment in open court. In the event Chief Justice Simpson, having noted that it was most inconvenient for all concerned, granted an adjournment until 6 April. This adjournment, effectively won for me by Kenneth over dinner at the Muthaiga Club, saved the lives of three men. In fact, my client went on to become prime minister of Kenya.

How had this case come my way? I was still two years away from getting silk when I was told I was needed in Nairobi by Gordon Breadmore, who had succeeded Walter Butler as our senior clerk. 'I am afraid it's another case of treason,' he added. My excitement was huge. In my early youth I had been excited by Africa and seeing those great East African plains teeming with game. I had been to East Africa twice and on both occasions I had been arrested and unceremoniously thrown out.

Shortly after the conversation with my clerk I had a conference with my instructing solicitors in chambers. It appeared that the editor of the Kenyan newspaper the *Sunday Standard*, together with two others, was facing the death penalty on charges of treason associated with the attempted Air Force coup of August 1982 against President Daniel arap Moi. It also became clear that the main evidence against my client, Raila Odinga, the son of a former vice president, was that of a witness who had already been convicted of treason and sentenced to death himself. Indeed, this witness had given evidence in other cases and a number of others had been sentenced to the gallows based on what he had said. This condemned witness had, during the preliminary investigation at the magistrates' court, given evidence against my client and the two others who now languished in prison awaiting the trial that was to determine their own fate.

Through my earlier exposure to the complexities of high treason and its development since the Treason Act of 1351, I was, of course, aware that up to 1870 anyone who was convicted of high treason in England suffered an extinction of civil rights; his blood was made corrupt and his estates and goods forfeited. The blood was corrupted both upward and downward. He could neither inherit as an heir nor transmit to descendants. He was, in fact, a non-person, civilly dead in law.

There was doubt as to whether the English Forfeiture Act of 1870, which did away with the corruption of the blood, was a statute of general application and, therefore, adopted by Kenya. If I was correct, then not only was this condemned witness unable to testify in court, but the Supreme Court in Nairobi had no jurisdiction to try the case, because the proceedings in which my client had been committed for trial had been flawed by being based on the testimony of this non-person. It was what we lawyers call a bad committal.

On the very first day of the trial I had intended to make a submission to the Chief Justice which was to be on these lines: 'My Lord, the blood of the witness is corrupt and he is suffering from a severe case of *civiliter mortuus* and there is, therefore, no jurisdiction in this court to embark on this trial as the committal proceedings are grounded in the evidence of a man who could not testify before the magistrate.'

However, I was thwarted in my aim by Harwood's disclosure in the Muthaiga Club that the prosecution were entitled to advance notice of fourteen days before such a point of law could be advanced.

In the adjournment granted by the Chief Justice, I returned to chambers in London where I set about preparing the notice I had to serve on the prosecution and a summary of my legal arguments on corrupted blood. On completion, I sent it through to the Attorney General of Kenya and looked forward to developing this esoteric argument before Chief Justice Simpson in the Supreme Court in Nairobi.

However, in a surprise move on 23 March, two weeks before I had to appear before the court in Nairobi, the government of Kenya decided to withdraw the treason charges against all three men. We had won without having to deploy the argument in court and I was delighted that lives had been saved. It was clear the government had made a political decision to avoid the trial and the subsequent drama in open court, in which a decision in my client's favour on jurisdiction would have had an impact on the cases of all of the others who had already been sentenced to death on the evidence of this accomplice.

In 2008, my client became prime minister of Kenya. He continues to this day to be a diehard supporter of Arsenal Football Club.

# 14

# 'You Will Hang in the Morning'

'FROM GOLF TO THE GALLOWS' said the *Times*.

'ANOTHER CASE OF WHITE MISCHIEF IN AFRICA' reported the *Independent*.

She was convicted of murder on my birthday. Mariette Bosch was to go down in history as the first white woman to be sentenced to death in the former British protectorate of Botswana. Mariette, whose husband Justin had died in a car accident, shocked and divided the tightly knit British and South African expatriate society who enjoyed the affluence of what was arguably the most robust economy on the African continent, where expansion had been fuelled by diamonds and tourism. With a lifestyle reminiscent of colonial days – large houses, swimming pools and an abundance of domestic staff – she was one of those who lived in the smart suburb of Gaborone, nicknamed Park Lane.

Unable to wait until her lover Tienie Wolmarans got a divorce, the prosecution said, she shot his wife, Ria – her best friend – twice in the head. The case was dubbed Botswana's White Mischief, after Lord Erroll's murder in Kenya.

In their armoury the prosecution had three deadly arguments. First, on the day before the shooting, Mrs Bosch had picked up the murder weapon, her late husband's 9mm pistol, from Pietersburg in South Africa; secondly, after the murder she and Tienie got engaged in secret; and, finally, after she had been charged with the murder, she married him in undignified haste.

In November 2001, totally oblivious to the existence of Mariette Bosch, I was making arrangements to spend Christmas on Taprobane with Katarina and Victoria. A call to my clerk, Robin Driscoll, from Edward Luke, Mariette's counsel in Botswana, threw my Christmas plans into total confusion. If I undertook to represent Mrs Bosch before the Court of Appeal in Botswana in January 2002, Christmas would be spent in England going through volumes of evidence, legal rulings and the judgment that culminated in her conviction; above all, drafting new ground of appeal.

My attention being entirely taken over by the Bosch appeal, I spent Christmas in Chelsea, wading through the evidence and the judgment. What struck me was that the judge had gone hopelessly wrong in law. I was quite confident that the Court of Appeal of Botswana, which was to include two British judges (Lord Cowie and Sir John Blofeld), would find that the trial of Mrs Bosch was a travesty of justice.

With her engagement and subsequent marriage to the dead woman's husband, Mariette appeared to me to have done her best to supply the prosecution with the only evidence of motive: jealousy and a passion that could not wait. In his judgment the trial judge, finding her guilty, said she had killed her best friend as a result of 'jealousy and infatuation'. After her arrest she had protested her innocence from the outset and, even as the sentence of death was being pronounced, those sitting close enough to the dock heard her muttering, 'I am not guilty. You are sentencing me for a thing I have not done!'

The night before my appearance in the Court of Appeal I received a telephone call in my suite. The caller informed me that Lord Cowie and Sir John Blofeld had been taken off the Bosch appeal and would no longer form part of the Appeal Court. I was flabbergasted, as I had been assured they would be two of the three judges who would determine Mariette's fate. 'Desmond, I am sure she will swing,' said my caller, 'because there is a growing local protest that the newspapers in South Africa and elsewhere are beginning to champion her cause. Many locals here believe this is only being done because she is white. If she was black they feel the outside world would not take this interest.'

Depressed at this news, I turned in ahead of meeting Mariette and beginning my arguments in the Court of Appeal the following day. Collected from my hotel by my junior, Edward Luke, I was driven at very considerable speed to Gaborone and the court. No sooner had I entered the court building than I ran into Sir John Blofeld, from whom I discovered that this was his very first visit to Botswana as an appeals judge. He confirmed he would not be on our appeal. Shortly thereafter I made my way with Edward to see my condemned client.

Sitting in a cramped cell was a woman who showed all the signs of having been in solitary confinement for nearly a year. With pale and tired skin, she looked frail. Her frock, once smart, hung on her as if several sizes too large.

Fixing me with a long and nervous look, she placed her right hand in mine. Her posture was tense. A tremor ran through her fingertips...Was the trigger pulled by one of those fingers?

Counsel in capital cases have three harrowing moments: when they meet their client for the first time; when a sentence of death is imposed or upheld; and the day of the execution.

'Do you think you can save me?' she said, in a soft South African accent.

'Edward and I will do our best for you,' I said, still holding her hand. Our exchanges thereafter were brief, as I had to be in court in fifteen minutes.

I made my way to the courtroom in which the appeal was to be heard. The corridors were packed with journalists. Outside the court building more journalists and photographers milled around vehicles with large satellite dishes.

In court the main gallery was packed. Counsel for the state and his team were already installed in their places. Just after I took my seat, Mariette was brought in, surrounded by female police officers.

We all stood as the three appeal judges came in. This was the first time I knew for certain the composition of the court. Instead of Austin Amissah, an outstanding lawyer and judge who had once been a pupil in our chambers, there was another presiding judge. His opening salvo was directed at me: 'Who are you and what are you doing here?' When I explained I was representing Mrs Bosch and that I had been admitted to the Bar of Botswana by the Chief Justice, who was sitting on his right, I was met with the response, 'You should have called on me this morning as a matter of courtesy.'

So this is how it is going to be, I said to myself, and made the apology that, having come out from England to represent Mrs Bosch, I had spent the few minutes I had before coming into court with my client. 'But I was sitting in my room, you could have spared me a few minutes,' he replied, not letting up. I was beginning to feel like a coconut shy. I apologized again with as much deference as I could muster and tried not to let it show that while he might have been sitting untroubled in his room my client was facing execution.

After this unseemly exchange we settled down to a fairly normal day in a Court of Appeal. Their Lordships listened attentively as I took them through the passages of the judgment in which the trial judge, as we lawyers say, reversed the burden of proof: applying a test that put the burden of proving her innocence upon the defendant. During the course of my address, one of Their Lordships intervened by saying, 'Mr de Silva, it is quite clear that the judge not only went off the rails but remained off the rails.' At which point, my junior, Edward Luke, in a stage whisper said to me, 'Desmond, I think we are winning.'

For three days the fate of Mariette was debated before the court; at the end I felt drained and exhausted. Unusually, the president of the court said to me, ominously, 'Mr de Silva, pray that we get our judgment right.' So saying, he rose, as did the other judges, and the court was adjourned for judgment to be delivered on a date to be fixed in the future. I did not share Edward Luke's confidence that we had won the day.

Returning to my hotel, I packed to leave for Johannesburg, and then London the following day. When I returned to my hotel there was a message awaiting me, from a clergyman I had met two days before. When I called him, he asked me if he could join me for breakfast the following morning. He did. To my utter astonishment, the cleric asked me not to surrender my suite in the hotel that day, but to let him use it instead. He undertook to take care of his share of the hotel bill when he eventually left.

'Why do you want my suite?' I enquired, rather puzzled by the unusual request. 'Ah,' he said 'I am rather well known here and it would be an awful giveaway if I booked a suite in my own name. You see, I have three girlfriends and the constant problem I have is to find a place without giving myself away to my wife and my family. Discovery would be awful.' Moved by the cleric's plight, I informed reception that I was not actually checking out, but would settle my account up to that morning and that another would be settling the account thereafter. The man at the reception desk seemed not in the least bit bothered as I made these curious arrangements, with the reverend gentleman at my elbow to ensure that there were no slip-ups that might interfere with his future pleasures. Perhaps the clerk at the desk had been through this routine many times before.

Some weeks after I returned to London I had a call from Botswana. It was Edward Luke. 'Desmond,' he said. 'I have some bad news. The Court of Appeal has upheld Mariette's conviction and confirmed the sentence of death.' Informing Edward that we had to start organizing an appeal for clemency, I got in touch with a doughty fighter for human rights, Anne Schofield, the wife of the English Chief Justice of Gibraltar. Anne was then attached to Radcliffes, a highly thought of firm of London solicitors. Within days she mobilized the likes of the brilliant Edward Fitzgerald, QC, a towering intellect in the law, with many contacts at human rights organizations around the world that opposed the death penalty.

A holding petition was filed while efforts were made by Anne Schofield and others to mobilize opinion through African organizations to plead for clemency.

I was having breakfast on a Monday morning in Hull, prior to going into court to represent the Leeds United footballer Lee Bowyer, when my mobile telephone rang. It took some moments to understand what the caller was saying. Between heart-rending sobs the quavering voice of a young girl told me, 'They have hanged our mother.'

As I was about to leave for court, I could not embark upon a long conversation with Mariette's daughter. What emerged, when I did, was a story of cruel, secretive and arbitrary conduct. Apparently Mariette's teenage children had gone to the Central Prison to see their mother on Friday 30 March. They were told they could not see her as the prison was undergoing some refurbishment, but could they please come back on Monday.

Within hours of the children leaving, an official entered her cell, in which a small window overlooked the prison graveyard. Handing Mariette her death warrant he said to her, 'Your application for clemency has been refused. You will hang in the morning.'

When Soné – Mariette's daughter – and her sisters turned up at the Central Prison on Monday to see their mother, they were told, 'Sorry, we hanged her on Saturday.' The decision to press ahead with the execution, just two months after she lost her appeal, was the shortest such period ever applied by Botswana's judicial authorities.

I was appalled, as I had been given an assurance there would be no decision taken until May, during which time a petition for clemency would be considered. Local press reports suggested that President Festus Mogae of Botswana had decided to bring forward the date of execution because of the growing international clamour for clemency. He was reported to have viewed such pressure as an infringement of Botswana's sovereignty.

As a storm of indignation swept through the world's press, I expressed my view that it was a shabby and indecent exercise to execute her secretly, in haste, without her husband, family or lawyers being informed. Any system of justice must have a human face, even when it comes to the execution of a death penalty. Condemned persons must have the opportunity to settle their affairs, make financial dispositions, take their leave of their intimate family and compose themselves with spiritual advice before they face the ultimate ordeal. Mariette Bosch was denied all of this.

## 15

# The Caesar Photographs

IN 2015 A GRUESOME EXHIBITION OF PHOTOGRAPHS DEPICTING VICTIMS of torture and execution, committed by the current Syrian regime were on display at the United Nations in New York. The photographs were supplied by a defector who worked for the Assad regime.

When the Syrian president, Bashar al-Assad, was asked about these pictures he responded by saying, 'Who took the pictures? Who is he? Nobody knows. There is no verification of any of this evidence, so it is all allegations without evidence.' The classic techniques of denial were now being put into play. Yet I met the defector, I gave him the code name Caesar and I saw the evidence he had smuggled out of Syria.

In January 2014, an unusual request came to me through the well-known London solicitors, Carter-Ruck. The instructions I received were to go to the Middle East where I would meet a defector from the Assad regime. My brief was to interrogate him to ensure he was a genuine defector and not an Assad plant. Of course, one of the classic methods of discrediting your enemy is to trap him into relying on evidence with which he is fed, in order to subsequently demonstrate conclusively that his propaganda based on that evidence is false.

As the country I had to go to was Qatar, and because Qatar financially and militarily supported a rebel group, or groups, against the regime in Damascus, I required of my instructing solicitors Cameron Doley and Saad Djabbar that I should head a team of my choosing. This was so that several pairs of experienced eyes could look at any evidence brought out of Syria and a collective view could be reached as to the true status of the defector himself. There was a strong element of scepticism with which, I believed, this particular task had to be approached.

In the cauldron that is war-torn Syria, where fact and fiction are difficult to separate, where allegations and counter-allegations are very much the order of the day and where disinformation is the currency of choice on all sides, it is a difficult task to be sure of anything, save that hundreds of thousands have been killed and myriad factions have their own agendas.

In Doha I met up with the two others I had selected for the team: David Crane, my former boss from Sierra Leone, who had a background in US intelligence; and Sir Geoffrey Nice, QC, who had prosecuted Slobodan Milošević for war crimes. We had all prosecuted heads of state and had been appointed by the international community to do so. Each of us had seen images of death, to the point that we could read a photograph to tell us, superficially at any rate, how death had been inflicted.

However, to ensure total professionalism of approach, I approached Chris Gregg at Axiom International, a former detective chief superintendent, for the best pathologists on their books. We were fortunate to get Dame Susan Black – a world-famous professor of forensic pathology – and the hugely experienced forensic pathologist Dr Stuart Hamilton.

The Free Syria Movement, one of the more moderate rebel groups fighting Assad, had spirited Caesar out of Syria under the cover of a mock funeral, held to mourn his murder at the hands of a rebel group opposed to Assad.

Caesar was, before the conflict to topple Assad, a crime scene photographer working for the Syrian government. After the conflict began the Syrian security services took thousands into detention. In detention they were tortured and executed. The significance of Caesar was that he was one of the photographers required to capture the images of those who had been executed.

Before we examined in detail any of the 55,000 images of corpses, we let Caesar give his account of the horrific images he had smuggled out of Syria. After our preliminary interrogation we, together with the pathologists, examined a large selection of the photographic images, to ensure forensic evidence corroborated the account Caesar was giving us.

According to Caesar, he had to take four or five photographs of each body. It is important to remember that the dead bodies shown in these photographs were in just one area. Of course, approaching the matter with a degree of cynicism, we all wondered why the regime in Damascus would require the bodies to be photographed. In dictatorships there is a need to ensure the orders given to execute individuals have been carried out. These photographic images were the proof the regime needed that no one had bribed a guard and escaped.

When our report was released it came as a bombshell. While stories abounded about executions in Assad's Syria, this was the first 'smoking gun' evidence by someone who worked for the regime and could testify to killings on an industrial scale. Here was the clearest proof, corroborated by photographic evidence, of war crimes and crimes against humanity being committed by the henchmen of the Assad regime. This is not to say that groups fighting Assad are free from the stain of war crimes.

The report was tabled before the Security Council in New York; the full wrath of the Syrian government and their backers in Moscow were turned on us. Their immediate response was to say the photographs were faked.

A large number of the victims had been starved before they were killed. With sunken cheeks, hollow eye sockets and ribcages showing under their skin, they resembled the emaciated bodies encountered by the Allies who entered Nazi concentration camps in 1945. It would have been impossible to fake these images and get them past our forensic experts.

These photographs are now in the Holocaust Museum in Washington. If Assad and his regime are ever brought before an international court for crimes against humanity, Caesar's evidence will certainly be centre stage.

# 16

# The Playboy Peer

'IS THAT MR DE SILVA?' ASKED THE GIRL AT THE OTHER END OF THE TELEPHONE.

'Yes.'

'Just a moment please. Dame Barbara would like to speak with you.'

A few seconds later I had the world's most prolific author on the line.

'Desmond,' said Barbara Cartland. 'Charles Brocket is in trouble and you must look after him.'

Barbara, the legendary creator of plots in which lively heroines were rescued from villains by dashing heroes, had taken up arms on behalf of her neighbour, Lord Brocket.

'His solicitor must be in touch with my clerk,' I said.

'I will tell him at once,' said the formidable writer.

The headlines that day in February 1995 had been about the arrest of Charles Ronald George Nall-Cain, the 3rd Baron Brocket. I had met him a few times at Camfield Place, Barbara Cartland's house. There were always several other guests and I could not really recall any conversation I had had with him. He just seemed an engaging sort of chap.

Very occasionally he was accompanied by his stunningly attractive wife, the former Vogue model, Isa, who I recall used to sit at table without saying a word. Charles Brocket had inherited a neighbouring estate to Camfield Place, the centrepiece of which was the magnificent eighteenth-century Brocket Hall. In its colourful history it had been home to the great Victorian prime ministers Lord Melbourne and Lord Palmerston. Palmerston died on the billiard table with a chambermaid beneath him. It was also the home of Byron's lover, Lady Caroline Lamb, who once had herself served up naked in a huge soup tureen before a startled Melbourne and his Cabinet. It was in the elegant ballroom of Brocket Hall that the waltz was first introduced to England.

Charles Nall-Cain, at the age of fifteen, had inherited the hall, but not the 5,000 acres that surrounded it. He succeeded his grandfather, whom he had only met once when he visited him at Eton. Having served for a spell in the 14th/20th King's Hussars, where his good looks and rakish charm got him into trouble with other officers' wives, he emerged from the Army and set about trying to preserve Brocket Hall. He borrowed huge sums of money to turn it into a sumptuous conference centre with a magnificent golf course. Twinned with his passion to keep the great house at all costs was his obsession with his collection of classic cars. At one stage the collection was valued at £20 million, but it was all bought on borrowed money. When classic car prices slumped, Charles found himself facing debts of some £16 million, with the collection no longer providing the banks with the required collateral. The banks were baying for their money.

When a deal to sell the cars to a Japanese businessman fell through, the peer was staring ruin in the face, mortgaged to the hilt, with his marriage in tatters. Before he could overcome one misfortune, he was beset by another. He was in the territory of despair. I have no doubt that when he cooked up the fake raid at Brocket Hall, in which he claimed that a 1952 Ferrari 340 America, a 1955 Ferrari Europa, a Ferrari 195 Sport and a 1960 Maserati Tipo 'Birdcage' had been stolen from his showroom, it was out of an escalation of panic. Once he had reported the theft of £4.5 million worth of classic cars, which in fact had been cut up into small pieces and buried on the estate, he was carried by the tide of what he had started and had to live with the dread of discovery. No false insurance claim could have been more ineptly choreographed.

The highly suspicious General Accident insurance company refused to pay out on his claim. It was not in the least bit surprising, as Brocket Hall had been turned into one of the most secure conference centres in Europe. Margaret Thatcher had greeted Gorbachev, Reagan and Bush there and it was used regularly for summits when Britain held the presidency of the European Community in 1992. Close-circuit television monitored everything that came in and went out. The Maserati and the three Ferraris were not seen leaving the grounds.

Arrested with four others for attempting to deceive an insurance company and a Lloyd's of London syndicate into paying out £4.5 million over a burglary at Brocket Hall, Lord Brocket pleaded guilty on 19 December 1995. At my request, Judge Daniel Rodwell granted Brocket bail pending his sentence, but warned him 'to be under no misapprehension whatsoever' that he would be sent to prison at the next hearing.

There was in fact no misapprehension on the defence side. Lord Brocket clearly accepted he would have to go to prison. The issue was, how long for? Some classic car enthusiasts felt he should be given life for destroying those fantastic handmade treasures.

Quite apart from the fraud itself, I felt that a sentencing judge who wanted to justify a heavier than usual sentence of imprisonment would latch on to the fact that Brocket had suborned two of his employees into taking part in the swindle, with the veiled threat that unless they participated they and their families would be thrown off the estate. As anticipated, in February 1996, when Brocket returned to court for sentencing, Judge Rodwell passed upon him a sentence of imprisonment. A term of five years made Brocket sway in the dock.

Given the public disgrace be had brought upon himself, the social ruin taken together with the collapse of his marriage, and the undoubted element of panic, a sentence of half that actually imposed would have been appropriate. However, as the Court of Appeal will do its utmost to uphold a sentence unless the judge has made a major mistake of principle, I realized it was unlikely to interfere with the sentence of five years. In fact it did not, and Brocket had to pay his dues in the harsh coinage of imprisonment. Indeed, to ensure it could not be alleged that he had enjoyed some special treatment on account of his status, I am sure that even his eventual move to Ford Open Prison was delayed beyond the usual.

# 17

# The Poisoned Daughter

MR JUSTICE STEPHEN MITCHELL WAS AN OUTSTANDING LAWYER AND compassionate judge. When, in 1994, I had what I consider to be one of the saddest cases that ever came to me, I was relieved to hear it would come before Stephen Mitchell.

The defendant, my lay client, was a West End bank executive. One day she returned home from work and poisoned her bright thirteen-year-old daughter with a cocktail of drugs cooked into her food. She then lay down with her offspring and cuddled her through the night. In the morning she kissed her dead daughter, leaving a visible lipstick mark on her cheek, and set about taking her own life with antidepressant tablets. She survived the overdose.

Charged with murder at the Old Bailey, the Crown accepted her pleas of not guilty to murder but guilty to manslaughter by reason of diminished responsibility. At her age, thirty-three, this assets and securities manager of a Piccadilly-based bank had found herself in the grip of a severe depression brought on by a stress-related illness. To use the language of a psychiatrist who had prepared a report on her, 'she had entered a spiral of mental decline in the hothouse of the financial sector.'

The details of her daughter's death were so harrowing that the judge took the rare step of allowing this poor woman to leave the dock of the Old Bailey and sit with a nurse. The sentence imposed upon her, eventually, was fairly minimal, but the impact that case left upon me, as to the ravages that can be brought about by fierce pressures of the office, was huge.

These days, such a sentence would be met with howls of indignation generated by the popular press, with loud calls for the resignation of the judge. The exercise of compassion in sentencing takes judicial courage and without that courage justice is diminished.

# 18

# Tom Clancy

Ray Pilley, who had left the RAF after narrowly escaping death when he had to eject from his Phantom jet fighter moments before it crashed, became a solicitor in England and set up a busy practice in Gibraltar. We met when I was prosecuting the extradition of Roderick Newall, after which Ray was good enough to instruct me in some of the bigger or more newsworthy trials that came his way in Gibraltar. Tom Clancy was one.

I always enjoyed going to Gibraltar, as I would often take a house in Sotogrande in Spain, which gave me a chance to combine a trial with a holiday. I could also renew the great friendships I had developed in Gibraltar with such marvellous people as Anthony Lombard, David and Marevic Daniel, Charles and Marie Sacarello and many others.

In 1995, when a brief arrived in chambers for me to advise Tom Clancy in Gibraltar, there was a flurry of excitement in the clerks' room. Was this the bestselling author who was catapulted into literary fame with his first novel, *The Hunt for Red October*?

When I opened the brief sent to me by Ray I learned that Tom Clancy, who had been feted in Gibraltar as the undisputed master of intricate plotting and razor-sharp suspense, spent his time on the Rock readily signing his autograph and inscribing copies of his books. He was there, ostensibly, to research his next novel. He also needed to make an insurance claim for the loss of a wardrobe of handmade Italian clothes, which he asserted had been lost on his way to Gibraltar. He took his problem to an old firm of Gibraltar lawyers who, in obedience to their client's instructions, set about making a claim on his behalf. This would end up with Lloyd's of London and Assicurazioni Generali of Italy, and amounted to tens of thousands of pounds.

After he had been there for some time, the celebrity status of my client was called into question by the eight-year-old son of one of the partners of the firm, who said to his father, 'I do not believe this Tom Clancy to be the famous author.' The boy narrowly missed being cuffed around the ears for his impertinence; his father had basked in the glow of having acquired such a celebrity client. However, as the weeks went by, owing to some of the habits displayed by his client, the boy's words came back to his mind. The lawyer was to get a shock. So, too, was his client.

The lawyer eventually called up Clancy's publishers in the US. To the lawyer's enquiry as to whether the famous author was in Gibraltar, there came the surprised response that the publishers sincerely hoped he was not, as they were expecting him to lunch in half an hour in New York. The eight-year-old boy was right.

Aflame with moral outrage that his firm had been the victim of a hoax, and now convinced that the impostor was making fraudulent insurance claims, the lawyer wasted no time in taking the Clancy legal files to the police station, alerting them to the client's insurance claim. Shortly thereafter, the man who became my client was arrested in Gibraltar and charged with a number of false insurance claims. He was charged in his real name: Tom Clancy. For five months Clancy was held on remand at the Moorish Castle before being granted bail.

So, as it turned out, I was being called upon by Clancy's new solicitor, Ray Pilley, to advise on the question of legal professional privilege. Here, the former solicitors had discovered facts in the course of their professional relationship with the client. What really seemed to upset them was that they had been made to look foolish by having lavished time and money on a celebrity client who turned out *not* to be the world-famous author. They were, of course, perfectly entitled to dispense with him as a client but could they, without his permission, hand over to the police all their files that recorded communications between lawyer and client? If a prosecution resulted from what the police discovered in the lawyer's files, could it give rise to an argument that the proceedings might be stayed, as they sprang from a breach of professional privilege? I had no doubt that a lawyer was under an obligation to reveal information in the event he reasonably believed the intention of his client was to commit a crime, and that the passing of the information was necessary to prevent that crime. Had this firm gone much further?

Having read my instructions, I flew to Gibraltar for a consultation with Ray and Clancy. There I formed the view that something was decidedly odd about our client that only medical science could make sense of. When the appropriate medical examinations had been made of the defendant, it became clear to the doctors that the defendant was suffering from a form of brain damage that would make it impossible for him to give proper instructions or, indeed, do himself justice in the witness box.

Deciding that it was not necessary to go into the issues of privilege and breach of confidentiality, Ray Pilley informed the prosecution that we were going to ask for a stay of the proceedings on the grounds of it being an abuse of the process of the court for any trial to commence or continue. Having served our medical reports on the prosecution, the matter was set down for a hearing in the Supreme Court before Chief Justice Derek Schofield on 16 July 1996.

There were no fewer than seven medical reports on Clancy, which included an MRI scan by Dr T. Cox, a consultant radiologist at the London Bridge Hospital. Dr Christopher Clough and Dr R. Abbott, both consultant neurologists in England, agreed that Clancy was suffering from cerebrovascular dementia. Dr Maskill, from Gibraltar, under whose care Clancy was placed, concurred. Despite the arguments of Ricky Rhoda, QC, Gibraltar's Attorney General, that the defendant was a confidence trickster and that this illness was put on, the Chief Justice stayed the proceedings on the basis that the defendant would not be able to give instructions or follow proceedings in this complicated fraud. Clancy was thus spared a trial.

Now freed from the worries of a criminal trial, Clancy walked out of court into the sunshine of Gibraltar, and spent the next month badgering Ray Pilley to obtain from the police the return of the clothing receipts seized by the police on his arrest. As I recall, the police refused to return Tom Clancy's receipts on the ground that they were forgeries. Indeed, it turned out that similar Sartoria Greggio receipts had been used many times before by the old rogue as a means of obtaining hundreds of thousands of pounds from various insurance companies.

The police also refused to return to Clancy a passport seized by them on his arrest. It was in the name of Forsyth: Frederick Forsyth.

# EPILOGUE

Memoirs tend to suffer from many flaws. The first is vanity of which, no doubt, I shall be accused. Self-justification is certainly a close second. However, this is perhaps to be found more in the domain of the political memoir, where retired politicians try to persuade us that their lives contributed to the commonweal. The opportunity to be malicious must certainly feature in the memoirs of any barrister. Day after day, Bar messes and robing rooms up and down the country echo to the sound of witty – and usually malicious – accounts of the conduct of judges, opponents and other barristers. In an effort to avoid an excess of waspishness in relation to judges, and some of my opponents, I have decided to leave any modest success I have enjoyed at the Bar to be written about by someone who has covered many of my cases for twenty-five years or more and has no motive to be malicious.

Paul Cheston, whom I have got to know in the past twenty-five years, has in fact written many of the front-page splash headlines in the *London Evening Standard* that accompanied the arrests of people long before I was instructed to either prosecute or defend in their cases. Bearing in mind the undesirable temptations that may beset a barrister writing about his own cases, I have written about very few, and on the whole concentrated on cases overseas, which Paul did not cover, or English cases where guilty pleas were entered. I am profoundly grateful to Paul for his own perspective on my professional life, which, happily, has been varied, satisfying and occasionally perilous. Indeed, when I first really got to know him, it was in Gibraltar, when he was covering an extradition murder case that had all the elements of an Agatha Christie thriller; there was even a witness I christened Miss Marple.

Reading what Paul has written has resurrected memories of cases that had long fled my mind but now, happily, bring back recollections of great human dramas that were played out in the courts.

Over to you, Paul.

# PART II

## 19

# A Newspaperman's Introduction to Desmond

*Paul Cheston*

SOME YEARS AGO I MET UP WITH DESMOND IN LONDON. AMONG OTHER things, I asked if he was going to write his memoirs. He told me that the problem was he had not kept a proper record of his cases, to refresh his mind about the trials in which he had appeared. It was at this point that I told him that I had the notes from a fascinating range of his cases that I had covered as the courts correspondent for the *London Evening Standard*, and would be happy to collaborate with him.

Having thought about it for some time, he agreed I could author a part of his memoirs, based on the material I had accumulated over the years. The thing that would spur him to write, he said, would be his mounting anger at the destruction, by successive governments, of the Bar that he loved, the independent Criminal Bar, which he saw as a pillar of the constitution.

He had been appointed for the past one and a half decades to high legal office by the international community to run United Nations-sponsored war crimes investigations, which had kept him away from England. He returned at the behest of David Cameron's coalition government, to carry out a year-long investigation into the alleged complicity by the security services in targeted assassinations in Northern Ireland during the Troubles. His report was tabled in the House of Commons. Following this, in 2014, he headed a team investigating a defector from Syria, code-named Caesar, who produced the first 'smoking gun' evidence of mass executions of detainees by the Assad regime. It provided critical evidence should that regime be tried for war crimes and crimes against humanity at some future point in time.

Desmond was knighted under a Tony Blair Labour government, while a Conservative prime minister, David Cameron, appointed him to be a Member of Her Majesty's Most Honourable Privy Council. Although he is now The

Right Honourable Sir Desmond de Silva, QC, the cases I recount are from a time when he was just Desmond de Silva, QC. I will refer to him simply as Desmond, as he would prefer.

Gibraltar has been a mixed blessing for me. In summer, as the Spanish *costas* bask in beautiful sunshine, the Levante cloud sits smack on top of the Rock, bringing a stifling tropical clamminess to the narrow, claustrophobic streets. Millions have been spent to brighten up the marina, but in the late 1980s there was an air of decay and shabbiness about the strategically vital, but otherwise anachronistic, colony bolted on to the end of Europe.

Four years earlier I had spent the best part of August on the Rock, covering the inquest into the SAS shooting of three IRA terrorists, so I was faintly dubious about returning in the autumn of 1992. This time it was to cover what was expected to be a straightforward extradition hearing for Roderick Newall, the handsome young Army officer from one of Britain's most fashionable regiments, accused of murdering his parents in Jersey.

Joining old press colleagues around the pool on the roof of the Holiday Inn, my spirits were not improved to hear that the proceedings could take days and would probably occur in chambers, with the press and public barred. Some might dream of lounging around the Mediterranean with nothing to do, but I knew my news editor would haul me back and kick me all over London if I could not file something and soon.

'What's the Crown's counsel like? Is he any good? Will he help?' I asked in despair.

The answer came in a chorus: 'You won't believe it!'

An hour or so later I understood why. We had adjourned to the hotel bar to line up the first of the day when I first saw Desmond.

He stands six foot three inches tall, with a more than substantial frame to match, olive-skinned and with an unmistakable voice, described by his old friend Mr Justice Henriques as, 'More English than any Englishman you have ever met.' It was a typical tease and far from faint praise, as one glance at Desmond's background would confirm.

In an appreciation of her life, the *Guardian*, in May 2000, produced a two-page spread of his father's sister, Minnette, referring to 'her social aplomb', which was a family trait, together with her 'grand contralto voice'. It was immediately clear that Minnette's nephew maintained the family trait. He is ear- and eye-catching enough, but it is his presence, a mixture of command and bonhomie, witty bombast and self-depreciation, which struck me.

In earlier chapters Desmond has described something of his background. To tread the path from junior barrister to legal stardom needs confidence. To delve deeper into the source of his self-assurance I decided to consult the College of Arms in London. This ancient institution, run by members of the royal household, keeps a record of all English Arms legally issued, and the names and pedigrees of those, wholly or partly of English and Welsh descent, entitled to bear them. I approached one of the thirteen 'Heralds in Ordinary' who make up the College of Arms, and who have been members of the royal household, directly appointed by the Sovereign, since 1484. According to Robert Noel, Lancaster Herald, not only does Desmond have the right to bear English arms, but his family tree is recorded in the College of Arms and appears in the official records of the college. One of his earliest English ancestors, shown in an unofficial pedigree drawn up by Sir Edmund Burke, was Henricus Rose, who was returned to Parliament for Great Yarmouth in 1322.

Crossing the lobby of Gibraltar's Holiday Inn, heading a pack of lawyers and policemen, he came striding across the room, straight for the bar. Slightly dumbstruck, I was introduced.

'My dear boy, I'm delighted to meet you. You must join us immediately,' was his instant reaction.

As the evening progressed the lawyers and policemen, well aware of Desmond's abilities, quietly slunk away to their beds, but a hard core of Fleet Street's finest, a profession never known for its aversion to a drink, decided to tough it out with the counsel for the Crown. We paid a heavy price.

Brought up on traditional Fleet Street values, I had quietly believed I could more than handle myself in this department, but next morning I had the hangover from Hades. Desmond had risen ridiculously early for a man who had, to my unreliable memory, appeared to have drunk his body weight in Armagnac the night before, and was already jauntily preparing for court. But, as I was to find out over many years to come – and as I will describe later – that was only a comparatively modest night for Desmond.

Through bleary eyes, the press pack eventually dragged itself the 150 yards to court to report the start of this truly sensational case. I will deal later with the

Newall saga and what was initially thought to be a straightforward extradition but turned into a marathon of twists and turns, tantrums and tailspins before this Army officer was jailed for life, seven years after the merciless double murder. But since that first meeting in Gibraltar I quickly sensed that things happened in Desmond's cases, and I kept an eye on the court lists around the country to watch this man at work. I was rarely disappointed; he was, and still is, box office.

Over the years I came to admire his precise grasp of the law and his ingenuity in handling it, the surgeon-like forensic skill in pinpointing the key issues and the way, by brilliant advocacy and sheer chutzpah, he would gently caress a jury toward a favourable verdict. But what was so appealing was his impishness. Inside this giant frame is a real schoolboy who cannot resist poking fun – very often at himself.

In court he would use it as a major weapon to disarm the opposition and charm the jury. It is a spontaneous gift which cannot be found in *Archbold* or learned in a law degree. Yet no one is perfect and certainly no one as colourful and extrovert, who has lived and functioned in a very public arena for so long, can get it right every time. One failing, which he is the first to admit, is his inability to resist a crack and a laugh in court, sometimes at the expense of a witness, very often at the expense of an opponent and occasionally at the expense of the judge. Advocates live in dread of being pulled up or reprimanded by the judge in front of the jury. Desmond treats it as an occupational hazard.

Another flaw is his impetuosity. His penchant for the politically incorrect remark, sometimes ill-considered, has caused offence to those who don't know him well. Once invited with his wife, Princess Katarina of Yugoslavia, to an audience with the Polish Pope John Paul II in his private quarters in the Vatican, at a time when Yugoslavia was still under Communist rule, he astonished the cardinals who surrounded the Supreme Pontiff with a Desmondian moment. Greeting his wife, the Pope said: 'I hope democracy will come to your country as it has done to Poland.' As he shook Desmond by the hand, the Holy Father was no doubt taken aback to be told: 'Your Holiness, I am delighted to see that you are a Pole first and a Pope second!' It is said that in the momentarily icy atmosphere the only sound came from the cardinals, imitating a dozen kettles with a sharp collective intake of breath.

What I find so strange is that this mischievous Anglo-Sri Lankan Puck functions comfortably at the heart of the British establishment; royalty, Whitehall, members of the intelligence services, the Conservative Party – his contacts are legion. When I approached Dame Elizabeth Butler-Sloss (now Baroness), the then president of the Family Division and Britain's most senior female judge, to ask her about Desmond, she told me how she had arrived at a restaurant in St James's: 'There was Desmond with our mutual friend, Anne Schofield (the wife of the Chief Justice of Gibraltar) and then there was Benazir Bhutto – I had no idea Desmond knew Benazir, but he certainly does know a huge variety of people.' Dame Elizabeth then went on to describe Desmond as being, 'larger than life, which could irritate a rather more staid English male at the Bar, of which there are a considerable number, but I think he is much more interesting than them. He has an extrovert personality which I think is great fun and he is very successful, but maybe that rubs people up the wrong way.'

But whatever your background, whether you are a defendant, an instructing solicitor, a newspaper reporter, or just a member of the public wandering in from the streets to sit in the gallery, what is clear is that this extraordinary character creates great courtroom theatre and – most importantly – he wins cases.

For thirty years the society and gossip columns of newspapers have described him as the 'fashionable silk', reflecting those contacts and a client list ranging from Lord Brocket and the baronet Sir Rupert Mackeson, to millionaire Premiership footballers. A measure of his success came in a *Financial Times* report in 2002, following the Leeds United footballers double trial, which showed him among that tiny number at the Criminal Bar to have then broken the £1 million a year barrier.

Yet money has never been his primary consideration. Although a consistently high earner at the Criminal Bar since he began to practise, he has, on occasion, been moved to waive his fee to undertake a defence, to avoid what he felt would be a great injustice. But he has never been part of that group of barristers who have gone abroad to do death row cases on a pro bono basis.

He once agreed to undertake a private prosecution for no fees when he was instructed by the solicitor, Christopher Stewart-Moore. Stewart-Moore was representing Winnie Johnson, whose daughter was one of the victims of the Moors Murderess, Myra Hindley. Unable to get a speedy decision out of the Director of Public Prosecutions – to prosecute those responsible at the Royal Academy for defiling its walls with a portrait of the murderess painted with the handprints of children – the mother of one of the child victims had instructed Desmond to bring a private prosecution. Desmond took the view that this ghoulish decision was made all the worse by the Royal Academy when it went on to invite to the exhibition the parents of those Hindley had murdered. Winnie Johnson, one of the mothers, was outraged.

Desmond felt that if a portrait of Hitler had been painted using the hands of little Jewish children related to those who perished in concentration camps and such a picture was publicly exhibited, it would be likely to provoke a breach of the peace. In that he felt lay the possible criminal charge that could be brought against those at the Royal Academy. The preservation of the Queen's peace is the most ancient prerogative of the Crown, and there is a breach of the peace whenever harm is done or is likely to be done to a person or property through an assault or other disturbance.

However, before a private prosecution could be mounted, the Sensation exhibition closed, and with it the distress caused to the victims' parents. Before the closure the picture had been attacked by someone incensed by its inclusion.

Desmond's willingness to go from being one of the highest earning criminal QCs at the English Bar to facing the dangers of setting up a war crimes tribunal 'in theatre' in Sierra Leone, where British forces had moved in to stop anarchy and a savage civil war, is typical of the man. In steamy West Africa, earning a fraction of his regular income, alongside the largest concentration of UN peacekeeping troops in the world, he tried and succeeded in bringing to justice some of the major warlords in the sub-Saharan region – including a head of state.

I have covered criminal trials for thirty-five years and it is obvious that the destiny of every case is governed by the evidence. However, it is how that evidence is found and deployed in front of the jury that can swing the really tight trials. The intuitive feel some advocates have for getting at the truth and, if necessary, peeling a dissembling witness like an onion, is the hallmark of the finer performer. Then, of course, there is the final speech – a critical weapon in the armoury of counsel. The ability to transform the mundane by a captivating speech is among the most potent of instruments available to the advocate in our adversarial system. Any experienced barrister will tell you that perhaps eighty per cent of contested trials are either won or lost on the established facts, even before a case arrives in court. It is in perhaps only twenty per cent of contested cases that the skill and persuasiveness of counsel determines the outcome. It is within this range that the truly exceptional advocate makes his mark and wins his case against the merely very good.

All barristers have a number of traits, the equivalent of a criminal's modus operandi. Some expect their solicitors or the Crown Prosecution Service to feed them all the relevant material. Rather than sit behind a desk in the Temple, Desmond always tries to go out to the scene of a crime to pick up its flavour and that of its surroundings. On a Sunday afternoon in Jersey, during the Newall case, I watched Desmond, who had kitted himself out in wellington boots, a Barbour jacket and a rather fetching trilby hat, tramp through the mud with the police, who were searching the isolated field where the bodies had been buried.

Similarly, he would want to test the account of every witness, not just to take their word for it on paper. Nigel Creasy, senior Crown prosecutor in Sussex, remembers a vicious murder in the resort of Hastings, when a key issue was the time it took to walk between the scene of the crime and a snooker hall, where the defendant had claimed to have been at the time of the murder. 'So Desmond and I walked from the house to the snooker hall; and our investigation would have had scientific merit if the eminent QC had not insisted on stopping to eat candy floss on the way,' he laughed.

'It is Desmond's determination to personally test the evidence that is one of his very best hallmarks. I can only remember one other site visit by any other barrister in all my experience. Another characteristic of Desmond's is the way he checks the police photographs of the scene. If a witness says he saw so and so, Desmond would go and see if it was capable of being true. Photographs often distort distances.' He went on: 'Desmond works and works and works. I first instructed him in 1987 and he has never lost a case for us, that's why we use him, and on top of that he is good fun; why should the boring people get all the work? He is loyal and generous; the sort of man you would follow anywhere.

'He has got a wonderful brain and if he senses a witness has fallen for his chuckling style he will suddenly fire in a clinching question. A dissembling witness rarely saw the trap that closed around him. Because he is such a good defender, when prosecuting he looks at a case somewhat differently to a normal prosecutor; that is another reason why we used him to prosecute so often. There was an insurance-fraud case and we had drawn up an indictment. Desmond came in and redrafted it on the basis of: what would I least like to face if I was the defendant? As a result they all pleaded guilty and Desmond had done himself out of a six month trial!'

After he was elected a councilman in the City of London in 1980, Desmond declined to take any instructions to prosecute frauds investigated by the City police or the fraud squad, as he felt that it would be inappropriate to be instructed by the City solicitor when he might have to serve on the Police Committee of the Council. The Corporation of the City of London looks after the Old Bailey, which at that time heard virtually all the big City financial frauds. The City has its own police force, fraud squad and, indeed, its own Commissioner of Police.

Desmond has also developed an extensive knowledge of ballistics and forensic medicine, to challenge the experts in court in their chosen fields. But if I was to choose any single quality I would say it is his mastery of court craft, the years of experience to cajole, threaten and unpick a hostile witness, encourage, placate and reward a useful one and charm, enlighten, amuse and, above all convince, a jury. Put simply, it is advocacy and rhetoric which give him the cutting edge in so many trials.

Of the many solicitors who have instructed him over the years, Steven Barker of the well-established West End firm, Barker Gillette, told me: 'Desmond is the best jury advocate in this country, and I have seen them all in action.' He, too, speaks of Desmond's infinite capacity for sustained work. When Barker instructed him to lead Raymond Lewis for the accountant, Robert Price, in the Roger Levitt £34 million fraud trial that rocked the City of London in 1993, they took a vast number of files and flew off to Corfu, where they stayed in Sir Christopher Benson's villa. In three days, according to Barker, Desmond, working fifteen hours a day, got to the heart of complex City dealings. 'Price was the only defendant to be totally exonerated,' says the solicitor.

Mel Goldberg, another West End solicitor who specializes in representing celebrities in the sports and entertainment world, described Desmond as 'one of the most respected QCs in the profession. Had he not been an eminent QC then he would almost certainly have enjoyed an outstanding career as a politician.'

Politician? I think Desmond would be lost in modern politics, his wit and spontaneity ruined by the thought that a jest, especially a politically incorrect one, could cost votes. An orator he certainly is, but he needs the big space, a live audience, the old-fashioned hustings, when today the intrusive nature of the television camera lens requires a more 'fireside chat' approach. His is a style of a different age – and best suited to a courtroom.

In *The Final Score*, a book Goldberg co-wrote with goalkeeper Hans Segers about the football corruption trial, Goldberg remembers a speech about the evil of drugs Desmond had made at the Conservative Party conference in Brighton in 1984, when he called for a life sentence for 'drug barons who kill, kill and kill again'. That day, Leon Brittan, the Home Secretary, announced that the government would raise the maximum penalty for trafficking hard drugs. The following day the *Financial Times*, reviewing the previous day's conference, called Desmond's speech, 'the most powerful and passionate speech of the day.'

It was that very night that the IRA had chosen to try and kill the prime minister, who was staying at the Grand Hotel. The bomb killed five people and narrowly failed to claim the lives of Mrs Thatcher and the Cabinet. Fortunately for Desmond, he had left the hotel bar barely ten minutes before the bomb detonated, to return to London to prepare for court in the morning. Despite the mayhem, his words had obviously struck home, for in 1985 an Act introducing life sentences for drug dealers reached the statute book to cover certain Class A offences.

There was another occasion on which an IRA bomb nearly claimed his life. In October 1992, when Desmond was dining with Lord Sudeley in his flat in Melcombe Street, Marylebone, IRA bombers exploded one of their devices. The heavy curtains in the peer's dining room protected those at dinner from the shards of flying glass. Apparently, Desmond was the worst affected, for the blast blew the chocolate pudding he was just about to consume straight off his spoon. The *Daily Mail* headline the following day inexplicably said, 'Terror Bombers Get Their Just Desserts'.

To the public, the most famous barrister of modern times was the late George Carman, QC. He and Desmond were friends, although not particularly close, and they would occasionally dine together. They clashed in court only once and it was Desmond who emerged the victor, in a cut-throat defence at the Old Bailey in which two co-defendants blamed each other for a bizarre fraud on the Bank of Nigeria. Desmond was representing a senior bank official and Carman an American fraudster called Jaquith, in a conspiracy which could have realized £50 million.

The Nigerian bank official claimed he was in thrall to witchcraft and had been placed under an occult spell by associates of Carman's client which, were it to be true, would amount to duress under English law. In court, Desmond argued that the threat of the curse had forced the unfortunate man to bend to their will and falsify documents in order to save his life, while Carman used his considerable skills to rubbish the whole concept of witchcraft. Desmond carefully brought out before the jury that one of the other defendants, who had originally been charged, was not in the dock because he had died in custody.

Nigel Lambert, QC, who was representing a third defendant, admits now to feeling uncomfortable about the evidence of voodoo that Desmond sought to establish. Desmond cross-examined a prison officer to show that the man who died had stood in the middle of a circle he had drawn and begged the prison officers not to take him outside the chalk mark. They did. Within a short time, he was dead. He, too, Desmond established, had been the recipient of a communication from Carman's client.

After all the evidence was heard and shortly before prosecuting counsel, Nigel Mylne, QC, was to make his final speech to the jury, Desmond rose to his feet. He took the extraordinary step of applying for the case against his client to be thrown out on the basis that 'no English jury could possibly understand the grip that dark mystical forces could have on the minds of those born and reared on such esoteric beliefs', and that the Crown had failed in cross-examining his client to challenge the evidence of duress when he was in the witness box.

Desmond's persuasiveness was such that, to the astonishment of the wily Carman and the amazement of Lambert, Judge Derek Holden promptly stopped the case and directed the jury to find Desmond's client not guilty. No doubt the jurors are still mystified to this day but then, this was a case about magic.

Carman was livid and applied for a retrial for his client on the basis that, by acquitting Desmond's client in those circumstances, he had 'invested that defendant with the mantle of truth' and, as Desmond's client had blamed his client for the duress, the jury were likely to conclude that his client was guilty. The application was refused and Carman's client was convicted and jailed for seven years.

Carman did, however, have the consolation of having his client's conviction quashed in the Court of Appeal, on the grounds that he should have been given a retrial. During the course of that appeal, Their Lordships were equally staggered that any Old Bailey judge could have been persuaded to halt a trial and discharge an alleged fraudster because of the hidden mysteries of witchcraft that did not lie within the comprehension of a London jury.

Looking back now, Lambert's main memory of the case was the sense of unease all the counsel felt about the voodoo and the dramatic cut-throat nature of the defence between Desmond and George. Something else sticks in his mind: 'I do remember that Desmond sat next to me. During a quiet part of the trial, when he was sitting down, he asked the police to let him have a look at an exhibit in the case, not yet produced for the jury. He was given a briefcase taken earlier from my client's home... to my horror, as I watched through the corner of my eye, he found in it, buried below a lot of papers, a most incriminating document against my client, missed by the police – and, I admit, by all of my team – but later to be used by Desmond to try and convict my client.'

Desmond succeeded.

Judges are enormously difficult to impress, but Mr Justice Rose (later Lord Justice Rose and vice president of the Criminal Division of the Court of Appeal) privately expressed his admiration for Desmond's advocacy in an unprecedented tribute in the middle of a trial.

Notu Hoon, a long-standing friend and colleague in his chambers, remembers the case as one of the most horrific murders imaginable: a husband cutting his wife's throat so brutally her head was almost severed from the body. Their small daughter, aged no more than four, had come downstairs to find her mother's corpse in the living room and tried to replace the head, hanging by a thread of the spinal cord, but only succeeded in putting it back the wrong way around. When a postman came to the door he could hear the plaintive cry, 'I can't wake my mummy up, I can't wake my mummy up.'

Said Hoon, 'It was the first time I had met Desmond and it was quite by chance, as we had been instructed separately. The defendant was a Pathan from the North-West Frontier Province of Pakistan and came from a highly respectable family. The defendant and victim had gone through the full rites of an Islamic marriage and costly wedding gifts had been forthcoming from his family.'

However, unknown to him, it was a bigamous marriage, as the English victim was already married to a British citizen working as a helicopter pilot for the United Nations. The victim went on to form an association with another man and was clearly stringing him along while he was staying in east London and she was living in Hinckley, Leicestershire. She aborted the defendant's baby, taunting him with the fact she had done so. Abortion is anathema in Sharia law, but as far as the trial was concerned there was no possible defence to the homicide.

Hoon went on, 'Desmond was absolutely brilliant, which is why I still revere him to this day. The issue was murder or manslaughter and he crystallized it in his own inimitable way. We ran the four horsemen of the apocalypse defence and all simultaneously – diminished responsibility, provocation, even an element of self-defence and then appealed to the jury for mercy.

'The prosecution's closing speech took one hour and was totally unmemorable. Desmond made a four and a quarter hour speech in which everybody was on the edge of their seats. It was the most fantastic speech I had ever heard and, thirty or so years later, I have not heard a speech like it. By the end his shirt was dripping with sweat from the effort. The jury had hung on every word.'

Mr Justice Rose had only recently been appointed to the red robe. The trial was in Leicester and he was invited by the local Bar as the guest of honour to a circuit dinner, which fell on a night when he was still summing up to the jury. Desmond, who was doing his first murder since taking silk, was another guest, but Hoon remembers he had to pay for his supper.

He continued, 'Rose made a speech which went along the lines of: "I apologize for not having been able to see more of you all but I have been engaged in trying a case of murder." Then in words I will never forget he added: "It is a trial in which my learned co-guest Mr Desmond de Silva, QC, has made a speech of such force and intensity that I believe that a serious miscarriage of justice may occur."

'It was almost unheard of to comment in such terms in the middle of a case in which he was the judge and he was only halfway through his summing up.'

The jury was out for a considerable length of time mulling over Desmond's speech in this otherwise straightforward murder and, eventually, the potential miscarriage of justice was averted as they convicted the defendant.

Humour is one of the advocate's greatest weapons but when it is heavy-handed, laboured and unfunny – and there are any number of barristers who suffer from this problem – it is plain embarrassing and counterproductive. When it is witty, well-timed and off the cuff it can create a relaxed and receptive mood among the jurors in which to put forward the arguments for their consideration.

Judge Zoe Smith remembers a typical example of Desmond's unique courtroom style when she was at the Bar: 'It was a four-month trial that concerned a conspiracy to manufacture millions of ecstasy tablets in a pill factory in Enfield,' she told me.

'The profits were going to be vast and, if convicted, the ringleaders were looking at terms of twenty years' imprisonment. The prosecution was represented by the future QC, Peter Clarke; Desmond was leading Colin Campbell for Verciglio, the Italian factory owner, with Alan Newman, QC, leading for the notorious drug dealer Stephen Raymond. I was for a man called Unstead.

'The star witness for the prosecution was a highly intelligent supergrass who had been in prison for some years – before he escaped. He was also an amateur chemist. I remember the trial for one outstanding moment. The supergrass was a tall, beaky man who loomed like a vulture with his talons out in the witness box. He was fixated with the film *Dune*, and kept using phrases from the film. Desmond cross-examined him destructively for four days, during which he came to examine the diaries the super grass had kept, which contained a mass of numbers the witness said were the telephone numbers of prostitutes.

'The defence, on the other hand, were trying to prove, using the last digit of each number, that these were the supergrass's coded offshore bank accounts, hiding profits from earlier dealings in drugs. In the course of his cross-examination Desmond put to the supergrass that as he had been in prison for a number of years, these figures could not possibly have been prostitutes' numbers. To this the supergrass replied, "As you may not know, Mr de Silva, you can get these numbers from the *Daily Sport* newspaper, which is available in prison." The witness then added sarcastically, "Do you know the *Daily Sport*, Mr de Silva?" Desmond's immediate response was, "Of course. But I only take it for the financial pages." The jury absolutely loved it. In the end Verciglio, Raymond and Unstead, who were the principal figures in the dock, were acquitted, while some four others were convicted.'

The first time Steven Barker briefed Desmond was a 1984 case, which was to turn into the longest-running charity fraud heard at Knightsbridge Crown Court. From the unpromising start of a thirty-six-charge indictment against a defendant matured a solicitor/barrister partnership which has lasted almost twenty years and has never lost a jury trial.

'I provide the bullets, he aims and fires the gun,' Barker, one of the hardest-working solicitors in London, told me. 'But whatever the bullets, you have to know how to fire them. I would have Desmond every time.' I know that Desmond is a keen shot and I expect he also calibrates the gun and, from the ammunition, selects an appropriate bullet depending on his prey.

Recalling this otherwise unremarkable case, Barker gave me three examples of Desmond's court craft which, small in themselves, played an important part in winning over the jury and achieving an acquittal for his client who, if convicted, was facing a very long sentence of imprisonment for preying on vulnerable charities by looting their funds while pretending to manage their affairs.

In the course of the trial the defence needed to call a forensic accountant to shed light on a complex monetary aspect of the case. Having given his evidence, this witness took a seat in court beside Barker, Desmond's instructing solicitor. No sooner had the witness sat down than the judge turned to Desmond for some assistance, as the judge was unclear as to what the defence case was. Desmond tried to summarize the calculations on which he hoped to persuade the court of the negligible benefit which would have accrued from the alleged fraud. Advocacy is one thing but mental arithmetic was clearly another and, as Desmond vainly battled with the pluses and minuses, and carrying over from one column to another, the accountant, sitting at the back of the court, was becoming visibly more and more agitated. In a combination of hoarse stage whispers and anxious body language, the expert was telling Barker in no uncertain manner that Desmond was getting it all wrong. Sensibly the solicitor knew better than to ever interrupt his counsel in full spate.

With things going from bad to worse and with Desmond mixing his long division and his three times table, and vainly casting around for the piece of paper containing the number he had first thought of, a woman in the front row of the jury, who had been following the evidence, pencil in hand, leaned forward and said: 'Mr de Silva, the answer is twenty-seven.'

'Thank you, madam,' he sighed with relief, 'Thank you very much!' He then pressed on with another point as the court settled down to accept the juror's calculation. It cannot have hurt his case to have had on his side this very self-satisfied-looking female juror who was clearly good with figures and who, no doubt, in the retiring room, played a significant part in the decision to acquit.

In the same case, the prosecutor, Ann Goddard, QC, later a highly respected judge at the Old Bailey, rose to her feet to object to one of Desmond's occasional habits of making a speech to the jury in the guise of asking a question and, as Barker recalls it, she said, 'I hesitate to rise to my feet, My Lord, but this is yet another of Mr de Silva's soliloquies.'

'Yes, Miss Goddard,' replied Judge Monro Davies, 'but I find this one particularly enlightening.'

The jury, having acquitted the defendant of thirty-five of the thirty-six charges, were unable to agree on the thirty-sixth. A retrial was ordered on the remaining charge, an allegation of obtaining bank borrowings by deception, in which the key witness was a bank manager who told the court that he had agreed to the loan at a meeting in his office in the bank, where the defendant had made representations that turned out to be false.

When it came to cross-examination, repeating every critical facet of his evidence, Desmond, metaphorically, took the bank manager down the garden path and closed the gate behind him.

Languidly, he asked the confident bank manager, 'And what date was this meeting?'

'August 26,' replied the witness.

'Are you sure?'

'Positive.'

'You could not be mistaken?'

'No, I remember it well.'

Turning to Barker sitting behind him, Desmond said solemnly: 'Fetch me the document.' Every pair of eyes in the court watched as the solicitor rose slowly from his seat and walked to the back of the court. He unlocked the filing cabinet, which held a vast number of documents, and extracted a desk diary. Locking up the cabinet behind him he walked back and passed it over to Desmond.

Handing it to the witness, Desmond said, 'Would you care to open it to 26 August and read to the jury the two words that appear beside that day in August?'

Turning to the relevant date, the manager's previously serene features suddenly began to look ashen and sickly. Replying in a faint voice, he said, 'Bank Holiday.'

'Sorry, I didn't quite catch that,' said Desmond.

'Bank Holiday,' repeated the witness.

'I'm afraid the jury may not have...'

'Bank Holiday,' he repeated, by now thoroughly crushed.

'Well, I don't know what happens at your branch on a bank holiday, but I know mine is closed all day!'

It came as no surprise to anybody when, once the judge had summed up the case to the jury, they returned with a verdict of not guilty in barely twenty minutes.

Overdramatic? Possibly. Cruel? Well, needs must when a client's liberty is at stake. There is an éclat about Desmond which would not have gone amiss on the stage. But then, an element of the actor is an essential part of every successful defence barrister, whose primary aim is to communicate his client's case to the jury as effectively as he can to achieve an acquittal. To the solicitor it was a spellbinding *coup de théâtre* which the jury would not forget; nor did he. This was the beginning of a very successful run of cases for Desmond from this West End firm of solicitors.

Other friends and Bar colleagues admire Desmond's unrivalled ability to produce the *mot juste* at exactly the right time. On one such occasion Desmond was cross-examining an undercover police officer who had infiltrated the Kurdish terrorist organization, the PKK, but was proving rather cocky in trying to score points off the defence.

Desmond began by asking: 'Tell me officer, it is right, is it not, that to infiltrate a terrorist organization is a very dangerous occupation?' The witness rather sneeringly replied: 'It depends on which organization you are trying to infiltrate.' Turning to the jury Desmond delivered the put-down: 'I dare say you would rather infiltrate the Salvation Army than the IRA.' Faced with mocking laughter, the officer gave no more trouble.

In 1982, Desmond lost a case in court, but his influence outside its walls saved a very different type of defendant from an unknown fate. He was retained to represent a young Tanzanian called Yassin Membar, one of five charged with hijacking a Boeing 737 on an internal Tanzanian flight, at gunpoint, and forcing it to land at Stansted. It was the first aircraft hijacking by a group who were escaping an African tyranny.

This group of students were demanding democratic elections in Tanzania and were being hunted by President Julius Nyerere's secret police. Fearing for their lives after being accused of plotting against him, they decided to hijack an internal flight within Tanzania and come to Britain. Here, they hoped to seek asylum and continue their campaign for democracy in socialist Tanzania. Yassin's older brother, Moussa, was the leader of the group. Intending no violence, Moussa used an imitation gun and candlesticks made to look like dynamite.

After a twenty-six-hour siege at Stansted, they gave themselves up without bloodshed, once they had received assurances that they would at least be considered for asylum. This gave rise to the very first aircraft-hijacking trial in Britain.

When the trial opened at the Old Bailey, before Mr Justice Woolf, later the Lord Chief Justice, all the defendants claimed that they had not only fled to save their lives but that there never really was a hijacking because the captain of the aircraft, who was sympathetic to their cause, was part of the plot and had agreed to help them leave the country. He had asked them to stage a fake hijack with the imitation weapons in order to protect his position back in Tanzania. Coming from Tanzania to give evidence at the Old Bailey, the captain steadfastly denied any such knowledge or collusion.

Desmond's cross-examination peeled him like an onion.

'You were on an internal flight within Tanzania?' he began.

'Yes.'

'For how many years had you been doing this internal flight?'

'A number of years.'

'Of course, you would have needed a lot of fuel to have got you to Stansted?'

'Yes.'

'In fact, you claim you were forced to refuel in Athens and then fly on to Stansted?'

'Yes.'

'When your flight bag was examined by the police, is it correct that by some marvellous coincidence it contained the landing charts for Athens?'

'Yes.'

'Likewise, it was a stroke of good fortune that your flight bag contained the landing charts for Stansted?'

'Yes.'

'Therefore, by accident, you just happened to have the charts for the two airports you landed at?'

'Yes.'

Desmond had established beyond any doubt that this captain was in on it and his questioning had the jury exactly where he wanted them. He then went on to suggest to the captain that he sympathized with the pilot's inability to be totally frank, as Tanzania was then a dictatorship and he had to return there.

However, this was one occasion when Desmond's adroitness was trumped by the judge, who directed the jury that they might well consider that the captain of the aircraft had voluntarily flown the defendants to London but that that was not sufficient in law, as control of an aircraft is also in the hands of ground control, and that there was not a shred of evidence to suggest that any of the staff on the ground had collaborated with the hijackers.

On that direction to the jury, conviction was inevitable. With a resourcefulness which was to characterize the future Lord Woolf, the judge had neatly pulled the legal rug from under what Desmond and his fellow counsel had felt was a complete defence. However, the judge went on to pass relatively light sentences of between three and eight years. Perhaps he had been won over to the conclusion that these young men were fleeing for their lives, and borne in mind Desmond's mitigation, which contained the memorable phrase, 'My Lord, all these young men ever wanted was the right to live in a free society – unhindered, unmenaced and unafraid.'

Yassin was released on bail in 1984 and allowed to stay in Britain temporarily, but Desmond used his undoubted influence in writing to Home Office minister David Waddington to fight for full asylum status. Against the odds, and to the anger of many Conservative MPs, Yassin was eventually granted indefinite leave to stay in Britain. Desmond was then on Mrs Thatcher's powerful think tank the Centre for Policy Studies, and did not hesitate to use his contacts if he thought the cause was just. Since then, Yassin has proved his worth to his new country by becoming a legal executive with a firm of London solicitors. However, an indication of what could have happened to him was the fate that befell his brother, who was returned to Tanzania. He was arrested, jailed for his political opposition to Nyerere, and died in hospital a relatively young man.

Another merciful outcome came in a case in which Desmond made legal history at the Old Bailey. A barrister had pleaded with Desmond to defend her father, who was charged with murder and attempted murder. Once a high-ranking officer in the Pakistani Army, Mustaq Khan had settled in Brighton, but on one night in June 1995 he took his old service revolver and went round to where his two sons lived. As they watched television he entered their flat, shot one of them dead and then shot the other. He left believing he had killed them both and returned home to sleep, but the second son was lucky enough to survive. When later arrested, he told the police: 'My sons do not care, they do not listen and they do not obey me.'

On the face of things this looked an open and shut case of intentional killing, a planned execution – murder. A tragedy certainly on the face of it; a proud man confounded and driven to distraction by children brought up in a different culture he could neither understand nor tolerate.

The defence accepted the fact that he had carried out the shootings, but Desmond argued that Khan was under the influence of a rare but frightening side effect of the drug Prozac, which the prosecution accepted had been prescribed by his doctors. This was the first time that the Prozac defence had been used in England. Wheelchair-bound, following a stroke after the shootings, Khan pleaded not guilty to the murder of one son, the attempted murder of the other and an alternative charge of causing grievous bodily harm.

In order to destroy the Prozac defence, the prosecution, led by Heather Hallett, QC, called as a Crown witness a scientist who specialized in drugs of this kind. He told the court that of the 30 million people who had been prescribed Prozac, there had been very few examples of a severe reaction leading to violence.

Desmond's cross-examination of the scientist began in this way: 'You say from your research that you know of 186 examples of violent reactions after taking Prozac?'

'Yes.'

'That's not much consolation if my client is the 187th, is it?'

'I suppose not.'

A later cross-examination went as follows: 'The whole drift of your evidence has been to suggest that Prozac is an absolutely safe drug?'

'Yes.'

'Prozac is made by the pharmaceutical company, Eli Lilly?'

'Yes.'

'By the way, do Eli Lilly make a contribution to your research programme?'

'Yes.'

'How much?'

'You will have to ask my accountants.'

In a trice, Desmond had thrown the evidence of the Crown's expert into doubt by skilfully showing he may not have been wholly disinterested in championing the cause of Prozac. Next he took the brave step of actually calling the surviving son, Zia, thirty-six, who told the jury he was bewildered by the shooting because his father was 'a committed family man' and his dead brother Sujad 'the apple of my father's eye'. Finally Desmond told the jury that these were 'motiveless crimes committed through illness, not wickedness; through abnormality of mind, not murderous purpose. The defendant is now a man broken by ill health and mentally tortured by remorse. He has been forgiven by his family because they, above all, were able to see the mental collapse from which the offences were born.'

The jury were out for days. They could not agree on the murder charge. They could not agree on the attempted murder charge. They could not even agree on grievous bodily harm. Eventually, the prosecution, in despair, accepted the defendant's plea of guilty to manslaughter on the grounds of diminished responsibility, which the defence had offered in the first instance but which the prosecution had refused to accept. A relatively lenient sentence was imposed, which led to his release about two and a half years later.

Not every case, however, goes according to plan – even when you win. In 1985, Desmond defended Alan McQueen, who was charged with the murder of an antiques dealer, Roy Porjes. Michael Worsley, QC, prosecuting, told the Old Bailey that the victim had 'vanished off the face of the earth' in Greece two years earlier on his 'European dream trip' and his body had still not been discovered.

But Desmond, acting on the firm instructions of his client, convinced the jury that McQueen was innocent of murder and been left to take the blame when his partner, Michael Latham, twenty-six, had fled to the United States. It was Latham who had delivered the fatal blows to Porjes in a caravan on a campsite outside Athens, said Desmond.

McQueen was acquitted of murder but convicted of manslaughter on the basis that he was party to an agreement with Latham to rob Porjes with the use of some low-key violence and that Latham had gone too far. He was also convicted of conspiracy to defraud, using cheques and credit cards belonging to the victim, and was sentenced to ten years' imprisonment.

Sentencing, the Recorder of London, Sir James Miskin, QC, said the victim, 'far away from home and family,' was killed, and robbed jointly by both men, who made a 'skilful and successful concealment of the body' and went on a spending spree with the victim's cheques and cards.

The case had only come to court because Sam Goodman, Porjes's stepfather and an Auschwitz survivor, had refused to accept the disappearance. He turned detective and discovered that £5,000 worth of cheques were being passed through his stepson's account, and that the motor caravan he had been driving around Europe had just been sold at a garage in the West Sussex resort of Bognor Regis.

Goodman showed the garage owner a picture of Porjes, to confirm it had been sold by an impostor, and a young mechanic remembered the mystery man had been accompanied by an attractive blonde, who worked as a receptionist at a local hotel.

Mr Goodman, then sixty-five, and his wife went to see the girl, Stephanie Belcher, and then confronted her live-in boyfriend, Alan McQueen, face-to-face. Police were called in and Belcher, who had met McQueen and Latham in Nice and travelled with them to Greece, turned against him and gave evidence for the Crown.

McQueen's own camper van, complete with the copiously blood-stained mattress on which Porjes had clearly been killed, was found in Yugoslavia, where the killers had abandoned it, but there was no sign of the body.

Angered that McQueen had been cleared of murder, and determined to find out where his stepson's body was hidden, Goodman kept up his campaign and maintained a vigil outside Blundeston prison, Lowestoft. Three years after the trial, McQueen cracked. From his cell on F Wing he asked his probation officer for a map of Greece, and drew crosses on the area where police could search for the body. In a letter to Goodman, he drew a diagram showing a curving road, trees and rocks, which he said should identify the exact location.

On prison notepaper he wrote: 'I cannot live a lie any longer and I know I must put your mind at rest, if that is at all possible... I am also writing to His Honour Judge James Miskin, QC, to set the record straight; I am guilty of taking your son's life.' He also wrote to Desmond, apologizing for giving him false instructions saying he had never touched the deceased.

Of course, the double jeopardy law then in force meant McQueen could not stand trial a second time for the murder, but never has there been such a stark and dramatic demonstration of the perennial dilemma faced by every barrister. All defendants have the right to expect the best possible defence and counsel have to follow the instructions they are given, even if they run the risk that what they are told turns out to be lies. Here, Desmond had secured the acquittal of McQueen on a murder charge that he was to confess to.

Barristers have their favourite courts, often associated with their more celebrated cases, or because they are situated in attractive and appealing locations. In Desmond's case, the Old Bailey is undoubtedly his favourite, the most famous court in the land, if not the world, memorably described by Rumpole's creator John Mortimer as 'le palais de justice.' Outside London he, like me, loves Lewes Crown Court, built in the shadow of the castle built by William de Warenne as a stronghold in Sussex.

During trials in Lewes, Desmond never commuted from his home in Chelsea but preferred to stay at the poet Shelley's old manor house, or at the historic White Hart. From the latter, all he had to do after breakfast was to cross the road to be under the pillared portico of this grand old courthouse; a few paces more and he was in the robing room.

Not long before Christmas 1994, I drove the few miles from my home to Lewes Crown Court to cover another murder that Desmond had been instructed to prosecute. It was an unremarkable killing – a domestic stabbing by a husband of his wife, the mother of his four children, as she put on the kettle for a cup of tea. Nevertheless, this case demonstrates the original and colourful way in which he was to explain a complex psychological illness, which psychiatrists call morbid jealousy syndrome.

Accepting the defence plea that this was manslaughter on the grounds of diminished responsibility, Desmond told the court the key to the case was a white handkerchief found by the defendant, which had convinced him – quite wrongly – that his wife was having an affair.

'It is clear beyond doubt that this frenzied killing of his wife was as a result of what can properly be called the Othello Syndrome,' he said, opening the case for the prosecution. 'A morbid jealousy took hold of his mind and led him to believe, quite wrongly, that this poor woman was being unfaithful to him. The paranoid delusions caused him to find proof of infidelity in such imagined evidence as a partly-opened window, through which he was convinced she had bidden her lover. One week before the killing he found a handkerchief, and his mind was fixed on the idea that it was contaminated by her lover.' Psychiatrists, said Desmond, had confirmed that the handkerchief had triggered the decision to kill and the accused was sent to a psychiatric hospital. To compare this domestic killing to a Shakespearean tragedy, committed when the accused was in the grip of Othello Syndrome, was typical of his use of imagery.

In 1997, I was sent to Preston Crown Court to cover the trial of a homeless drug addict called Terence Storey who had stabbed to death a talented young vicar – a Wykehamist with a double first from Oxford – on the altar of his church. Amid the huge publicity that greeted this terrible crime, there had been a great deal of speculation about the background to the relationship between the vicar and his assassin, but nothing had been substantiated. Sitting in the press gallery, I was not alone in anticipating that many of the unanswered questions would have to be cleared up in open court.

Storey made the rare plea of guilty to murder and the case was opened by Richard Henriques, QC, who very properly stuck intently to the facts of the murder, without explaining anything of the background to the case.

Desmond was defending and, in the press box, we felt certain that his mitigation must delve deeper, to explain why Storey had murdered this vicar. However, he rose to his feet and told Mr Justice Kay, 'Everything I need to say in mitigation to you, My Lord, I will submit in writing for the purpose of your recommendation to the Home Secretary for the minimum term of the mandatory life sentence this young man must serve before he is considered for parole.'

We were all aghast! We felt cheated. As a result, my potential front-page story was relegated to page eighteen. On reflection, of course, Desmond had, no doubt, served the best interests of his client, as well as ensuring that the Church of England and the victim's family were spared all embarrassment.

In his chambers at the High Court, his opponent that day, by now Mr Justice Henriques, remembers being staggered by Desmond's nerve. 'That was the only time I have ever seen it done, I have never encountered anybody trying that before,' he told me. 'Some judges would say: "This is a public court of law, the public are entitled to hear the mitigation." I would be tempted to take that course; think what would happen if everybody did it! But no doubt it was a hyper-sensitive case and I'm sure he acted quite properly in doing so.'

No profile, analysis or assessment of Desmond's life at the Bar could be complete without chronicling some examples of his astonishing capacity to consume a huge amount of drink into a frighteningly late hour and still emerge next morning bright and eager for battle in court. Some stories have entered into legend and some are open to exaggeration to the bounds of urban myth; but I shall concentrate only on a selection of stories, which have been independently verified.

Desmond was defending in a long-running drugs case at Lewes in the early 1980s when the Crown was led by Hubert Dunn, QC, a very proper and intensely serious counsel, who was in the habit of rising at 6 a.m. to take a walk on the downs in order to clear his mind and think over the legal complexities before court at 10.30. As he set out, according to my source at the Crown Prosecution Service, he would regularly meet Desmond emerging from a taxi after a hard night's wassailing in Brighton. Both parties would gaze at each other with a look of total incomprehension at the other's chosen lifestyle.

Again, in Lewes, Desmond was prosecuting in a trial which became known as the Tea Dance Murder. His junior was a pleasant but homely barrister, Bernard Phelvin, who admired Desmond's skills at the Bar but was somewhat terrified by Desmond's reputation for living it up outside court.

Desmond had told him that he believed in having two large whiskies before lunch, as well as claret with the meal and a couple of double brandies after, before they all returned to court, and that he expected his guests to keep him company. And that that was just for the normal adjournment between 1 and 2 p.m. Imagine the face of this poor man, halfway through the morning of the trial, when a psychiatrist failed to arrive and the defence had run out of witnesses and his leader turned to him with a look of glee and, rubbing his hands in anticipation, announced at 11.54 a.m.: 'Luncheon, dear boy?'

In Gibraltar for the Newall extradition proceedings, author and journalist Barry Wood and *Daily Telegraph* reporter Paul Stokes found themselves caught up in a mammoth session, which finally ended in Desmond's suite at 5 a.m. By 9 a.m., Desmond was down and awaiting a substantial cooked breakfast of three poached eggs, four sausages and several rashes of bacon, prior to a busy day in court. The two hacks were so *hors de combat* that Wood did not emerge from his hotel room for three days and the only sign of life was the occasional plaintive call to room service for a bottle of mineral water. Stokes swore never to be entertained by Desmond again.

The wonderful old inn by the cloisters of Winchester Cathedral, the Wykeham Arms, was the base for two of the defence teams in the Grobbelaar football corruption trial, in which Desmond defended Wimbledon goalkeeper Hans Segers. Both Rodney Klevan, QC for Grobbelaar, and Desmond settled into the Wykeham Arms, along with prosecution counsel, David Calvert-Smith, while the two future QCs, Jerome Lynch for Richard Lim and Trevor Burke for John Fashanu, rented a house that Desmond was to label the Love Shack.

At the Wykeham, Desmond used to hold court most nights until 3 a.m. One night the beleaguered landlord came down in his pyjamas and begged: 'Mr de Silva, we love having you here but, please, think of my staff!' A sensible compromise was soon worked out, with the bar staff handing over the keys with which Desmond was to lock up the establishment before he turned in. The empty bottles were totted up in the morning to calculate his bill.

The then prosecutor, now Sir David Calvert-Smith, QC, for five years the Director of Public Prosecutions and then a High Court judge, looks back on the out of court hours with half a smile and half a shudder. 'We were all living out of a suitcase in the Wykeham Arms and nights there with Desmond were not something that people of a frail constitution like me could do more than once a week,' he told me. 'I was fairly insulated, as my room was in the Bakehouse on the other side of the road to the pub, and I could withdraw tactfully when Desmond was ordering the Armagnac.'

In midtrial, a diary reporter from my own newspaper, the *London Evening Standard*, managed to see the bill and reported, I thought rather unsportingly, that Desmond had consumed over £2,000 worth of Armagnac in just two weeks. The reporter even rang his wife Katarina at home in London, but she took the news without turning a hair and, while pointing out her husband was an enormously generous man, who entertained his friends, blithely suggested that she thought the bill could have been higher.

Such stories contribute to a rounded picture of Desmond, but there has never been one judge, barrister or instructing solicitor – let alone client – who has ever complained that his legal skills have been impaired in any way, either in or out of court. He has never appeared to live within the boring confines of middle-class life.

## 20

# The Man Who Would Be King

FOR LONDONERS CRAMMED ON TO TRAINS, TUBES AND BUSES AS THEY made their way home on the cold night of 27 January 1995, the attention-grabbing splash headline on the front page of the *London Evening Standard* would have been irresistible – 'ROYAL AIDE ARRESTED'.

The running royal scandal at the time was only the latest in a series of highly public and clearly damaging recent episodes; not least the Princess of Wales's alleged affair with the antique dealer, Oliver Hoare. Loyal subjects who saw the billboards that day would have sighed, republicans would have chuckled with glee.

John Kennedy, the trusted chief of staff to Prince Michael of Kent, and a young public relations consultant, Anthony Bailey, had been arrested and interviewed by Special Branch over allegations of an alleged plot to blackmail a member of the Libyan royal family – the al-Senussi family – which had ruled in Morocco, Algeria and Libya at various times since the end of the eighth century. They had been ousted from power in Libya in 1969, by Colonel Muammar Gaddafi, at a time when King Idris was having medical treatment abroad.

In 1995, midway between the Queen's *annus horribilis* and the death of Diana, the public's interest in the highs and lows of royal life was at its zenith. The press scented the prospect of a spectacular Old Bailey trial that would take readers into the corridors and state rooms of Kensington Palace itself, with the possibility of a member of the royal family having to go into the witness box. In the background to the story lay allegations of cash being paid for a parliamentary Early Day Motion, signed by forty-one almost exclusively Tory MPs, at a time when John Major's government was being swamped by sleaze.

If the case reached the Old Bailey it would be one of the memorable trials of the decade; a potential disaster for the royal family, at a time when they could least afford it, and possibly the last straw for a crippled government – then in power with a majority of just one. However, as committal proceedings were subsequently to prove, all the allegations were based on a lie; but it was a lie that brought danger close to the heart of the government, and caused considerable anxiety at both Kensington and Buckingham Palaces. Something had to be done.

A matter of days after this story broke in the *London Evening Standard*, the *Times'* Diary reported that Desmond de Silva, QC had been retained for the defence. To many, including the Fourth Estate, it came as no surprise. Desmond, whose wife was the Queen's niece and cousin to Prince Michael of Kent – Kennedy's employer – was the obvious choice. Within six months of this appointment, the reputations of the unfortunate Messrs Kennedy and Bailey had been restored and the palace and the government had escaped calamitous revelations.

The press and public were deprived of their trial but more importantly, a complete charlatan, the self-styled 'Prince' Idris al-Senussi, was exposed as a vain, ruthlessly ambitious, arrogant, deceitful and dangerous rogue, prepared to lie and cheat his way to power.

Behind the newspaper headlines and the police investigation lay a tale of princes and politicians, policeman and spies; above all there was to be the unmasking of a fake claimant to a Middle Eastern throne and international power politics from Washington to Whitehall, Baghdad and Tripoli. The story had all the hallmarks of a Victorian plot from Britain's imperial heyday, when rulers abroad were brought down or Britain's nominees were put upon thrones.

As he terminated the case, the east London stipendiary magistrate Inigo Bing described the evidence he had heard as encapsulating 'duplicity and intrigue which has taken us from Pall Mall to Libya, from Westminster to Qatar.'

The story began in 1989 and 1990, when Saddam Hussein was growling his threats to neighbouring Kuwait. Idris al-Senussi, a rich businessman and member of a cadet branch of the Libyan royal family, spotted a chance to seize power for himself in his homeland, and cunningly decided to exploit the developing international situation to his own advantage.

Ever since he had taken power in a military coup, Gaddafi had espoused his own political system – a combination of socialism and Islam. Within that system he held a tight grip on Libya, and used its oil revenues to promote subversion and terrorism abroad: the Lockerbie bombing and the shooting of WPC Yvonne

Fletcher in London being just two of the outrages associated with Libya. To the West he was a threat worth removing and, should that happen, Idris wanted the support of Washington and London to promote himself as the alternative head of state. After all, had not a British military government ruled Libya after the defeat of the Germans and Italians in World War II? Had not Britain played a major part in the creation of the Kingdom of Libya in 1951? And, did not King Idris, who had ascended the throne, then have the full support of Britain?

With all these thoughts uppermost in his mind, Idris al-Senussi went about spinning his web of intrigue to restore the Libyan monarchy, with himself as King. In reality he was no nearer the throne than being the second son of the sixth son of the second son of the younger brother of the last king's father. He was not even entitled to use the title of HRH. As Desmond was to say, graphically, in his final submission to the court, 'Idris began his ascent to the throne of Libya on a ladder of lies, the rungs of which have been exposed in this court.'

In truth, were there to have been a restoration of the monarchy, the heir to the throne was the son of Crown Prince al-Hassan of Libya who, 'by his Will' appointed his son, Mohammed, the next Crown prince and head of the royal house of Libya. Unfortunately, after the overthrow of the royal family in 1969, most of its members, including the true heir, Mohammed, were kept either under house arrest or thrown in prison by Gaddafi.

Idris, the false claimant, took advantage of the confusion that prevailed and the fact that the royal family had dropped from sight. Living in Italy, be began to promote his own claims. In February 1990, he put out a press release in Venice to the effect that he was the heir to the throne of Libya and was willing to return as its spiritual and political leader. He had calculated that if Iraq invaded Kuwait, to which Saddam had laid claim, Gaddafi might support his fellow Arab dictator. Indeed, when Iraq did invade Kuwait, the Libyan president claimed there were 'thousands of Libyans offering to fight for Saddam.' Idris thought the United States and Britain would drive Saddam's troops out of Kuwait and then go on to Baghdad. Then, perhaps, they might even take the opportunity to topple Gaddafi as well.

This was Idris's big chance; it was well within the bounds of possibility that the West, as it was later to do with Afghanistan, might look for a replacement leader from the deposed royal family. So Idris put his plan into operation. He hired public relations consultants in London to promote himself as the rightful heir and the one to replace Gaddafi, while holding himself out to be a friend of the West and condemning any support of terrorism.

On 26 April 1990, members of both Houses of Parliament assembled in Committee Room 16 of the House of Commons to hear Idris spell out his vision for the future of Libya, and the role that Britain could play in helping him on to the throne. In an impassioned plea he told them the time had come for Gaddafi to be overthrown in favour of the monarchy, which would bring stability to the country and be widely supported by the people. What's more, he was the man to be King. A total of forty-one MPs were so impressed by this wealthy, well-dressed man, with a Learjet and homes in Mayfair, Rome and the south of France, that they lost no time in signing an Early Day Motion hailing Idris as 'the heir presumptive to the throne of Libya.'

Not long afterward, when Saddam invaded Kuwait in August 1990, everything seemed to be on target for Idris's plan. Even Gaddafi had begun to make the noises supportive of Iraq that Idris had shrewdly anticipated.

Emboldened by the MPs' unquestioning support, Idris wrote a letter to the *Times* claiming to be the grandson of the late King Idris. It was a patent lie and a falsehood which was to haunt him in the witness box years later, as Desmond exposed this fraudulent claim. But when the first Gulf War ended, with Gaddafi having failed to throw his troops behind Saddam, Idris found himself back at square one. Far from the coalition forces overthrowing Gaddafi, they did not even enter Baghdad to overthrow Saddam Hussein. Idris, however, was not going to be blown off course. With Gaddafi continuing to threaten the West's interests, Idris sensed that there may be another chance to place himself as number one contender to head any new regime in Tripoli.

Waterman & Associates of Washington are a fashionable and influential firm of international and political consultants. With Charles Waterman – a former CIA officer and vice chairman of the National Intelligence Council – as its president; Edward Peck – a former US ambassador to Teheran and Baghdad – as a director; and having another director with extensive combat and political experience, Michael E. Dash, Idris had found the firm he needed. They came up with a $2.5 million proposal to 'portray His Highness as a genuine alternative to Gaddafi' with a further assessment that, 'There exists a genuine and broad-based desire among most top-level Clinton administration officials for Gaddafi's removal from power.'

Now Idris needed help in London. Two years earlier, in Montenegro, he had met John Kennedy, a distant relation to the Montenegran royal family, while he was attending the reburial of King Nikola, whose remains had been brought to Montenegro from Italy. In his drive to secure political support, Idris decided to hire Kennedy's public relations company, Thunderbolt, to relaunch a lobbying campaign in Parliament. Also in Thunderbolt was the former Conservative MP Harold Elletson, and leading authorities on Middle Eastern affairs, including a Church of England vicar who had close connections with the ruling houses of the region, was fluent in Arabic and was thought to be a former member of MI6. Idris entertained MPs lavishly at Claridges, and invited them to his St Tropez home. There and elsewhere he blithely, and falsely, told them, not only that he was the rightful heir to the throne, but that the government recognized him as such. No one questioned his claims of meetings with the Foreign Secretary and other senior ministers.

Idris also wanted to use Anthony Bailey, then a twenty-three-year-old accounts director for PR giant Burson-Marsteller. Bailey had a list of clients from heads of state in Africa to crowned heads of Europe. Apart from the Italian royal family he also, on matters touching on public relations, advised the exiled kings of Greece, Bulgaria and Ethiopia, as well as the Vatican. In Britain he had organized the official visit to Peru by Prince Michael of Kent in November 1994. It was on that flight to Lima that John Kennedy offered to introduce him to Idris al-Senussi.

Learning that Prince Michael of Kent was paying an official visit to the Sultan of Oman in 1994, Idris not only offered to loan 'his' jet for the trip but, when that offer was accepted, he insisted on coming along too.

Bailey, who was also acting as press secretary for Crown Prince Mohammed, had previously had a bad experience with Idris, when the impostor had gate-crashed a private luncheon Bailey had arranged at the Travellers Club in Pall Mall, attended by King Simeon II of Bulgaria and Prince Michael.

Crown Prince Mohammed, being very conscious that Gaddafi could only profit from any confusion over the royal succession, had agreed that Bailey could promote Idris as a spokesman for their country; but not as the heir apparent.

Try as Idris might, Bailey would not budge from his loyal support for Mohammed as the true Crown prince, and he warned Idris that he had to stop challenging the rightful heir. A furious Idris, hoping to put paid to Bailey's support for Mohammed, went to the police and made the allegation that Bailey and Kennedy were blackmailing him and demanding money by menaces. He claimed that Bailey, using Kennedy as a conduit, had demanded £250,000, under the threat that he would ruin Idris's reputation with the smear that he had paid the Tory MPs £110,000 to sign the Early Day Motion. This was at the height of the 'cash for questions' crisis that was engulfing John Major's beleaguered government.

Once Idris had made his allegations, the police moved in and carried out their arrests. Bailey, a young man, faced a substantial prison sentence if convicted of blackmail, which the law has always regarded as particularly abhorrent. He was in desperate straits and retained the services of Desmond de Silva. Together with Desmond, Bailey's solicitors, Barker Gillette of Wimpole Street, instructed John Causer. Kennedy also retained the same counsel. Bailey told me later: 'For a twenty-three-year-old, having such a prominent QC was wonderful. He saved me. It was a very unpleasant, in fact a frightening experience, and Desmond came to my rescue. I will never forget it.'

Four months after the arrests, the Crown Prosecution Service dropped the case against Kennedy, who had never been charged. There were widespread rumours that the intelligence services had been so alarmed by the blackmail allegations against the royal aide that they had bugged Kensington Palace, and were eavesdropping on royal conversations that were not intended to be the subject of surveillance.

Why did Desmond have a personal meeting with the head of MI5, Stella Rimington, in her Millbank office, just before the Crown Prosecution Service abandoned the case against Kennedy? We shall never know. John Kelsey-Fry, then a senior Treasury counsel, who prosecuted Bailey, never knew the answer, even though he teased Desmond about it in court. 'Desmond, in that wonderful Desmondian way, with an eye to the great public good and the interests of the nation, thought he ought to point out that there was a problem with this case, and knocked on the door of a certain woman,' Kelsey-Fry told me over a drink in the Howard Hotel, near his chambers.

'I can't remember how I discovered it. It came to my attention some way or the other. It made me smile, and I did tease him about it. What surprised me was that he had the nerve to do it, even knowing everything I know about him.' Kelsey-Fry's comment illustrates my own assessment of Desmond: he has access to those at the highest levels, which he would use if he thought it right.

'I always understood that charges are dropped if there is insufficient evidence or if it is not in the public interest. Now it seems there was a new criterion. Two people can do the same thing and you react in different ways. If certain people had done that I would have blown my top, but with Desmond, I smiled,' said Kelsey-Fry.

A month later, in June 1995, Kennedy tendered his resignation to Prince Michael and issued a statement thanking Prince Michael for his 'unstinting support'. In the statement he felt the need, mysteriously, to deny publicly that he had ever blamed his arrest on an MI5 smear.

In July, Bailey and Desmond were able to face Idris across a court, packed with press, for a committal hearing which would decide whether the case would go to the Old Bailey for trial. In those days, before fast-track committals were introduced, evidence could be called at this stage and witnesses cross-examined to test the prosecution's case.

Thames Magistrates' Court is one of London's dingier corners for the dispensing of justice. Located on the Mile End Road, it was certainly unused to seeing the stellar legal talents of a senior QC and the soon-to-become-silk Kelsey-Fry, together with a defendant who represented royalty and a millionaire star witness for the prosecution with pretensions to be a royal head of state.

Kelsey-Fry opened the Crown's case, revealing how Bailey had been secretly taped with a body mic worn by Idris; the resulting recordings demonstrated 'blackmail demands, and their accompanying threats,' said counsel for the Crown. It was not long before the Crown's principal witness, and the alleged victim of the blackmail, entered the witness box. Desmond tore into the so-called prince. He started by informing the bench that he proposed to establish in cross-examination that the 'alleged victim was a fraud and impostor who had sought to inveigle Anthony Bailey into promoting his spurious claims to the throne of Libya.'

Through deft cross-examination of the alleged victim, he went on to demonstrate that Idris had lied to the police about his dealings with Bailey and leaders of other Arab countries. In addition, suggested Desmond, Idris had deliberately taped selected meetings with the defendant to give a one-sided view favourable to his allegations.

On the key tape, which was meant to prove Bailey's guilt, Idris had asked a series of leading questions about the potential threat from his enemies. Far from making menaces, Desmond established that Bailey was merely giving Idris his assessment of possible future dangers. Having got Idris al-Senussi to repeat, on oath, that he was the rightful heir to the throne and that, in a letter to the *Times*, he had described himself as the grandson of King Idris, Desmond forced him into a corner from where he had to acknowledge that he had lied to the court and in the *Times*; the King had died childless.

The *coup de grâce* to Idris's reputation was provided by another witness, David Williamson, co-editor of Debrett's *Peerage and Baronetage* and one of the world's greatest authorities on genealogy, having in 1977 and 1980 compiled the copious genealogical sections of the two volumes of *Burke's Royal Families of the World*. He had already provided a statement confirming that 'to the best of our knowledge and belief the rightful claimant to the royal throne of Libya is His Royal Highness Crown Prince Mohammed' and that 'no other member of the al-Senussi family is entitled to be styled prince and Royal Highness.'

Asked by Desmond: 'What would happen if you were to shake the Libyan royal family tree?' Williamson replied, 'Idris would be the first thing to fall out!' With the whoosh of laughter across the court still taunting him, Idris immediately left the court building and flew out of the country to the Middle East on his private jet.

At the end of the three-day hearing, having heard submissions in law from Desmond on behalf of Bailey and from Kelsey-Fry for the prosecution, the stipendiary magistrate threw the case out, with a ruling that was brief but damningly to the point.

'There have been bizarre allegations of corruption in public life, both in this country and the Middle East,' he said. 'In the cloak-and-dagger tale which provides the background to this case we have dealt with image, deception and make-believe. The court has to decide whether it amounts to a criminal offence.

'The world of make-believe has absorbed Mr Idris al-Senussi in this case. He wishes people to believe he is the heir presumptive to the Libyan throne… It is a case of hope exceeding expectation. There have been a number of untested assertions bandied around as fact. There have been allegations of an attempt to corrupt MPs. There is not a shred of evidence in court that any MP was corrupted, or paid cash for asking questions, or promoting the interests of Mr al-Senussi.'

He added: 'I have thought long and hard about these submissions. If it is true, as Mr al-Senussi has said, that there are no skeletons in his cupboard, then it is improbable that he is a blackmail victim. However, if he has committed some blackmailable acts and wanted to promote the image of being the heir apparent, then more reason for hiring the services of a public relations company. I do not consider there is a case which I should send for trial.'

Kelsey-Fry emerged from court at a loss to explain the case. While admiring Desmond's skill in his advocacy and cross-examination, which had won the case, he was baffled why he had lost.

'The fact is that whether Idris was a pretender or not affected his credibility, but not the evidence of what was on the tape. The magistrate's job was to rule on whether there was a case to answer; the evidence was on the tape and whether there was entrapment or not was a matter for a jury,' he told me. 'The credibility of Idris was neither here nor there to the magistrate's decision. It can only go to credit and credit is not an issue. I remain bemused as to how the hell Desmond managed to do it.'

Whatever the legal niceties for one man, nothing was more important than winning or losing. Bailey had been saved from ruin. Exonerated and unburdened by the threat of prison, Bailey now runs a very successful company offering 'international diplomacy, reputation management and public affairs'. In 2007, Bailey married Princess Marie-Therese von Hohenberg, the great-granddaughter of Archduke Franz Ferdinand of Austria, whose assassination led to the outbreak of World War I.

Kennedy fought and lost a second general election campaign for the Conservatives, at Halesowen in 1997.

Not long after disposal of the case, it was reported that the Queen had been deeply concerned about the blackmail allegations and further credence was given to the suggestion that one of her palaces had been bugged. John Causer, Desmond's junior in the case, recalls that leading up to the committal hearing, Desmond 'decided that this case needed some additional royal input, and so, on one memorable day, he arranged a conference in the morning with King Simeon of the Bulgarians at the Travellers Club and another in the afternoon with Crown Prince Victor Emmanuel of Italy at the Connaught.

'Those were the days when it was usual for clients to "attend on" counsel at chambers for pretrial conferences except, of course, when they were in custody. Huge, leather-bound diaries would in those days read "Conf. in chambers" or "Conf. elsewhere", with the details often filled in afterward.

'On this occasion, when we returned to chambers,' said Causer, 'the senior clerk, Robin Driscoll, raised a rather quizzical eyebrow: "Now Sir, which prison was it where you saw these gentlemen?"'

Apparently Desmond had requested these conferences because private conversations between these royals and members of the House of Windsor had been picked up in the tapping of the palace telephones, undertaken by the security services after Idris's allegations against the equerry. They were, no doubt, seriously shaken by what he had to say, but who better than Desmond to reassure them and ensure that nothing untoward seeped into the public domain? After all, his wife was the niece of Queen Elizabeth, King Simeon was her godfather and cousin, and Crown Prince Victor Emmanuel was another cousin.

The British Foreign and Commonwealth Office was to say, 'Her Majesty's government had never recognized Mr Idris al-Senussi's claim to the Libyan throne,' and confirmed that Idris had never been welcomed at the FCO.

And what of Idris? He was arrested in 1998 and charged with blackmail, kidnap and false imprisonment, over allegations of abduction at knifepoint and a robbery of £50,000 earmarked for a *coup d'état* in Libya. He was cleared, along with three other defendants, when the Crown offered no evidence, after the alleged victim was found to have told 'demonstrable untruths'.

According to reports of the case at Middlesex Guildhall Crown Court, Idris was, even then, still claiming to be the rightful heir to the throne of Libya.

Gaddafi was, as the world knows, later to be overthrown by his own people in a coup more than tacitly supported by the Western powers.

## 21

# The Perfect Murder

IT WAS A CAT THAT FIRST ALERTED THE WORLD TO WHAT HAD BEEN planned as the perfect murder. If no crime is suspected, no culprit is sought. The perfect murder, therefore, is one committed according to a plan that ensures the victim is never missed and death never suspected. In this case, however, a cat exposed the perfect murder by doing what cats do best: being curious.

On the clifftops where the Greenwich Meridian leaves the south coast of England, almost midway between Brighton and Eastbourne, stands Peacehaven. Trapped between the South Downs to the north and the English Channel to the south, with just one main road, the A259, in and out, Peacehaven is a home for the retired and those who work in and around Brighton.

To this unprepossessing town came John Haycroft, from London. He was looking for a second home, and what better place than one with some spectacular but exposed views across the Channel? Aged forty-nine, and a computer analyst, he lived from Monday to Friday in a comfortable home in Hillingdon, in Middlesex, then worth about £300,000. In addition, he had about £300,000 invested in stocks and shares: a tidy sum which, in the heady days of booming stock markets, would have given him the comfort of looking to an eventual retirement as a stock market millionaire. A fortune even more likely to be made and preserved, as he was a miser who rejected the comforts that money could buy. He went around in scruffy clothes, drove a Robin Reliant and, when he bought the modestly priced weekend home in Malines Avenue, he let rooms in it to two lodgers. It was a wealthy retirement he never lived to enjoy.

To his family and work colleagues at Lambeth Council, there was a simple reason why no one had seen John Haycroft for three months. Had he not written in, resigning his position and saying he was taking early retirement? Had not the council written to him expressing their gratitude for the many years of service, and wished him well for the future?

Haycroft never received these good wishes from his superiors, nor indeed had he written to resign from his employment. One night, when he had come to his home in Peacehaven, he was bludgeoned with a hammer and strangled with a garrotte. The body was then buried under a plastic goldfish pond. His murderer set about becoming John Haycroft himself.

Those who put him in that makeshift grave were his lodgers: Thomas Longhurst and Peter McDonald. Whereas the latter was only involved in the illegal burial, it was Longhurst, a driving instructor, who made the garrotte and waited for his landlord to make an unanticipated rendezvous with death.

Longhurst had already spent months practising his victim's handwriting and set to work on a resignation letter to his council employers and postcards to Haycroft's few remaining family, to give the impression he was off travelling abroad. He negotiated a £45,000 mortgage on the bungalow, and had the money paid into five accounts he had opened in Haycroft's name; he then planned to raise £160,000 from a remortgage on the £250,000 Hillingdon house. The plundering of the murdered man's assets had begun. To avoid unmasking, when it came to selling stocks and shares, Longhurst studiously avoided speaking to the partner at the stockbrokers who handled the dead man's investments. Instead, having discovered the name of that partner, he began by calling the switchboard and asked to speak to another partner, through whom he would negotiate the sale of shares.

It was when the pair were in Malaga, where Longhurst had found a yacht on which he paid a deposit, that the local cats arrived in the garden of the house in Malines Avenue and began to extract the goldfish for immediate consumption. Despite the fact that there were no more goldfish left, one particular cat, no doubt believing that an inexhaustible source of food lay hidden beneath, started scratching around the plastic pond.

Unfortunately for this evil pair, it was not just the feline animal in the garden that was to prove their downfall. Unable to gain entrance by ringing the front doorbell, a postman decided to try the back of the house, to see if anyone could take the package he was carrying. Arriving at the rear of the house, he noticed that the sun on that summer morning was glinting off something beside the pond. As he strolled over to look at what had caught his eye, he was confronted by a ring on a decaying human finger pointing up at the sky. It was protruding out of a hollow scratched by the curious cat.

When Longhurst and McDonald arrived back at Gatwick, they were in for a rude shock. Awaiting them were the police. Having been discovered, Longhurst put Plan B into operation; he readily confessed to the killing, but stunned detectives by calmly telling them about his book, an unpublished fifty-page short story. A police search found the manuscript, and his lawyers soon found psychiatrists who would support the claim that he had been 'taken over by the character he had created' and was in 'an unreal state', acting out the murder scene from this work of fiction.

Thomas Longhurst was to produce one of the most original defences ever put forward in court: not guilty of murder on the grounds he was only acting out the plot of a fictional story he had written. A story in which the killer is never caught. Longhurst, fifty-one when he stood trial, was a driving instructor, but he had greater ambitions: to be rich and become a bestselling author. What's more, he had his own ideas on how to achieve both aims, fast.

The trial began at Lewes Crown Court before Mr Justice Alliott in July 1990, with the well-known Eastbourne firm, Mayo & Perkins, instructing Dan Hollis, QC to lead Richard Cherrill for Longhurst. Longhurst pleaded not guilty to murder, but guilty to manslaughter on the grounds of diminished responsibility. Desmond, who was briefed for the prosecution and leading Howard Vagg, took the view that the psychiatrists were talking rubbish. Unfortunately for him, most of the Crown's psychiatrists came to the conclusion that Longhurst *had* been 'taken over'. Desmond decided to give the prosecution psychiatrist's reports to the defence and rely on his own common sense, rather than attempt to obtain any further evidence for the Crown.

Opening the case for the Crown Desmond told the jury: 'This was a premeditated killing for gain, a highly complex crime and not the product of a diminished mind.' He went on: 'Longhurst conceived a fiendish plan to perpetrate the perfect murder. He would kill, and then assume the identity of, the slain man, thereby allaying any suspicion that Haycroft had been done to death.' He told the court how Longhurst had been arrogant in his recorded interviews with the police and 'displayed a complete lack of remorse.'

The defendant had told the police: 'I murdered Haycroft by striking him three times with a nine-pound hammer and then strangling him. I had a terrible job burying him. Later I decided that, as he had gone, I might as well use the money.' That's where the fraud and deception came in. He described Haycroft as 'a big wally,' adding, 'I never liked the bloke.' Asked by the police in his interview why he had killed Haycroft, Longhurst replied: 'It seemed logical at the time.'

From the witness box, Longhurst mounted a masterclass in deception. He clearly had his act worked out in detail, every point covered, every twist anticipated and linked to the plot in his book, to give the impression of an obsessed and deluded mind. Haycroft was 'mean, messy and smelly' and 'drove me crazy' with his untidiness, he said. On the night of the killing he had come in feeling 'grotty' after a hard day driving in bad weather, and was horrified to see that Haycroft had arrived unexpectedly to stay overnight.

He cracked when the landlord washed his filthy hands just after he had washed the bathroom basin. 'He started to wash his face and just died... I just did it, he'd driven me crazy. I struck him between the shoulders with a club hammer which was lying on the floor and he turned around and said: "Why are you doing this to me?"'

Longhurst told the police that, after hitting him, he went into the bedroom for a garrotte of wire and wood he had created weeks earlier as part of the research for his book, and then went back to strangle his victim. 'If somebody had told me two seconds before I killed that he would die at my hands I would not have believed them.'

He gave his evidence in confident tones and, encapsulating his defence in a single sentence, he concluded with the punchline: 'It was like acting in a play you'd written and directed yourself. It wasn't real, it just happened.'

It was a tour de force, a brilliant performance, and Longhurst clearly believed he had convinced the jury. Sometimes the lie is so big an ordinary person would find it inconceivable that it could not be true. He could have got away with it in real life too, but for the single question he had never expected, and which cracked his meticulously constructed plan and exposed the real motive of this most arrogant of murderers.

Desmond pricked that bubble of self-confidence with his very first question in cross-examination. It was a deadly question. 'Would you have killed Mr Haycroft if he was a pauper?' Which way was the witness going to answer? The atmosphere in court was suddenly more than tense; it was electric.

Longhurst paused, for the first time in self-doubt. He looked uncertain. Hesitatingly he finally answered with a cautious 'yes.' Desmond pounced. 'But your fictional hero only killed for money; so why do you say you were taken over by the character you had created?' As Desmond continued to pound him, the links between the crime and the book fell away and the jury could see the degree of calculation behind the plot.

One Crown lawyer involved in the case described this seminal moment as a typical Desmond ploy. 'He has the rare ability to think laterally, to always ask himself: "What if?" That's why he always prided himself on starting many cross-examinations with a bang, to put the witness on the back foot,' he said. 'That was the one question Longhurst had not thought of and by putting it to him straight away, he was finished.'

Longhurst had been demolished, but there was still the expert evidence, represented by no fewer than four psychiatrists. The first, Dr Michael Heller told the court he had diagnosed a 'psychopathic personality' in Longhurst, characterized by obsessional behaviour, conceit and a display of extraordinary detachment from the crime. Under close cross-examination by Desmond, he admitted he had found no evidence of delusion, hallucination or specific mental illness. The others gave similar evidence when cross-examined.

Desmond was able to call, in rebuttal, Dr Patricia Williams, who made it very clear she believed the story of the book 'coming alive' was 'very flimsy'. She insisted that Longhurst had known exactly what he was doing when he killed and that in his interviews with the police he showed no signs of mental illness. He had an obsessional character disorder, but not a state of mind that would impair his responsibilities, she said.

Longhurst's daughter, Susan Forth, still clung to the wreckage of her father's shattered defence. 'I don't think he meant it. It was the murder book he was writing that made him subconsciously do it,' she said, dutifully.

Six days after the trial opened the jury returned a verdict of guilty to murder and Longhurst was jailed for life. McDonald, his hapless stooge, was jailed for four years. He said he had arrived home late in a drunken stupor to find Haycroft dead, and had been pressed into service by the stronger personality of his fellow lodger to help bury the body.

As the jury came back into court after their retirement, and as the verdict was returned, Longhurst's girlfriend, Pat Jones, burst into tears and vowed she would marry him in prison and ensure that the book would be published. If she succeeded in that latter aim it is safe to say, more than a dozen years later, that it has yet to reach a place on the bestsellers list as the murderer had craved.

Had it not been for the cat that exposed the finger, no one would have suspected that Haycroft had been murdered. Using Haycroft's address book, Longhurst had sent postcards to members of Haycroft's family, and a selection of his friends, saying that he was selling up in England and going to live abroad. They all believed that the forty-nine-year-old bachelor had retired to some sunny part of the world and wished him well.

## 22

# The Clock Tower Alibi

IF ANY NOVEL, PLAY OR FILM PORTRAYED THE EVENTS OF THIS TRIAL, IT would have been met with laughter and derisory disbelief. Yet this particularly horrifying murder trial was stood on its head, exactly at the moment when the killer came within an ace of establishing a foolproof alibi that would have led to his freedom.

Matthew Speare, a jobbing gardener, was charged with the murder of an eighty-four-year-old widow who had lived in a picturesque cottage in the Old Town area of Hastings, in Sussex. Speare, who had occasionally worked for a Mrs Hutcheson as a gardener, was arrested for her murder after it was discovered that he had sold the deceased's locket to a jeweller in Brighton. Although his fingerprints were found in her cottage, this was by no means conclusive evidence of him being her assailant, as Speare had done odd jobs for Mrs Hutcheson and been into the house.

The case for the Crown turned on two particular pieces of evidence: the sale of the locket by Speare, and contradictory accounts given by him to the police after his arrest. At first he told the police he had been in a snooker hall at the time of the killing and had not been near the cottage that day. His account later changed and he told the police he found some jewellery, including the locket, in a bag at Mrs Hutcheson's back gate. He lived nearby. He admitted he had sold the jewellery in question for a paltry £10.

Desmond was retained to prosecute for the Crown, with Bernard Phelvin as his junior. The trial took place in July 1988, at Lewes Crown Court, before Mr Justice Peter Pain. Despite his contradictory accounts to the police, Speare at all times maintained his innocence. Desmond opened the case by explaining that, in the Crown's view, as there was no evidence of a break-in, Mrs Hutcheson had very probably been attacked by someone whom she knew and had let in. She was clubbed to the ground in her kitchen, with a series of blows from a heavy object, and then stabbed. Desmond continued, 'To ensure that she did not survive this brutal attack, a knife taken from her own kitchen drawer was driven through her left ear into her brain.' He went on to tell the jury, 'The killing of this old lady took place in order that her assailant could make off with a few bits of jewellery. Taken from her neck was a silver locket, which she always wore – a locket that contained family photographs. Also, torn from her finger, was her wedding ring.'

When Desmond called the evidence for the Crown, the victim's daughter, Diane Sinclair, told the court that her mother had vowed she would never be parted from the Edwardian locket, because it contained a photograph of her late husband, George, who had died three years earlier, and her daughter. 'It could not really have been more precious to her. So much so that she made me and my children promise that, when she died, it would be buried with her,' said Mrs Sinclair.

As for her wedding ring, arthritis had prevented the victim from taking it off for many years, an indication of the brute strength that was used to rip it from her finger. Mrs Hutcheson's precious locket had, according to the records of the jewellers, been sold by Speare at 5 p.m. As Desmond put it to the jury in his opening, 'it was torn from her neck in death as she would never have parted with it in life,' so it followed that the Crown had to establish that the killing had taken place no later than 4 p.m., to allow Speare time to make his journey to the jewellers with the locket.

Speare, who did not give evidence, relied on his interview with the police, in which he had asserted his innocence by saying, 'I would hardly get into trouble for killing an old lady for a tenner. I have never hit anybody. It is an unfortunate coincidence, but it wouldn't be the first time someone has dropped items from the burglary in a panic.' Indeed, the prosecution could not show that all the other items taken from the cottage had been found or sold by him. His defence was simple: he was the victim of a terrible misfortune. Someone else had killed her and stolen her property, dropping some of it in making his or her escape. His only involvement was to find some of it and sell it.

To a large extent, the outcome of the case looked as if it was going to be determined by the exact time of the murder. It appeared that she had been killed shortly after she had put some potatoes to boil on a gas cooker. When her body was discovered, the gas was still on and the saucepan had boiled dry.

The Crown had to carry out exhaustive tests as to how long it took for a pan of that size to boil dry, using different quantities of water. In addition, there was the time involved in the walk between the house and the snooker hall where the defendant had claimed he had gone. It was on this occasion (as described earlier) that Desmond ruined the timing exercise by stopping off to buy candy floss. However, walking times for the distance in question were eventually agreed between the prosecution and the defence.

The real bombshell came when the defence case began; they produced two utterly respectable witnesses who knew the deceased and were unshakeable in their view that they had seen her beneath the clock tower in Hastings town centre, when the clock was showing 6 p.m. This was a good hour after Speare had sold the locket and by which time, according to the Crown, she was already a corpse. If that evidence was correct, Speare could not have been the murderer.

It was at this point, when the witnesses had given their evidence about seeing Mrs Hutcheson under the clock tower, and all seemed lost for the prosecution, that the court was electrified by a shout from the gallery, 'But my mother had a double!' Everyone looked upward and there in the gallery was the upstanding figure of Mrs Sinclair, who repeated, 'My mother had a double.' The stunned silence in court was broken by Desmond who, swinging round and pointing upward to the gallery, responded: 'Madam, come down and testify.'

Pure melodrama. In the theatre or the television it would have been unbelievable hokum. But it did really happen. As it was, the jury were sent out while Desmond, as astonished as anyone else, had to persuade the judge that Mrs Sinclair should indeed be allowed to 'come down and testify'. The strict rule is that witnesses are not allowed into court to hear proceedings before they give their own evidence. The reason is obvious: having heard how the case is going, they could tailor their evidence accordingly. But Mrs Sinclair had already given evidence and was perfectly entitled to sit in the public gallery thereafter. New evidence, as long as it is relevant and admissible, can be introduced at any time in a trial, subject to the leave of the judge. In this case, the jury had heard the witness cry out and would have been frustrated if they were not allowed to hear her explain what she said and, indeed, face cross-examination. The alternative would have been a new trial.

In the event, the judge gave the prosecution leave to recall Mrs Sinclair to rebut what would otherwise have been cast-iron defence evidence. Entering the witness box for the second time, she told the jury how, since her mother's death, she had often seen her mother's double in Hastings. Not only did this other woman look exactly like her mother, but she even dressed so similarly that the sight of her would send shivers down her spine.

Desmond established that Mrs Hutcheson used to wear glasses but, because she was constantly falling over, her daughter had, shortly before her mother's death, got her contact lenses. Indeed, the contact lenses were in her eyes when her body was discovered. The lady beneath the clock tower was wearing glasses.

The jury unanimously found Speare guilty of murder and he was sentenced to life imprisonment.

## 23

# The Tea Dance Murder

A few years later, Desmond was instructed by the Crown to prosecute a case the press dubbed the Tea Dance Murder. Sometimes an otherwise prosaic trial is transformed by the people involved. This was a murder case that went back in time, bringing out class differences last prevalent in the 1950s, and deep and deadly sexual passion.

Aged fifty-two, the auburn-haired divorcee June Cuxson had hit the singles scene, seeking companionship while awaiting her divorce. At the Mid-Sussex Divorced and Separated Club Dance in a quiet Sussex town, she met sixty-eight-year-old Ted Martin, who taught her the waltz and the quickstep. Gradually a reward of a kiss on the cheek at the next week's tea dance became a kiss on the lips. They began seeing each other regularly and became an item, according to the story that later unfolded in court. The relationship, however, cooled when Mrs Cuxson realized that Martin was seeing a second woman, divorcee Doris Dennington, whom he had met at another tea dance. Mrs Cuxson, however, continued to see Martin; but then she met Warwick Batchelor, an eighty-year-old retired Unilever executive who had been a major during the war, and possessed the manners and outlook of a more courtly age.

On a warm summer's evening in August 1994, Warwick Batchelor was found stabbed to death outside his garage in Hassocks, West Sussex. Ted Martin, from Burgess Hill, who had been a lance corporal during the war, was arrested for the murder, when detectives spotted him trying to hide a bin liner stuffed with blood-stained clothing, a pair of woollen gloves and a 76.2 centimetre screwdriver that had been sharpened to a deadly point. Hassocks and Burgess Hill, two towns nestling in the Downs, could hardly be quieter and a less likely setting for such a violent murder; but then even old-aged passion can run deep, particularly when faced with the prospect of ending your life in loneliness.

The trial took place at Lewes, before Mr Justice Michael Wright and a jury. Michael Lawson, QC, was leading Alan Kent, for Martin. Leading Bernard Phelvin for the Crown, Desmond opened the case to the jury by telling them that they would hear of a 'classic love triangle' in which the ageing Romeo had threatened the senior suitor to 'lay off my girl'. He continued, 'You will enter a world of singles clubs for the not so young, of genteel tea dances, simmering jealousies and violent death.'

Having met June Cuxson at a University of the Third Age bridge party, she and Batchelor became increasingly close. 'I found Mr Batchelor very attractive,' Mrs Cuxson told the court. 'He was physically very strong for an eighty-year-old and he didn't seem to have a wrinkle on his body... As soon as I saw Warwick, I was attracted to him. When I realized he was eighty, I tried not to like him, but it does not always work out when you try not to be attracted to someone.'

Said Desmond, 'As Mrs Cuxson's feelings for Mr Batchelor got stronger and deeper, so she tried to scale down her relationship with the defendant, and in fact told him that she was not in love with him. Sadly, some people cannot take no for an answer and the Crown says that this man plotted a terrible revenge.'

However, she still kept seeing Martin from time to time as her dance partner and, despite the fact that they waltzed and danced rumbas together, he became more and more bitter, until he finally confronted the object of his love and said to her, 'It's either me or Warwick.' He wrote a letter to her pleading, 'Do not let our friendship die like this. I know we both need each other.' But by then, he had lost his place in her heart and Mrs Cuxson started to make plans to go on holiday to France with Batchelor, after which, she told the court, they hoped to move in together.

The contrast between the two men was vast. Batchelor, despite being the older man, was fit and handsome. He was an accomplished chef, knew a great deal about wine and was a lively companion with a quick mind. He had effortless charm and a sizeable pension, which could help Mrs Cuxson out of her money problems following her separation from her husband Alan, an international business executive. Martin was strictly working class and a former Army NCO, and while a good dancer, had no great skills that extended beyond helping Mrs Cuxson out in her house and garden.

The proposed trip to France was just too much for Martin. Having sharpened a huge screwdriver into a deadly weapon, he lay in wait for Mr Batchelor outside the latter's garage in Hassocks, on an evening in August 1994. When the victim arrived and parked his car, out of the darkness disaster struck. Martin stabbed him repeatedly. As Desmond was to tell the court, 'it was a callous and premeditated murder.' However, Martin's defence was that he had taken this terrible weapon simply to warn Batchelor off, and to have it in case the latter attacked him.

In a taped interview with the police, which was played to the jury, Martin made no effort to hide his love and jealousy: 'I was very, very fond of her. We kissed and fondled each other but never had sex. We got very close but she kept saying, "We shouldn't be doing these things." But I think she had some Italian blood in her, you know. I meant to say, a man of my age doesn't like to miss an opportunity with a younger woman like that.'

He admitted that his jealousy was so intense that, 'every time she mentioned his [Batchelor's] name, I used to get upset.' On the eve of the French trip he had seen Batchelor's car parked outside her house and he was filled with fury. He admitted that he had driven to his love rival's home in order to wait for him to return.

'I was going to tell him to keep his hands off her. He was much too old for her. I was so jealous. I knew he was bigger than me so I took this screwdriver with me in case he started on me. As he got out of the car I said, "Warwick." He said, "You bloody imbecile," and came at me.'

Martin claimed the two men had wrestled each other to the ground. 'The last thing I remember is that I was on his back somehow stabbing him in the shoulder. He was saying, "Help, help – I am being attacked." Then he said, "I'm dead, I'm dead." I thought he was going to kill me.'

Cross-examined by Desmond, Martin admitted his jealousy had been inflamed by Batchelor being so much older than himself, and that the class difference between them had played its part in his losing June Cuxson. He also admitted that the first stab wound was in Batchelor's shoulder and from the angle of penetration Martin was forced to admit it was consistent with him stabbing Batchelor from behind. Gradually, Desmond took Martin through all the twenty stab wounds and asked him why he had taken a change of clothes with him to the scene where the killing took place. It was, suggested Desmond, because Martin knew full well that he had intended to kill his rival in love, and to do so in a manner that required him to change out of his blood-stained clothing, which the police subsequently found with the murder weapon.

'If all you intended to do was talk to Mr Batchelor, why did you take a pair of gloves with you on this warm summer night?' asked Desmond, who then put it to Martin that it was to leave no fingerprints on the screwdriver, thereby underlining the Crown's case that this was a premeditated murder.

After a trial lasting little more than a week, the jury unanimously convicted Martin of murder and he collapsed in the dock. In sentencing him to life imprisonment, Mr Justice Wright said to him, 'The explanation of your offence at the end of a long respectable life is only too clear. You were overcome by an overwhelming jealousy toward a man you perceived as a threat.'

Mrs Cuxson, it is said, lost her taste for afternoon tea dances, and Ted Martin was to die in prison.

## 24

# Brothers in Blood

A DOUBLE MURDERER ON THE RUN FROM JUSTICE IS ARRESTED ON THE high seas by a British frigate and brought to a British colony in chains, to be returned home to stand trial; it sounds like a tale of derring-do, when Britannia ruled the waves and piracy was rife.

It would have been a lot simpler if it had taken place in an age of rough justice, without the legal niceties of today, for it was to take two more years for Roderick Newall to finally face the court which was to jail him for life. In the seventeenth and eighteenth centuries, when piracy was widespread, the Royal Navy was empowered to board ships on the high seas and seize pirates for trial in England – whatever their nationality. However, in living memory, no one could recall an instance of British warships or frigates being ordered to put to sea by the Foreign Secretary in order to effect an arrest in international waters and bring back an individual for trial.

Newall, who had murdered his mother and father in Jersey, and buried them with the help of his brother, Mark, had escaped arrest for five years, through luck and lack of evidence, when he was intercepted off the north coast of Africa and brought to Gibraltar. It was to be one of Desmond's greatest triumphs that, in the teeth of all manner of difficulties and indeed threats on his life, he was finally able to get the murderer extradited back to the Channel Islands. In this case he was leading Ian Christmas. He had to survive a contract taken out on his life, the shadowy presence on the Rock of a former MI6 agent in a homburg hat, covert bugging of his own conference room, as well as every conceivable legal obstruction thrown in his path.

In court, Desmond faced not some sophisticated well-spoken silk from the Temple but the local legal street fighter, Christopher Finch, on his own patch, far from the law courts of London. It was the classic match-up, the boxer versus the slugger, and perhaps even Newall, the murderer, does not know how close he was to getting away with it.

This is a story which crosses the globe, with violent deaths, million-pound fortunes, spying, fast cars, expensive yachts, beautiful girls, courtroom dramas and the remarkable discovery that Interflora can sometimes be better at keeping tabs on a fugitive than Interpol.

Roderick Innes Nelson Newall was tall, blond and charming. After Sandhurst he was commissioned into the Royal Green Jackets. He was just twenty-two when he battered his parents, Nicholas and Elizabeth Newall, to death with a pair of martial arts rice flails in their own home, after they had all returned from a family dinner in a local restaurant in October 1987 to celebrate his mother's birthday.

Nicholas, fifty-six, a retired schoolmaster and author, and Elizabeth, forty-seven, had sent their two sons to the English public school Radley, where both had been unpopular. Roderick had told contemporaries he intended to join the Army 'because I want to kill people', and Mark was known as 'a shit among shits'.

Roderick Newall never spoke in public about the murder and eventually submitted only one statement to court, in which he claimed he had hit out when 'bitter childhood memories' had been re-awoken by a drunken row after dinner. During school holidays the parents would shower their sons with presents, but pack them off to relatives in England and Scotland. There was money but no love and affection; but that could never explain murder.

Today, those wishing to settle in Jersey have to show assets of £10 million or more. It is the intention of those who run the affairs of Jersey to keep it as a welfare state for the really rich. When the Newalls settled in Jersey the monetary requirements were less – but, it was still a hideaway for millionaires.

The truth, according to some, was that the parents' money was running out. In the 1980s, and for some three centuries before, being a name at Lloyd's of London had been considered a safe investment and a gentleman's way to make an income. All that began to change because of unexpected claims in the US for asbestosis and pollution, often in relation to policies written decades previously. These impending losses were about to devastate the Lloyd's syndicate of which Nicholas was a member. With a legacy from a rich relative going first to their father before it could reach them, Roderick and Mark knew their inheritance would be wiped out within a matter of months. Only their father's death could avert the financial ruin.

When, after years of denials, Roderick finally made an official statement admitting double murder, he claimed that Mark, his younger brother by two years, had not been in the house at the time. In a self-serving statement Roderick claimed he had rung Mark immediately after the killings and together they had wrapped the bodies, still in the clothes they had worn for dinner, in plastic sheeting, bundled them into a van (conveniently hired earlier that day by Mark) and using tools identical to those acquired that day by a man answering Roderick's description, driven to a deserted meadow near their childhood home to bury them by moonlight. He gave few more details, but what is undisputed is that the pair returned to the house to spend all night clearing up the blood, before leaving the property with the central heating turned up to maximum to dry out their murderous handiwork.

The alarm was eventually raised and the parents were reported missing. By that time, Roderick and Mark were back in England. The police examined the house but it was not considered to be a murder scene until much later. Only then were tiny blood stains, some barely visible, others microscopic, discovered. The brothers were the only suspects, but by then they had their story pretty off pat and the police were unable to prove anything without the bodies or a murder weapon or any incriminating evidence.

The brothers were pulled in for questioning repeatedly but, smug and confident that the police had nothing, they arrogantly kept to their cover stories, sneering at the police's lack of success. Roderick left the Army and set sail around the world, while Mark resumed his career in the City, where he was to turn the brothers' uncontested £1 million inheritance into a massive fortune.

The police were frustrated but did not give up. Detective Inspector James Adamson, a dogged Scottish officer on the Jersey force, endeavoured to keep track of Roderick's whereabouts through Interpol. But he found the worldwide police agency's information was usually a month out of date by the time it reached the Channel Islands. Adamson discovered that the dashing former Army officer was in the habit of sending his girlfriends a floral gift from his every port of call. A quick call to the best-known flower delivery service and now he was getting news of Roderick's movements within twenty-four hours.

As the deadpan detective told Desmond, 'I came to the conclusion, sir, that Interflora was more effective than Interpol.'

Roderick left Britain in May 1988, and for the next three years travelled to the Far East, Australia, New Zealand and the Falkland Islands before arriving in Brazil where, in January 1991, he learned that his parents had been officially declared dead and the inheritance was now his and Mark's.

In Porto Alegre ('Port of Happiness') he met a local beauty called Helena Pedo, who was to become a key figure in the case. In July, while they cuddled around the fire in the South American winter, Roderick asked her to fetch a book, the Nobel prize-winning novel *Magister Ludi* by Hermann Hesse and to read a passage. Desmond was to read the same passage to the Gibraltar court more than two years later:

> Oh! he thought in grief and horror, now I am guilty of his death. And only now, when there was no longer need to save his pride or offer resistance, he felt, in shock and sorrow, how dear this man had already become to him. And in spite of all natural objection he felt responsible for the Master's death, there came over him, with a premonitory shudder of awe, a sense that this guilt would utterly change him and his life, and would demand much greater things of him than he had ever before demanded of himself.

Once she had finished reading he burst into tears, shook his girlfriend by her shoulders and repeated over and over again, 'I am a murderer, I am a murderer.' He pointed to a bottle of whisky and said, 'That was responsible for what happened.' When, years later, Desmond read the passage in court, Newall nodded to him from the dock.

However conscience stricken Newall was in 1991, he was still a long way from giving himself up, and he took off again on his lonely seafaring, back to the Falklands. In May 1992, he returned to Helena and took her to Miami to meet Mark, who had flown over from Paris. The brother, a cold and calculating man, could sense that Roderick might become a liability in preserving the secret of the cold-blooded murders, and warned him never to return to Britain, where the police were still suspicious.

The night Mark flew back to France, Roderick took Helena to see the film *Cape Fear*, starring Robert De Niro and Gregory Peck, who, coincidentally,

Desmond knew. Emerging from the cinema, she told him she had hated the film but he replied, 'It's good to live in fear.' He told Helena he had a continual banging inside his head, but when she suggested a psychiatrist he refused, because he had read a book in which two brothers had committed a murder, and gone to see a psychiatrist, who had betrayed them to the police. He told her she didn't know what it was like to be him. Despite the warnings of his brother, Roderick decided to chance things and return to England.

A month later, he landed at Heathrow and, after visiting friends, dropped in on an aunt, Nan Clark, in London, who persuaded him to drive to Scotland to speak to Stephen, his late father's identical twin. Word got back to the police in Jersey and detectives set off in a mad scramble to get to the meeting place first.

Stephen agreed with the police that he should be secretly tape recorded when he confronted Roderick about the missing parents. The meeting took place in the Dunkeld House Hotel outside Perth, 'with a fourteen-man surveillance squad, some hidden in the grounds, others posing as guests and at least one as a member of the hotel staff.' But what was expected to be a showdown started anticlimactically, with hours of family gossip, and boredom began to set in among the officers who were listening. The uncle, Stephen, however, discharging his role brilliantly, began to play upon his nephew's feelings of remorse. Suddenly, the dam burst and, as Desmond was to graphically tell the court in Gibraltar, 'As this accused gazed into the face of his father's identical twin, there spilled from his lips the pent-up guilt that he had harboured for so long and which finally broke its banks in a series of admissions that point inescapably to the conclusion that he was responsible for patricide and matricide.'

In a long mea culpa, Roderick told his uncle the bodies were wrapped in plastic and well concealed, still wearing the clothes which would 'pin it down to the night', that he carried an equal blame with another, that there were no mitigating circumstances and that if the police moved in he had a suicide plan, but when it came to legal advice, 'I don't think I'd mind too much paying the price.'

He added that he was quite looking forward to seeing his parents 'on the far side.' Asked by Stephen to 'say you are sorry', Roderick replied, 'no.'

Desmond told the court, 'Taken individually or together this amounts to the clearest confession to being involved in murder that a person could make, short of the use of the phrase "I did it."'

But whatever Roderick had said to Stephen he was not going to give himself up. While the police sent tape transcripts off to the Jersey Attorney General for an arrest warrant, the trained soldier drove south at breakneck speed, quickly spotting the unmarked police car tailing him and giving it the slip on the M6. As the Jersey authorities dithered over the warrant, Newall headed for the English Channel, picked up his sixty-six-foot twin-masted yacht, the *Austral Soma*, and headed for the open seas again.

Police turned their attention to Mark and found he had booked a flight to Tangier, via Paris and Madrid. Covert surveillance by undercover officers located the *Austral Soma* moored in Tangier harbour, and the fateful decision was taken: wait until he gets into international waters, then arrest him; better to extradite him from Crown territory in Gibraltar than an unpredictable jurisdiction in North Africa, particularly Morocco, which had no extradition agreement with Britain.

When Roderick set sail from Tangier, the undercover officers, who were billeted on the top floor of a brothel, sent their signal. HMS *Argonaut*'s refitting in Gibraltar was scrambled and Operation Snowbird was underway. *Argonaut*, a veteran of the 1982 Falklands campaign and armed with Exocet and Seacat missiles, antisubmarine torpedoes and a Lynx helicopter, was a lucky ship. It had been hit twice by Argentine bombs, which had not exploded. As Captain Bob Stevens steamed through the straits of Gibraltar, some crew members on shore leave were flushed out of the Rock's many bars and bordellos and flown out to the ship by helicopter, at a cost to the taxpayer of some £200,000.

The *Austral Soma* was tracked by another British frigate, HMS *Ranger*, which had a firearms unit from Gibraltar aboard; they waited for *Argonaut*, which arrived at the rendezvous point, some 160 miles off the Rock, at 5 a.m. on 5 August 1992.

The terms of engagement were drawn up at the highest level and authorized by Foreign Secretary Douglas Hurd; the arrest must take place in international waters and only if Newall was flying the Red Ensign or was flagless. But everyone had overlooked one thing. It was a matter that gave rise to a serious legal problem for Desmond later on. A British warrant could not be executed in international waters.

The more immediate difficulty was that the *Austral Soma* was a steel-hulled icebreaker and Newall could ram and sink the frigate quite easily. He was an experienced soldier and Captain Stevens believed Newall might have been carrying a heavy calibre weapon aboard.

The ruse hatched was for the *Argonaut* to pretend to be taking part in an exercise and to challenge Newall to row over and present his documents for a routine safety check. Ships of the Royal Navy have the right to interrogate any vessel flying the Red Ensign.

At first he refused to acknowledge the signal – it later emerged he was busy hiding his cannabis stash – but he responded, oblivious to the danger, by asking if they could make him 'a nice cup of tea'. He was certainly provided with a warm welcome when, dressed in a baggy T-shirt and cut-off jeans, he came aboard, was escorted across the flight deck, round the corner and into the armed reception committee. Just before Newall saw the six armed men with their weapons pointed at his head, the officer escorting him turned to him and said, 'We have got a surprise for you, old boy.'

After a desperate struggle he was forced to the deck, handcuffed and after six years Jersey police were finally able to read the arrest warrant to him. *Argonaut* then altered course and headed for Gibraltar at full speed.

On the Rock he asked for his Jersey lawyer, David Le Quesne, and indicated he would be looking for a quick route home. And that was the impression the press pack from Fleet Street had when we arrived in Gibraltar for the first extradition hearing. But sometime after his arrest, when he was being held in the Moorish Castle prison, one captive had whispered to Newall the words every prisoner is reputed to pass to a newcomer: 'Get Finch.'

Christopher Finch was forty-two then, a hugely self-important man who revelled in his reputation as a long-standing pain in the side of the British establishment. He had acted for the families of the three IRA terrorists shot dead by the SAS in 1988, and represented the most controversial witness at the inquest, Carmen Proetta. He then took delight in taking her around Fleet Street, cleaning up a small fortune in libel awards as a result of injudicious reports on her activities.

Gibraltar was his turf and he thought he was the unchallenged king of law on the Rock. Gibraltar Attorney General John Blackburn Gittings told me, 'I suppose most people in the world who get arrested 160 miles south-west of Gibraltar have the name of Chris Finch on their lips. If they are in trouble they want him. His reputation is that well known.'

Finch was certainly not going to recommend to his new client that he should look for the quick route home, not without fighting the extradition all the way; and he more than lived up to that promise. The Crown sent for Desmond, bearing in mind the complicated issue of an arrest in international waters.

Meanwhile brother Mark, knowing Roderick's arrest jeopardized his own freedom, had not been idle either. He rang Stephen from Paris to say Roderick wanted him to withdraw the evidence. 'How many more people need to die?' he asked his uncle. 'What are you going to achieve? You by your actions are going to lead to his (Roderick's) death.' With his wife Gay taking notes on the extension line, Stephen asked Mark straight out: 'You could tell us where the bodies are?' to which Mark put on a feigned air of hurt: 'I can't even remotely understand your perspective. I am very, very sad.' After putting the phone down on his uncle he tried the same tactic on Nan Clark, telling her to speak to Stephen. Both relatives were disturbed but neither would budge.

When the Gibraltar hearing opened, in November 1992, Finch won the first round by persuading magistrate Felix Pizzarello to hear proceedings in chambers, out of sight of the press and public. Two days later the press were allowed in to hear the magistrate's ruling, when Pizzarello dropped his bombshell.

He ruled that the taped confession made at the Dunkeld House Hotel was inadmissible because it had been gained in a 'sneaky way'. He attacked the 'loaded and leading questions' put to Roderick by his uncle. He accepted that the tape was 'in the nature of a confession, but in the exercise of my discretion and in the circumstances of this case I disallow it.'

He went on: 'It is unfair to the defendant and more importantly it was brought into being by the calculated act of the police, through the agency of persons who could lull the defendant into a false sense of security... I do not believe the police acted improperly in the investigative sense, but it is clearly improper in the forensic sense, for they used an avenue in a sneaky way to circumvent the right to silence.'

Newall was remanded in custody for another five days. Pandemonium broke out. Desmond was totally flabbergasted, wondering just how the 'sneaky' principle had suddenly entered English law; Finch was cock-a-hoop, telling everyone he would have his client out at the next hearing and free to sail the seven seas again.

I flew back to London and found Finch on the same flight. 'Congratulations,' I said. 'I expect you will be putting your fees up now.' A self-satisfied smile crossed his face, 'If I did that then only person who could afford me would be the Queen of Sheba.'

Back in Gibraltar, the Crown's plans were in tatters, and Desmond had to buy time. His strategy, as it turned out, was to stay the proceedings, by applying for a judicial review of the magistrate's ruling, and get hold of Helena Pedo in Brazil. Detectives had tracked her down after Newall's arrest, when they found her number in his Filofax aboard the *Austral Soma*. She had told them about the fireside confession but she was too scared to cross the Atlantic to give evidence. Now the Crown had no choice. Desmond instructed officers to leave for Brazil immediately and persuade her to give evidence against her former lover. Because of fears for her own safety she was promised a twenty-four-hour protection squad and relocation after she gave evidence.

Finch, unaware of Desmond's moves, demanded that Newall's passport be brought to court, while the murderer's friends were preparing the *Austral Soma* for a fast getaway as soon as he was released.

When the case resumed the court was packed. Desmond indicated that leave to stay the proceedings had been granted by the Supreme Court, on the grounds that a committing magistrate's job is not to assess the weight of evidence but, rather, to decide if there was sufficient prima facie evidence to grant an extradition. He applied for Newall to remain in custody pending a full hearing of the appeal on the tapes. Casually, he dropped into his submission the fact that the Rock's Chief Justice, Alister Kneller, had set aside three days for the hearing in a month's time. Finch went ballistic, accusing the Crown of going to the Chief Justice, 'like thieves in the night while I was away from Gibraltar', and demanded bail.

If bail was granted, Newall would have fled and the Crown would have lost its chance to bring him to justice. It was a close call, but Desmond won his breathing space. Finch's bravado was dented but he was not broken. Over the following weeks and months he kept up a stream of further bail applications, on the grounds that Newall was being kept in barbarous conditions in the Moorish Castle.

With the prospect of immediate release snatched away, Newall tried new ways to attract attention, starting with a hunger strike. In April 1993, he sent the authorities a handwritten statement, reproduced for the first time here, in which he announced in pretentious and doom-laden terms, 'I, Roderick Innes Nelson Newall, late of the ship *Austral Soma* before being dragged to Gibraltar at gunpoint, wish to make clear that I wish to receive no medical treatment of any kind or any food or liquids, either in prison or hospital or anywhere else I might be taken. I write this in sound mind and have requested that my attorney, Christopher Finch, continues to see that these requests are carried out should I not be able to communicate due to any reason including unconsciousness.'

Desmond took steps to have some Mars bars and a beaker of water placed in Roderick's cell as he contemplated his death fast. The temptation proved too strong and the fast didn't last long, so the prisoner turned to a succession of suicide attempts. Some were more dangerous than others, but somebody on the outside was clearly trying to help him as syringes, drugs, a blade and even a surgical knife were smuggled in to him. He was kept on suicide watch – the Crown didn't want to lose him this way, either. Intercepts had been placed on his phone calls in prison since his arrival on the Rock, and they revealed the plots the Newall brothers and their friends were hatching.

Security information reports (disclosed for the first time) show two calls Newall received on 17 October 1992. The officer's report noted: 'At 1400 hours I monitored a call to Newall from a lady called Leslie [sic]. As he was expecting a call from his brother he did not want to accept the call, but Officer [redacted] authorized him to have a few words, as the lady in question said she had a very important message for him.

'It went as follows: Leslie: "Rod, if you get a decision (in court) which is not favourable, don't commit suicide or do anything irreparable; just give it a few days, shall we say ten, and something is being prepared."

'Newall: "I understand and thank you for everything. I cannot contact you because everything I could tell you would be censored."'

An hour later the call Newall was expecting from his brother Mark was put through. The security report noted that Mark told him, 'I have the man in London on hold, he has a reasonable and substantial amount of men in London and over there in Gibraltar. Don't worry, we have the best shots in London. We have paid for the next few weeks but we do not want to go to big expenses if it is not necessary [meaning if the court released Roderick].'

Newall replied: 'I will have a lengthy meeting with Finch on Monday and he will contact you later.'

Mark clearly had a number of options. Plan A was financing Finch with enough money to hopefully get Roderick released on legal grounds. If not, he was preparing two choices: 1. Help his brother commit suicide; 2. Get hired guns in position for a shoot-out. If the shoot-out succeeded and Roderick escaped everything was fine and dandy; albeit that the police would never rest and pursue him around the world to recapture him. If Roderick died, either by his own hand or in the gunfire, Mark knew the case against him would collapse and he would never be prosecuted.

As Desmond was analysing the intercepts, word came from Special Branch that a contract had been taken out on him too. He hurriedly despatched his wife Katarina and their eighteen-month-old daughter, Victoria, who were visiting him on the Rock, back to Britain. Around this time a transmitter had been discovered in the Crown's main conference room, embedded into the back of a gilt frame that surrounded a picture of the 1779 Siege of Gibraltar. Inspector Adamson's room had also been burgled.

Intense security measures were adopted inside and outside the prison – Newall was the most guarded prisoner in Gibraltar's history. Around the Crown's team security was significantly tightened over and above the high level already existing. In Brazil, police from Jersey ensured that Helena Pedo was moved to a safe house.

Brother Mark, now living in some luxury in Paris, was pumping money into the legal battle. For the judicial review of the admissibility of the tape, Finch briefed Brian Leary, QC, a heavyweight counsel from London, at a cost of £2,000 a day and a huge brief fee. Although Leary flew into Gibraltar, his yacht, on which he was to live and entertain during the case, arrived before him and lay moored in the marina.

Leary's vast experience and success at the Criminal Bar had earned him the soubriquet of Gangbuster when he was a senior prosecuting counsel. His first act, appearing for Newall in the Gibraltar Supreme Court, was to complain that Desmond had not supplied him in advance with a skeleton argument of the Crown's case.

'If you want a skeleton, I suggest you ask your client,' snapped Desmond.

The court ruled that the magistrate was wrong, but the legal wrangling was to continue through the winter, spring and summer of 1993. It seemed that every time Finch made an application he would win in the lower court, but Desmond would triumph when it was referred to the higher court.

In March 1993, Desmond decided to put a stop to the flow of money and ordered the arrest of Mark on a warrant for double murder. It was a gamble because, in putting the younger brother in the dock on his own, the Crown had practically no evidence to prove the charges. It was only if the two brothers were put on trial together that the prosecution could use all its evidence.

But Desmond's hand was forced when he heard that Mark was planning on moving to the United States, from where extraditions are famously tortuous. Jersey detectives collected the correct documents and made their way to the French capital, where they met the diminutive but dynamic Odile Fraisse, head of the Paris murder squad. She stood less than five feet tall in her stockinged feet, but was something of a legend among French police. She led the armed police unit to Mark's luxury flat in the Rue Paul Valery, close to the Arc de Triomphe. They persuaded the concierge to ring his doorbell claiming to have a parcel, for which he had to sign. When he answered the door they overpowered him.

Inside, amid the expensive bachelor trappings of a luxury apartment, including a spiral staircase and roof garden, they found on the mantelpiece in his living room the original restaurant bill from the 'last supper' the brothers had shared with their parents before the murder, five and a half years earlier. Unlike his brother, Mark immediately agreed to extradition back to Jersey, where he fought bitterly and unsuccessfully for his trial to take place before Roderick could be brought back.

By now Helena Pedo had agreed to travel to Jersey, to swear an affidavit in front of the island's Attorney General about the fireside confession, giving Desmond vital back-up material if the taped confession should come under fresh legal challenge. But in court, Desmond was still complaining in vain about 'the legal paralysis of the case' as Finch redoubled his efforts, now claiming the arrest at sea had been unlawful, using a recent House of Lords case, R v Bennett, as the hearing once again headed for the sandbanks. To the Crown team of Desmond and Ian Christmas was added Brian Jubb, who had been junior counsel in the Bennett case.

Tempers started to fray as Finch described the arrest as 'modern day piracy', adding, 'why bother with international law if you just send out a gunboat and bring him in?'

Desmond replied, 'It makes no difference whether Newall had been pulled out of the sea on a fish hook or brought in by the tide on a broken-down vessel; once he was in the jurisdiction he had been lawfully arrested.'

Finch then claimed his client could no longer get a fair trial in Jersey because of the prejudicial publicity the case had generated over the past years, and cited a case decided just a day earlier in which a judge at the Old Bailey had thrown out charges for that very reason, against police officers accused of corruption in their investigation of the Birmingham Six. That argument failed too and, as summer dragged on into autumn, Finch applied for legal aid. Desmond pointed out his client still had a £200,000 yacht. Here was the first indication that the Gibraltar street-fighter was starting to think the game was up.

On 1 October 1993, Finch took Desmond to one side and offered a deal, and they went off to negotiate. The defence were still threatening to take the case to the Privy Council, which would add untold months to the proceedings; perhaps a deal giving the Crown one and a half birds in the hand, rather than the chance of losing two in the bush, was a good idea.

When an agreement seemed near they took lunch at a restaurant, which, in the Mediterranean sunshine, with copious amounts of food and, especially, drink, continued through the afternoon into the early evening before Finch lurched to his feet with every intention of going home.

Virtually the entire Bar in London and most Commonwealth countries know that lunch with Desmond can be hazardous. Unfortunately, the word had clearly not reached Finch. Manoeuvring himself on to the pavement he failed to spot a skateboarder, was knocked aside and landed in an agonized heap. As an ambulance carried him to hospital, with his leg broken in two places, the whole scene was captured by the unforgiving eye of a Channel Island television crew who, having shown the events to their viewers at home, happily provided free and hilarious viewing of the incident for the press for the rest of the night.

The terms of the deal negotiated by Desmond, and fully approved by the Jersey authorities, were:

> Newall to end his legal challenge to extradition and agree to return to Jersey; to plead guilty to two murders and show the police where the bodies were buried.
>
> No further charges to be brought.
>
> No order for costs to be enforced.
>
> Mark Newall to plead guilty to being an accessory after the fact, and murder charges against him to be dropped.

The Attorney General to recommend Mark Newall receive a six-year sentence.
No further charges against him and no order for costs.

Finally, fifteen months after we had all gathered for the first extradition hearing, Desmond could open the case for the Crown in open court. His speech was a sensation from the moment he began: 'It is the case for the Crown that Roderick Newall, then an officer in a fashionable regiment, was an assassin of his parents, Nicholas and Elizabeth Newall, on or about 10 October 1987.'

For this final hearing, Finch turned up in a wheelchair, and Desmond wished him a speedy recovery and paid him a typically generous compliment: 'He is known for his passionate oratory on behalf of his clients, and he has proved himself to be a master of court procedures, which enabled him not only to prevent the extradition for so long, but also brought him close to having his client discharged on legal grounds.'

The final cost of extraditing Newall was £2.5 million, of which the people of Gibraltar's share was £70,000, the taxpayers of Jersey picking up the rest. Newall's legal costs, mostly funded by Mark, have been estimated to be close to £250,000.

Newall was on his way back to Jersey and the threat of a shoot-out, and the attempted assassination of Desmond, had been averted. The senior Jersey police officer, Detective Superintendent Paul Marks, said, 'The inspiration for the whole team for virtually all of the fifteen months in Gibraltar was down to the incredible intellect and hard work of Desmond de Silva, QC. He is unbelievably brilliant at his job and he kept us going with his work and wit.'

Newall did help police find the bodies, and Desmond was there to watch a ghoulish moonlight reconstruction, to help the murderer get his bearings in relation to a light he remembered seeing in a nearby house, overlooking the makeshift gravesite. He did plead guilty and was sentenced to life imprisonment in August 1994, and Mark did receive six years; some of the ten jurors who made up the sentencing panel wanted more, but were outvoted.

True to his money-grabbing nature, Mark tried to block Stephen's understandable attempt to deprive the brothers of the inheritance they had won through murder. 'Greedy and distasteful,' he called his uncle, although he withdrew his objection later.

But the story was not to end there for Christopher Finch. Four years later, almost to the day, he flew into Heathrow and was arrested by Scotland Yard detectives engaged in Operation Cotton, a four-year operation targeted at drug dealers and money laundering on the Rock. He was charged with conspiracy to supply cannabis and launder the proceeds of drugs between 1 January 1995 and 13 August 1998, the date of his arrest. But five years on, in 2003, after even longer court proceedings than the Newall extradition, the Crown was forced to drop the charges against him and eight other defendants, after a judge ruled there had been illegal police entrapment.

## 25

# The Traitor Who Never Was

THE WORLD OF ESPIONAGE IS MURKY, BLURRED AND FULL OF SHADES, with no primary colours, let alone black and white. Millions have enjoyed John Le Carre's tales of 'the Circus', a game of bluff and counter bluff a million miles from the goodies and baddies in Ian Fleming's James Bond mythology. Only those involved in real-life espionage knew the truth of what went on in the dangerous decades after the end of World War II and the iciest days of the Cold War.

In the early 1980s, Desmond was involved in a trial that caused an absolute sensation. It was full of spies with secret cameras, codebooks, radio transmitters, invisible ink and more cloak, dagger and intrigue than any spy-novel reader could wish for. But, as time went by, what had seemed wrong then now started to seem right and, more and more intriguingly, the very real question was: had our intelligence service conned the highest law officer in the land to maintain a cover to hoodwink the KGB?

As the decade dawned, Ronald Reagan secured the White House, in a victory for the hawkish side of right-wing Republicanism, and the Iron Lady had already started her three-term premiership in No. 10. Brezhnev was succeeded in the Kremlin by the former KGB head Yuri Andropov, a clear sign of Soviet intent; the battle lines of both East and West were still clearly drawn.

In January 1980, a small story appeared on the foreign pages of the better broadsheet newspapers: a Canadian professor had admitted to spying for the Russians. Professor Hugh Hambleton, fifty-seven, a professor of economics at Laval University in Quebec, had confessed he had been an unpaid Soviet secret agent for thirty years. Hambleton was Canadian born, but a British subject, holding dual nationality and a British passport. He had been educated in Britain and had a British father and grandfather.

It was reported he had fought for General de Gaulle's Free French forces during World War II, and been recruited post-war by the Russians when he worked for Canadian military intelligence in the then newly-created West Germany. He had not become an active agent until 1961, when he was contacted by the KGB in Spain, it was said. The Royal Canadian Mounted Police (RCMP) counter-intelligence unit had seized a short-wave radio at the home of his ninety-one-year-old mother and had also taken maps, the diary in which he recorded his missions, a large number of books and an empty five-gallon gasoline container.

Interesting, if mysterious, news. But the reason it was hidden away on the foreign pages was the blasé way in which the case was being handled. Hambleton himself was quoted in later reports as confidently predicting he would not be charged, because the information he had passed was not classified as secret.

'On that basis I don't think I'm in any real danger. I had no access to secret documents, I had no information that they [the Russians] could not have got from a dozen other places,' he was reported as saying. 'I never got any money and I never asked for any. Once you start accepting money they've got you.'

He sounded supremely confident, after apparently being fully debriefed by the RCMP. Its spokesman also seemed totally relaxed about the matter and, when asked about possible charges, replied off-hand that that would be down to the Justice Department, which would make a decision within a few weeks. When nothing more was heard it seemed clear that the Canadian government had struck some deal to sweep the embarrassing revelations under the carpet and say no more about them.

There came a point when Hambleton wanted to visit an aunt in England. It was made quite clear to him that if he did come to England he would most certainly face prosecution. Two years later, Hambleton suddenly turned up in London and was arrested at his hotel. He was taken to Rochester Row police station and charged under Section 1 of the 1911 Official Secrets Act. Police objected to bail and the sixty-year-old was remanded in custody.

The allegations against him consisted of communicating NATO secrets to 'an enemy'. 'Enemy' in law was taken to mean a potential enemy with whom Britain might someday be at war. The Soviet Union in the Cold War days certainly fell into the category of an enemy power. Not long after Hambleton's arrest, Desmond was retained as defence counsel.

When Desmond visited him for a conference in prison, he raised with the client the issue of why on earth he had come to England after being warned that he was likely to be prosecuted. 'I did not think I would be arrested,' said the professor later, 'particularly as I had an immunity granted to me by the Attorney General of Canada.'

When I interviewed Desmond about this case, he remembered saying to his solicitor that it was an interesting legal position that an Attorney General under the Crown could give a man an immunity which another Attorney General, under the same Crown, need not heed. This might provide the defence with an opportunity to argue abuse of process. How about advancing the argument at committal, 'one Crown, one immunity'?

Although as a matter of law there may have been good constitutional arguments to the contrary, Desmond remembers instructions being taken from the client on this specific matter. While it would be a breach of professional privilege to disclose what transpired in conference, what can be said is that the point was never taken. To the non-lawyer that Hambleton was, it might have seemed like a perfect solution to his plight – 'one Crown, one immunity'. To a journalist such as myself, looking back, the clear inference was that for some reason, Hambleton did not want the point taken, which might result in his release at the committal proceedings before the magistrate. But why?

Not being a QC at that stage, Desmond selected John Lloyd-Eley, QC, to lead him at trial at the Old Bailey. Lloyd-Eley, who had led Desmond many times before, had been in military intelligence during World War II.

When the case arrived at the Old Bailey in November 1982, Hambleton faced two charges, extending the allegations of his spying activities right up to 1979:

> That between September 1 1956 and October 31 1961, for a purpose prejudicial to the safety or interests of the United Kingdom, you communicated to a Russian agent information, namely top secret, secret and confidential material belonging to the North Atlantic Treaty Organization, which was calculated to be, or might have been intended to be, directly or indirectly useful to an enemy.

> That between September 1 1956 and November 5 1979, for a purpose prejudicial to the safety and interests of the United Kingdom, you obtained information which was calculated to be, or might have been or was intended to be, directly or indirectly useful to the enemy.

There was nothing like the prospect of a spy trial to set the pulse racing, but the press were puzzled. Hambleton had clearly secured a deal in Canada, presumably for immunity from prosecution in exchange for telling all he knew about what he had passed on to the Russians, who he knew and how he had done it. If that was the case, why was he being prosecuted here, in the jurisdiction of the same Queen who had granted immunity in Canada? Surely it would be a simple matter for the defence to have the charges thrown out before the trial even started.

The Hambleton case was listed for 2 p.m., after another spy trial at 10.30 a.m. This one was a real old-fashioned case, a sort of male version of Mata Hari, in which a young woman, Rhona Ritchie, working at the British Embassy in Tel Aviv, had fallen in love with an Israeli agent and supplied him with as many secrets as she could lay her hands on. She pleaded guilty and was sentenced to fifteen years. Confident that a corking story had been filed for tomorrow's papers, and anticipating that the Hambleton case could not possibly match it and, anyway, would probably be mired in unreportable legal argument, the press wandered off to the Magpie and Stump, across the road from the court, for well-earned refreshment.

By 2.30 p.m. there was a stampede back across the street, when word had emerged that not only had the Hambleton case started, in front of Mr Justice Croom-Johnson, but the Attorney General, Sir Michael Havers, QC was on his feet, telling the jury an incredible story that made the Ritchie case sound tame by comparison.

Far from being the low-grade informant the professor had so confidently described to reporters in Quebec in January 1980, the court was told he now admitted he had had dinner in a Moscow flat with Andropov, just seven years before, when the Russian was head of the KGB. At that dinner, Andropov had offered to finance the professor's election campaign to become a Canadian MP.

Sir Michael, who had been closely involved in the prosecution of two other traitors, Geoffrey Prime and Michael Bettaney, told the jury Hambleton had admitted 'spying for the Russians over a period of thirty years' and was alleged to have photographed 'maybe 300' NATO documents. He had been detained in Canada and 'not prosecuted' but, on coming to London, he had been rearrested by Special Branch and interviewed for three days. The first thing the Special Branch superintendent had told him was, 'You have not been given immunity', even though Hambleton said he possessed a letter stating that no action would be taken against him, the court heard.

What accrued from those interviews were details of meetings with Soviet agents in Paris and Vienna, messages in dead letterboxes, coded instructions received on a short-wave radio receiver, a special camera to photograph secret documents, and messages in ink that were invisible until treated with hydrochloric acid and cigarette smoke.

Sir Michael showed the jury a piece of equipment Hambleton had called 'a light'. When this was plugged into the earphone socket of a radio, 'the number of the code going over the radio lights up so you can read off the numbers.' He added, intriguingly, 'There is an interesting fact about that decoder. It is not an entirely Russian invention.'

The court heard that Hambleton's first contact with the Russians was a diplomat named Vladimir Bourdine, at the Soviet Embassy in Canada. He had often visited the family's house, as Hambleton's mother was studying Russian. In 1956, at the instigation of the Russians, Hambleton had joined the NATO staff in Paris under John Licence, director of the economic section, who had contacts with the British traitors, Guy Burgess and Donald Maclean. Licence was a homosexual, but Hambleton was not certain whether he was also an agent for the Russians. From May of that year Hambleton had regular meetings with his contacts, both in Paris and Vienna, where he moved in 1958.

Sir Michael said Hambleton had access to documents dealing with the economies of particular countries, but not to military matters. Economic data, to the trained eye, can be highly revealing in assessing military defence capabilities. The Russians had told the professor they were interested in 'original authentic documents of the highest classification.'

Hambleton had said that dinner with Andropov was arranged after he had travelled to Vienna to meet a contact named Paul. He was met at a rendezvous by the Danube and given a Russian diplomatic passport, containing his photograph, and driven to the Russian Embassy in Prague. He flew in a Soviet aircraft from a military airstrip outside Prague, via East Germany and Poland, to Moscow, where he was taken to a third-floor flat in the city centre.

The next morning he met Paul and another man known as 'the American', because he dealt with American affairs. That evening the KGB chief came to the flat, accompanied by seven or eight other men. Over a convivial meal,

Andropov asked him what he thought of the Common Market (now the EU) and Hambleton said that he had replied that he did not think it would last long. None of the other people present spoke during the meal because 'they were all afraid.'

Andropov went on to ask about the United States' defence spending, and the attitude of the young in the West to the Soviet Union. He said he hoped Hambleton could play a role in the world's trouble spots, providing political and economic assessments, and he would like him to become an MP and would pay for his election campaign.

Asked by his interrogators why he had worked for the Russians, Hambleton replied that he was ideologically sympathetic to their cause; it gave him 'a sense of belonging' and he identified most with their officer class.

It was a sensational start to the case and there was more to come the next day, when Sir Michael continued his opening speech, detailing what Hambleton had told Special Branch. The professor said the Russians had given him radio equipment so they could contact him in rapid Morse code on a fixed medium-wave frequency at 8 p.m. on Friday evenings.

He said they also asked him for NATO documents, using the internal reference numbers. 'That was a very significant answer. This is the Russians asking for documents by the documents' own reference number,' the Attorney General told the jury.

When in Paris, Hambleton admitted, he had taken home more than eighty economic documents of the most secret classification, and photographed them overnight before handing over the film to his contacts, usually at brief meetings, often on the Metro.

'These were documents of the very highest secrecy. So important that their disclosure would result in exceptionally grave damage,' continued the Attorney General, who then asked for the court to be cleared and go into camera so he could outline 'the details of the damage caused.'

Hambleton entered the witness box, after the court had been re-opened to press and public, and told the jury he had been a double agent, passing false NATO documents to the Soviets for four years, in an operation masterminded by the French secret service.

He said he had reported his first contact with Bourdine to his uncle, who was a friend of the RCMP commissioner, and his father-in-law, who was a leading official at the Canadian Defence Department. When he went to the University of Paris and the Russians renewed their contact, he again went to the authorities. He was visited by a man who introduced himself as Jean Masson, an agent of the French Service of External Documentation and Counter Espionage. It was he who suggested applying for the job at NATO, which the Russians were to welcome warmly.

Masson also suggested Hambleton give the Russians false information by doctoring the documents they had asked for. 'He would bring me documents which I would photograph and hand over to the KGB. Out of every ten pages, eight would be absolutely genuine and two would be altered in some way,' the professor told the court. He described how nervous he was when taken to Moscow to dine with Andropov. 'I thought I would disappear without trace,' he said. 'I was put under considerable pressure when I was leaving; I was searched very thoroughly.' He insisted he had kept his contacts at home fully informed on his return. 'I thought these things would prove invaluable to Western intelligence,' he added.

Over the next years, Hambleton continued his academic life, and was to gain two doctorates, and attend numerous courses at universities around the world, in a distinguished career. In 1978, he received instructions from the Russians to defect, but he refused to go. At the same time he learned that his wife had revealed his double-agent status to the Russians, but they were not convinced.

He came to Britain after being asked to present a paper at Exeter University on petrochemicals in Saudi Arabia. He was advised by Canadian intelligence not to go because 'they [Britain] had not been put fully into the picture.' He said he had ignored the warning that 'the strongest action' would be taken against him because, he insisted, he had committed no offence.

Until now Hambleton had appeared confident and relaxed, often smiling at the jury and judge, although there was a clash over naming certain agents in open court, which the professor thought would compromise them. It was agreed finally that he should write down their names and addresses and pass them to the judge. He was also keen to put details of what he insisted was his double-agent life in the context of its time. He would prefix many answers with the words: 'You have to remember...'

But the atmosphere changed on the sixth day of the trial, the second day of cross-examination, when his confidence was worn away and he cracked, confessing that far from being 'run' by a French intelligence agent who provided the documents, he had personally selected eighty per cent of them. And not just the 300 documents the Crown had alleged; Hambleton now confessed to betraying 'thousands' of secrets, both economic and military.

It is hard to convey now the shock that was felt then of such a devastating disclosure, ten years or so before the collapse of the Iron Curtain. What is more, here was a defendant confessing in the witness box in the middle of a trial. Not even two-bit thieves put their hands up in the middle of a cross-examination. Old Bailey veterans say nobody before or since has done such a thing.

It was wrung out of Hambleton by Sir Michael Havers, not just the principal law officer of the government, but a man who, during his career at the Bar, was known as a fearless and destructive cross-examiner. The son of the judge who had sent Ruth Ellis to the gallows, and father of Philip Havers, QC and the debonair actor Nigel, Sir Michael wore glasses over a beaky nose and had a slightly dated air about him. He liked to give the impression of slightly muddling through, questioning in a charming and not terribly hostile way, before attempting to pull the rug from beneath the defendant's feet.

Yet even he must have been stunned by Hambleton's sudden caving in. Sir Michael told the jury the professor had started to alter his evidence once he realized the Crown planned to bring members of the RCMP to court to testify. 'Is it because this lying story you were telling is difficult to remember?' he asked. 'Is it because you realize you have boxed yourself in completely?'

Hambleton replied, 'I boxed myself in the moment I took the plane to England.'

SIR MICHAEL: 'Even at this late stage you are still anxious to protect your friends, like Andropov, Paul and Bourdine? Are you still pro-Russian?'

HAMBLETON: 'I am not pro-Russian.'

SIR MICHAEL: 'Do you still identify with them and find it a thrill to be run by them?'

HAMBLETON: 'I said I tended to identify with the officer class; I did not say with the KGB.'

The professor agreed he had passed over increasing numbers of documents because of pressure from the Russians. 'Once you passed one document, you are in a vice are you not?' pressed Sir Michael.

'Yes,' Hambleton replied.

'That is why you passed thousands and thousands of documents?'

'I was under pressure, yes.'

Sir Michael said these answers made 'utter nonsense' of Hambleton's claims to be a double agent. 'If you were a double agent it would not matter a tinker's cuss if the Russians said you were a spy, because you were in fact a double agent.'

Leaning closer, the AG went on: 'Do you have qualms or regrets about passing thousands of pages of confidential NATO documents under pressure to the Russians?'

'Yes sir,' Hambleton replied.

'Then you were spying for Russia?'

'I suppose it could be classified that way.'

'There is no other answer.'

'I suppose not.'

In view of the admission he had made, John Lloyd-Eley and Desmond advised Hambleton to change his plea to guilty. Sir Michael left court with a sense of triumph at an outstanding and brilliant victory. The next day the spy was sentenced to ten years' imprisonment, a light sentence for ostensibly such a damaging traitor, but one which reflected his age, the late change of plea and the fact that the offences dated back nearly thirty years.

The heads of Canadian and French security services were in court to see the judge tell Hambleton he had committed, 'a very grave offence which has to be recognized; although it is a very long time ago you committed those acts, they caught up with you in the end.'

Sir Michael told the court, 'There was no question of this man ever being a double agent. Allegations of member states of NATO running an agent, in view of the firm undertaking given by all member states, is of such gravity that it is essential, in spite of the plea, to say those allegations have no justification at all, damaging no doubt as they were.'

Instantly, MI5 and Special Branch set about putting their spin on proceedings. Security sources were quoted in the papers describing the professor as 'a major spy'. One source told the *Times*, 'He undermined the very fabric of NATO for five years; he was very, very big indeed. After all, Andropov would not have dined with any old agent.' It was said that he had spied 'for the fun of it'; he had 'travelled the world as Moscow's eyes and ears and ended his career as an important conduit for spies in North America, because he enjoyed the glamour and excitement.'

Details of the passwords he had used in meeting his contacts were leaked to inflate the sense of a spy novel come to life. In Vienna, Hambleton had arranged to meet a KGB officer who would ask him, 'do you have any etchings of Paris?' to which he would reply, 'not in Paris but in London.'

It was said Hambleton had deliberately gone public in 1980 to play down his role, knowing the Canadians were having trouble framing charges against him. He had been exposed by a Czech defector to the West, but the FBI were furious at the way the Canadians were dragging their feet. Hambleton was arrogant and, having got away with it for so long, never believed he would be prosecuted.

All this was pumped into the papers unchallenged as the professor was locked away. Indeed, a few months later, it was reported that he had provided the Russians with evidence that Israel was manufacturing atomic bombs, and his reports were regarded as so important that every member of the Politburo read them.

But after the trial things started to change. In June 1986, Hambleton was driven from Gartree Prison, Leicestershire, where some of Britain's nastiest criminals were housed, to Heathrow, where he was put on a flight to Toronto. The Home Office said it was part of a new repatriation scheme, so he would serve the rest of his sentence near his ninety-five-year-old mother. Hambleton was the first prisoner in a British jail to benefit under the new scheme. Then, in October 1987, it leaked that he had been released almost as soon as he had arrived back in Canada, and now enquiring minds on both sides of the Atlantic started putting two and two together.

Around that time glasnost and perestroika became the new flavour of international diplomacy; Gorbachev had risen as a force in Russia and Mrs Thatcher declared she could do business with him.

Had the whole Old Bailey trial been a charade to persuade the Russians into thinking that the material Hambleton had been passing them was entirely genuine? Once glasnost had arrived, the paramount need to continue hoodwinking the KGB disappeared. If there had to be a show trial to convince the Russians that he was not a double agent, then Hambleton's collapse in the witness box in the face of Sir Michael's triumphant cross-examination could not have been better scripted. But surely the highest law officer in the land could not go into open court and say to one of the country's most senior judges, 'there was no question of this man ever being a double agent… it is essential to say those allegations have no justification at all.' Those words, spoken by the Attorney General, would have served to comfort the KGB that Hambleton was always one of theirs. The collapse of the professor in the witness box destroyed his account that he had been planting disinformation on the Russians. That, too, must have reassured the KGB that all the information they had from their trusted agent was genuine. Looking back at the sequence of events – his coming to England, his arrest, his trial, which led to Sir Michael denying that Hambleton was anything other than a KGB spy – to many it has the hallmarks of a put-up job in the great Cold War game of deception.

The other, less likely, inference is that Sir Michael did not know, and the intelligence services had concealed material from him which led him to believe he had pulled off the greatest victory of his career in a hugely expensive Old Bailey trail, when it was all stage managed to protect the overall Western intelligence effort. The rooster taking credit for the sun coming up?

# 26

# The Trusted Mole

STAN LAUREL AND OLIVER HARDY WERE TWO OF THE GREATEST STARS of Hollywood comedy; their grainy 1930s black-and-white two-reelers are still loved and enjoyed today. From a later era there was Abbott and Costello. During the terrible conflict in Bosnia, their names were pinched by a corporal and two British officers who had to disguise their Serb names and operate undercover. One of them was Major Mike Stanley, who flew out as Captain Laurel but was in fact born Milos Stankovic. His father, Radomir Stankovic, was an officer in the Royal Yugoslav Army who, having fought the Germans and the Communists, had to escape after the Communist takeover in Yugoslavia in 1945. His mother, half-Scottish, half-Serbian, was in the Special Operations Executive (SOE) during World War II. They settled in England, where Milos was sent to public school and distinguished himself, ending up as head boy, before going on to Sandhurst and a commission into the elite Parachute Regiment.

As Captain Stankovic, he found himself in the midst of the horror of Balkan savagery, working alongside the commander of BRITFOR – Brigadier Andrew Cumming, and then Generals Sir Michael Rose and Sir Rupert Smith, who picked him as someone who could act as a conduit between themselves and Radovan Karadžić, the self-appointed president of Republika Srpska, and General Ratko Mladić.

For two years he proved to be one of the most effective agents in the area, working with the appropriate authorities to provide vital information on leading Bosnian-Serb war criminals. He also conducted rescue operations to repatriate Muslims, Serbs and Croats caught on the wrong side of the ethnic divide, which was codenamed Schindler's List. Promoted to major and decorated by the Queen with an MBE, Stankovic suddenly found himself arrested under the Official Secrets Act 1989, on suspicion of passing information to the Serbs that might endanger the lives of British soldiers. All who knew him, even remotely, or who had heard of his reputation, were stunned.

When he was given bail, a friend in Special Branch advised him to seek the services of Desmond de Silva, QC. It was advice he did not regret. Together the QC, solicitor Steven Barker and client recognized that Stankovic was the victim of a power play between Britain and the United States in Bosnia. Stated simply, they could see that the Americans were undoubtedly helping the Bosnian Muslims, in order to appear pro-Muslim (at least in Bosnia) to help with the coalition of Islamic states that the US had built up against Saddam Hussein. The Americans viewed the British as not sufficiently anti-Serb and for the British General Rose to have a Serb – as they saw Stankovic – at his right hand was too much. In addition, a local Sarajevo newspaper supporting the Muslims called Stanley the 'Trusted Mole', trusted by Rose and the Serbs. The inevitable happened. The Americans began to put it about that Major Stankovic was a spy for the Serbs, which led to his arrest by the Ministry of Defence Police, who proved themselves to be hopelessly out of their depth in dealing with the Byzantine complexities of this Balkan war. Fortunately, a powerful team of people was assembled to ensure that the gallant major was not to be a legal victim of an American obsession.

Desmond led the defence in law, bringing in, on the military side, General Sir Mike Jackson, then commander-in-chief of Britain's land forces. He took up the torch, while Virginia Bottomley, Stankovic's constituency MP and Martin Bell, the MP who had met the major in Bosnia and covered so much of the fighting for the BBC, were to lead the charge in Parliament. In fact, Martin Bell had already raised the whole affair in the House of Commons. Again, he drew on lengthy first-hand experience of Bosnia, an advantage not shared by anyone else in the House.

To quote from the chapter 'A Soldier's Story' in Tim Slessor's book, *Ministries of Deception*:

> Major Stankovic's job was to deal with the Serbs – the most difficult of the three ethnic groups – and he did so. His job was to get to know them, and he did so. In the Bihac crisis he was personally responsible for freeing fifty Canadian UN hostages held by the Serbs and unblocking convoys and the airport. He did that alone. He saved the life of a Muslim woman wounded by sniper fire in the town

> of Vitez. He scooped her up and took her to hospital and saved her life. He was awarded the MBE. He received his medal from the Queen. Beyond the line of duty, Major Stankovic took part in humanitarian endeavours. I cannot specify exactly what he did, though if charges are laid against him, I may have to do so, because they bear on his courage and his character.

Had this case come to the Old Bailey, the distinguished lines of generals and politicians trooping in and out of the witness box would have ensured it was a treason trial unequalled for a long time. One hundred years after the notorious Dreyfus Affair, here once again was the danger of another disgraceful miscarriage of justice in the military. Faced with the disturbing echoes of history, Desmond and Barker decided that they could not simply let things happen, and so formed an aggressive, proactive strategy. Desmond took the view that, in the next interview with the MoD Police, the major would have to disclose matters not just classified, but which potentially could imperil the lives of 'assets' still in place. To quote Tim Slessor again:

> Steven Barker, Desmond de Silva, QC, and the major started to put together a detailed document. It almost certainly leaned on information from those army officers who knew Milos Stankovic and, even more relevantly, knew what he had done in Bosnia. When finished, the file would be delivered to the Director of Public Prosecutions and the Attorney General, so that those two Crown authorities could see the strength of the defence. And, presumably, weigh it against the relative weakness of the MoD case. At the same time, Barker was repeatedly asking the MoD Police for information regarding who had made the original allegations about Major Stankovic and what, in reasonably specific terms, those allegations were. He never got any reply that made sense. To Dreyfus one could now add Kafka. It was a fair bet that the MoD policemen were appreciative of neither. Maybe they thought they were Muslim enclaves somewhere in Bosnia.

Before facing the police questions, Desmond, Barker and the major carefully went through their tactics. On the appointed day it was down to Surrey and the police station. When the police turned up, there were four of them. It seemed they intended to operate in two shifts over the next two days. They told the Guildford custody sergeant that, as yet, they had insufficient evidence to lay any charges against the major. This was after two years of inquiries (they had spent a year on a covert investigation before the arrest). Now, they wished him held in custody while they questioned him in order to get the evidence, so that they could lay specific charges. They were fishing.

Everyone sat down. The senior of the four policemen slid a multipage list of questions out of a file and looked around the room to see that everyone was ready. The two tape recorders were switched on. He was about to lead off with his first question when Major Stankovic got in first. It had been planned the night before. Quickly identifying himself, and speaking with a deliberation that made sure the tapes would not miss a syllable, he began:

> I would like to address your detective chief superintendent, as I recognize him to be the senior investigating officer in this case. I heard your detective sergeant here tell the custody sergeant that he does not have sufficient evidence to charge me. That does not surprise me. It doesn't surprise me as I know you don't have it. I know you don't have it because I have done nothing wrong. I can tell you another thing: you can investigate this case for the next two years and all you are going to come up with is a box of contradictions.
>
> I am not going to sit here and have my life – my professional life and my private life – dissected when you have had two years to investigate me. Two years! One year of which was after my arrest, during which time you have pored over every single scrap of paper that you could find in my house or in my room at Bracknell. During which time you have interviewed close to 300 people, and during the course of that you have tried to debunk me and tarnish my name and blacken me with some of the witnesses.
>
> And what have I had to do in the meantime? I have had to fight for my right to get access to this documentation, which you seized over a year ago. And you, at every twist and turn, you have tried to deny me this. Then, in a letter, you tell me that you are prepared to give us the statements of eighty-two witnesses. Then you change your mind and give us a synopsis. Then you give us a second synopsis, because the first has mistakes in it. Then at the eleventh hour and fifty-ninth minute you toss us four statements. I haven't had time to deal with these statements because you did it at such a late hour. It is symptomatic of everything that has gone on this last year. It's a cheap and dirty trick.

> I tell you, two days is not enough time to discuss Bosnia. I could sit here for two weeks, two months even, trying to build the sort of picture to place all of this stuff in context. And in so doing I would have to tell you things that would make your eyeballs pop out. Things that even the generals don't know about.
>
> I'll tell you another thing. The British Army was my life, and, not only was it my life, it was my soul. I gave everything to that Army – everything. I committed myself wholly to it and you have destroyed that. You and your chief constable have taken that away from me. Your chief constable insisted that I was removed from Staff College. And you have destroyed my career – along with these other people and their shadowy allegations that you won't even tell me about.
>
> And not only have you destroyed my career, you have also destroyed what is left of my family. My father died because of the pressure and strain that I put him under simply because I was out there in Bosnia. He died a bitter, old man who should be alive today. And I have the burden of that. No one else. And you have come close to destroying me as well.
>
> I can tell you now, you have done nothing this past year to convince me that this is a fair investigation. I am sorry – I do not trust you and I do not trust the motives in this investigation. You have to take what I am going to say seriously. I am not going to say anything to you. I am now going to sit here and this is the very last thing that you are going to hear me say to you in this police station.

Two large files, wrapped and sealed, were put on the table. One addressed to the Attorney General – Sir Nicholas Lyell, QC, MP, a friend of Desmond's for thirty years, and the other to the Director of Public Prosecutions – Sir David Calvert-Smith, Desmond's old adversary in the Grobbelaar, Fashanu, Segers football-corruption case. The sealed files were transmitted to Lyell and Calvert-Smith under the strict condition that the MoD Police and the Crown Prosecution Service would not see any part of their contents. Indeed, such was the sensitive nature of some of the material that a plaintive request from the MoD Police to look at parts of the secret files was refused.

Finally, after five months of painstaking analysis of the files, Calvert-Smith made a decision. There was insufficient evidence against the major. According to Desmond, there was not a shred of evidence against his client, who for two years lived with the agony of being destroyed on the rocks of international politics.

General Sir Mike Jackson, who became chief of the general staff, was hamstrung by his position to describe at length his true feelings about the case, which he referred to somewhat euphemistically as 'quite sensitive ground'. But from his desk in Whitehall he made it quite clear how shocked he was at the arrest of Stankovic, particularly as he had first-hand experience of his decency and even-handedness from a personal family connection.

'In the spring of 1992 we, as in the Jackson family, engaged a young Bosnian Muslim girl as an au pair for our then very young son. Her parents were at that time in Sarajevo, which in 1992 was under siege and continued to be so for some time,' he said.

'She was very upset and it was very hard for her to watch the TV news and so forth. It crossed my mind to help by asking one or two people if they could take a small package to her parents, containing food and some personal items and some bird food for their canary or budgerigar. Milos was then in Bosnia and volunteered to see if he could get the package delivered, which he was able to do.

'They were a Muslim couple and he started quite a friendship with them. That's what hit me about the personal family nature of it. On one of my visits to Sarajevo I went with Milos to see the old couple and it was quite emotional.

'So when Milos was arrested, allegedly for spying for the Serbs I was very shocked. I had personal proof that he had been very kind, at some risk to himself, to this elderly Muslim couple. I gave a statement to the MoD Police underlining much of what I have told you and being of the view, not having seen any of the evidence so I could not make a judgment, that I could help with the man I know.

'For Milos it was very difficult. I had great sympathy for the position he found himself in. As events unfolded, the allegations were unfounded, because he was never put on trial.'

General Jackson has high praise for Desmond for doing 'a very good job for Milos', adding, 'This was not just a case for Desmond because he felt personally very strongly about it.'

Three years later, when his term as Director of Public Prosecutions was almost over, Sir David, who went on the High Court Bench thereafter, told me of his admiration for the approach adopted by Desmond and Barker in this case. 'I thought the work Desmond and his solicitor put in was excellent and indeed I did tell Martin Bell that it was first-class work which, should it be emulated by other defence counsel, would make the decisions I and my staff had to make much easier and justice much speedier,' he said.

In defending, counsel have a tough decision to make, whether to go on the attack – 'your cutlass in your teeth' to quote a favourite phrase of Desmond's – and run the risk of exposing your position, inviting possible criticism of giving the game away. Many counsel would take the attitude of let the Crown come to us and see whether we want to give evidence or not, and not put our cards on the table, in the hope of persuading the prosecution that it hasn't got a strong case.

The views of the chief of the general staff were echoed by Sir David-Calvert Smith. 'Desmond's approach has to be commended because, if you are innocent, why not say so? It is a high-risk policy if you are not innocent and, of course, counsel may suspect but cannot possibly know, but it was typical of Desmond that he was bold and that he took the decision, which paid off.'

To this day there sits in the solicitor's firm of Barker Gillette a safe supplied by the Ministry of Defence, within which they insisted the papers in this case should be secured. Only Barker and Desmond knew the combination. Whereas the MoD may have forgotten about this safe, the major can neither forget nor forgive, for reasons described in detail in his critically-acclaimed account of the war, *Trusted Mole*, said by the *Times* to be 'by far the best book to have come out of the Balkan wars…'

# 27

# This Sporting Life

How can someone who takes pride in his total ignorance of our national sport come to be described in a two-page profile in the *Times* as Football's Greatest Defender? He wasn't being compared with Rio Ferdinand or Bobby Moore, but with the finest performers in wig and gown.

Desmond revels in his total lack of interest in the beautiful game and is much more of a rugby man. Indeed, before arriving in the cathedral city of Winchester, to undertake the defence of former Wimbledon goalkeeper Hans Segers in a sensational football corruption case, Desmond had never watched a football match, even on television. Before the trial, one newspaper assigned a reporter to find out which team each of the leading counsel supported. Rodney Klevan, QC was happy to declare his allegiance to Manchester City; Trevor Burke and Jerome Lynch came up with suitable answers. But when the reporter asked the fourth barrister, 'And who do you support?' Desmond barked, 'My wife and child.'

The simple answer to the question of how he became so revered in a world whose ebbs and tides moved him so little, is that any advocate as good as he can master any brief. Basic human behaviour and motivations, which lie at the heart of criminal trials, are the raw material with which the criminal barrister works; the rules of evidence by and large remain constant. In the course of his career, Desmond acquired expert knowledge in ballistics and forensic medicine without having to go down to the morgue or the shooting range; he did the same for football without having to sit with 50,000 others for ninety minutes on a Saturday afternoon. But Desmond used his disinterest in football as a badge of honour and part of his armoury of charm, to claim the empathy of other non-football lovers on the jury, particularly women, but in such a stylish and humorous way as not to alienate the genuine fans.

What is more, Desmond clearly relished every moment in the limelight that football brought him; a stream of successful and financially very rewarding cases provided him with some of his finest moments. In the space of just a few years he defended one of the most famous managers in the Premiership, a Premiership coach, two future England players and an international goalkeeper, as well as advising the England rugby captain, one of the country's favourite jockeys, and saving its most successful woman jockey. If the case came to a contested trial, Desmond won.

His incredible run of sporting cases started at Winchester Crown Court in January 1997, where the dock was filled with such football talent as Liverpool's immensely gifted, if erratic, goalkeeper, Bruce Grobbelaar; John Fashanu, an England international, once of Wimbledon and later Aston Villa; the Dutchman Hans Segers, who played as goalkeeper for Wimbledon; and a Malaysian businessman, Richard Lim.

Grobbelaar, Fashanu, Segers and Lim were all charged with conspiring with others to take cash to fix the outcome of matches. Grobbelaar also faced a further charge of accepting £2,000 from his friend Chris Vincent to throw a game. Upon the outcome of thrown games – the Crown was to allege – millions of pounds were made by shadowy Far Eastern gaming syndicates. It was a case that put on trial the very integrity of English football itself.

The allegations had arisen from a sting operation carried out by reporters at the *Sun* newspaper into the Liverpool goalkeeper after a tip-off from Vincent, a man so corrupt himself that when accused in court of being 'a viper', he answered, 'correct'. A secret camera was planted in a Southampton hotel room in an attempt to catch Grobbelaar taking the bribe from his friend.

The covert recording having been made, reporters then confronted Grobbelaar just as he was flying out to Zimbabwe and the story was splashed across their newspaper. The police followed up the published account and uncovered what they believed to be a flow of money on behalf of a Far Eastern betting syndicate being paid to the two goalkeepers, via Lim and Fashanu. Grobbelaar was said to have been paid the biggest single bung: £40,000 to throw the Newcastle United v Liverpool match in November 1993, which the home team won 3-0.

Some of the results of matches where money was supposed to have changed hands did not quite fit the intended outcome. For instance, Liverpool had been 3-0 down against Manchester United in a match Grobbelaar was meant to have thrown, but came storming back to level at 3-3, at which time the Liverpool goalkeeper made a number of stunning saves.

When the trial began, before Mr Justice Tuckey, the jury was told that the defendants would be guilty if they were proved to have received or agreed to take money on the understanding that the results would be fixed, even if it didn't work out that way through their own efforts or those of other players.

Charts were produced by the prosecution showing the number of mobile phone calls between the defendants before and after key matches, and large sums of money being paid into their bank accounts. Lim, the alleged middleman, was said to have received more than £500,000 as a slush fund for bribery from sources in Indonesia and Singapore. This was a mere bagatelle considering that vast sums, according to the prosecution, were made by corrupt syndicates betting on a fixed result.

Desmond was defending Segers, who was known as one of the most consistent and reliable keepers in the Premiership. At the heart of the Crown's case against him was the allegation that he and Fashanu, then teammates at Wimbledon, had put more than £80,000 in cash into Swiss bank accounts only days after suffering three heavy defeats. This was just one instance of infusion into their accounts.

Segers had never met Grobbelaar off the field but, like every Wimbledon player, he was in thrall to Fashanu, the powerfully-built ex-Barnardo's boy who actually hated football, but claimed he played the game solely to make money. A martial arts expert, he had been the dominant personality in the dressing room when a player and, after retirement through injury, became a ruthless and successful businessman.

The big problem for the defence was that Segers – whose Crazy Gang teammates at Wimbledon had told him his head 'was as wooden as his clogs' – had, when arrested, regaled the police with a pack of lies. He was the only defendant to answer their questions and, without legal advice, had panicked and told them the money had come from a fantasy life of crime as a teenage car thief in Holland. It was all sheer nonsense but it strengthened the prosecution's case against him immeasurably for, as the Crown was able to claim, this pack of lies was told by Segers because he had to cover up the real source of this money – corruption.

Desmond's tactic was clearly to keep his head down while the major battle was being fought between the Crown – who were trying to prove their core allegation that Grobbelaar was crooked – and Klevan, who was busy ripping to shreds the prosecution's star witness, Vincent.

But far from riding on their coat-tails, Desmond had to neutralize the very damaging evidence of the lies and the Swiss bank account. In the witness box, Segers admitted immediately that he had told the police 'absolute rubbish' and that the money had come from a tie-making company he had been involved in, some work for Dutch TV and forecasting Dutch football results for Lim. He pointed out that the 1993/4 season, when many of the fixed games were supposed to have taken place, had been Wimbledon's most successful year, when they finished in the top six, their best ever league position; hardly likely if their goalkeeper was taking money to lose matches.

A succession of expert witnesses, including former Arsenal goalkeeper turned TV pundit Bob Wilson, were called to take the jury through endless videos and show that none of the goals Segers conceded could have been deliberate.

The trial was also the scene for two of Desmond's most famous faux pas. In the course of a stream of witnesses, all of them household names, internationals and premiership stars, Desmond asked one, in his normal stentorian tones: 'You were playing in a match involving Wimbledon and Queens Park Rovers?' Amid the laughter the judge reminded the blushing barrister that the west London team renowned as QPR are, of course, Queens Park Rangers.

Later he asked Joe Kinnear, the well-known manager of his client's own team Wimbledon, to confirm to the jury that his name was Roy Kinnear – in fact the name of the then recently deceased roly-poly actor. Segers' solicitor, Mel Goldberg, believes the first error may well have been deliberate. In the book *The Final Score* he co-wrote with Segers, he asks was it, 'a mistake or a very calculated slip of the tongue to warm up the audience or jury?'

The second was more likely to be a slip as, exasperated with himself, Desmond recovered by turning to his junior, the Tottenham Hotspur-supporting Steven Berrick, and waving his notes, berated him, 'How do you expect me to read your handwriting?' to renewed hoots of laughter and more warm smiles from the jury.

Desmond's next bon mot was a brilliant piece of calculation and spontaneous wit. Leading counsel for the Crown was David Calvert-Smith, later a QC and the Director of Public Prosecutions before becoming a High Court judge.

This neat and precise advocate, who had captained the school football team at Eton, rose to make his final speech to the jury, knocked a jug of water and sent its contents flying across the table, flooding his notes and spilling cascades over the expensive trousers seated alongside him. As he made desperate and mostly futile attempts to mop up the deluge with his silk handkerchief, Desmond's voice boomed, 'But David, you told me your case was watertight!' a remark greeted with hoots of laughter in court.

After two days' deliberations the jury was unable to agree a verdict and a retrial started a few months later. It was held in the same court, but in front of a different judge, Mr Justice McCullough, who adopted a much tougher approach than that taken by Mr Justice Tuckey, who allowed a certain latitude, which suited the defence.

McCullough clamped down straight away on what he deemed to be celebrity-style behaviour of the defendants, particularly Fashanu, playing to the gallery and signing autographs. He even withdrew the defendants' bail over lunchtime on the first day so they had to eat in the cells. He was determined to stamp his authority on the proceedings and not allow defence counsel to win over the jury with the stream of jokes and banter that had characterized the first trial.

In the second trial Desmond was determined to block a gap in the defence over the tie business. The Crown planned to call Segers's business partner in the company, Alphonsus Thuys, who had denied paying the goalkeeper as much money as had been claimed. But under cross-examination by Desmond, Thuys was forced to admit that he actually still owed Segers money. From that point onward his credibility crumbled, as it became apparent that he might have an interest in seeing the man to whom he owed money, imprisoned.

The focus of any allegedly thrown game must always be the goalkeeper. After all, without him letting goals in, the corrupt plan would never work. Desmond emphasized this in one of his finest final speeches.

He began by describing the role of a goalkeeper in captivating language. 'Between the goalposts and under the crossbar there are those who stand alone. They stand between the glory of victory and the agony of relegation. They are the ones who stand alone.' The object of this imagery was to highlight to the jury that it was almost impossible for 'a man who stands alone' not to be spotted if he deliberately let in goals, when 50,000 pairs of eyes were watching him on the pitch and countless millions more on television.

The jury was out for a week and on their return they acquitted all the defendants on the conspiracy charges. However, they were unable to agree a verdict on Grobbelaar and the £2,000 in the *Sun*'s sting and, as two trials had failed to produce a guilty verdict, the Crown followed the convention of dropping the charge.

Desmond had been picked to represent Segers by the solicitor Mel Goldberg, one of the sporting world's most famous legal names, with a clientele including footballers such as Paul Gascoigne, Roberto Baggio, John Fashanu, Paul Merson, Ray Parlour, and Stan Collymore; and boxers such as Chris Eubank and Joe Calzaghe, among many others. The extraordinary range of his contacts was shown by the guest list of his wedding in Mexico in 1970. Although a relatively small affair, he had as his witnesses the then England captain, Bobby Moore; the most famous England captain of the 1950s, Billy Wright; the Arsenal manager, Bertie Mee; and international footballers Charlie Cook and Danny Blanchflower. In *The Final Score* Goldberg wrote, 'Desmond is one of the most impressive lawyers I have ever met. I admire him enormously and it was a privilege to work with him. To borrow football parlance, he is a megastar of the legal profession.'

He described Desmond's closing speech to the jury as, 'a masterpiece: powerful, carefully thought out and delivered in clear, precise tones. There was no room for misunderstanding.' He added, 'Desmond never lost sight of the human factor, the common touch, with a wicked sense of humour. If I had to choose a counsel to defend me on a murder charge… I would want Desmond in my corner. There are many fine advocates but, to coin an Alan Hansen-ism, Desmond is the business.'

Segers was equally complimentary. In that shy way footballers have with words, he limited the tribute to his QC to three words: 'A mighty man.'

Having been cleared, Grobbelaar decided to sue the *Sun* for libel and for a third time faced a jury under cross-examination, this time from the newspaper's counsel, the formidable George Carman, QC, appearing in his last major trial. The jury awarded the goalkeeper £85,000 in damages, a decision which Carman went to his grave believing to be totally inexplicable. In January 2001, the Appeal Court took the unprecedented decision to overturn the libel jury's findings in favour of Grobbelaar, which the judges described as 'an affront to justice.'

The Law Lords allowed the jury verdict to stand, but reduced the damages to just £1, and ordered Grobbelaar to pay the *Sun*'s costs of £500,000, which left him bankrupt.

Even though he had played no part in the civil proceedings, Sir David Calvert-Smith described the appeal court ruling as one of the sweetest personal moments of his five years as Director of Public Prosecutions. Looking back on the two criminal trials, Sir David told me there was nothing he regretted about the way the Crown had run the case.

'I thought the second trial in particular went as well as it could have done as far as I was concerned, so to get three acquittals and the fourth defendant discharged after two deadlocked trials was disappointing,' he said. 'I have no regrets; looking back I would not do anything differently if the case was to start again. But I had a real go at Segers, a real go at Grobbelaar and was deprived of having a go at Fashanu because he did not go in the witness box. I thought Lim did himself no favours at all. I remember he admitted he had bought a shredder and when the question was put to him about the whereabouts of some missing papers, I could hear the whisper from the back row of the jury, "In the shredder," and I thought we were home and dry.

'Whether it was Desmond's closing speech or Rodney Klevan's closing speech that pulled it round, I don't know. In all these sorts of trials there is a danger of being star-struck. Personally I thought the trials were enormous fun. I know that sounds the wrong thing to say, but when do you get the chance to speak to witnesses like Alan Ball? I mean, he has won the World Cup.

'I am a Middlesbrough fan, not a particularly comfortable world at the moment I'm afraid, but I am a very keen sports fan and most of us turn to the back pages of the papers over the breakfast table. But Desmond is not, hence his now famous solecisms, although he is such a skilful advocate I would not put it past him to have done that deliberately. I simply don't know.'

A few years after the trials, Sir David found himself on the same plane bound for Greece as Segers, when the Crown prosecutor was en route to a family holiday and the goalkeeper, then with Tottenham Hotspur, was flying out for a preseason friendly. 'It was my wife who spotted him first in the departures hall; in fact she spotted Glen Hoddle, then she pointed to a man who had his back to us,' he said.

'Segers did recognize me, but not immediately; at first he kept looking at me as if he had seen me somewhere before. On the plane he was three or four rows ahead of me and suddenly there was a lot of animated conversation among the Spurs lot, turning their heads in my direction.

'When we landed and we were waiting for our suitcases on the carousel I just said to him, "How are things going? I hope your life has not been totally ruined?" He said "No." I said, "Have you got a good squad this season?" and he replied, "Really good, we have spent money on some very good players and there's a good spirit in the squad." I said, "Top ten finish then?" He replied, "I never make forecasts. Not now, Mr Calvert-Smith."'

# 28

# Bojangles's Handshake

One of the defence witnesses in the Grobbelaar trial was the colourful football manager Ron Atkinson, a cavalier Scouser known as Big Ron and Mr Bojangles for his chunky jewellery, permanent suntan and love of champagne. But his record as a manager, particularly at West Bromwich Albion, Manchester United, Aston Villa and Atletico Madrid, demanded the greatest respect.

A year after the Winchester epic, he was in need of help over a road-rage case in Birmingham, and Desmond was able to rescue him. In a Court of Appeal judgment, Lord Lane stated that the habit of drivers getting out of their cars, losing their tempers and manhandling other road users was increasing. In such circumstances, the court directed that prison sentences should follow as a matter of course. Given the facts of this case, Big Ron was in serious peril of imprisonment.

An insurance salesman, Martin Player, claimed that when he had stopped at traffic lights Atkinson had got out of his Jaguar, gone over to Player's car, opened the driver's door, grabbed his hair and threatened to 'punch my lights out' after an incident in rush-hour traffic in Digbeth, Birmingham.

The clash made front-page news in the tabloids; the thirty-three-year-old driver claimed the manager had cut him up and, when he had given a blast on his horn, Atkinson had come at him 'red in the face and furious – other motorists were open-mouthed.'

Player went on, 'He held my head down for a few seconds and it was very painful. He is built like a brick outhouse and is way over six feet tall. I am just 5ft 8ins so I wasn't going to put up a struggle.'

Atkinson, at that time director of football at Coventry City, had been driving home from a Variety Club lunch for the Midlands Sports Personality of the Year. He was quoted as saying: 'I never touched him, I just ticked him off.

I didn't cut him up either, but I admit I went to his car to apologize in case he thought I had. He then made a very rude gesture to me and I simply told him not to do it again. There was no question of any violence.'

Although this case was to be heard in a magistrates' court, given the celebrity status of the defendant, and above all the prevailing mood that road rage had to be stamped out by sentences of immediate custody, Atkinson's solicitors retained Desmond to defend.

Atkinson was charged with common assault and the case was listed at 10 a.m. at Birmingham Magistrates' Court in February 1998, by which time he had become manager of Sheffield Wednesday. In one of the most bizarre sequences in a courtroom, the prosecution opened the case and called the alleged victim as the first witness; but after just twenty minutes of cross-examination by Desmond the trial was halted, and soon afterward it was all over.

John Davies, prosecuting, took Martin Player through his evidence and it was plain that his witness statement to the police was almost word for word what had appeared in the press.

Desmond quickly established that Player had gone to the *Birmingham Evening Mail* with his story before he had reported it to the police, and suggested he had been motivated by greed and self-promotion.

Player denied he was exploiting Atkinson's fame to seek publicity, claiming he had believed it was a genuine news story, although in reply to Desmond he accepted that if the incident had involved a 'nobody' he would not have bothered.

At this point the senior stipendiary magistrate, Bruce Morgan, leant forward to intervene. 'Is this a case where you could go outside, shake hands and call it all off?' he asked. He adjourned for fifteen minutes to await the outcome. In the event, it took forty-five minutes: Player had to consult his wife.

When Player conceded, Mr Morgan commended him as 'very courageous' and the compromise took place at the back of court. 'Well done,' said Atkinson, shaking his hand. 'Cheers,' replied Player.

'The first criminal court case settled by a handshake,' said the *Times*.

Atkinson was understandably overjoyed and could not speak highly enough of the magistrate. 'What do you think of the judge, Ron?' he was asked on the steps of the court by the press. 'He was great, I hope he is reffing us on Saturday,' he shot back.

However, for a football manager to compare anyone to a referee obviously sent out mixed messages, so by the time he was asked again, 'Would the magistrate make a good ref?' Atkinson decided there should be no doubt of his high regard. 'No, he's too sensible,' was his considered response.

In the helter-skelter finish to the case, many had forgotten that Atkinson had pulled a masterful stroke even before the case came to court. When the police needed to take a statement from the alleged suspect, they decided not to pull him into the station but to go round to his luxurious house in Barnt Green, Worcestershire.

They set up the tape recording equipment required by law, turned the machines on and began to read Atkinson the official caution. The tape was played to the court and when the officer got to the point '...you don't have to say anything...' Atkinson butted in: 'Well stop hitting me, then.' The police could be heard laughing as they continued with the usual words '...but what you do say will be taken down and may be used in evidence against you.'

With one light-hearted line, Atkinson had taken the advantage away from those sent to formally interview him about an alleged assault and put himself in a position to take charge of the interview. Blinding, as he would say in the strange language of footballers.

## 29

# Leeds and Violence

In the years following the Grobbelaar trial, Premiership wages skyrocketed and an outcry grew over spoilt, overpaid young players and their drunken antics. The headlines were full of reports of drink-fuelled violence by the idols of the football pitch who, it was widely said, had too much money too young. By the time a group of Leeds United players were arrested in January 2000, after a young Asian student was chased through the city centre streets, caught and given a sickening kicking and beating, public anger was demanding that something be done.

One of the footballers was Lee Bowyer, an immensely talented, slimly built midfielder who had been the most expensive teenager in Britain when he was bought by Leeds from Charlton Athletic for £3.5 million. By the age of nineteen he was earning £18,000 a week. He had a reputation on the field as a niggly, even snide player, far from loved outside Yorkshire, but a hero to the local supporters.

Bowyer had a previous conviction for affray from his Charlton days, when he smashed up a fast food restaurant at 5 a.m., injuring and racially insulting an Asian worker. If anybody was going to be used as a scapegoat to bring these footballing hoodlums to heel, he fitted the bill. Bowyer's solicitor, Steven Barker, brought Desmond in straight away, together with Steven Berrick; and this trial, with the clamour of a witch hunt ever present in the background, was to be one of the most difficult of his career – and not just in court. Desmond's first task was to get the venue right. The Crown wanted the trial moved out of Leeds because of the likelihood the jury could be packed with Leeds United fans, at a time when their team was challenging for the Premiership title, as well as having a storming run in the European Champions League.

The Crown wished it to be transferred to Sheffield: but that happened to be the home of United's fiercest local rivals. Desmond went to court with a timetable of the arrests and crowd violence in recent years at matches between Leeds and the two Sheffield teams, Wednesday and United. He achieved an important victory in ensuring the trial was moved to Hull, where the home team was languishing in the Third Division but where a substantial number of Leeds fans lived.

In the prolonged legal argument before the trial started, Mr Justice Poole went to great lengths to stress that neither he nor the Crown believed the attack to have been racially motivated, and he would come down hard on anyone who suggested it was during trial.

In March 2001, Nicholas Campbell, QC, leading Adrian Waterman, opened the case against Bowyer and teammates Jonathan Woodgate, who had played once for England, Michael Duberry and Tony Hackworth. Duberry and Hackworth were represented by Clare Montgomery, QC and Charles Bott, respectively. The two non-footballers in the dock were Woodgate's friends; Paul Clifford, represented by Nigel Sangster, QC, and Neale Caveney, represented by Aidan Marron, QC, leading Philip Creighton. Campbell, in opening the case for the Crown, told the jury how Sarfraz Najeib, 20, and his brother Shahzad, both non-drinkers, had enjoyed a night out in the Majestyk club, where a large number of footballers had gathered on a pub crawl. Outside the club a scuffle broke out and the two Asians were suddenly chased and beaten to the ground in Mill Hill.

Woodgate was said to have jumped up and down on the prone body of Sarfraz and Bowyer had joined in the attack, which had left him with spots of Shahzad's blood on his jacket. Bowyer was caught on CCTV being hugged by one of Woodgate's friends 'in a visible display of emotion aroused by the violence and victory they believed they had won.'

All but Duberry, who had not been drinking that night, were accused of affray and inflicting grievous bodily harm with intent. All but Bowyer and Hackworth were also charged with conspiracy to pervert the course of justice by mounting an alleged cover-up.

Desmond's problems started almost immediately, when a national radio station broadcast Bowyer's criminal record in a phone-in programme. It was a blatant contempt of court and potentially terminal for the defence, if the jury were to hear what Bowyer had done just a few years earlier. The judge was furious but he was to get even angrier with the media before the trial finished.

On the field, Bowyer was somehow able to ignore the courtroom pressure and find the best form of his career. Two days into the trial it seemed the whole of Hull was watching Leeds United's televised Champions League tie against Anderlecht of Belgium, in which Bowyer scored the winner in a 2-1 victory.

Every single northern edition of the national newspapers next morning carried a front-page picture of adrenalin-filled Bowyer's face as he celebrated; eyes bulging, fist clenched, his face, flecked with blood from a nose injury, distorted into a grimace of rage and triumph. Of course, this was an image from the football field, but no single image could have better served the Crown's case of Bowyer being at the heart of the beating in Mill Hill. However innocently done, and delighted as Desmond was at his client's success, this was another potential prejudicing of the jury that the defence could have done without.

The most damaging evidence against Bowyer was the blood on the jacket and one strong witness, a barmaid granted anonymity, who gave a good description of the footballer 'kicking the victim in the head over and over.' However, in the witness box she said she had also seen Bowyer bite the victim; yet the teeth marks were clearly proved to be Clifford's. Desmond kept getting her to repeat in different ways that it was Bowyer who was the one who left a savage bite mark on the victim's cheek. Finally he put it to her, 'Miss X, if you are wrong in your identification of Bowyer as the biter – do you agree that your evidence may be seriously incorrect?' The witness agreed.

The blood marks proved trickier to counter. The first thought was that the blood could have been transferred on to the jacket in the hug caught on CCTV by someone who had been involved in the attack. Forensic scientist Mark Webster also told the jury Bowyer could have slipped and fallen into a pool of Shahzad's blood on the ground.

This was good rebuttal evidence, but if Bowyer was to be cleared he would have to go into the witness box and convince the jury himself that he had not been involved. Footballers are rarely known for their loquaciousness and he soon found himself saying, 'I was not involved in nothing that night.'

But he cleverly abandoned any false modesty and told the jury, 'I am not very clever, it's how I speak. What I have told you is what happened on the night and it might be jumbled up but I cannot help that. I am sorry. I am not very good with words.' The one fact that the defence concentrated on was that, from the first interview with the police, Bowyer had always denied entering Mill Hill, where the victim suffered his terrible injuries.

Slowly and carefully he explained how he had been celebrating his birthday, a week late, with other players, including Michael Bridges and Harry Kewell. He emphasized that he was not a regular drinker and that five or six glasses of wine had made him 'tipsy but not drunk'. Becoming separated from Woodgate's group, he left the club and jogged after them in a direction pointed out to him by the doorman. Indeed, the CCTV footage entirely corroborated him in this regard. In the course of running he had fallen over, because he was not looking where he was going, and received a 'whack on my face and my head hit the floor.'

Stunned, he picked himself up and saw a group of people running from Mill Hill. They brushed past him. He said he had no memory of the CCTV embrace with Caveney or why he had done it. He had never entered Mill Hill.

When he was arrested, Bowyer had been asked to hand over the clothes he had been wearing on the night of the attack. The shoes he submitted bore no blood stains and the Crown claimed they were different to the ones he could be seen wearing on CCTV footage at the entrance to the club, which looked as if they had buckles. There were white patches to be seen between the trouser legs and the shoes. These were buckles, said the Crown. It was a critical area of the case for, if the jury came to the conclusion that the Crown was right that Bowyer had handed in the wrong shoes, the inference was clear: he had done so because he was fearful of handing in the pair he was actually wearing on the night.

Desmond asked Bowyer to change into the trousers and shoes to prove that what looked like a buckle was in fact a patch of bare white skin, visible to the camera because the footballer never wore socks.

Desmond told him, 'I want you to put these trousers on,' and Desmond reassured him, 'Don't worry, the jury can't see you.' Bowyer replied sheepishly, 'I am not wearing any underpants.' Desmond spluttered, 'What, you don't wear underpants either?'

Bowyer changed outside court, walked up and down in front of the jury and the judge and the prosecution, then changed back. Whether the floor show proved anything conclusively did not particularly matter, because the little exchange had shown a side of Bowyer's character; that, far from being a reckless thug, he was a shy boy with a cheeky grin. If Desmond had planned the whole routine in advance it was unlikely his 'stooge' was in on it, as he responded so spontaneously. It had an impact outside court as well. On the following Saturday at Elland Road the new terrace chant was: 'He's here, he's there, he wears no underwear – Lee Bowyer, Lee Bowyer.'

Desmond and Steven Barker were working fourteen hours a day on the case as the police and Crown lawyers, under intense pressure to secure a conviction, served box after box of additional evidence to be sifted and analysed. Whether the long hours were to blame for Desmond's fall, on the Saturday night before closing speeches were due to start, is difficult to assess. His wife Katarina found him at the bottom of the stairs at their Chelsea home and took him straight to hospital. They stitched the back of his head up but he discharged himself before they could give him a scan.

The next day Barker picked him up to drive back to Hull, and en route could clearly see he was unwell and disorientated. He drove him straight to Hull Royal Infirmary and told the doctor, 'Can you tell me the size of this man's brain because I've been briefing him for twenty years and I know how good it is. I want to know how big it is.'

Desmond was diagnosed as suffering from concussion and ordered to rest for seven days. Barker left him in hospital, returned to the hotel and rung prosecutor Campbell with the bad news. On the Monday morning, Campbell agreed to apply for a week's adjournment, to allow Desmond to recover, when in through the door strode the man himself, with his wig covering the evidence of his injuries.

Desmond was absolutely determined that nobody should have to stand in for him at this crucial stage of the trial. He refused to take a step back even though nobody could possibly accuse him of letting his client down. Barker was so concerned for his health he sat in court all day 'unable to take my eyes off him'.

In fact the final words of Desmond's closing speech proved controversial. 'Bowyer may have a glittering future ahead of him in the great game of football, and the great prizes of life in that game may still be open to him,' he said. 'One day the dream he has spoken of, the dream of seeing England to victory by scoring the winning goal in a future World Cup, I hope, will come true. On the evidence you heard in this case I invite you, ladies and gentlemen, to help him achieve that dream for himself and for England.'

My editor at the time, Sir Max Hastings, was not alone in the media world in believing that this was an appeal too far in terms of naked patriotism and emotion. However, I have not met a single lawyer who did not think it perfectly fair and, if they had thought of it themselves, would have used it in similar circumstances.

Said Barker, 'Any jury, any time responds to the character, wit and decency of Desmond. He plays on their affections and emotions shamelessly but oh so effectively. This speech was clever because, if you were a football fan on the jury, you might not support Leeds but you would support England, and if you didn't like football you were likely to be a patriot and would not want to harm England's chances.'

By the time the jury retired, Hackworth had already been discharged and Duberry and the other defendants were soon to be cleared of the cover-up. But while jurors were still deliberating over their verdict on the attack itself, the *Sunday Mirror* published a long interview with the victim's father, commenting on the case, and insisting the attack on his son had been racially motivated. As soon as at least one juror had confirmed he had read the article, the judge had to discharge them all.

All the defence counsel applied for the case to be stayed or postponed indefinitely, on the grounds that this publicity had made a fair trial impossible. Desmond, irritated by the possible collapse of the trial, suggested the judge should summon the editor of the *Sunday Mirror* before him 'and that he should be asked to bring his cheque book.'

Mr Justice Poole rejected the applications, ordered a retrial and reported the newspaper to the Attorney General. He also rejected a cheeky application from Campbell to have the trial location moved again, although there would be a new judge for the second hearing.

The second trial took place in the autumn of 2001, with David Fish, QC, now leading for Woodgate and Raymond Walker, QC, leading David Lamb for Caveney. The second trial was prefaced by a concerted attempt to prove that the mountain of prejudicial reports in the media – five separate clear contempts of court, including the *Sunday Mirror* article, radio broadcasts and websites – had made it impossible for Bowyer, in particular, to have a fair trial. Barker had brought in rising star Ben Emmerson, QC to argue the application, but the new trial judge, Mr Justice Henriques, would have none of it; although, for the first time he did accept for consideration an expert academic paper on the subject that Barker had commissioned.

The replay attracted far less publicity as the evidence remained much the same; although the barmaid this time accepted she was mistaken in having told the first trial that Bowyer was the biter.

In mid-December, the second jury retired and this time cleared Bowyer of affray and GBH, and found Woodgate guilty of affray but acquitted him of GBH. He received 100 hours of community service, as did Caveney, for affray, while Clifford was jailed for six years for affray and GBH.

Bowyer did go on to play for England. A few days before the jury had retired he had left the field at Elland Road with a farewell wave to the crowd, fearing he had played his last game; a guilty verdict would mean an inevitable prison sentence and possibly the end of his career at twenty-five.

In response to a letter from me, Mr Justice Henriques wrote a charming handwritten letter, describing himself as 'a great admirer of Desmond' and looked forward to meeting me 'to discuss the great advocate'. In his office high up in the Royal Courts of Justice, the judge told me the Bowyer trial had been one of the greatest examples of Desmond's skill. 'He was brilliant; the defence was meticulous,' he said. 'There was a lot of fairly difficult scientific evidence but he did very well on the blood and very well on the shoes.

'One of Desmond's great qualities is that juries like him enormously, but then so do judges and co-defendants and particularly clients. I felt he showed great ability to allow Bowyer to do justice to himself, which was very important.

'He is also extremely courteous in his cross-examinations; he never bullies a witness – although I have known him rough up the odd policeman – he never alienates a jury in the way he asks his questions. His forte is also his closing speech; he has a grasp of the way jurors' minds work and an ability to focus on the points that decide the case and completely ignore everything that is unlikely to assist the defendant.'

The eminent judge remembered two episodes in the trial which showed the endearing side of Desmond and the fondness which had developed between the two men who, before the elevation to the bench, had fought each other in trials over many years.

'For the legal argument, Desmond's solicitor brought in Emmerson, one of the finest criminal lawyers, as opposed to advocates, particularly in the field of human rights. His argument took about two weeks and I also had to hear from Clare Montgomery, QC who is similarly talented in that field; she was arguing that it would be an abuse of process for the Crown to call her client, Duberry, as a prosecution witness.

'After the legal argument was over and the trial started, Desmond was back leading the defence and a very mundane point of law arose – I think it was over Bowyer's identification parade – and the jury had to retire while I heard it.

'I, tongue in cheek, inquired whether Emmerson would be coming back to argue the point, and Desmond replied with masterful sarcasm, "Your Lordship will be amazed to know that I have been entrusted with this weighty point."'

The judge went on, 'During a long trial the Bar traditionally entertains the judge – if he has been behaving himself – and the judge returns the compliment at a later date. On this occasion we had a very good evening, but there was some concern when Desmond insisted on continuing the party back at the hotel for a few more hours.

'The next morning there were further concerns about Desmond's wellbeing and even a suggestion that the judge might want to sit for shorter hours if Desmond was not able to cope with the rigours of the night before. Well, you can imagine, Desmond was in scintillating form that day, razor sharp in his questions and truly on the scent. Those who did not know him were staggered but those who did found it entirely predictable.'

30

# Chelsea and Violence

DESMOND'S NEXT FOOTBALLER CLIENT FACED THE DANGER OF A LONG sentence, perhaps eight years' imprisonment or more, if convicted. Chelsea defender John Terry was charged with wounding with intent to cause grievous bodily harm, unlawful wounding, possession of an offensive weapon and affray.

The charge against Terry was that he used a bottle to inflict injury to the face of the alleged victim. There is a legitimate public expectation that those guilty of such offences should be severely punished, to bring home to the offender the gravity of the offence and to deter others from similar behaviour. If such punishment did not follow, public confidence in the administration of criminal law would be weakened.

By August 2002, the outcry against rich, drunk footballers had, if anything, intensified and a year earlier Terry, along with his co-defendant Jody Morris, had been very publicly named and shamed as being part of a pack of Chelsea stars who had insulted grieving Americans at a Heathrow hotel on the night of the 9/11 attacks.

Terry, Morris, Frank Lampard and Eidur Gudjohnsen had just had their European game called off as a mark of respect for the dead; so they went on a five-hour drinking spree in which they were reported to have stripped naked and vomited. They were fined two weeks' wages, a total of £130,000, by the club which was donated to the US victims' fund.

After the failure to achieve any guilty verdicts on the most serious charges in the Grobbelaar and Bowyer trials, the public pressure was even greater to find a scapegoat to be taught a lesson. Once again Terry, one of England's most promising young defenders, or Morris, a spiky midfielder and former England under-21 international, would make an ideal sacrifice. The other defendant, Des Byrne, then playing for Wimbledon, was less well-known.

All three had been on a night out in January that year, just three weeks after the Bowyer trial had ended, which concluded in the private Wellington Club in Knightsbridge. Morris, who was injured, had just become a father, but Terry was due to play for Chelsea in an FA Cup tie at Norwich and was breaking a prematch curfew, for which he would be fined by his manager, Claudio Ranieri. Byrne was Morris's friend.

The Wellington Club was said to have been the last licensed premises visited by Lord Lucan before his disappearance in 1974. The footballers were not members; the club's clientele included Sophie Dahl, Kate Moss, Gwyneth Paltrow, Jude Law, Mick Jagger and Bono, but their status as footballing celebrities was enough to win the defendants access. They were drinking B-52s, a potent mixture of Kahlua, Baileys and Cointreau. A fight broke out, a doorman was seriously injured and the police were called.

The urbane Jeremy Donne, opened the case for the Crown at Middlesex Guildhall Crown Court, before Judge Fabyan Evans. Desmond was leading Daren Samat for the defence of Terry. Jody Morris was represented by Sonia Woodley, QC and Des Byrne by Simon Pentol together with Andrew Payne. Donne told the jury of the trouble that had started when Morris insulted the club's manager and was asked to leave; he was seen to spit his drink on the floor and stagger into a wall, looking as if he was about to be sick.

Morris was 'winding himself up into an aggressive mood' and taunted the staff with 'don't you know who we are? I could get you sacked' and 'I earn more in one day than you do in a week.' Terry was said to have demanded, 'Why are they letting foreigners in?' in front of a group of Japanese patrons. Violence erupted in the reception area and one of the muscular doormen, Trevor Thirlwall, was hit with a bottle, causing 'an explosion of pain' in his eye which temporarily blinded him, said Donne.

Terry was said to have struck him with a bottle which 'miraculously did not break on impact as it is terrifying to think what could have happened if it had.' He was found to have an injury to his hand 'consistent with having punched somebody'. Terry and Byrne told police they had acted in self-defence and Morris denied any part in what he said was 'a scuffle.'

The forensic evidence was clearly going to be important, but in fact the outcome of the trial hinged on Desmond's cross-examination of the doorman, Thirlwall, who had already given an interview to a Sunday newspaper under the headline: 'He could have blinded me'.

Desmond immediately attacked him as 'an arrogant thug' who had goaded the footballers into a fight. He accused him of fabricating his story to make money from the press and to make a claim against Terry for compensation. He said the doorman was desperate for money because he had been caught with heroin. 'I think you have your facts wrong,' the witness replied.

Under pressure from Desmond, Thirlwall admitted lying to the police by telling them that his brother Matthew, a professional boxer, had not been present at the incident and went on to deny that he was lying to protect his employers, the Panayiotou family, who would suffer 'catastrophically' if they were to lose their drink license as a result of late-night brawling.

'You are an arrogant thug in the employ of shady people,' said Desmond.

'That is slanderous, I disagree with that,' was all the bemused bouncer could reply.

Desmond established in court that the family had previously owned the celebrity haunt Browns, in Great Queen Street, which was raided by police in June 1999; large amounts of cocaine were discovered. Angelo Panayiotou had been cleared at a trial of allowing Browns to be used for the supply of cocaine, but was jailed for two years on five charges of possessing a firearm.

Thirlwall admitted he had been employed at the club at that time. It was a devastating cross-examination which changed the course of the trial. Said Barker, 'This was a classic example of Desmond getting to the heart of the issues: how did this man conspire with his employers to put a bottle in John Terry's hand? Desmond provided the answer. In order to hide the fact that the boxer and brother had started the violence, which would have imperilled the club's licence, it was necessary, said Desmond, to blame the guests, and to put the principal injuries suffered by him down to the best-known footballer in the dock. I provide the bullets and he fires them, but it is the way you fire them that is crucial.'

Desmond was intent on impressing two things on the jury: that the Wellington Club was operating out of hours, beyond the limits of its license; and that Thirlwall was not licensed as a bouncer by Westminster Council. Having proved his points he turned to the jury and said, 'All this talk of licenses has made me rather thirsty,' and raised a glass of water which the jury probably wished, for his sake, was full of something stronger.

Terry, his liberty at stake and his career in the balance, gave at times tearful evidence insisting he had acted 'only as a peacemaker', to defend a friend who was being beaten up. He denied being drunk; 'Although we were all over the drink-drive limit we were in a good mood, just having a drink.' Thirlwall had racially abused the Irishman, Byrne, and as he was trying to separate them he was put in a headlock and lashed out. 'I was being attacked by three of them, I was being ganged up on and it was then that I threw a punch.' He never touched a bottle, he said.

Desmond asked him if he had trouble with foreigners. 'No, over 90 per cent of the Chelsea team are foreigners,' he replied.

The clinching argument came from the forensics. Desmond and Barker had been impressed by an expert, Professor Christopher Milroy, who had been called by the Crown in the Bowyer case and given effective evidence. This time they called him for the defence and he showed the jury that the bottle said to have been wielded by Terry could not have been used in the way the Crown claimed, because the injuries would have been different. Terry wept again when he was cleared of all charges. Like most defendants facing very serious charges and the uncertainty of a jury decision, he had prepared himself for the possibility of prison by bringing a packed case to court. He also bought a copy of the former England and Arsenal captain Tony Adams's book on alcoholism and his own prison term for drink driving. Since the trial Terry went on to play for and, indeed, captain England and proved himself one of the best defenders in Europe, although not entirely escaping trouble and controversy off and on the pitch.

But at the time he said, 'I had a good think about what I was doing and I've changed my lifestyle around now. I haven't drunk alcohol for six months and that's the way I think it will stay. I realize I have a responsibility to myself, the club and the kids who follow the club to behave in a proper manner, and I have learned my lesson.'

Morris and Byrne were also cleared of affray; Byrne was convicted of possessing a bottle as an offensive weapon and was fined £2,000.

## 31

# Cocaine and the Captain

LAWRENCE DALLAGLIO WAS ENGLAND CAPTAIN AND IN 1999 HE WAS THE biggest name in British rugby; the sport was booming in commercial terms, with a World Cup looming – the first after the sport had turned professional. The clean-cut, phenomenally fit, Ampleforth-educated back row forward had succeeded Will Carling as the game's highest profile figure, with the promise of all the riches that that could bring to such a commercially attractive sportsman.

In a sport full of big men, he stood out for the awe and presence he commanded on the field; and the dignity with which he bore the death of his sister, Francesca, a nineteen-year-old ballerina, who had died on the *Marchioness* river boat disaster.

Then, in May 1999, he very nearly threw it all away in a classic sting operation by undercover *News of the World* reporters. He was trapped on tape claiming that he was a drug dealer, and had taken ecstasy and cocaine with other players on the recent British Lions tour of South Africa. Two reporters, posing as executives from Gillette interested in sponsorship deals, plied him with champagne at a hotel reception and later encouraged him to talk about 'any experience of the drug scene.'

Dallaglio, obviously keen to fit in to what he perceived to be their lifestyle, to make himself more eligible for whatever sponsorship deal was in the pipeline, made the biggest mistake of his life. According to the next Sunday's front-page splash, with extra pages of background material inside, he told them, 'I no longer take cocaine but I might make an exception on tonight's occasion.'

'Grinning and bragging,' he went on to say that, when he was nineteen, he made his money dealing drugs before going into rugby. He described driving 'from one end of London to another' dodging the police to deliver supplies. He said addicts 'were so desperate for a fix they would bombard me with calls around the clock.'

When the story broke, Desmond was spending that weekend with Lt. Col. James Baxter and his wife, Sharon, at Catterick, where Baxter was commanding his regiment. During the course of the morning one of the house guests, going through the Sunday papers, spotted the Dallaglio exposé, and drew Desmond's attention to it, with the suggestion that it looked as if he had a new sporting client. Everyone was amazed when, an hour later, solicitors tracked Desmond down to the Baxters' home and asked him to come up to London that day for a consultation. Desmond caught a train immediately and went to London to meet up with Dallaglio and his solicitors.

As a result of that meeting, and acting on Desmond's advice, Dallaglio resigned as England Captain and gave a press conference the next day setting out his position. During another consultation, Desmond discovered that there was a professional conflict of interest that prevented him from acting for his professional client any further.

In the fallout from the story, Dallaglio was hounded so much he had to lay low at the home of the England coach, Clive Woodward. There were calls for a police investigation and the governing body, the Rugby Football Union, charged him with bringing the game into disrepute, when he was represented by George Carman, QC.

The wisdom of Desmond's advice to Dallaglio, to resign the captaincy immediately and fight for his career, was proved right four years later when he was re-appointed England captain, albeit briefly, in succession to Martin Johnson, who retired after leading his country to victory in the 2003 World Cup. The disgrace of the bogus drugs confession was forgotten, as the London Wasps back row forward was rewarded by coach Sir Clive Woodward for his sterling performances in the tournament, in which he was the only England player to play every minute of every match.

Dallaglio retired from international rugby after the following World Cup, in 2007, and within ten years, newspaper stings carried out by the *News of the World* and later its replacement, the *Sun on Sunday*, were totally discredited when their star reporter, Mazher Mahmood, was jailed for perverting the course of justice.

32

# Jamie Osborne

Another knock-on effect of the Grobbelaar corruption trial was the fear that fixing and betting coups were equally rife in other sports; the obvious target being horse racing.

In the late 1990s, the Jockey Club and the police were extremely active in investigating what they believed was organized collusion between jockeys and millionaire gamblers and betting syndicates, including criminals attempting to launder money through fixing races.

The police inquiry was to last years and a number of National Hunt racing jockeys were arrested and interviewed; including Graham Bradley, who made no secret of his close friendship with the multimillionaire drug baron Brian Wright, known as The Milkman, because of the reputation that he 'always delivers'.

The hugely popular rider Jamie Osborne was arrested in January 1998. Such was Desmond's reputation among sporting personalities it was inevitable he would be called in, together with Steven Barker as his solicitor.

The police were particularly intent on examining a race at Exeter in March 1997, the HMS Exeter Novices' Handicap Hurdle, in which Osborne was riding a horse named Avanti Express. Only two horses were considered to have a chance of winning the race in the eleven-strong field: Avanti Express, trained by Charlie Egerton; and Give and Take, ridden by champion jockey Tony McCoy and trained by Martin Pipe.

When the betting opened, Avanti Express was 5/4 on favourite, but the sheer weight of money placed on its rival meant that it drifted and started the race only second favourite. It ran so badly that Osborne had to pull it up long before the finish, and neither jockey nor trainer could provide any explanation to a stewards' inquiry.

Later analysis of a urine sample found the presence of the doping agent ACP, which depresses the central nervous system, producing a mild sedation which can last for four hours. Osborne was understandably furious at being suspected to have been involved in doping a horse he was due to ride. He pointed out that hurdling and steeplechasing was quite dangerous enough, without willingly sitting on a hundredweight of horse, travelling at thirty to forty miles per hour, full of drugs.

Five professional gamblers were later charged with conspiracy to defraud bookies, and others who may have lost money, by interference with the fair running of horses by doping. The charges covered the Exeter race and one at Plumpton in the same month. Both Osborne and Egerton appeared as witnesses for the Crown, but the case collapsed in September 2000.

During the investigation, Osborne was approached by an ex-detective turned private eye, Robert Harrington, who asked him for £2,500 to bribe a policeman into dropping any possible charges. Harrington also approached Detective Sergeant Richard Wall, who was then heading the inquiry into Osborne, and offered to become an informant.

Having consulted his solicitor and Desmond, Osborne immediately reported it to the police, who secretly taped a further meeting between the jockey and Harrington, at which the private eye said he required a £500 sweetener for Wall to recommend to the Crown Prosecution Service that the case be dropped, and at another meeting asked for a further £2,500. Wall, like Osborne, was entirely innocent of any corruption.

Harrington was arrested and Osborne was the key Crown witness at the Old Bailey trial, in January 2000, which resulted in the ex-detective being jailed for attempted corruption and deception.

## 33

# The Lady Jockey

FIVE YEARS EARLIER, DESMOND HAD HELPED ANOTHER JOCKEY TO WALK free; this time from charges of defrauding banks and credit card companies in a £2.5 million conspiracy.

Jacqui Oliver was Britain's most successful woman jockey, as well as a friend of Princess Anne. At her trial in Birmingham Crown Court, in January 1995, she was represented by Desmond and another member of his chambers, Lady Ponsonby. By then Jacqui had ridden in the Grand National, won the £25,000 Mecca Bookmakers' race at Sandown and entered the *Guinness Book of Records* as the first woman to win three professional races in a day.

Her father, Henry, was a racehorse owner and trainer, and the family friendship with the princess led Jacqui's brother, also Henry, to later date Zara Phillips. But Jacqui became another victim of a *News of the World* sting. The newspaper sensationally reported that she was 'making a fortune by masterminding a huge credit card swindle.' It went on to accuse her of being 'a cocaine-snorting cheat who admits slowing down a horse to fix a race. Her parents, Sally and Henry – both respected figures in the racing world – are cocaine users.'

The reporter was Mazher Mahmood, who later became the paper's investigations editor and was responsible for a whole range of sting operations which have fallen apart in court. They included the gang said to have planned to kidnap Victoria Beckham and her children.

His stock in trade was posing as a wealthy Arab sheikh, or an agent of such a potentate, offering the chance of riches or lucrative business while tape recording the unwary, who would be prepared to say anything to secure what he had to offer. Other victims included Sophie, Countess of Wessex, the Queen's daughter-in-law, who in her PR days made some unwise comments about Tony and Cherie Blair; and John Alford, the star of *London's Burning*, who ended up in prison.

Desmond had the chance to cross-examine Mahmood, who sat arrogantly in the witness box, lolling backward to answer his questions. All the evidence against Oliver was on the secret tapes, but Desmond exposed the degree of enticement which had taken place, with Mahmood dangling the fictitious prospect of regular rides on the world's best horses as a jockey attached to the fake sheikh's stables. Gullibly, Oliver agreed to do and say whatever Mahmood suggested to keep him sweet. As Desmond told the court, for a jockey still fighting to make her way in a sport dominated by men, it was a temptation so irresistible that she succumbed to it.

Judge Iain Black agreed and ruled the tape recordings inadmissible against his client, resulting in the Crown dropping the charges against her and a verdict of not guilty being entered. Outside court she was so relieved she gave Desmond a tip to back her next ride at Cheltenham the next day; unfortunately, it lost.

Four others, including her then boyfriend Kay Sander, went on to face trial over the fake credit cards and voucher fraud. They were convicted and ended up in prison.

# AFTERWORD

If there is one thing Fleet Street teaches you it's that you can't beat a good courtroom drama. Hollywood has done its best, but nothing can recreate the sheer theatre of a devastating cross-examination, a sensational twist in the evidence and ultimately the heart-pumping, adrenalin-filled tension of the slow single file of a jury entering court to deliver a verdict everybody can guess at but nobody can possibly know.

Life and death cases – the epic murder trials – are usually the ones that stick in the nation's consciousness for generations. Even though it is more than fifty years since capital punishment was abolished, the public imagination remains riveted by true life laid bare in high-profile cases. Thanks to television, which is banned from taking its cameras into court, the advocates who feature in such cases are repeatedly filmed walking in and out of court, and have become familiar faces to the viewing public.

Just as the late George Carman, QC will always be remembered for his mastery of libel trials, I suspect Desmond's successes will mostly be cherished by sports fans for saving one sporting personality after another in trials where the evidence appeared stacked against them. But it would be wrong if the preceding chapters gave the impression that Desmond's career has been an unbroken chain of successful results; no barrister could ever claim that.

Like any silk, he has suffered the depressing feeling of impotence and ineffectiveness when going down to the cells to commiserate with a client, perhaps to explain why the jury took against him, and wish him well for the next few years he will have to spend at Her Majesty's pleasure. Desmond himself will accept that the Brocket hearings, for instance, were not his finest hours. The evidence was overwhelming, a guilty plea the only option and mitigation found no favour with an uncompromising judge.

Desmond takes many cases because he cares. I have heard it said that he cares too much, even that he wears his client's cause on his sleeve. It might be some unfortunate who faced jail for a crime he didn't commit. It might be the government facing a threat that certain revelations would give powerful PR ammunition to the nation's enemies. It sometimes means operating behind the scenes. As the old cliché has it: it's dirty work but someone has to do it, and there are cases he has taken and interventions he has made which – to this day – are too sensitive for publication.

The difference between Desmond and many at the Bar, whose first thoughts are money and media profile, is that he acts in a particular way because he believes it to be the right thing to do.

When the news broke of Saddam Hussein's capture by the Americans, I switched on the midday news. It came as no surprise to see Desmond's unmistakable features. The screen was split. On the left, Desmond was giving his expert opinion on how Saddam could be dealt with and the sort of tribunal which could be formed to try him; and on the right there were pictures of the bemused and bearded tyrant being humiliated by an American doctor taking DNA samples from his mouth.

I had to smile. Having spent so long thousands of miles away from the media spotlight, he had returned to Britain for Christmas and landed right in the midst of the world's headlines.

However, by this time Desmond was operating on the international legal stage, having been personally picked by the Secretary-General of the United Nations to be the chief prosecutor of a UN-sponsored war crimes court. With Desmond bringing about the arrest of the tyrant Charles Taylor for war crimes, his reputation spread worldwide.

# ILLUSTRATION CREDITS

Charles Taylor (Pascal Guyot / AFP / Getty Images)
John Terry (Central News)
Lee Bowyer (John Giles / PA)
Jamie Osborne (Neal Simpson / PA)
*Times 2* front page (*The Times* / News Syndication)
Roderick Newell (PA)

Wedding photograph full caption:

*Front row left–right*: HRH Prince Nikola, HI&RH Archduchess Valerie of Austria Margravine von Baden, HRH Princess Margarita von Baden, the author, HRH Princess Katarina carrying HRH Prince George, HRH Prince Tomislav of Yugoslavia carrying HRH Prince Michael, HRH Crown Princess Katherine of Yugoslavia with HRH Prince Peter, HRH Prince Alexander and HRH Prince Philip, HRH Princess Mandi von Baden

*Back row left–right*: HRH Prince Leopold , HRH Prince Maximilian Margrave von Baden, Count Bertil Bernadotte, the Earl of Inchcape, HRH Crown Prince Alexander of Yugoslavia, HRH Prince Ludwig von Baden

# INDEX


2 Paper Buildings 10–12, 13, 22, 24

Abdullah, Abdullah Ahmed 42
Abraham, Joe 161
Adama (cook) 68
Adamson, DI James 242, 250
Adeniji, Ambassador 47, 52
aircraft-hijacking trial 206–8
al-Assad, Bashar 177
Aldrin, Dr Buzz 154–5
Aldrin, Lois 154–5
Alexander, HRH Crown Prince of Yugoslavia (DdS's in-law) 122–3, see wedding photograph
al-Hassan, Mohammed 218, 220, 222
Allen (gardener) 49
Alliott, Sir John 228
al-Qaeda 38, 42, 54, 78, 81
al-Senussi, Idris 217–25, 222–3, 225
al-Senussi family 216, 217
al-Zarqawi 81
Amissah, Austin 173
Andropov, Yuri 255, 259–60
Annabel's 122
Annan, Kofi 80, 84
Anyah, Morris 88
Archer, Lord (Jeffrey) 7, 148–50
Archie (gardener) 99
Argyle QC, His Honour Judge Michael 20
Armah, Kwesi 29–30
arrests 11, 129, 162–4
art, DdS's mother's 112–13
Artamonov, Nikolai Fedorovich 135–41
Assad regime 177–9, 191
assassination, close calls with 39, 115–16, 166, 240, 250
astrology 111
Athar, General Syed 60
Athwal, Pin 81
Atkinson, Ron 281–3
Austin, Lt. Col. Dick 55
Avory, Rt. Hon. Sir Horace 133
Axiom International 178

Bahamas 15
Bailey, Anthony 216–17, 220–3
Baker QC, His Honour Judge John 10–11
Baldry, Right Hon Sir Tony 48, 71
Balkan conflict 266–72
Ban Ki-Moon 145
Banjul 158, 159, 163, 163–4
Bar, career at the *see* legal career of Desmond de Silva
Bar, nature of the xii–xv
Bar Council 17
Barker, Steven 36, 198, 203–5, 267, 268, 271, 284, 288, 289–90, 294, 298
Batchelor, Warwick 236–9
Battle of Ceylon xii, 101–4
Baxter, Brigadier James 36, 297
Baxter, Sharon 36
Beccles-Davies, Justice 133
Belgium 98
Bell, Martin 267, 271
Bellinger, John 81
Bernadotte, Bertil Count see wedding photograph
Benghazi 42
Benson, Sir Christopher 198
Bergin, Lt. Col. Desmond 70
Berkeley Castle 115
Berrick, Steven 276, 284
Bevin, Ernest 11
Bhalla, Bitu 65
Bhutto, Benazir 65, 195
Biddle, Keith 39, 45, 47, 54, 56
Biddle, Sue 54
Bin Laden, Osama 78

Bing, His Honour Judge Inigo 217
Birkett, 1st Baron (Norman) 23
Black, Dame Susan 178
Black, His Honour Judge Iain 301
Blackledge, QC, G. G. 6
Blackstone, William xiii
Blizzard, Colonel David 39
Blofeld, Sir John 172
Blom-Cooper, Sir Louis 30
Blow, Amaury (DdS's nephew) 115, 116
Blow, Detmar (DdS's nephew) 50, 109, 122–3
Blow, Detmar (senior) 115
Blow, Helga (DdS's sister) 110, 112, 115
Blow, Isabella 123
Blow, Jonathan (DdS's brother-in-law) 115
Blow, Selina (DdS's niece) 115
Bockarie, General Sam 'Mosquito' 48, 50, 52, 53–4, 57
Bolton, Ambassador John 80
Bombay 117
Bosch, Mariette 26, 171–6
Bosch, Soné 175
Botswana 26, 171–6
Bott QC, Charles 285
Bottomley, Baroness (Virginia) 267
Bourdine, Vladimir 259, 260
Bowyer, Lee 175, 284–91
Breadmore, Gordon 22, 155, 169
Brezhnev, Leonid 137, 140, 255
*Bridge on the River Kwai, The* (film) 152–3
Bridges, Sir Phillip 130, 133, 159
Brimelow, Lord (Thomas) 134
Broadlands 106
Brocket, Lord (Charles) 180–2, 195, 303
Brocket Hall 180–1
Brooks's Club, London 48, 49, 50
Bruce, Lt. Colonel Duncan 36
Buretown Beach 57
Burgess Hill 236
Burke QC, Trevor 28, 215, 273
Burkina Faso 46, 58, 76, 91
Burns, MP, Conor 149, 150
Bush, President George 77, 81, 83, 84
Butler, Walter 3, 11, 22, 23–4, 27, 30, 169
Butler-Sloss, Right Hon, Baroness Elizabeth 69, 195
butterflies 113–15
Buttrose, His Honour Judge Murray 20–1
Byng, Lady Mary 156
Byrne, Des 292, 292–5

Caesar photographs 177–9, 191
Cairns, Earl 121
Caldecott, Sir Andrew 102
call to the bar 3, 5, 32, 124
Calvert-Smith, Sir David 28, 215, 270–2, 276–7, 279–80
Cameron, Rt Hon David 191
Cameron, Rosamund 31, 113–14
Camfield Place 180
Campbell, Colin 203
Campbell, His Honour Judge Bruce 18
Campbell, Naomi 87–92
Campbell QC, Nicholas 285, 289
*Cape Fear* (film) 152, 243–4
capital cases
  Gambia, The 160–7
  Kenya 168–70
  Mariette Bosch (Botswana) 26, 171–6
  Sierra Leone 11, 126–34
Carlton Club 18, 50
Carman QC, George 25, 28, 199–200, 201, 278, 297, 303
Carmon, Daniel 144
cars 93–4, 105, 119, 181
Carter-Ruck solicitors 177
Cartier-Bresson, Henri 111
Cartland, Barbara 180
Cassa, Corporal 163–4
Cassel, His Honour Judge, Sir Harold 25
Castlereagh, Viscount 120
Causer, John 161–2, 166–7, 221, 224, 225
Cavalry and Guards Club 64
Cavendish, Anthony 49, 61
Cavendish, Elspeth 61
Caveney, Neale 285, 287, 289, 290
Centre for Policy Studies 208
Ceylon
  birth of DdS in xi–xii, 5, 101
  early life in 93–107
  film-making in 151–7
  Kandy 93, 94, 95–6, 98–9, 151
  use of old name xii
  World War II 101–4
Ceylon National Congress xii, 101, 107
Ceylon War Council xii, 102
Chad 76
Chadwick, Daniel 115–16
changes in the legal system xii–xv, 15–16, 17–18, 31–3, 191
Chaveas, Ambassador Peter 55, 57
Cherrill, QC, Richard 228
Cheston, Paul 187
child soldiers 43, 76
Christmas, Ian 240, 251
Churchill, Right Hon Sir Winston 102–3, 104

CIA 73, 76, 136, 137, 138, 140–1
City of London councilman 153, 158, 198
Clancy, Tom 184–6
Clarke, Arthur C. 154, 157
Clarke QC, His Honour Judge Edward 20
Clarke QC, His Honour Judge Peter 20, 203
Cleland, Agnes 119
Cleland family 116–17, 119–20
 *see also* Rose-Cleland
clerks, chambers 22–3, 27, 162
clerks of court 6
Clifford, Paul 285, 286, 290
close protection 36, 43, 56, 68
Cold War 135–41, 159, 255–65
Cole, Chief Justice 127
College of Arms 193
Colombo Museum 99
common law, English xiii–xiv, 5
Compaoré, Blaise 76
compassion in sentencing 124, 183
Conan Doyle, Adrian 109
Constantine, Lord (Learie) 13–14
contract on DdS's life 250
Copaken, Richard 138–9
Corkery QC, Michael 25, 31
Corr, Annie 166
Coté, Luc 80
Cote d'Ivoire 48
Council of Europe 33
councilman, elected 153, 158, 198
Courville, Cindy 81
Coward, Noel 152
Cowie, Lord 172
Cox, Meineke 120–1
Crane, David 34, 37, 38, 39, 43, 46, 50, 56, 58, 59, 66, 68, 74, 75, 77–8, 80, 178
Creasy, Nigel 197
Creighton, Philip 285
Crespi QC, James 25, 26, 27
Crick, Michael 149, 150
crimes against humanity
 Middle East 142, 179
 Sierra Leone 40, 73, 77
 victims as clients of the prosecutor 74
Crockfords 27, 29
Croom-Johnson, Rt. Hon. Sir David 258
cross-examination
 DdS's skill in 203, 205, 207, 209, 222, 224, 228–9, 230, 290, 294, 301
 defendant confessing during 262, 265
Crown Defence Service 16, 32
crown of Kings of Kandy 98–9
Crown Prosecution Service 16, 32
Cumming, Brigadier Andrew 266
Cussen QC, Edward 6–7, 25
Cuxson, June 236–9
cycle of impunity 41, 58–9, 78

Dallaglio, Lawrence 296–7
Dallaire, Major General Roméo 75
Daniel, David 184
Daniel, Marevic 184
Dash, Michael E. 219
Davidson-Houston, Brigadier Patrick 37, 43, 44
Davies, John 282
Davis, Captain Pippa 55
Davutoglu, Ahmet 144
de Fonesca, Catharina Petronella (DdS's great-great-great-great-grandmother) 108
de Gaulle, President Charles 122
de Mauny, Count Maurice 100, 156
de Meuron, Count 108
de Murville, Couve 122
de Silva, Agnes *see* Nell, Agnes (grandmother)
de Silva, Esme Gregg (DdS's mother) 112–13, 116, 118–19, 122, 124
de Silva, Frederick (DdS's father) 94–5, 109, 110, 112, 118–19, 121–2, 156–7
de Silva, George E (DdS's grandfather) 5, 12, 93, 93–107, 109, 110–12
de Silva, George 'Sunny' (DdS's uncle) 100–1
de Silva, Helga (DdS's sister) 110, 112, 115
de Silva, Marcia (DdS's aunt) 97
de Silva, Minnette (DdS's aunt) 97, 151, 152, 153, 192
de Silva, Percy (DdS's uncle) 100–1
de Silva QC, Harendra 14
de Silva, Right Hon. Sir Desmond
 birth 5, 95–6, 101
 City of London councilman 153, 158, 198
 early years 95, 101, 106, 117–18
 family history of lawyers 5, 94, 108–9
 genealogy 193
 humour/ wit 194, 202–3, 276–7, 278, 291
 impetuosity 194
 knighthood 191
 marriage 106, 115
 move to England 117–18
 natural history, interest in 113–15, 116–17, 157
 not going into the church 94–5
 personality 194–5, 197
 physical appearance 192–3
 political incorrectness 194
 Privy Council 191
 reading legal biographies 109
 schooling 116–17, 118

de Silva, Victoria (daughter of DdS) 156, 171, 250
de Soysa, Edward 93
de Worms, Baron Charles 113–14
de Worms, Baron Henry 113
Deanstone 100
Déby, Idriss 76
Defence Intelligence Agency (DIA) 81
Del Ponte, Carla 73, 83
Delves Broughton, Sir Jock 123
democracy, and the rule of law 33
Dennington, Doris 236–9
Devlin, Lord xiii
di Portanova, Baron Enrico 122
diamonds
 in Africa 38
 and Charles Taylor 87, 88–90
 and Naomi Campbell 87, 87–92
 Sierra Leone 41–2, 70, 72, 76, 78
Diplock, Lord (Kenneth) 13, 28
Divisional Court 29
divorce work 25
Djabbar, Saad 177
Dobbs, Geoffrey 157
dock briefs 7–8
Dold, Sir Gilbert 3–5
Doley, Cameron 177
Dönitz, Grand Admiral Karl 34, 72, 79
Donne, His Honour Judge Jeremy 293
Dorchester, The 154
Doss, Alan 52, 81, 84
Doss, Soher 52
double jeopardy 129, 211
Downing Street 3
Dr Johnson's Buildings 6
Dr Nico (witchdoctor) 67–8
drink, capacity for 27, 53, 68, 193–4, 214, 215, 252, 291
Driscoll, Robin 22, 171, 225
Du Cann, Charles 7
du Cann, QC Dick 25, 26
Duberry, Michael 285, 289, 291
due process 32–3
Duke, Donald 82
Dulwich College Prep School 118
Dunn, QC His Honour Judge Hubert 214
Durand QC, Victor 25

El Vino 23, 24, 25, 26–7, 28, 29, 131
*Elephant Walk* (film) 152
Elias (senior houseboy) 111
Elizabeth of Toro, Princess 12
Ellery, Brigadier James 43–4, 45, 46, 47, 50, 51, 52, 53, 60, 63–4, 65
Elletson, Harold 220
Emmerson QC, Ben 289, 290–1
England, Ray 63
English Forfeiture Act of 1870 169–70
English Treason Acts (1351, 1553, 1695) 127, 160, 169–70
Erroll, Merlin, 24th Earl of 123, 171–6
Erroll, Josslyn, 22nd Earl of 123, 171–6
espionage cases 135–41, 255–65, 266–72
European Convention on Human Rights 33
Evans, His Honour Judge Fabyan 293
Evans, John 70

Falkender, Lady (Marcia) 61
family history of lawyers 5, 94, 108–9
Farrow, Mia 87, 89, 90, 91
Fashanu, John 215, 274, 275, 277, 279
'fashionable silk' label 195
Feingold, Russ 46
Fellowes, Julian (Lord) 156
Finch, Christopher 240–1, 246, 247–9, 251–3, 254
Finch, Peter 152
Fingland, Sir Stanley 129
Fish QC, David 289
Fitzgerald QC, Edward 175
Fletcher-Cooke QC, Sir Charles 11, 14, 126
Flynn, Joseph 138, 139
Foot, Lady (Dorothy) 12
Foot, Right Hon. Isaac 10
Foot, Right Hon Sir Dingle 3, 10, 12, 13, 14, 23, 30
football cases 28, 175, 195, 199, 215, 270, 273–80, 284–91, 292–5
forensics, knowledge of 95, 178, 198, 273, 295
forgery, ancestor accused of 120–1
Fraisse, Odile 251
France 121–2
Francis, Ted 148–9
Frank, Mel 153–4
Franks, Robbie 36, 56, 84, 85–6
fraud trials 17–18, 181–2, 197, 198, 199–201, 203–5, 298–9, 300–1
freedom, and the English legal system 32–3
Freer, Major General Adrian 47, 55, 62, 66
Fulford QC, Sir Adrian 62

Gaddafi, Colonel Muammar 37, 42, 69, 76, 160, 216, 217–18, 219, 220, 225
Galle Face Hotel 105
Gambia, the 76, 127, 158–67
Gandhi, Kasturba 96–7
Gandhi, Mahatma 96, 111

Gardner-Thorpe, Col. Sir Ronald 158
Garrick Club 13, 29
Gaza 142–7
Gdynia, Poland 135–6
George of Yugoslavia, HRH Prince
(see wedding photograph)
Getty, Paul 31
Ghailani, Ahmed Khalfan 78
Ghana 13, 29–30, 57–8, 59, 77
Gibb, Frances 71
Gibraltar 14, 184, 192, 214, 240–54
Gittings, Mr Justice John Blackburn 18, 246
Glasse, Jennifer 64
Glazebrook, Captain Sally 64
Gleeson, Ian 47
Goddard, Lord 12–13, 26
Goddard, Her Honour Judge Ann 205
Goldberg, Mel 198–9, 276, 278
Goldstone, Richard 142–7
golf 70, 111, 159
Gomez, Eddie 161
Goodman, Sam 211
Gordievsky, Oleg 139–40
Gratien QC, Noel 131–3
Gray QC, Gilbert 25, 28
Greenstock, Sir Jeremy 63, 70
Gregg, Chris 178
Gregg MacGregor, Rev. John William (DdS's
great-grandfather) 120–1
Grenier, Sir Samuel 94
Grenier KC, Joseph 94
Griffiths Jones, Mervyn 22
Griffiths QC, Courtenay 88
Grobbelaar, Bruce 28, 215, 270, 274–80
Grosvenor House 153
Gudjohnsen, Eidur 292–5
Guinea-Bissau 163
Guinness, Alec 152–3
Gulbenkian, Nubar 31

Hackworth, Tony 285, 289
Hague, Lord (William) 148, 150
Hague, The 33–4, 62, 72, 82, 86
Hailsham, Quintin, Right. Hon Lord 18, 27
Haines, Joe 61
Hallett, Right. Hon. Lady Justice Heather 209
Hamas 142
Hambleton, Prof. Hugh 255–65
Hamilton, Dr Stuart 178
Hanratty case 126
Harman, MP Right Hon Harriet 71
Harrington, Robert 299
Harris, Chris 71
Hart, Wendy 68
Harwood, Nicholas 168, 170
Hassocks 236–9
Hastings 232–5
Hastings, Sir Max 289
Hastings KC, Sir Patrick 109
Haussman, Cynthia 137
Havers, Lord (Michael) 29, 258–9, 262–5
Havers QC, Hon. Philip 262
Hawkins QC, His Honour Judge Richard 7
Haycroft, John 226–31
Hayes, Jerry 11
Haywards Heath 159
head of state immunity principle 58, 78–9
Heald QC, Mervyn 133
Heller, Dr Michael 230
Helms, Richard 141
Henderson, Arthur 98
Henriques QC, Hon. Sir Richard 192, 213,
289–90
Hezbollah 38
Hilles House, Stroud 115
*Himalaya, SS* 117
Hindley, Myra 196
Hirst, Rt. Hon. Sir David 25
HMS *Argonaut* 245–6
HMS *Iron Duke* 47
HMS *Westminster* 44
Hoare, Oliver 216
Holden, His Honour Judge Derek 200
Hollis, Brenda 34, 87, 88, 90
Hollis, Dr Michael (uncle of DdS) 16
Hollis QC, Daniel 228
Holmes, Major General John 37
Hood, Gavin 65
Hoon, Notu 14, 201–2
Hopkin, Sir David 16
Hopkins, Stanley 23
Horovitz, Sigall 88
horse racing case 298–9
Horsham 49, 61
Hough, Richard 134
House of Lords 4
Howard QC, Bill 25
Howarth, Kathryn 88
Hudson QC, Barry 24, 25, 26–7
Hudson-Phillips QC, Karl 145, 146
human nature, understanding of 73, 84, 273
Humphreys, His Honour Judge (Travers)
Christmas 21
Hurst, Dickie 101
Hurt, Henry 136
Hussein, Saddam 69, 217, 219, 267, 304

Hutcheson, Mrs 232–5
Hutchinson, Lord (Jeremy) 30
Hutchinson, Malcolm 36

identity impersonation case 184–6
immunity, Crown 58, 78–9, 257
Inchcape, Earl of (DdS's Best Man)
see wedding photograph
independent advocacy, erosion of 31–2
information-gathering systems 75–6, 83, 178
*see also* intelligence services
Inner London Quarter Sessions 21, 27
intelligence services 73, 75–6, 78, 83, 221, 255–65, 265
Interflora 242–3
International Criminal Court (ICC), The Hague 33–4, 80
International Criminal Tribunal for Rwanda (ICTR) 35, 74, 81, 142
International Criminal Tribunal for the former Yugoslavia (ICTY) 35, 62, 74, 81, 83, 142
international law career of Desmond de Silva
apprenticeship 74
Caesar photographs 177–9
capital case in Kenya 127, 168–70
chief special prosecutor in the Gambia 76, 158–67
deputy prosecutor role 74
Gibraltar 184–6
Mariette Bosch (Botswana) 26, 171–6
Middle East 142–7
personal danger, being in 36, 37–8, 43–4, 48, 63, 75, 81, 166–7, 250
salary cut 35
Special Court for Sierra Leone 33–4, 33–71, 35–71, 79–86, 92
UN fact-finding mission 145–7
International Tribunals (Sierra Leone) Act (2007) 86
Interpol 242–3
IRA bombs 27, 199
Iraq 48, 70, 218
Ireland 116–17, 119
Israel 142–7

Jackson, General Sir Mike 267, 271
Jafferjee QC, Aftab 14
Jawara, Lady (Chilel) 160, 164–5
Jawara, Sir Dawda 158–60, 161
Johnson, Dr Samuel 142
Johnson, Jim 80
Johnson, Winnie 195–6
Johnson Sirleaf, President Ellen 81–2, 85, 86
Jones, Alan 47, 50, 52, 53, 57
Jones, QC, Sir Elwyn 12
Jubb, Brian 49, 251
Jubb, Susan 49
Judicial Committee of the Privy Council 15
judicial review xv, 248
juju 51
juries, skill with 198, 289, 290
jury system xiii–xiv

Kabaka of Buganda (King Freddy) 12
Kabbah, President Ahmad Tejan 41, 56
Kalugin, Oleg 140, 141
Kamara, Brigadier Brima 56
Kandy 93, 94, 95–6, 98–9, 151
Kansteiner, Walter 57
Karadžić, Radovan 73, 83, 266
Karu QC, Lee 14
Katarina of Yugoslavia, HRH Princess (DdS's ex-wife)
and Arthur C. Clarke 154
audience with the Pope 194
on DdS's bar bills 215
at Hilles House 115
at Marlands 49
marriage 106
and the Newall case 250
related to British Royal Family 217, 225
at Royal Wedding 158
at Taprobane 171
Katherine of Yugoslavia, HRH Crown Princess (DdS's in-law) 122–3
Kellock QC, His Honour Judge Tom 10–11, 27, 29, 30, 126
Kelsey-Fry QC, John 221, 222, 223, 224
Kennedy, John 216–17, 220–2, 224
Kent QC, Alan 237
Kenya 15, 123, 127, 168–70
Keyt, Flavia 95
KGB 136–7, 140, 141, 255, 258, 259–60, 264
Khan, Aga 122
Khan, Mustaq 208–10
King Tom, Sierra Leone 39
Kings Bench Walk 6, 23
Kinnear, Joe 276
Kitson, Sir Timothy 148–9
Klein, General Jacques 66
Klevan, Hon. Mr Justice Rodney 28, 215, 273, 276, 279
Kneller, Sir Alister 248
knighthood 191
Knightsbridge Crown Court 125, 135, 203–4
Kobonella 100

Kochnov, Igor 141
Kondewa, Allieu 54, 55, 56
Konuzin, Ambassador Alexander 63
Koroma, Johnny Paul 50, 53–4, 55, 60, 62
Koumjian, Nicholas 88
Kueneman, Peter 110
Kurdish terrorism 206

ladies of the night 131–3, 162
Lagoonda 43–4
Lamb, David 289
Lamb, Lady Caroline 180
Lamb Building 12
Lambert QC, Nigel 200–1
Lamont, Lord (Norman) 65
Lampard, Frank 292–5
Lamport, Sir Stephen 49
Lane, Lord (Geoffrey) 281
Lansana, Brigadier David 126–7, 131, 133–4
Lansbury, George 98
Latham, Michael 210–11
Law Lords 4
Lawrence, Lady (Gloria) 11
Lawrence,QC, Sir Ivan 11
Lawson QC, His Honour Judge Michael 237
Layton, Admiral Sir Geoffrey 102, 103
Le Cercle 49, 65
Le Quesne, David 246
Leakey, John 118
Lean, David 152–3
Leary QC, Brian 25, 250
Leeds United case 284–91
Lees-Milne, James 156
legal aid 7, 8, 31, 32
legal career of Desmond de Silva
    *see also* international law career of Desmond de Silva
  appointment as deputy circuit judge 124
  arrests 11, 129, 162–4
  call to the bar 3, 5, 32, 124
  chief prosecutor of international criminal tribunals 72–86, 87–92
  continuing although concussed 288
  court craft 198, 202–3, 204–5, 253, 272, 290
  cross-examination skills 203, 205, 207, 209, 222, 224, 228–9, 230, 290, 294, 301
  destiny as a lawyer 5
  early leanings towards 95
  Ethics Committee 149–50
  family history of lawyers 5, 94, 108–9
  'fashionable silk' 195
  first capital case 11, 126–34
  first case 5–6, 7–9
  first case abroad 13
  first junior brief in House of Lords 29
  first junior brief in Old Bailey 29
  first jury trial 26
  first murder case as silk 202
  first Old Bailey case 18–19
  first time 'being led' 24
  first time in jail 11
  focus on criminal Bar 25, 94
  forensics knowledge 95, 178, 198, 273, 295
  guided by Magna Carta ch. 29 33
  head of chambers 15–16
  humour/ wit 194, 202–3, 276–7, 278, 291
  judicial reprimands as occupational hazard 194
  juries, skill with 198, 289, 290
  lateral thinking 230
  little preparation for international criminal court 73
  long working days 67, 198, 288
  not moving into civil service 16
  pro bono work 195
  prosecutorial work 197
  pupil master of President Kabbah 41
  pupillage 3, 5–7
  scene of crime visits 197
  speaking skills 196–7, 198–9, 202, 205–6, 277–8, 288–9, 290
  taking silk 27, 28
  testing of the evidence 197
  understanding of human nature 73, 84, 273
  on 'Yard List' 22–3
legal principles, as great English export 32–3
Leigh, Vivien 152
Leopold von Baden, HRH Prince
    see wedding photograph
lepidoptery 113–15
Levitt trial 198
Lewes Crown Court 212, 214, 228, 237
Lewis, Raymond 153, 198
libel 25, 155
Liberia 37, 38, 42, 50, 53, 57, 57–61, 66, 72–86, 225
Libya 69, 76, 91, 216, 217–25, 222
Licence, John 259
Lim, Richard 274, 275, 276, 279
Lloyd-Eley QC, John 257, 263
Lombard, Anthony 184
Longhurst, Thomas 227–31
Lord Mayor of London 158
Lords Chancellor 18, 27, 31–2, 61, 121, 125, 155
Luke, Edward 171, 172, 174
Luke, Rob 85

Lussick, Mr Justice 34
Lyell, Lord (Nicholas) 270
Lynch QC, Jerome 28, 215, 273

MacDonald, Ramsay 98
Macdonald QC, Lord 90
Machel, Graça 89
Mackay, Bruce 50, 56
MacKenzie, Major General Lewis 75
Mackeson, Sir Rupert 195
magistracy xiii
magistrates' courts 16–17
Magna Carta xiii, xiv, 33
Magpie and Stump 257
Mahmood, Mazher 297, 300
Major, Rt. Hon. Sir John 23, 149, 216, 221
Malabar Hill 117
malaria 130
Mandela, Nelson 89, 91
Mandi von Baden, HRH Princess
see wedding photograph
marabouts 162
Marder QC, His Honour Judge Bernard 6
Margarita von Baden, HRH Princess
(DdS's mother-in-law)
see wedding photograph
Margai, Sir Albert 127
Marie-Therese von Hohenberg, Princess 224
Marion Hill 100
Marks, D/Supt Paul 253
Mark's Club 49, 65
Marlands 49, 61
Marriage QC, James 25
Marron QC, His Honour Judge Aidan 285
Marshall, Frank 58, 64
Marshall Hall, KC,Sir Edward 23, 109
Martin, Ted 236–9
Marx Brothers 153
massacres 43, 48, 72, 77
Massey, Col. Hamon 64
Masson, Jean 261
Mathews, Frank 59
Mathews, Harriet 59, 65
Matthew, John 25, 30
Maude QC, His Honour Judge John 18–19
Maugham, Viscount (Robin) 155–7
Maurice (chimp) 53
*Mavi Marmara* 143–4, 147
Maximilian von Baden, HRH Margrave
see wedding photograph
McCullough, Hon. Mr Justice Thomas 277
McDonald, Peter 227–31
McElligott, Mike 17
McKinley, Lt. Col. Graham 68
McQueen, Alan 210–12
Melbourne, Lord 180
Membar, Moussa 207, 208
Membar, Yassin 206–7, 208
Metropolitan Police 31
MI5 221, 263
MI6 76, 120, 139, 220, 240
Michael of Kent, HRH Prince 216, 217, 220, 222
Michael of Yugoslavia, HRH Prince
see wedding photograph
Middle East 142–7, 177–9, 218, 223
Middlesex Crown Court 137, 138
Middlesex Quarter Sessions 7, 26
*Million Pound Note, The* (film) 151
Milošević, Slobodan 178
Milroy, Prof. Christopher 295
Milton Margai Blind School 71
Minor, Ambassador Bob 129
Miskin QC, Sir James 210–11
Mitchell, QC, Sir Stephen 183
Mitchiner, Dr John 68, 70
Mladić, General Ratko 73, 83, 266
Mogae, President Festus 175
Mohammed, Fazul Abdullah 78
Molly (chimp) 53
Monro Davies, His Honour Judge William 205
Monrovia 54, 58, 61, 62, 77, 78
Montagu QC, Hon. Ewen 8–10
Montgomery QC, Clare 285, 291
Moore, Major General Bill 47
Moors Murderers 23, 195–6
morbid jealousy syndrome 212–13
Morgan, Bruce 282
Morissette, Gilbert 38
Morris, Jody 292–5
Morris QC, His Honour Judge Gwyn 17–18
Morrison, Herbert 98
Mortimer QC, Sir John 29, 212
Mountbatten of Burma, Admiral of the Fleet
Earl 105–6, 133, 134
Munyard, Terry 88
Murray, Nigel 19, 126, 129, 130
Muthaiga Club, Nairobi 168
Mylvanganam, Paul 14
Mylne, QC, Nigel 200

Nagumo, Vice Admiral Chuichi 102, 104
Nairobi 15, 78, 168–70
Najeib, Sarfraz 285
Najeib, Shahzad 285, 286
Nall-Cain, Charles (Lord Brocket) 180–2
Napley, Sir David 18

Nassau 15
Nathanielsz, Lorna (DdS's aunt) 110
Nathanielsz, Ray (DdS's uncle) 112
Natural history, interest in 113–15, 116–17, 157
Nell, Agnes (grandmother) 93–4, 96, 97, 100, 102, 108, 109–10, 151
Nell, Frederick August 108, 119
Nell, George (DdS's great-great-great-grandfather) 108–9
Nell, George Frederick 108–9
Nell, Louis (DdS's great-great-grandfather) 109, 121
Nell, Mrs Louis 97
Nell, Paul (DdS's great-grandfather) 100
Newall, Mark 240–54
Newall, Roderick 14, 152, 184, 192, 194, 197, 214, 240–54
Newman QC, Alan 135, 203
Nice QC, Sir Geoffrey 178
Nicholl-Cadell, Lt. Commander Robert 97
Nigeria 64, 77, 78, 79, 82, 83–4
Nikola of Yugoslavia, HRH Prince see wedding photograph
Nkrumah, Kwame 29
Noel, Robert 193
Norman, Samuel Hinga 47, 48, 54, 67
Northern Ireland 191
Nuremburg trials 34, 35, 72, 79, 105
Nyerere, President Julius 206–7

Obama, President Barack 88
Obasanjo, President 66, 77, 82, 83–4
O'Brien, Mike 69
Odinga, Raila 169–70
Old Bailey
  DdS's favourite court 212
  DdS's first junior brief in 29
  history of 14, 20–1, 25, 28–9
  IRA bomb (1972) 27
Old Street Magistrates' Court 17
Oldfield, Sir Maurice 120
Oliver, Jacqui 300–1
Olivier, Laurence, Lord 152
Olivier, Hon. Tarquin 152
Onoshko, Walter 136
Operation Barras (Operation Certain Death) 37, 40
Operation Cast Lead 142
Operation Overlord 104–5
Orentlicher, Diane 79
Osborne, Jamie 35, 298–9
*Our George* (Russell, 1981) 94
*Outcasts of the Islands* 153

Paddy's Bar, Freetown 47
Pademba Road Prison, Freetown 45, 55, 134
Pain, Hon. Sir Peter 232
Palmer, Sir Geoffrey 145, 147
Palmerston, Henry, 3rd Viscount 180
Panda, George 126–7
Paper Buildings 10–12, 13, 22, 24
Paramount Hotel, Freetown 128, 131
Parker, Lord 31
Parker, Malcolm 129
Parkinson, Lord (Cecil) 149–50
Parnell, Lt. Col. Bob 50
Passani, Veronique 151
Payne, Andrew 293
peace building 41, 74, 143
Peacehaven 226–31
Peacekeeper's Handbook 75
peacekeeping operations 37, 75
Pearl Harbor 102–3
Peck, Edward 219
Peck, Gregory 151–2, 243–4
Pedo, Helena 152, 243, 248, 250, 251
Peter of Yugoslavia, HRH Prince see wedding photograph
Pentol, Simon 293
Peradeniya 106
personal danger, being in 36, 37–8, 43–4, 48, 63, 75, 81, 166–7, 250
Pethick-Lawrence, Lord 98
Pettitt, Tracy 36, 39, 49, 53, 57, 64, 68
Phelvin, Bernard 214, 232, 237
Philip of Yugoslavia, HRH Prince see wedding photograph
Pilley, Ray 184, 185
piracy 14, 240
Pirbright, Lord 113
Pizzarello, Felix 247
PKK 206
Player, Martin 281, 282
Poland 135–6
Ponsonby, Lady (Maureen) 300
Poole, Hon. Mr Justice David 285, 289
Pope John Paul II 194
Porjes, Roy 210–11
Porter, Brigadier Simon 70
Potter, Mr Justice Kenneth 15, 168
Preston Crown Court 213
Price, Robert 198
Privy Council 3, 12, 15, 23, 191, 252
Prozac defence 209–10
pupillage 3, 5–7
Purnell QC, Nick 7
Purnell QC, Paul 7

Qatar 177–9
Queen's House, Colombo 102

*R v Bennett* 251
racehorse (DdS's) 35–6
racing (horse) 122, 298–9
Radcliffes (solicitors) 174–5
Ralston, Leonard 137, 139
Ramsbottom, Norman 49
Rapp, Stephen 34, 88
Rathgael 116–17, 119–20
Raymond, Stephen 203
Reagan, President Ronald 255
Reed, Carol 153
Reid, Lord 4
Renouf, Lady Michèle 154
Reticker, Gini 72
Revoltier, Rene 54
Revolutionary United Front (RUF) 42, 54, 91
*Rex v Disney* 133
*Rex v Molloy* (1921) 133
Rhoda QC, Ricky 186
Rhynern 116
Richard, Lord (Ivor) 11–12
Richards of Herstmonceux, General Lord 37, 68
Rifkind,QC, Sir Malcolm 52
Riley, Commander 166
Rimington, Dame Stella 221
Robertson Justice, James 152
Robertson QC, Geoffrey 41, 67
Rochas, Clio 65
Rodwell QC, His Honour Daniel 181–2
Rogers-Wright, Cyril 128, 130
Rohsler, Caron 65
Roscoe, James 85
Rose, General Sir Michael 266, 267
Rose, Henricus 193
Rose-Cleland, James Dowsett (DdS's great-great-great-grandfather) 116, 119, 120
Rose, Lord Justice 201, 202
Rose, Lt Richard (DdS's great-great-great-great-grandfather) 119
Rothschilds-Worms family 113
Royal Academy 195–6
Royal Courts of Justice 31
Royal Wedding (1981) 158
rubber estates 100, 101, 104
rugby case 296–7
rule of law 32–3
Russell, Jane 94, 98, 105, 111–12

Sacarello, Charles 184
Sacarello, Marie 184
Saho, Lamin 162–4
Samat, Daren 293
Sandinistas 76
Sands QC, Prof. Philippe 79
Sangster QC, Nigel 285
Sankoh, Foday 76
Sanyang, Kukoi Samba 76, 158, 160, 163
SAS 37, 40, 63, 160, 192, 246
scene of crime visits 197
Schofield, Anne 174–5, 195
Schofield, Chief Justice Derek 186
Scotland Yard 22–3
Seaton QC, Reggie 21
Seaview House 37–8, 39, 40, 44, 50
security concerns in Gibraltar 250
security concerns in Sierra Leone 36, 37–8, 43–4, 48, 63, 75, 81
Security Council Resolution 1315 40
Segers, Hans 28, 199, 215, 273, 274, 275–80
Select Committee for International Development 48
senior clerks, role of 22–3, 27
sentencing 124, 183
Shadrin, Ewa 135–41
Shadrin, Nicholas 136
Shanthi Dairiam 145, 146
Sherrard QC, Michael 126
Sierra Leone
  DdS first visit to 38
  DdS in 11, 33–5, 196
  diamonds 41–2, 70, 72, 76, 78, 91
  first visit to 126–34
  Special Court for Sierra Leone 33–4, 35–71, 79–86, 92
Simeon of the Bulgarians, HM King 220, 224
Simpson QC, Robin 25
Sinclair, Diane 233–4
Slessor, Tim 267–8
Smith, Derek 68
Smith, General Sir Rupert 266
Smith, Her Honour Judge Zoe 203
Somerville, Admiral Sir James 104
Soviet spies 135–41, 255–65
Speare, Matthew 232–5
Spearman, Terry 39
Special Branch 11, 14, 166, 216, 250, 258, 263, 267
Special Court for Sierra Leone 33–4, 35–71, 79–86, 92
Spencer, QC, Sir Derek 23
spy cases 135–41, 255–65, 266–72
Sri Lanka *see* Ceylon
St George's (grandparents' house) 94, 99–100, 102, 105–6, 110, 151, 152

St Paul's, Kandy 96
St Thomas's school 116
Staker, Christopher 66, 80
Stankovic, Major Milos 36, 265–72
Stankovic, Radomir 266
Steadman, Karen 139
Stevens, Siaka 127, 128, 130–1, 134
Stewart-Moore, Christopher 195
Stokes, Paul 214
Storey, Terence 213
Stormont Castle 120
Straw, Right Hon Jack 58
Sudeley, (Merlin) Lord 199
Supreme Court xiv, 7
surveillance, being under 43, 250
Sweeney, Hon. Sir Nigel 17
Syria 177–9, 191

Tafrov, Ambassador Stefan 63
Taft, George 81
Taliban 54
Tambiah, Justice 133
Tanzania 127, 206–8
Taprobane Island 100, 156–7, 171
'target number one' status 39
tariff penalties, going against 124
Taverne, Lord (Dick) 11, 24–5
Taylor, Charles Ghankay
  appeal 91–2
  conviction of 91
  crimes 76–7
  ECG tests 84–5
  escapes 83, 86
  exile 77, 78
  indictments against 77–9, 88
  legal team 88
  in Libya 76
  medicals 84–5
  and Naomi Campbell 87, 87–92
  at Nelson Mandela's house 89
  not guilty plea 86, 88
  and the Special Court for Sierra Leone 34, 35–71, 80–4, 85
  transfer from Nigeria 79–80
  trial at The Hague 87–92
Taylor, Admiral Rufus 136
Tea Dance Murder 214, 236–9
tea estates 100, 113, 117, 119
Tejan-Sie, Sir Banja 128
Tenet, George 73
Terry, John 292–5
Terry, Terrence 67, 79
Thames Magistrates' Court 222
Thatcher, Right Hon Margaret 65, 181, 199, 208, 255, 264
Thirlwall, Trevor 293–5
Thiruchelvam, Sharmini 153
Thomas, Rosemary 65
Thompson, Sir Lionel 27–8
threats to life 39, 115–16, 166, 240, 250
Thuys, Alphonsus 277
Tipperary (Ceylon) 100
tobacco 45
Tokyo trials 35
Tomislav of Yugoslavia, HRH Prince (DdS's father-in-law)
  see wedding photograph
Tower of Silence, Malabar Hill 117
Treason Acts 127, 160, 169–70
Trengove, Stadler 85
Trimble, Lord (David) 146
Trincomalee 104
Trinity College, Kandy 116
Trusted Mole (racehorse) 35–6, 266–72
truth, getting at 135, 142, 196
Tuckey QC, Rt. Hon. Sir Simon 275, 277
Tudor Price, Hon. Mr Justice David 135
Turkel, Jacob 146, 147
Turkey 146, 147
TV appearances 69, 304

Union House 37, 44, 53, 66
United National Party 107
United Nations
  chief prosecutor role must deal with 73, 75
  fact-finding mission 142, 145
  'hazard postings' 39
  Human Rights Council (UNHRC) 144–5
  and intelligence 75–6
  international criminal courts 35
  Secretary-General 40, 47, 80, 145, 147
  Security Council 80, 82, 86, 143, 144–5, 179
  United Nations Mission in Sierra Leone (UNAMSIL) 43

Vagg, Howard 228
Valerie, HI & RH Archduchess of Austria, Margravine von Baden
  see wedding photograph
Vickers, Lt. Col Robin 64
Victor Emmanuel of Italy, HRH Crown Prince 224
Victoria, HM Queen (great-great-great-great-grandmother of DdS's daughter Victoria) 105, 113, 156

Vincent, Chris 274
Vincent, Robin 39, 50, 52, 53, 56, 59, 68

Waley QC, His Honour Judge Felix 7
Walker QC, Raymond 289
Walker-Macran, Douglas (DdS's cousin) 121
war crimes
  horror of 43, 48, 54, 56, 72, 77
  Iraqi war crimes tribunal 70
  Middle East 142
  Special Court for Sierra Leone 33–4, 35–71, 79–86, 92
  'in theatre' trials 40, 41, 74–5, 196
  victims as clients of the prosecutor 74
Waterloo Ball 31
Waterman, Charles 219
Waterman & Associates 219
Waterman QC, Adrian 285
Watt, Ian 134
weapons of mass destruction (WMD) 69
Webster, Mark 286
Weligama 110
Wellington Club 293, 294
West African Court of Appeal 130, 133
West Side Boys 37, 40
White, Alan 38, 50, 52, 53, 55, 59, 60, 78
White, Carole 87, 89
White Elephant on the River 27
White Hart, Lewes 212
*White Mischief* (film) 123
White's Club 50
Williams, Dr Patricia 230
Williams, Rosamund 115
Williamson, David 222
Williamson, Ambassador Richard 63
Win Min Than 151–2
Winchester 215, 273, 274
Winn, Lady 6
Winn, Rt. Hon. Sir Rodger 6
witch doctors 67–8
witchcraft 200–1
witness protection 74, 248
Wolmarans, Tienie 171
Wood, Barry 214
Woodgate, Jonathan 285, 287, 289, 290
Woodley QC, Sonia 293
Woodward, Sir Clive 297
Woolf, Lord (Harry) 207, 208
World War II 101–4
Worms, Maurice 113
Worms family 113, 116
Worsley QC, Michael 28, 210–11
Wright, Sir Michael 237
Wrotham Park, Barnet 156
Wykeham Arms 215

Yard List 22–3
Yeaten, General Benjamin 52–3
Yurchenko, Vitaly 140